MUSIC AND WONDER AT THE

Medici Court

Frontispiece. Costume design for planetary gods (*intermedio* one) by Bernardo Buontalenti. From left to right: Mercury, Apollo, Jove, and Astraea. I:Fn, Palatina C.B.3.53, vol. II, c. 29r. By permission of the Ministero per i Beni e le Attività Culturali della Repubblica Italiana and the Biblioteca Nazionale Centrale, Florence. Further reproduction of the image by any means is forbidden.

Musical Meaning and Interpretation
Robert S. Hatten, editor

Music and the Early Modern Imagination
Massimo Ossi, editor

MUSIC AND WONDER AT THE
Medici Court

The 1589 Interludes for
La pellegrina

NINA TREADWELL

INDIANA UNIVERSITY PRESS
Bloomington and Indianapolis

This book has received the Weiss/Brown
Publication Subvention Award from the
Newberry Library. The award supports
the publication of outstanding works of
scholarship that cover European civilization
before 1700 in the areas of music, theater,
French or Italian literature, or cultural
studies. It is made to commemorate the
career of Howard Mayer Brown.

This book is a publication of

Indiana University Press
601 North Morton Street
Bloomington, IN 47404-3797 USA

http://iupress.indiana.edu

Telephone orders	800-842-6796
Fax orders	812-855-7931
Orders by e-mail	iuporder@indiana.edu

The paper used in this publication meets the
minimum requirements of American National
Standard for Information Sciences—Permanence
of Paper for Printed Library Materials,
ANSI Z39.48-1984.

Manufactured in the United States of America

Library of Congress Cataloging-in-Publication Data

Treadwell, Nina.
  Music and wonder at the Medici court : the 1589 interludes
for La pellegrina / Nina Treadwell.
      p. cm.—(Musical meaning and interpretation)
  Includes bibliographical references and index.
  ISBN 978-0-253-35218-7 (cloth : alk. paper)   1. Intermedi—
Italy—Florence—16th century—History and criticism.   2. Fer-
dinando I, Grand-Duke of Tuscany, 1549–1609—Marriage.
3. Christine, of Lorraine, Grand Duchess, consort of Ferdinand
I, Grand Duke of Tuscany, 1565–1636—Marriage.   4. Barga-
gli, Girolamo, 1537–1586. Pellegrina.   I. Title.
  ML290.8.F6T74 2008
   782.1—dc22   2008005575

1   2   3   4   5   13   12   11   10   09   08

TO JAMES TYLER
Lutenist, scholar, teacher, and mentor
With deep respect and appreciation
and
Alla mia meraviglia
JEANNE JACKSON

Contents

Illustrations

Acknowledgments

James Tyler first introduced me to the music of the *Pellegrina* interludes in 1993. After venturing to the United States (from Australia) to study baroque guitar with him, it was clear to me within a matter of weeks that I should complete a masters in early music performance at the University of Southern California. I had the privilege of learning from him, playing in his ensemble, and later becoming his duet partner. I learned by doing; he threw a lute in my hands and I managed to play the instrument (at a funeral) two days later. Jim ignited the passion I developed for Italian theatrical music, and for continuo playing on theorbo in particular. I can only now partly articulate the wonder of playing continuo that I gleaned from him instinctively: it is about a relationship, preferably (for me) with a female singer, and you need to be ready for anything.

Reading Jim's book *The Early Guitar* prompted me to write to him in the first place; I thank him (self-centeredly) for writing this book because the contact I had with his ideas led to a series of events and interactions that essentially changed my life. I chose to study with Jim because he was a true scholar-performer; that foundation has proved to be the backbone of much of my thinking and writing about music making. I thank him for the numerous conversations we have had over the years about music—the many hours on the phone—which continue to invigorate me. I also thank him for telling me to never believe anything I read in a book, and of course his advice applies to this book too. Although performance practice per se is not the focus of this book, I dedicate it to him with deep gratitude.

This book was written over the course of my affiliation with three academic institutions. The ideas for the project began germinating while I was an assistant professor at Grinnell College. I would like to thank Jon Chenette for his support during this period, and my partner in crime, ethnomusicologist Roger Vetter, from whom I learned a great deal, especially while co-teaching the course "Music, Culture, Context."

From 2002 to 2004, I held an Andrew W. Mellon Postdoctoral Fellowship at the UCLA Humanities Consortium. The fellowship gave me the opportunity to begin work on this project and to engage with an interdisciplinary group of scholars. I would particularly like to thank Kirstie McClure from the political science department, who always kept me on my toes, and Vincent Pecora, then the director of the Humanities Consortium. Also important during this period was the hospitality of UCLA's musicology department, where I was given several opportunities to teach a graduate seminar in Renaissance performance practice. For their encouragement and support I especially thank Elisabeth Le Guin and Susan McClary, and acknowledge the wonderful graduate students who enriched my intellectual and personal life during that time period.

Long before I spent time at UCLA as a postdoctoral fellow, Susan McClary encouraged my research interests when I was a graduate student by welcoming me into several of her graduate seminars. A 1997 article in *Women and Music* on the *Pellegrina* interludes began life in one of these seminars. Later, she graciously agreed to come across town to serve on my dissertation committee. I thank her for her continued encouragement and support of my work.

At my present institutional home, at the University of California, Santa Cruz, I am fortunate to work in a music department where the intersection of scholarship and performance is nurtured, and collaborative projects are actively encouraged. I have greatly benefited from opportunities to collaborate with Amy Beal, Linda Burman-Hall, and Nicole Paiement, and by watching the theatrical wizardry of Brian Staufenbiel. I wish to thank Leta Miller for her generosity with time, her guidance, and her unstinting support, and David Cope for his wise counsel.

My colleagues in the Visual and Performance Studies research cluster at UCSC have welcomed me with open arms. I thank them for their support, both personal and professional, and the intellectual stimulation made possible by their commitment to interdisciplinary exchange. In particular, my heartfelt thanks go to Mark Franko, Tyrus Miller, Deanna Shemek, and Catherine Soussloff. The exchanges that took place within the context of VPS seminars helped me to find suitable ways to frame and theorize a number of the ideas presented in this book.

My research has been supported by faculty research funds granted by the University of California, Santa Cruz. In addition, the Arts Research Institute at UCSC funded permission costs for pictorial images and the recording of the accompanying CD. I also acknowledge the Publication Subvention (from the Gustave Reese Publication Endowment Fund, 2005) that I received from the American Musicological Society to support the CD recording. The inclusion of almost thirty plates, many of them color, was made possible by a Weiss/Brown Publication Subvention Award (2006) from the Newberry Library.

Some of the material in this book first appeared in somewhat different form in journal articles in *Women and Music: A Journal of Gender and Culture* 1 (1997); *Cambridge Opera Journal* 16/1 (2004); and *Current Musicology* 83 (2007). I thank these journals for permission to rework material.

Although my doctoral dissertation did not concern the *Pellegrina* interludes per se, since my dissertation research in the late 1990s I have spent considerable time in Italian libraries and archives. I wish to thank the directors and staff who have made materials available to me, without whose assistance this book would not have come to fruition. In Florence, I would particularly like to acknowledge the staff at the Biblioteca Riccardiana, who made it a pleasure to work there (even in extreme heat), and Dott.sa Paola Pirolo at the Biblioteca Nazionale Centrale, who generously allowed the reproduction of many of the costume and stage designs contained herein. In Modena, I spent many hours at the Biblioteca Estense and benefited greatly from the helpful staff. At the Archivio di Stato in Modena I acknowledge Angelo Spaggiari and Lucia d'Angelo, whose interest and friendliness made it a pleasure to work there. Finally, my friend Elisabetta Parrulli continues to provide me with a second home in Modena. I surely would not live and work so happily in Italy without her friendship and generosity.

I am indebted to numerous scholars and friends. Carol Williams from Monash University was the first to encourage my efforts in musicology. Joyce Tyler always had her finger on the pulse and essentially managed my career as a graduate student, beginning with the plethora of introductory faxes to final graduation. I am deeply grateful to Giulio Ongaro, who has selflessly offered his time and assistance with Italian texts and translations over the course of the past fourteen years. I thank him for sharing his love of Italian language and culture, for our always-engaging phone and email conversations, and for his ongoing support of my work. Margaret Rosenthal nurtured my interest in Renaissance women and put me in touch with Deanna Shemek, who by a lucky twist of fate became my valued colleague at UCSC.

My life has been deeply enriched by numerous musical collaborations over the past ten years (including the recording of the accompanying CD) with Voxfire's three sopranos: Samela Beasom, Christen Herman, and Susan Judy. Susan and I have had numerous opportunities to ponder and perform the solo music from the *Pellegrina* interludes, and she kindly typeset all of the book's musical examples. More recently, Ralf Dietrich offered an "ear" when it was needed and provided generous and speedy responses to my questions regarding German translations. Bruce Brown and Richard Freedman were kind enough to comb my French translations. Massimo Ossi has provided generous feedback on my work in general over the years, and supported this project from the outset, for which I am extremely grateful. A formative moment occurred when I read Suzanne Cusick's article "Thinking from Women's Lives: Francesca Caccini after 1627" in *The Musical Quarterly*. Suzanne's article and her work in general opened possibilities for scholarship in musicology that I was struggling to envision. Without her example in the discipline of musicology my path would have been a far more difficult one. I think she must know how much I admire her work and value her support.

I wish to express my gratitude to all those at Indiana University Press who have shepherded this book to publication. Every step of the way I have received the utmost of care and professionalism in a process that I understand, from hearsay, is not always so smooth. In chronological order, I thank Gayle Sherwood Magee, who, as music editor during 2003, enthusiastically encouraged me to submit a proposal to Robert Hatten's series, "Musical Meaning and Interpretation." I felt from the outset that Robert's series was an excellent fit for my work, and I was gratified that he felt likewise. I am grateful to him for supporting this project, giving me the latitude to develop the ideas contained herein, and for reading the entire manuscript with a fine-tooth comb. IUP music and humanities editor Jane Behnken had the insight to know exactly how much leeway was needed for me to develop the project fully, but was also able to keep me on track, especially as the project neared its end. I especially thank her for her flexibility and for overseeing the final stages of this project with such efficiency. Thanks also go to assistant music editors Donna Wilson and now Katherine Baber, for timely and helpful responses to all my queries. Before submitting the manuscript, I was lucky enough to come into contact with Karen Hiles, doctoral candidate in musicology at Columbia University, and editor-in-chief of *Current Musicology* (2005–07). She agreed to read the book in its entirety; her helpful questions and comments were invaluable.

Finally, I would like to thank my family and friends. My mother, June Treadwell, has had to put up with numerous visits to the United States when the book was "almost finished, but not quite." I thank her for her patience and her support. The friendship of Giulio and Cheryl Ongaro and Susan Judy has provided continuity amidst the vicissitudes of daily life. Our dear friends Linda LeMoncheck and Jed Shafer continue to enrich our lives in so many ways; I know Linda will recognize the theoretical framework of this book that she helped me to first articulate in her feminist theory class at USC in 1996.

Dame Edna Everage (aka Barry Humphries), iconic Australian cross-dresser and one-time talk show host, once described her/his talk show as "a monologue interrupted by strangers," thus positing the guests as strangers who were lucky if they got a word in edgewise. While writing this book, I have sometimes thought of Dame Edna's phrase in relation to my life partner, Jeanne Jackson, to whom this book is also dedicated. She has survived more monologic outbursts regarding the politics of *meraviglia* than I dare to remember. Yet it has been the dialogue (not monologue) surrounding the politics and wonder of everyday life and our journey together that has kept me going. I would particularly like to thank her for the red tie.

Notes to the Reader

Dates

During this period the Florentine calendar began on the Feast of the Annunciation, March 25. I have converted dates in the *stile fiorentino* to their modern counterparts.

Appendices

The sources transcribed in the appendices have been chosen because they are not readily available for consultation or because existing sources are unreliable.

Transcriptions of Italian Texts

All transcriptions retain the original orthography, including inconsistencies within sources. Original punctuation, accents, and use of upper or lower case letters have been retained. The letters *u* and *v* have been converted to conform to modern usage, and the letter *j* is rendered as the letter *i*. The tilde has been resolved accordingly.

Notated Musical Examples

With the exception of Giulio Caccini's "Io che dal ciel cader," all musical examples are transcribed from the 1591 publication of the *Pellegrina* interludes compiled by Malvezzi, *Intermedii et concerti*. The partbook designations in square brackets, though sometimes seemingly irregular, correspond to the parts as they appear in the print. Bar lines have been inserted or regularized, but note values have been retained, except where they extend across the measure. Accidentals have been modernized (e.g., sharp signs have been replaced by a natural where appropriate). Editorial accidentals have been added above given notes. Text has been supplied where "ij" is indicated in the original.

Accompanying CD: The Pellegrina Project

The excerpts were selected, partly, in response to available resources. Though it was not possible to include numbers requiring large-scale musical forces, the CD is central to an understanding of many of the key points in the book, especially regarding the importance of texture and timbre in the *Pellegrina* interludes, for which musical notation provides an inadequate representation. The CD is also intended to demonstrate my claim regarding the performative efficacy of the *Pellegrina* interludes (in 1589), and to facilitate an understanding of this argument to an interdisciplinary readership.

Abbreviations

Archives and Libraries

A:Wn	Vienna, Österreichische Nationalbibliothek, Musiksammlung
B:Bc	Brussells, Conservatoire Royal, Bibliothèque
D:W	Wolfenbüttel, Herzog August Bibliothek, Handschriftensammlung
F:Pn	Paris, Bibliothèque Nationale de France
I:Bc	Bologna, Civico Museo Bibliografico Musicale
I:Bu	Bologna, Biblioteca Universitaria, sezione Musicale
I:Fas	Florence, Archivio di Stato
I:Fn	Florence, Biblioteca Nazionale Centrale
I:Fr	Florence, Biblioteca Riccardiana
I:MOe	Modena, Biblioteca Estense
I:MOs	Modena, Archivio di Stato
I:Rasv	Vatican City, Archivio Segreto Vaticano
I:Vas	Venice, Archivio di Stato

MUSIC AND WONDER AT THE

Medici Court

Introduction

ON MAY 2, 1589, the Medici court staged the most costly and elaborate entertainment yet produced in Florence. In the Uffizi theater, the *intermedi* (interludes) performed between the acts of Girolamo Bargagli's comedy *La pellegrina* were the high point of a series of celebrations mobilized by the newly proclaimed Grand Duke of Florence—Ferdinando I de' Medici—for his wedding to Christine of Lorraine. An account of the opening of the first *intermedio* by one commentator, Simone Cavallino, described the scene:[1]

> [When] the first cloth fell, a cloud remained in the air, in which there was a lady dressed as an angel, who in the manner of an angel sang so sonorously, and with most beautiful accompaniments that everyone remained in wonder and stunned; and that cloud, having descended little by little, disappeared. . . . [2]

Scholars and students familiar with the opening of the *Pellegrina* interludes will know that Cavallino's report differs in at least one important respect from the official, Medici-commissioned description of the event written by academician Bastiano de' Rossi:[3] the Medici court's directive elite intended Cavallino's "angel" to represent the allegorical figure of Dorian Harmony—an allusion lost on Cavallino, whose (mis)identification is one of numerous perceptions by unofficial commentators that do not concur with official Medici-generated accounts.[4]

Cavallino's brief description brings a number of issues to the fore regarding the *Pellegrina* interludes that have remained largely unexplored. James Saslow recently dubbed the issue of audience perception as "the Pavoni factor," after Giuseppe Pavoni, another seemingly misinformed commentator who chronicled his impressions of the *intermedi*.[5] During the performance, to what extent did audience members register the veritable "symphony of meanings" that Rossi outlined in his official written account?[6] As scholars have pointed out at least in passing—beginning with Aby Warburg's seminal study of 1895—much of the erudite classical and Neoplatonic imagery detailed in Rossi's description went completely over the audience's heads.[7] Rather than dismissing unofficial sources entirely, however, I consider the significance of the sometimes contradictory impressions embedded in these accounts as part of the meaning-making process surrounding these extraordinary performances. At times, unofficial accounts appear to represent brief snapshots of performative moments remembered, while at other times portions thereof are evidently influenced by post-performance communications (by spectators hoping to glean information from those "in the know") or are clearly derivative of other written sources.[8] As such, unofficial sources are imbued with both a sense of an event remembered and of impressions and information that commentators *desired to convey,* and thus memorialize through the written word. The memory of the performance experience was thus informed by the background and interests of those who witnessed the *intermedi,* in the same way that Rossi's official report reflected an albeit more self-conscious account of Medici preoccupations.[9]

The picture and sound-world presented in this study both intersects and departs from Medici-sponsored accounts.[10] It is both a reconstruction—in the traditional sense of a piecing together of an array of sources, to indicate plausible inferences—but also a deconstruction, in the more general sense of the term. By deconstructing, my intent is to expand a field of inquiry that has privileged authorial intent (the stated intentions of the *Pellegrina* interludes creators) and to interpret "reconstructive findings" in ways that both confirm the performative efficacy of Medicean absolutism (especially through music), but that also show how meanings were negotiated by the spectator-auditor, and as such were ultimately less stable than official sources would lead us to believe. In addition, the narrative that emerges in this book is inevitably structured around my own interests and methodological preferences, including my fascination with the experiential dimension of performance, that is, with the experience of hearing and witnessing performance: as Elaine Sisman recently noted, "[T]he current popularity of reception studies reflects our interest in imagining audiences because of identification with our own emplacements."[11] Similarly, my interest in gender studies constitutes a recurrent theme throughout the course of the book. The prominence given to the Florentine court's three *prime donne* is important in and of itself because of their presence on the stage of a large court theater at a time when female singers typically performed in more private settings. I focus here on the ways in which contemporary gender ideologies informed the interludes' conceptions and signified (or were intended to signify) in the context of performance; in addition, I consider the meaning-making process vis-à-vis gender from the perspective of the spectator-auditor.

By now the reader should realize that my intent is not to provide an ency-clopedic summation of the *Pellegrina* interludes that might account for each and every variable in the sources (of which there are numerous: for example, were there fifteen or sixteen Sirens in *intermedio* one?), nor to evaluate details in unofficial accounts that might be conceived of as correct or incorrect using the official Medici-commissioned sources as a gauge. In his study of the 1589 Medici wedding festivities in their entirety, James Saslow referred to "the multiple readings that various components of the audience made of this visual-verbal 'text.'"[12] While my study addresses the *Pellegrina* interludes specifically, my emphasis is primarily on the spectator-auditor's experience through the lens of a visual-*aural* "text"; in other words, I advocate the per-haps contentious claim that, for the spectator-auditor, the music's text was frequently superfluous to the generation of meaning in the performance con-text of the Uffizi theater. Nevertheless, the music could be entirely efficacious, even if the words were misunderstood or not understood at all.

In light of the *Pellegrina* interludes' status as landmarks of the music-historical canon—frequently posited as precursors of the "invention" of opera in Florence several years later—it is surprising that so little detailed interpre-tive work has been devoted to the music. The question of performance is paramount here, because stripped of meaningful performance context, the music for the interludes seems, understandably, to fall short of much contem-poraneous nontheatrical music. The complex textures and representations of subjectivity manifest in late Cinquecento chamber madrigals spring to mind[13] by way of contrast to the broader brush strokes that characterize much of the interludes' ensemble music with its avoidance of complex polyphony, largely homophonic textures, and diatonic harmonies—none of which has elicited substantive musical commentary. On the other hand, the solo songs of the *Pellegrina intermedi* have come in for a certain amount of criticism, not least, I think, because they fail to bolster the text-oriented aesthetic that is so cen-tral to the birth-of-opera narrative.

A secondary deterrent to serious consideration of the music seems to have been the nature of the Medici-commissioned musical publication that contains the compositions of the various contributing composers, which in notational form are essentially arrangements by Malvezzi (published in 1591, some two years after the performances took place).[14] As one of only two such (extant) Medici-sponsored publications of *intermedi* from the sixteenth century, with an invaluable *nono* (ninth) partbook that includes information about the per-formers and musical instruments involved, the source is nevertheless prob-lematic as a guide to sonic experience. The music as distilled on the printed page provides only a skeletal impression of the aural dimension as it must have been experienced in full-*bodied* performance. Essentially, the kinds of musical textures and sonorities so fundamental to the efficacy of the interludes' music could not (and cannot) be adequately conveyed through the medium of musical notation. The surviving music is thus only a starting point for understanding the sonic experience; in order to flesh out the sonic dimension I have provided listening examples for the reader on the accompanying compact disc, and also have deferred to other types of sources and perspectives (including those of performance practice) in order to provide insight into the viscerally charged experience of hearing the music of the *Pellegrina* interludes in performance.

One particular type of source—the seemingly aberrant manuscript and printed descriptions of the *intermedi*—gives unexpected emphasis to the aural dimension of the spectacle. This is striking, considering the relative brevity of most of these sources—(compared to Rossi's seventy-two-page booklet)—and the centrality given to visual perception in general during this period.[15] These sources often help to flesh out aspects of the musical experience omitted from Rossi's account, and on a grander scale attest to the significance of music as a medium for projecting wondrous effects. Historians of theater, art, and stagecraft have rightly emphasized the visual component as a means of evincing *meraviglia* (wonder), but as the above-cited excerpt by spectator-auditor Cavallino attests, for some audience members the music was as wondrous as the stagecraft. I thus take seriously contemporaneous claims regarding the music's efficacy, and attempt to explicate the experiential dimensions of musical *meraviglia*. Further, I consider the perception of the mutually productive intersection of sonic and visual media as a primary mode through which the *intermedi* worked their wonders.

I also link *meraviglia* with the bodily practices of musico-theatrical performance because these practices structure the contours of human interaction, exerting influence on spatial and temporal perception. More specifically, I show how the use of different styles and juxtapositions of musics in the *intermedi*— emanating from bodily contingents of various configurations—were capable of ordering the perceiver's experience of time and space. This raises the question of the profoundly political dimension of the *Pellegrina intermedi* to which I have already alluded. It was precisely during the late Cinquecento and particularly during the reign of Ferdinando I that the rhetoric of divine-right theory began to enter Medici-generated discourse.[16] The purpose of the absolutist project was "to create legitimacy by assimilating the ruler to a sacred realm and fixed authority outside earthly space and time."[17] Further, the absolutist prince's power was posited as "a mystery of state," and, as Mario Biagioli elaborates, "the 'mystery' of the source of the prince's power . . . [was] aimed at shielding his power from being discursively probed."[18] A set of court *intermedi*—staged within the controlled environment of a closed court theater—was the medium par excellence for demonstrating mastery of the environment, particularly through the manipulation of perceptions of time and space, thereby generating an impression of the prince-as-god. One of the central strands of this book, then, demonstrates how musical *meraviglia* served the interests of nascent absolutism. In addition, although the influence of Neoplatonism in Florentine *intermedi* is well known,[19] there has been little attempt to demonstrate how Neoplatonic philosophy (as well as the politics of absolutism) played out in performative terms.

While my aim is to articulate the cultural work of musical *meraviglia*, which is easily linked to the interests of Florentine absolutism, I am also interested in explicating how *meraviglia* functioned in unanticipated ways or did not "work" at all. Unofficial sources demonstrate that the spectator-auditor was no mere receptacle for the subtle (or not so subtle) messages that contributed to the notion of the prince-as-god. While references to the sacred and ineffable pepper accounts that, on the one hand, register the success of the absolutist project, many of these same accounts are engaged with more distanced observational and pragmatic concerns, demonstrating that the sensual and cognitive "shock and awe" associated with *meraviglia* was not all-consuming. These concerns include an interest in the mechanical workings of the sets and scenery (there are frequent references to pulleys and ropes, even though the devices mostly appear to have remained unseen), references to technical features of the music, and recognition that the musicians on the stage were palpable human beings with particular qualities and skills.[20] These and many other kinds of observations deflect attention away from wholesale absorption in the mythical realm that the Medici court was concerned to project.

In his study *Bodies and Selves in Early Modern England*, Michael Schoenfeldt disputes the terms of New Historicism, with its Foucauldian backdrop, by demonstrating that the individual was not merely prey to "the power that circulates through culture" through institutions, practices, and sociocultural discourses.[21] He argues that looking closely at the past allows us instead to see what "individuals made of the materials of their culture, and their bodies, as well as what their cultures and bodies made of them."[22] In other words, Schoenfeldt entertains a dialectical approach that favors neither the complete autonomy of the individual nor the monolithic power of cultural forces. While *meraviglia* was an aesthetic and political force to be reckoned with within the context of the Uffizi theater, the testimony of the spectator-auditor conveys that there was more to *meraviglia* than met the eye (and ear).

Rossi explains one form of *meraviglia* that involved the evisceration of a preceding image—provoked, for example, by repeated viewings of Florence's incomparable *duomo* or by witnessing one wonder trump another in the

Pellegrina interludes—thereby inspiring "nuova maraviglia" (new wonder) in the viewer.[23] This evisceration destabilized the viewing process, registering the fleeting quality of meaning and the difficulty of proscribing credential knowledge through visual means. So too, sound, as a source of *meraviglia,* was inherently unstable due to its transience. The exertion of power through the aural medium at once referenced the intended power source—Duke Ferdinando—at the same time as the diffusion of sound demonstrated a lack of containment, suggesting that meaning was difficult to control. Thus, through the ambiguities and/or failures of *meraviglia,* the spectator-auditor commanded a central position in the meaning-making process.

In his essay on monarchical performativity at the French court, Mark Franko argues that the performance itself sustained "the ambiguity and contradiction of personal sovereignty . . . [leaving] it with the audience to carry away or resolve."[24] A similar conclusion was reached by one of the eyewitnesses of the premiere performance of the *Pellegrina* interludes, the German visitor Barthold von Gadenstedt, who, after a comparatively detailed account of his impressions, leaves final reckonings regarding the interludes' music to the auditor: "[A]ll who understand and appreciate music can judge and ponder for themselves what sort of music this was."[25] Presumably this "ponder[ing]" occurred after the performance took place. The performance experience did not lend itself to sustained thought, nor gaze-like absorption, although I do suggest that the opening number of the interludes came closest to mesmerizing the audience.[26] Experiencing performance is the aural equivalent of what Norman Bryson differentiated in *Vision and Painting* as the glance, not the gaze.[27] In the case of the *Pellegrina* interludes, not only was displacement and deferral structurally embedded in the viewing process (more so than in the act of viewing a painting),[28] but the spectator-auditor could direct attention toward any number of places (including other audience members) or to any number of considerations (for example, was the singer who performed in *intermedio* one—the prima donna Vittoria Archilei—the same woman who appeared at the opening of *intermedio* four?)[29] or toggle attention between various media. While major structural junctures seem largely determined by the interludes' creators—although even here Cavallino creates his own set of interludes by conflating some and individuating parts of another[30]—spectator-auditors engaged in their own form of "mental editing," privileging some parts of the experience, while discarding or ignoring others. As such, the production of *meraviglia* could not be guaranteed, although Rossi's precipitous account—which was still "in press" when the premiere performance took place—would have the reader believe otherwise.

Brief Overview

Part 1 of this study sets the stage by addressing broad political and aesthetic concerns that influenced the nature of the *Pellegrina* performances. I position these concerns as those of the Medici family and Duke Ferdinando in particular. Chapter 1, "The Politics of Dynasty," explores the Medicean impetus to establish political legitimacy. I examine the ways in which the Medici dukes strengthened their political and cultural status, particularly through international diplomacy. I also examine the perceptions they sought to generate through various types of propagandistic discourse and the relationship of that discourse to the performative mode. I consider Duke Ferdinando's "backstage" role as the *Pellegrina* interludes' theatrical arbiter.

Chapter 2, "The Aesthetic of Wonder," begins with a general consideration of *meraviglia* in the early modern period, including links with theatrical practice. More specifically, I consider a Neoplatonic conception of wonder filtered through the ideas of the contemporaneous philosopher, Francesco Patrizi, as a means of understanding how *meraviglia* functioned in light of the inability of many spectator-auditors to understand the words of much of the interludes' sung music. Finally, I consider the attempt to posit Duke Ferdinando as Neoplatonic Magus (in sharp contrast to his "hands-on" role as theatrical arbiter).

Chapter 3, "Court *Intermedi* at Florence," examines conceptions of the *intermedio* as a genre during the Cinquecento and in recent scholarship. I address the relationship between theory and practice, and situate these questions within broader debates regarding aesthetic preferences for unity and/or variety. The chapter concludes with a summary of what is known of each of the *Pellegrina* performances in terms of their constituent audience members, and of the commentators themselves.

Part 2 of the study offers sequential readings of each of the *Pellegrina* interludes. Each chapter balances the available sources in different ways, enabling the interpretative emphases suggested therein. The very nature of the subject matter demands an interdisciplinary approach. The reader will find elements of the following in each chapter: (1) an evaluation of the relationship between Rossi's *Descrizione,* eyewitness and unofficial reports, Malvezzi's musical print, costume and scenic designs, and other related sources, and (2) a consideration of possible motivations for the creators' musical and staging decisions not offered by official accounts. This consideration is threefold, addressing (a) elements omitted from Rossi's account (because his publication does not include last minute changes), (b) aspects not included by Rossi because of his (apparent) lack of interest in (or knowledge of) the performative *effects* of musical *meraviglia,* and (c) intentions deduced from the *Memoriale e ricordi,* the production logbook kept by Girolamo Seriacopi, and other "behind-the-scenes" sources. James Saslow has written of the "interlocking complexity" that underpins the wide-reaching interest in Renaissance festival.[31] With musical performance and *meraviglia* as central threads of a complex web, I hope to add to this complexity, showing how meaning and interpretation can come from the most unlikely (yet obvious) of sources: those individuals themselves who experienced the performance(s).

PART ONE
Medicean Theater

Aesthetic
and
Political
Underpinnings

CHAPTER ONE

The Politics of Dynasty

The Medici Grand Dukes: Consolidating the Duchy

FROM LATE APRIL through early June 1589, a series of ritualized events were staged for the wedding celebrations of Ferdinando I de' Medici (1549–1609) and Christine de Lorraine (1565–1636).[1] Royal weddings were carefully weighed diplomatic maneuvers that served to negotiate and renegotiate power relations in the constantly evolving sphere of international politics. Ferdinando's bold choice of a Valois princess marked the first step in a policy that sought to check Florence's dependence on Habsburg Spain. Sensing that Spain had passed its prime (the defeat of the Armada in 1588 was one indication among several), Ferdinando began by abrogating his father Duke Cosimo I's pledge that Medici alliances should meet the approval of the Spanish king. He was also no longer willing to unconditionally supply Spain with loans that were rarely repaid, and demanded that Phillip II give up his claim to the State of Siena. That the Spanish ambassador not only attended the Medici wedding celebrations (presenting Ferdinando with a letter of congratulation) but also relinquished Spain's claim to Siena is testament to the duke's political acumen. Further, the duke retained his influence in Rome after renouncing his cardinalate, using his contacts to negotiate a careful equilibrium between Spanish and French interests. Ferdinando's reign is generally characterized as one of consolidation: it brought the Florentine *principato* (principate) an unprecedented independence in foreign affairs and greater control over internal affairs, the latter accomplished chiefly through Ferdinando's centralization of government.[2]

Despite Ferdinando's obvious successes, the period of the wedding festivities during May 1589 were just the early days of his reign. It is easy in hindsight to trace an irreversible trend toward Medici consolidation, but to at least some of his contemporaries present for the wedding festivities, Ferdinando's success was by no means assured. In the early years of the Medici *principato* the family's rise in fortune must have seemed easily reversible, especially to the powerful families of the mercantile oligarchy such as the Strozzi and Salviati.[3] Throughout the sixteenth century there still existed strong anti-Medici senti-ment among aristocratic families with ties to broader-based economic and political systems. With French support, these families exercised a kind of "po-litical countersystem" that Cosimo had difficulty controlling, even with the help of the Holy Roman Emperor. The terms of the Medici's restoration in 1530 by Pope Clement VII (with the help of Charles V and his imperial troops) had left Cosimo a legacy of judicial ties and encumbrances. Thus, Cosimo's reign was necessarily characterized by a vigilant safeguarding of Florentine in-dependence. In part, it was through careful control of the diplomatic sphere— most notably through negotiations with leading European superpowers—that Cosimo was able to gain protection without stooping to subservience.[4] He used a complex diplomatic web of personal and clientelistic relationships to help shore up his dynastic prerogative at the international level which fed into the consolidation of his governmental apparatus at home: the men who com-posed the upper echelon of Cosimo's government were largely funneled through his diplomatic corp. In other words, the domestic and international spheres were inextricably connected, and the insights gleaned from diplomatic service were brought to bear on internal politics.[5]

Some of Cosimo's most important successes at the international level hinged on his relationship with Emperor Charles V, whose power was not to be underestimated. At Charles's coronation by Clement VII, the pope de-clared him "Emperor of the Romans and Lord of the Whole World"; as as-pects of the decorations for Cosimo's wedding festivities indicate, the emperor's dominions extended from Peru to the Black Sea. Indeed, one of Cosimo's key political aims at his own wedding celebrations was to demonstrate his loyalty to the emperor.[6] The relationship was reciprocal. In exchange for assistance against Turkish pirates, Charles relinquished his hold over several Tuscan fortresses, including the one manned by Imperial troops in Florence. In the mid-1550s Cosimo aided the Emperor through the conquest of Siena, which had set itself up as a republic in opposition to Imperial rule. The effort paid off: after two years of Spanish rule the State of Siena was partly relinquished to the Medici. The culmination of Cosimo's push to gain status at the inter-national level was perhaps the legitimization of the new politico-territorial organization granted by Pope Pius V in 1569. Cosimo was crowned Grand Duke of Tuscany, a political status that assured him preeminence over other dukes and rulers of autonomous states. Seven years later during the reign of Cosimo's son, Francesco I, the Emperor officially recognized the grand-ducal title. These were all important moments in a general campaign for increased political independence, but were by no means *faits accomplis*.

While international and domestic affairs were in many respects intertwined, Cosimo's internal reforms set a pattern that was to dominate the Medici principate: the duke reorganized the political economy—in particular, the guilds, treasury, mint, and tax system—in order to bring it under his direct supervision. In practice this meant that governmental officials oversaw (and could therefore more easily manipulate) economic domains that had previously maintained some degree of autonomy. Further, Cosimo established for himself the right to intervene and prevail in matters even at the expense of his own governmental officials. This was no piecemeal adjustment of minor aspects of the economy, as Judith Brown has argued, but rather a wholesale and systematic overhaul of the economic mechanism that firmly placed the reigns of control in a governmental apparatus that gave Cosimo himself absolute jurisdiction.[7] In this respect, Cosimo can be considered an absolutist prince, notwithstanding the diffuse channels through which absolutist power was necessarily maintained and exercised.

With this in mind, it is perhaps surprising to note that Cosimo's actual court was of quite modest proportions, one might even say provincial, by European standards. To be sure, there were high-profile public celebrations at court for weddings and other dynasty-affirming events, but day-to-day courtly life was by no means extravagant.[8] The court remained largely a private affair consisting of Cosimo's next-of-kin and faithful secretaries and advisors, with little involvement from the older aristocracy, whom Cosimo, like his son Ferdinando, was careful to keep at bay.[9] Alessandra Contini has suggested that the pinching and scraping to conserve funds might have opened up political advantages abroad, enabling Cosimo to finance European superpowers in exchange for increased recognition in the international sphere.[10] In keeping with the desire to secure international prestige, Cosimo ensured that when Ferdinando became cardinal at Rome, his son's court displayed the necessary grandeur that would reflect positively on the Medici *principato*. Ferdinando arrived in Rome in 1569 with such an enormous retinue that the Farnese cardinal was moved to remark: "he has come with such an entourage that he shall humiliate us."[11] While the reasons for Cosimo's decision to constitute a court of such magnitude for Ferdinando (while maintaining comparatively frugal practices in his own) were likely multifarious, it appears that in the context of the powerful political networks of the Roman curia, self-representation through conspicuous consumption was considered paramount.

When Cosimo's son Francesco died in 1587 after a fourteen-year reign that produced no eligible male heir, Ferdinando renounced his cardinal's hat and returned to Florence. Unlike Francesco, who apparently had more interest in alchemical experiments than in advancing Cosimo's administrative or economic policies, Ferdinando vigorously pursued commercial interests, sponsored experimentation in the areas of science and technology, and further consolidated the principate's international diplomatic ties.[12] Ferdinando also channeled funds toward conspicuous areas that would bolster his international stature, but like his father he too was known for his frugality and financial efficiency.[13] Indeed, he used the occasion of his own wedding to centralize the administration of all the artists, craftsmen, and musicians at court, installing Emilio de' Cavalieri as superintendent of fine arts (with a requisite bureaucracy) in the Uffizi.[14] This brought the fine arts in line with other governmental agencies, whose centralization Cosimo had orchestrated. Cavalieri became a central figure in Ferdinando's broader scheme to situate Tuscany's arts and industries beyond dependence on foreign states. At a more immediate level, the authority that Ferdinando vested in Cavalieri—who was a relative newcomer to Florence, sharing the duke's Roman background—had profound artistic and political implications for the 1589 wedding celebrations, and particularly for the performances of the *Pellegrina intermedi*.

Princely Magnificence

Although shrewd with regard to expenditure, Ferdinando's court was a greatly expanded one compared with that of his father, even the court that Cosimo maintained during the latter years of his reign in the late 1560s and early 70s. In 1588 the Venetian ambassador Tommaso Contarini noted that Ferdinando "has enlarged the court and given it much greater *magnificenza* than it previously possessed. . . . He is arraying the court with men who are noble and give it splendor."[15] The key word here is *magnificenza* (magnificence), not only as it applied to material culture but also to the princely attribute or virtue that prompted such manifestations. In the fifteenth century, the notion of magnificence was the most frequently cited justification for the building of permanent structures that adorned public spaces. Aristotle and Aquinas were the authorities cited to bolster the view that virtuous use of money by people of "high birth and reputation" was connected to "greatness and prestige"; Aristotle's *Ethics* confirmed that *magnificenza* was the demonstrable indication of a great spirit or magnanimity.[16] Through reference to this philosophical position, Florentine humanists provided a rationale for the building projects of Cosimo il Vecchio (1389–1464), the "old" (or "first") Cosimo, as later Medicean writers and historians described him. The 1589 account of the Medici wedding festivities by Bastiano de' Rossi is permeated by references to *magnificenza;* indeed, he introduces the concept at the outset of his *Descrizione,* and several pages later refers to Cosimo il Vecchio's works as a manifestation of the "true example" of *magnificenza*.[17]

As the reference to Cosimo il Vecchio in Rossi's account indicates, the concept of *magnificenza* was closely linked to the issue of political legitimacy through precedence. I will elaborate this connection below. Here, I would like to observe that the term *magnificenza* was not only associated with the construction of permanent structures such as buildings, but could also provide a rationalization for conspicuous consumption more generally. In line with Aristotle's emphasis on the correct use of wealth, *magnificenza* could inspire ephemeral manifestations such as spectacles, feasts, and other displays through which the prince asserted his public image.[18] Indeed, the concept found its way into theatrical treatises, such as that of Sebastiano Serlio, who in a discussion of scenery for satyric scenes made the following comments:

> And these things, when they are more expensive, they will be so much more praiseworthy, because in truth these [things] belong to generous, magnanimous, and wealthy lords, the enemies to ill-favored penny-pinching. I already saw some scenes of this type with my own eyes, prepared by the knowledgeable architect Girolamo Genga at the urging of his lord, Francesco Maria, Duke of Urbino, where I witnessed as much liberality in the prince as judgment and skill in the architect.[19]

The Jewish playwright, dramatic theorist, and director Leone de' Sommi expressed similar sentiments. In the fourth dialogue of his *Quattro dialoghi,* the interlocutor Massimiano refers to the superb *apparato* (set-up or decorations) for the tourney that took place in the courtyard of Duke Guglielmo Gonzaga's castle as part of his wedding celebrations.[20] De' Sommi (who conceals himself under the pseudonym of Veridico) goes so far as to suggest that the duke's magnificence was greater for having spent so many thousands of ducats on the *apparato,* but then destroying it as soon as it had served its purpose.[21]

Intermedi were singled out for their connection to princely *magnificenza* by the poet G. B. Strozzi the Younger (who contributed poetic texts for the fourth *intermedio* for *La pellegrina*). After a summary of the original purpose of interludes in his work known as "Prescriptions for Intermedi,"[22] Strozzi states: "But today the *magnificenza* of princes, and here particularly in Florence, has made *intermedi* so great and elevated, that it shows that their purpose is to amaze every viewer with their greatness. . . ."[23] Evidently disapproving of the extravagances of the *intermedi,* yet mindful of the need for deference where princes were concerned, Strozzi softens his prefatory remarks by stating that he "will not question if this [the elevation of the *intermedi*] should or should not be the case" and mentions "honoring in these matters the highness of great souls [i.e., princes]. . . ."[24]

As an indication of Duke Ferdinando's princely *virtù* (virtue) and magnanimity, Rossi frequently emphasized the duke's magnificence in his

1589 *Descrizione.* With regard to the specific occasion at hand, Rossi makes clear that the performance of Girolamo Bargagli's comedy *La pellegrina* with its *intermedi* was intended as the crowning jewel of the festivities, as the highest expression of the duke's *magnificenza:*

> [R]egardless of what type of magnificence, he [Duke Ferdinando] is not at all inferior to anybody else in his most serene family. And nevertheless wanting to show with works how much he is a lover of this virtue—besides the other splendid festivities made in his happy wedding, which filled with unprecedented wonder and amazement all those who saw them, in order to honor them and make them even more magnificent—he also wanted to present a representation of a comedy that for the beauty of the *apparato,* for the variety and beauty of the scenery, for the nobility and richness of its customs that are used in the *intermedi,* for the quantity of ingenious and wonderful machines [in the *intermedi*], was not inferior to any comedy, that might have been at any time whatsoever, ever recited in this city.[25]

Rossi's comments on Ferdinando's *magnificenza* provide a glimpse of the multifaceted task that he faced as official commentator. One task was to capture in prose, for commemorative purposes, the temporal musico-theatrical event that took place in the Uffizi theater.[26] The medium of print allowed Rossi to document details that were all but impossible for the spectator-auditor to retain in the rapidly evolving context of performance. As such, Rossi's text served as an index to the prince's magnificences. The ephemera that he catalogued—from the intricate details of costume designs, to the frequent listings of musical instruments, to the eleven-page description of the Uffizi theater's *apparato*—all testify to Ferdinando's *magnificenza.* The exhaustive details not only provided an inventory of the prince's magnificences that could be passed on to those who did not witness the performances, but may even have overwhelmed the reader in the same way as the performances were designed to overwhelm the audience. By saturating his text with intricate description, the reader may have been pushed to experience something like the awe of the spectator in the performance context of the Uffizi theater during May 1589. Stated another way, the effect of Rossi's rhetorical strategy on the reader was somewhat akin to the intended effect of this multi-media spectacle on the spectator-auditor: both sought to overwhelm and thereby arouse *meraviglia* (wonder) in the perceiver. In this respect, the concept of magnificence was closely allied with the evocation of wonder (see chapter 2, section entitled "The Currency of *meraviglia:* Inside and Outside the Theater"). Yet while the reader could contemplate Rossi's elaborate explication of material culture at leisure, the spectator-auditor had little time to consciously grasp the effects bombarding multiple senses. As such, the testimony of commentators suggests that the spectator-auditor mapped a course through the performative terrain that both registered (some) aspects of the Florentine court's politico- artistic agenda at the same time as actively defining their *own* meanings in light of a variety of considerations and identifications. Part 2 of this study traces these identifications and charts their meanings.

Shoring Up Dynastic Prerogative: Precedent and Continuity

It is a well-known fact of Medicean political history that during the transition from republic to *principato,* the family pursued policies and modes of self-representation that emphasized precedent and continuity as a means of shoring up their dynastic prerogative.[27] This project—which manifested itself through Medici-commissioned art works, ephemeral *feste,* and written texts such as funeral orations, *descrizioni,* or even more blatantly propagandistic works such as G. B. Strozzi's *Della famiglia de' Medici*—began with Duke Cosimo I and continued through the reigns of his successors. I will not rehearse this material here; instead I will briefly elucidate some of the ways in which this strand of Medicean self-representation informed Duke Ferdinando's wedding festivities. One of the more prominent manifestations was the series of arches and street decorations constructed for the entrance of Christine of Lorraine into the city of Florence.[28] Adorning these structures were stucco sculptures and paintings arranged along a trajectory of increasing monarchical perfection.[29] The first arch, for example, included a series of scenes from the alleged founding of Florence by Imperial Romans, and culminated with a canvas personifying the city of Florence, donning regal attire similar to the grand ducal habit. Thus, the first arch was given a ducal gloss—as if the Medici *principato* had been preordained—in what was presented as a sequence of "historical" events. The second arch presented a seamless and inevitable progression from republic to *principato* by depicting a series of Medici marriages from both regimes, up to and including that of Ferdinando.

These are only two brief examples from the arches constructed for Christine's entry into Florence that demonstrate the way visual art was utilized in the service of Ferdinando's political agenda.[30] It is evident from eyewitness accounts that spectators were generally able to "read" the political program suggested by the arches,[31] that is, they were able to readily identify the series of historical figures presented. This process was aided by the availability of book two of Raffaello Gualterotti's two-part guide to the street decorations,[32] which included corresponding illustrations.[33] Furthermore, the nature of outdoor arches and street decorations granted the viewer considerable observational autonomy, quite distinct from the act of viewing transitory imagery in the context of a closed court theater performance, such as those staged in the Uffizi.

In a similar vein, the act of reading Bastiano de' Rossi's commemorative *Descrizione* allowed the reader to contemplate the text at will, but it also allowed Rossi, through the medium of print, to create a cohesive chronological narrative that masked gaps in Medicean ancestral continuity (as he did in the preface of his booklet).[34] Indeed, the virtue of *magnificenza* as it applied to Medici rulers in general becomes the linchpin that holds the opening of Rossi's narrative together, allowing him to emphasize precedent as a means of legitimizing the current Medici regime. Not only does he use the overarching virtue of *magnificenza* as a means of blurring distinctions between all types of political systems (regardless of time or place),[35] but this leveling tactic provides a firm foundation on which to proceed with a degree of specificity: the city of Florence is posited as the "true" successor of the *magnificenza* of Imperial Rome, with its games, spectacles, and extraordinary theater that could hold some 8,000 people.[36] Humanist pretensions are thus brought into play, with continuity asserted through the imitation of ancient practice. Rossi later reiterates the connection between Florence and ancient Rome by suggesting that the city of Florence—due to its own magnificences—"will be sure to be the worthy daughter of such a mother [i.e., Rome]."[37]

The importance of ancient precedent, and particularly that of Rome, originally figured into the performative experience of the *Pellegrina* interludes, but the idea appears never to have come to fruition. Rossi's account indicates that there was a definite intention on the part of the creators of the spectacle to suggest a sense of continuity between the more distant past and present by presenting a view of Rome at the very opening of the entertainment, just prior to prologue of the first *intermedio*. Rossi clearly believed that spectators would recognize the city (he recounts the scene in the past tense as if recounting the reaction of audience members), which incorporated the city's well-known ancient structures. According to Rossi

> [t]he spectators believed that the scenery that was shown to them when the curtains fell—in which they could immediately recognize Rome—was going to be the one where they were going to represent the comedy. And they believed that there was not going to be any other scenery, and that the plot would begin in Rome. So much had the designer done with the excellence of his art, representing reality so well, that he was able to put at the back of the scenery, far from the eyes [of the spectator], the most noble and most wonderful ancient buildings, and modern ones of the sovereign city, and to give the impression that under the buildings would be the stage where the actors would be. He not only represented that [Rome], but the perspective seemed entirely realistic.[38]

Rossi focuses on the surprise factor here—that spectators were "tricked" into believing that they were witnessing the set for Bargagli's comedy *La pellegrina,* when in fact subsequent action would prove them wrong. Not only would the comedy use another set—replicating the Medici-ruled city of Pisa—but the entertainment would begin with the first *intermedio,* not the comedy. Saslow provides an additional perspective on this opening gesture: when the stage curtain and wall hangings in the auditorium instantaneously dropped, the Corinthian stage design and wall decorations mirrored each other, suggesting the conflation of stage and social life.[39] As Clifford Geertz has suggested with regard to ritual in general: "[T]he world as lived and the world as imagined, fused under the agency of a single set of symbolic forms, [would] turn out to be the same world."[40] Certainly, the Roman setting would have helped to reify long-standing myths regarding Medicean dynastic prerogative: not only was Florence the "worthy daughter" of Rome, but Ferdinando's marriage would usher in a newly articulated, all-encompassing vision for the city based on the notion of Florence as a "new Rome."[41] In addition, the city of Rome had obvious personal significance for the newly appointed duke, who had spent nearly two decades there as cardinal and was intent on preserving his political influence among the Roman curia. (Indeed, the splendorous entourages of Roman cardinals provided a highly visible presence among Ferdinando's invited wedding guests.) There also seems to have been some intent to blend the "real" and the mythic by blurring the scenic demarcation between comedy and interlude. The realistic Roman scene was to become the backdrop for the mythical prologue of *intermedio* one, in which a lone singer descended on a cloud.[42]

Despite the elaborate plans and expectations for the opening of the entertainment, the idea for the Roman set seems not to have been followed through. Rossi's source is the only one that mentions any such opening scene.[43] The intent, however, speaks to the relationship between myth and reality, because an identifiable depiction of Rome had both contemporary significance as well as links to a Medici-envisioned mythic past.

By way of contrast to the use of a realistic set of a city for the comedy—Pisa provided the setting for *La pellegrina*—the *intermedi* transported the perceiver into a mythical realm of gods and goddesses that had little *overt* connection to an identifiable past and the sense of continuity such a reference might provoke. This point is important because it speaks to subtle changes in political ideology that, by 1589, found their most efficacious manifestation in the context of the performances of the *Pellegrina intermedi.* In order to highlight these changes, I will briefly discuss the set of *intermedi* performed exactly fifty years earlier—in 1539—for Antonio Landi's play *Il commodo.* The entertainment was performed as part of the

wedding celebrations of Duke Cosimo to Eleanora of Toledo, daughter of
the viceroy of Naples.

The setting for Landi's play, like that for Bargagli's, was the city of Pisa.
Unlike *La pellegrina,* however, *Il commodo* was performed in a courtyard
setting—the second *cortile* (courtyard) of the Palazzo Vecchio. The performance followed a banquet for invited guests under the loggias of the first
cortile.[44] While this *cortile* was smaller and more contained than the space at
the Uffizi, it was not a purpose-built venue for theater, and of course the considerable technological advancements that would be made in the intervening
fifty years were unavailable to Cosimo's designers.[45] I will not discuss the
subject matter or mythological content of the *intermedi* for *Il commodo* here,
as those topics have been treated at length elsewhere[46] and my interest is in
the non-mythological aspect of the entertainment.

Kelley Harness recently drew attention to the significance of the theater
decorations for the *intermedi* for *Il commodo,* which included a series of twelve
large paintings (measuring some sixteen by ten feet each) positioned on the
east and west side of the *cortile.*[47] The paintings on the east side pertained to
Cosimo il Vecchio and his republican successors (with particular emphasis on
Neapolitan relations), while the set on the west side concerned important moments in the life of the current Grand Duke Cosimo I. The size of the paintings not only ensured their visibility but also allowed the spectator to readily
identify key Medici protagonists. While the paintings themselves were obviously stationary, it was the sun's movement from east to west during the
course of the performance (marking also the entertainment's passage through
time) that served to highlight the progress (via identifiable images) toward a
new dawning of Medicean prosperity. At the end of the entertainment, as the
sun set in the west over the final painting of the nuptials, the journey through
Medicean "history" was complete.[48]

Shoring Up Dynastic Prerogative: The Prince as God

During the performance of the 1589 *Pellegrina* interludes there was no such
overt gesture articulating the seemingly inevitable progression from the republic to the *principato,* let alone one that provided a unifying frame for the
entire entertainment in the manner of the *intermedi* for *Il commodo.* Let us
begin by considering the *apparato* for the Uffizi theater itself. What is striking
is that the decorations—described at length by Rossi[49]—did not lend themselves to easy interpretation without the aid of his text, which was not available for the premiere performance. Aside from a few obvious references to the
bride and groom, it is notable that most commentators, including eyewitness
ones, only describe the very general effect of the theater on the viewer, with

little if any reference to precise details of iconography. Generally speaking, commentators stress the use of color and light in the hall, emphasizing its richness and magnificence.[50] Evidently, the average viewer had some diffi- cultly ascribing precise meaning to much of the Uffizi's decorative content. For example, a series of statues variously based on themes associated with comedy and poetry would have been difficult, if not impossible, to interpret without the aid of Rossi's commentary.[51] One also wonders whether more obvious iconographical features—such as the coat of arms of Ferdinando and his bride attached to the sixteen chandeliers—would have even been clearly visible at such height.[52] Despite his detailed descriptions, various comments by Rossi suggest what is plainly evident in most other written accounts: dur- ing the performance, the iconographical details collectively produced an overarching impression of "the extraordinary greatness and magnificence of this wedding," rather than pinpointing distinct personages or images that could be identified with the Medici.[53] (It is also notable that the 171-page de- scription of the 1539 performance includes the entire script of the comedy [with only very brief descriptions of the interludes], whereas Rossi's booklet is almost exclusively dedicated to the *Pellegrina* interludes.)[54]

An emphasis on abstract generalities in 1589 points up a new strand of Medicean self-representation that historian Samuel Berner has tied to the late Cinquecento in general, and in particular to the reign of Ferdinando. By ex- amining the rhetoric of ducal funeral orations, Berner identifies a gradual shift in tone from a conceptualization of the prince as a palpable, recogniz- able human being into a figure who is beyond human concerns and thereby elevated to the celestial realm. According to Berner, the funeral oration deliv- ered by Bernardo Davanzati to the Accademia degli Alterati depicted Duke Cosimo I moving "through a real, historical Florence and not through the nebulous sublunary expanse to which the divine right theorists of the end of the century will assign Duke Ferdinando."[55] Berner argues that the "lack of verisimilitude as well as the references to the divine-right theory of kingship" that emerge in Lorenzo Giacomini's 1587 funeral oration for Duke Francesco "find their full[est] expression in the orations delivered on Duke Ferdinando's death in 1609."[56] Berner has discussed the language that characterizes the discourse surrounding Ferdinando, noting that the metaphors and images used—references to vast expanses of ocean or the mysteriousness of human events, for example—served to both distance the "real" Ferdinando from his subjects as well as align the duke with the infinite and divine.

The characterization of an almost disembodied duke in official discourse found material manifestation in the make-up of Ferdinando's court. Com- paratively few Florentines were employed within the inner circles at court, and even fewer Florentines of the patrician class found favor at court.[57] The physical distance that Ferdinando maintained between his person and the greater majority of Florentine patricians meant that they were denied regular access to the courtly context, the arena through which favor and privilege could be sought. Only on an infrequent basis were patricians invited to attend occasions at court, such as the festivities of 1589, and even then they were not given first priority as audience members (see chapter 3, section entitled "The Performances in the Uffizi Theater"). On these occasions, the duke and his retinue were typically given visual prominence, but actual physical proximity to the ruler was limited by strict codes determined by rank and gender. In all cases, Ferdinando's public appearances were carefully stage-managed and one can be sure that a politics of representation informed descriptions in court records of even his most "natural" appearances. For example, Ferdinando's historian and genealogist, Scipione Ammirato, marveled at one of the duke's most public displays when he personally took to the streets of Florence unguarded and muddied, distributing grain to the needy after the floods of October 1589.

> You may be certain Your Excellency . . . that I have never seen with my eyes a more noble sight than this, that of Grand Duke Ferdinando unguarded, with few horsemen and [even] fewer men on foot, going through the city all muddied, performing that duty which is truly princely. And as I usually say, the most beautiful building that Grand Duke Cosimo made was that of the porch at the Ponte Vecchio in order to walk through his [aerial] corridor to the Pitti [Palace], because when that citizen denied him the passage above his house, he did not want to exercise his power; thus I truly say that I have no hope of seeing the Grand Duke in a more beautiful or more stately act than that, in which it was my good fortune to chance upon and witness that day, that it drew tears from my eyes. Thus I assure you in good faith, that if my overly great timidity had not held me back I would, from the infinite affection that I felt being stirred to, go to embrace him and kiss his feet.[58]

I will defer discussion of Ammirato's reference to the Medicean aerial corridor momentarily. Instead, I will focus on Ammirato's representation of Ferdinando's godlike beneficence. The ancient belief that a successful crop yield depended on the efficacy of the monarch's supernatural power would have made the duke's appearance on the street with grain in hand a strategic public gesture that literally demonstrated his ability to provide sustenance to less fortunate Florentines. There is an aura of *meraviglia* embedded in Ammirato's account—the image of the magnanimous duke who in a rare public appearance deigns to descend from on high to tend to the needs of the poor. The duke's unexpected and seemingly miraculous appearance no doubt helped to bolster his general popularity. Indeed, Ferdinando was known to have been well liked by the populace at large.

A more frequent occurrence, however, was the *invisible* presence of the duke. At the public Baldracca theater, which could be reached via bridge directly from the Uffizi, the duke engaged Buontalenti to install a private balcony and grill, from which he could view theatrical proceedings while preserving, in James Saslow's words, "a sacral aura of aloof mystery."[59] It was to this secluded viewing position that the duke appears to have allowed Cesare d'Este access during the period of the wedding celebrations, prior to the performance of the *Pellegrina* interludes.[60] Duke Ferdinando had numerous posts, in fact, that allowed him the opportunity to engage in incognito surveillance not just of theater, but of various other kinds of activities as well. The desire to see but remain unseen was perhaps best epitomized by the possibilities wrought by the half mile elevated corridor (mentioned by Ammirato) built by Giorgio Vasari in 1565.[61] The corridor eventually connected the Medici residence at the Palazzo Pitti in the Oltrarno with the family's administrative headquarters at the Palazzo Vecchio.[62] Cosimo had commissioned the enclosed aerial walkway in conjunction with the marriage preparations for his first son, Francesco, to Joanna of Austria, and the structure was apparently completed in record time—a mere five months, according to Vasari.[63] The initial structure only went as far as the Grotta Grande in the Boboli gardens, but prior to Ferdinando's wedding celebrations (from October 1588 to May 1589), an extension was completed which took the corridor over the northeast garden wall, along the Piazza dei Pitti, and finally into the palace with doorways into the second floor, which housed the duke's apartments.[64] The timing of the extension allowed the duke and his highest-ranking wedding guests, who were housed at the Pitti Palace, to make their way directly to the Uffizi theater in complete privacy.

Not only would the aerial scene amaze distinguished wedding guests during the festivities—Duke Ferdinando took particular advantage of the passageway's power in this respect[65]—but its practical usage had also been envisaged as more long-term: it allowed the Medici dukes to cross the Ponte Vecchio and other parts of the city unseen and in complete security. At the same time, the corridor's various grated windows enabled the dukes to observe others while remaining unseen. On the city side, the corridor was fitted with small bull's eye windows that ensured that those inside were not observed by onlookers in nearby palaces along the Lungarno degi Archibusieri; the river side, on the other hand, had large square windows that gave occupants of the corridor an unimpaired view.[66] Despite the privacy the corridor afforded the Medici, there seems to have been little attempt to hide the actual structure itself from external view, although its integration into the contours of existing buildings meant that only the portions on the Ponte Vecchio and along the Arno were conspicuously visible. Nevertheless, the existence of the passage, with the implication of a potential Medici presence at any given time, projected an image of an omnipresent duke that literally walked above his subjects in an invisible, godlike fashion.

Of all the entertainments staged for Ferdinando's 1589 wedding festivities, the performance of the *Pellegrina* interludes were most clearly poised to present the prince as a god. By the late Cinquecento a set of *intermedi* staged within the confines of a purpose-built court theater was the medium par excellence for demonstrating control of the environment as metaphor for the absolutist prince's control of his dominion and beyond. One obvious manifestation of the godlike prince's power was the subject matter of the *intermedi,* which were "peopled" by gods; analogies between the gods and Ferdinando (and his bride) were numerous and frequently articulated in the sung texts of the Pellegrina *intermedi,* beginning with the very opening number ("Dalle più alte sfere"). This was nothing new, of course; allusions to the "divinity" of Medicean royal couples had been the standard textual conceit for decades.[67] Yet as I will demonstrate, especially in part 2 of this study, the texts of the sung music appear not to have been understood by many audience members; likewise, although courtly audiences were apt to interpret visual imagery in allegorical fashion, their identifications only rarely corresponded with the details supplied in Medici-sanctioned sources. How, then, was the duke's godly power communicated? I would like to suggest that performances of courtly *intermedi* during the principate attempted to *actualize* the duke's power, most especially during the 1580s, when advances in technology pressed each element of the multi-media genre to its most extreme manifestation.[68] This actualization, as I will describe it—in which the duke's (seemingly) divine power was not merely symbolized but enacted through performance—resonated with the conceptual premise of Ficinian Neoplatonism, a dimension that will be addressed in chapter 2.[69] With its emphasis on effects, including musical ones (rather than an overarching concern for unity, continuous plot, or text clarity), the *Pellegrina intermedi*—more so than early opera[70]—attempted to make manifest the duke's seemingly godlike powers. Machines, in particular, were used to evoke the impression that supernatural forces were at work in performance; court diarist Francesco Settimani noted that the *Pellegrina* machines were *quasi soprannaturali* (almost supernatural)[71] and later theorist-practitioners stressed machines as key to the evocation of the supernatural.[72] But as I will demonstrate in detail in part 2 of this study, music was also central to the actualization of the miraculous, as unofficial accounts attest.

With Ferdinando posited as sacred monarch, he could be viewed as the generating force behind the *Pellegrina* interludes, as well as the generator of the projected *semidei* who would secure the Medici line.[73] This explains, in part, the considerable weight that rested on the performances of these *intermedi,* and the amount of time and resources invested in them.[74] Indeed, this was Duke (as opposed to Cardinal) Ferdinando's first and most public demonstration of his power to the world beyond Tuscany. With the eyes of the international community resting on the performance of a set of *intermedi* some three years earlier, it is little wonder that Ferdinando's brother, Duke Francesco, had the Uffizi secretly searched from top to bottom because of a premonition that bombs would explode during the performance, sabotaging the entertainment.[75]

The Medici family were most concerned to impress foreign powers— friendly or otherwise, and it was with this broader audience in mind that they mobilized their seemingly unlimited resources and power.[76] In this regard, the success of the performances could be measured by the extent of the viscerally charged wonder and awe evinced in the auditor-spectator.[77] Here we are not discussing ritualized behaviors of court culture whereby subjects were inculcated through patterns of iteration. On the contrary, spectacles of this magnitude were only mounted on an occasional basis, and attempted to be "one of a kind." By stressing the singularity of the *Pellegrina* interludes I am not suggesting that foreign guests would have been unfamiliar with the kind of spectacle offered by the Florentine court; as we will see, the performances' efficacy depended on the spectator's familiarity with the kinds of spectacles that characterized display by European monarchs[78] (though of course the 1589 festivities were intended to "outdo" them), as well as a more general appreciation of wondrous discourse in various guises. What I am suggesting is that for most spectator-auditors, witnessing the *Pellegrina intermedi* would have constituted a rare, possibly "once in a lifetime" experience. Like travel narratives that recounted experiences in distant or "exotic" lands, unofficial accounts of the *Pellegrina intermedi* emphasize the "truth value" of direct experience.[79] The most persuasive evidence for the extraordinary nature of the performances lay in the indelible impression they were able to exert, through sensory perception (most especially through the eyes and ears), on those present. In effect, the performance experience constituted a credible source for knowledge claims regarding the potency of the Medici dynasty and would help lay the groundwork for a vision of renewed prosperity under the newly installed grand duke.

The Duke as Theatrical Arbiter

How easily I could have moved your souls to wonder, speaking about the splendor of his [Ferdinando's] court . . . of the entertainments, of the spectacles, which were not always premeditated—but were always elaborate, always stately, always wondrous, always worthy of a king. How much I could have said about the pomp and the magnificence of his wedding. . . . [There follows mention of the various weddings over which Ferdinando presided.] The superb decorations [*apparato*], the sumptuous show, the artful invention of priceless machines, the wondrous spectacles, which not only surpassed the expectations of all men everywhere, but also the imagination of the most expert and wisest men; not only were they [the spectacles] impossible to envision in our minds before they were performed, but once performed, and seen again, they could not be grasped by our minds. The expense was incredible, the artifice unimaginable, the inventions most noble, and their glory, and that of the prince, was fulfilled when everyone, by general consensus, admitted that they were wonderful, and that they could not be seen anywhere else but in Florence, nor anywhere else but in Florence could [such things] be arranged, nor could they be staged by any other prince than by the Grand Duke [Ferdinando].[80]

Upon Ferdinando's death in 1609, Giuliano Giraldi of the Academia della Crusca wrote these words in his funeral oration for the grand duke. Giraldi casts Ferdinando as the godlike architect of the various entertainments over which he presided during his reign. The apparent inconceivability of these spectacles was felt not only by mere mortals but also by the connoisseurs who remained mystified despite repeated "viewings." At the same time, the suggestion that the festivals were "not always premeditated"—yet nonetheless elaborate and wondrous—projects a sense of miraculous spontaneity or *sprezzatura,* appropriate for an absolutist prince. In other words, Ferdinando could direct proceedings without (or with very little) apparent labor, a stance that is characterized in a number of the posthumous engravings by Jacques Callot that celebrated the duke's accomplishments (see plate 1 and plate 2). In plate 1, the duke, at the left, is elevated above a scene depicting an assault on two fortresses. The cane in his extended right hand commands the viewer's attention, signaling his authority over the proceedings, but is mirrored by the extended rifles of the Florentine soldiers who are performing the "real" work. The duke's gaze is directed *away* from the battle scenes, with head and eyes inclined in a sympathetic gesture toward the youthful innocence of a young page carrying his helmet (note that the duke does not actually wear his helmet, which is cradled by the page's right hand). Likewise, the duke's left hand rests on the grip of this sword, which nevertheless remains stationary by his side. As the duke and page incline toward each other, the symbolic space created through the meeting of their eyes seems to register a more idyllic place beyond the violence and carnage of the battlefield. Plate 2 is a less ambiguous depiction of *sprezzatura,* showing the fortification and expansion of the port of Livorno. As in plate 1, the duke is positioned above the labor that is taking place (to his right) and his gaze averts the scene. In plate 2, though, a seated and reclining Ferdinando engages with an eager, energized attendant who presents him with what appears to be a (partially completed?) model of one of the port's fortifications. At the risk of over-interpreting this scene, the duke's nonchalant communication with his attendant—his self-assured upward glance and the gesturing hand of his barely raised left arm—suggest that (miraculously) the work is almost complete as busy workers continue their tasks. (Note the state of the two fortifications actively under construction: both "outdo" the truncated model held by the duke's attendant.) A slightly different interpretation would have the duke languidly directing his attendant's attention toward the workers' laboring, thus indicating effortless control, and deflecting physical effort away from his person.

But to return to the entertainment at hand: behind the scenes, of course, the duke took an active role in monitoring the preparations for his wedding festivities, especially for the *Pellegrina intermedi.* There were direct lines of communication between the duke and several of the key figures who oversaw important aspects of production—especially Cavalieri, Buontalenti, and Girolamo Seriacopi—in order to ensure that arrangements were proceeding according to plan. The *Memoriale e ricordi,* Seriacopi's logbook, records commands by the duke that were channeled through Cavalieri or Buontalenti.[81] For example, on December 25, 1588, Seriacopi notes:

> This morning Signor Emilio de' Cavalieri told me that he had [received] a letter of charge from His Most Serene Highness to press him to do all of the things related to the royal festivities for the arrival of his most serene bride. And for this reason work should start as soon as possible on the wooden walkway that goes from the great hall [in the Uffizi] for the comedy [*La pellegrina* with *intermedi*], passes above the roofs and along the church of S. Pietro Scheraggi, and reaches the painted great hall [the Sala dei Cinquecento in the Palazzo Vecchio] where the banquet is to be held.[82]

At the conclusion of the performance, Ferdinando's aerial walkway enabled the audience to proceed directly to the Sala dei Cinquecento, where the banquet ensued.

Regarding the preparations for *La pellegrina* specifically, the duke's commands (as noted in the *Memoriale*) included everything from production details and hall décor to the scheduling of specific rehearsals for the duke himself to attend. It seems that the latter were arranged so the duke could check that preparations were running according to schedule, but also so that he could exercise his politico-artistic authority directly. On April 13, the duke commanded that about 70 *braccia* of flesh-colored cloth should be used to cover the windows of the gallery that overlooked the hall,[83] presumably to maintain an aura of secrecy regarding the impending performances. (The flesh-colored cloth to which the duke referred was evidently intended to match the cloth that had been previously selected to cover the walls of the auditorium.) The duke was also kept abreast of certain production mishaps, such as those involving the fourth *intermedio* (as noted in the *Memoriale* on March 3).[84] It is also highly likely that the duke was involved with last-minute changes to the sixth *intermedio* related to the grand finale "O che nuovo miracolo."[85]

Several of the duke's appearances at rehearsal are mentioned in the *Memoriale*. As the following notification by Cavalieri indicates, the duke's demands were quite specific and his anticipated presence at a rehearsal in early April helped to push the production closer to its finished form:

> His Highness wants to come [to a rehearsal] on Wednesday, and he wants to see the entire comedy, with the costumes, and that it be recited with all the machines and the first *intermedio* of Vittoria [Archilei]. He does not care about the lights, because he wants it to be cool, so that everything possible should be finished [by then] and everything possible should be done. Show this [letter] to the executant [Seriacopi].[86]

The rehearsal that the duke saw did not take place until April 16, but immediately following this one he ordered another that took place on April 25.[87] Ferdinando must have been confident that by April 25 the production was close to its final form, because a dispatch of April 29 by the new Ferrarese ambassador Girolamo Gigliolo indicates that all the Roman cardinals and foreign visitors in Florence at that time attended the dress rehearsal with the duke, even though he was still actively involved in overseeing the proceedings. Gigliolo explains to his patron the Duke of Ferrara, Alfonso d'Este, why he was unable to secure an audience with Duke Ferdinando for that particular day:

> [B]ecause the Grand Duke was busy in assisting at the rehearsal of the comedy that will be staged when the bride comes (where also were all the cardinals and foreign guests who are here at present) we cannot meet that day.[88]

When the premiere performance finally took place on May 2, the duke was of course no longer visibly assisting in preparations but firmly positioned with the ducal party on their raised platform. It was from this position that, according to Rossi, Ferdinando himself visibly gave the cue (to Buontalenti) for the performance to begin,[89] although no eyewitness or other commentators observed the gesture. The duke's potentially surreptitious cue—his last act of labor—signaled the transition from his role as theatrical arbiter to that of Neoplatonic Magus.[90]

CHAPTER TWO

The Aesthetic of Wonder

The Currency of *meraviglia:* Inside and Outside the Theater

IN ROSSI's official *Descrizione* of the *Pellegrina* interludes, notions of *magnificenza* and *meraviglia* are closely intertwined.[1] The description's six-page preface—essentially a panegyric to the Medici linking their achievements with those of the ancients—incorporates a discussion of the magnificence of public buildings in which the rhetoric of wonder is close to the surface. Florence's cathedral, Santa Maria del Fiore,

> placed in the middle of the city with its distinguished bell tower (called by historians "the marble bell tower") and with the superhuman construction of its dome, which, and with great reason is, both for the excellence of its architecture, for the wealth of the finest marble, and for its incomparable height—which bares comparison with the nearby mountains—and always leaving new wonder in those who view it, can be placed ahead of any other building ever built or imagined. . . .[2]

The idea that a stationary structure such as the cathedral's dome can inspire "new wonder" in those who contemplate it—that multiple viewings do not jade its effect—is somewhat analogous to an experience of *meraviglia* in the *intermedi* where one wonder appears to trump another during the course of the performance. Further, Rossi's account of the superhuman feat of constructing the cathedral's dome finds numerous resonances in unofficial descriptions of the ephemeral act of performance where staging effects and performances by musicians are described as beyond human capability. And finally, Rossi's comparison of the cathedral's dome to the nearby mountains resonates with a familiar trope in descriptions of the *intermedi* (in both Rossi's account and unofficial accounts), whereby the artificially constructed theatrical space is favorably compared to the natural world. The *intermedi* not only mimicked aspects of the natural world (*imitatione*), but their technologies demonstrated mastery over that world and, very often, surpassed the "real," thereby engaging with the mannerist realm of *invenzione* (imagination).

As the unofficial accounts indicate, aesthetic criteria central to Rossi's account of the *Pellegrina intermedi* had broad cultural currency. The aesthetic of wonder that lay at the heart of the *intermedi* was readily articulated in contemporaneous literary and artistic cultures, as well as in the natural sciences and philosophy. Although an interest in miracles and marvels was by no means confined to the late Cinquecento, from the mid-sixteenth century onward European culture was distinguished by an increased fascination with the wondrous or marvelous, which Joy Kenseth defines as "those things or events that were unusual, unexpected, exotic, extraordinary, or rare."[3] The term *meraviglia* was also used to refer to human responses to the marvelous, including expressions of astonishment, surprise, admiration, or fear.

The early modern penchant for the marvelous was partly derived from lingering medieval beliefs in the supernatural and the miraculous,[4] but ancient sources provided a renewed and expanded understanding of the wondrous during the Renaissance. Ovid's *Metamorphoses,* which provided the subject matter for several of the *Pellegrina intermedi,* was one such source, describing wondrous transformations of humans, gods, and natural phenomena. This expanded view of wonder was also fueled by the ideas contained in Aristotle's *Rhetoric* and *Poetics* (the latter only became well known in the 1530s and 1540s). Aristotle emphasized the importance of surprising effects or extraordinary events, a tenet that became central to sixteenth-century literary criticism, but eventually spread beyond the literary sphere. His views regarding the didactic function of *meraviglia* were also influential.

European contact with the New World and other distant and "exotic" lands during the late fifteenth and early sixteenth centuries did much to continue the vogue for the marvelous.[5] In addition, advances in science and technology during the final decades of the century facilitated heightened evocation of wonder, enabling designer-engineer Bernardo Buontalenti to create even more spectacular scenic effects in the theatrical context than had his predecessors, including scenic metamorphoses that took place in front of the spectators' very eyes.[6] The latter effect raises the question of verisimilitude with regard to the *intermedi.* The visual and aural technologies marshaled by the interludes' directive elite were enlisted to create wondrous effects that would test the boundaries of the natural and artificial worlds, hence G. B. Strozzi's dictum in his "Prescriptions for Intermedi" that the genre reproduce the verisimilar at the same time that invention and judgment be clearly apparent.[7] While unofficial commentators frequently expressed wonder at how lifelike the fabricated visual effects appeared, the aural dimension—particularly the solo voice—was often experienced as that which exceeded the humanly possible. Indeed, though the lion's share of the solo songs in the *Pellegrina intermedi* required virtuosic performances by female sopranos, the inclusion of the castrato Onofrio Gualfreducci as soloist—whose surgical "modifications" literally embodied the emerging dialectic between the natural and artificial—attested to the willingness to flout nature's bounds for the purpose of increased virtuosity.[8]

Performances demonstrating superior technical skill or virtuosity were not restricted to the musical realm, of course; as John Shearman demonstrates, mannerist works in the visual arts were "conceived in the spirit of virtuoso-performances."[9] Giorgio Vasari—well known for his account of the lives of the artists but also as the artist-engineer of earlier Florentine *intermedi*—begins his biography of Leonardo da Vinci by retelling a story to demonstrate the artist's ability to invoke *meraviglia* through virtuosity. Given a small, round shield by his uncle, Leonardo allegedly decided to paint something on it that would "terrify anyone who saw it and produce the same effect as the head of Medusa."[10] According to Vasari's account, Leonardo assembled a conglomeration of unusual creatures, such as locusts, bats, crickets, and butterflies and, from these various animal parts, created a "fearsome and horrible monster" that "belch[ed] forth venom from its open throat, fire from its eyes and smoke from its nostrils in so macabre a fashion that the effect was altogether monstrous and horrible." Upon completing the painting, Leonardo invited his uncle to a room that he had darkened, save for a light spotting the painted shield. When his uncle saw the painting he was taken by complete surprise, initially unaware that the spotlighted "monster" was Leonardo's contrivance. According to Vasari, the artist's uncle ultimately "thought the painting was indescribably marvelous and he was loud in his praise. . . ."[11] This story raises the issue of the monstrous and the unexpected in relation to the evocation of wonder; both elements will later be explored as they have special relevance for interludes three and four (see especially chapters 5 and 6). What I would like to consider here, however, is the value Vasari (and other contemporary visual artists) placed on elements of technique and style that produced the effect of marveling in the viewer. Qualities such as clarity of execution, the precise rendering of detail, and the ability of the artist to produce miraculous, seemingly magical results resonate closely with qualities deemed desirable in the aural medium, particularly the techniques and effects associated with the interludes' virtuoso solo singers.

The rapid glottal articulations employed by virtuoso singers to execute intricate passagework or *passaggi* could transfix the auditor, as the seemingly superhuman nature of the feat and the projection of triumph over *difficultà* (difficulty) induced a state of *meraviglia*. The precision of execution required of the virtuoso painter to produce the effects Vasari described was paralleled by the requirement that the virtuoso singer possess *dispositione di voce,* a vocal disposition that made the singing of florid *passaggi* possible.[12] According to the Roman singer Giovanni Luca Conforti, disposition was possessed by few singers;[13] it was a means of articulating embellishments with the throat supported by a steady stream of air from the diaphragm that, when successfully rendered, could result in clear, precise, and rapid glottal articulation. Good disposition allowed the execution of seemingly impossible embellishment, often involving leaps and repeated notes in unrelenting scalar passages sung at lightning speed. In and of itself the experience of hearing a singer endowed with this ability seems to have been cause for certain wonderment. Giovanni de' Bardi admitted as much upon hearing an extraordinary bass singer in Rome, despite criticizing the indiscriminate use of the practice in his discourse on ancient music and good singing.[14] Aside from a few brief comments in the Medici-commissioned musical publication *Intermedii et concerti,* unofficial accounts of the soloists (such as Jacopo Peri and Vittoria Archilei) in the *Pellegrina* interludes attest to the evocation of the marvelous, most often through an appeal to the humanly impossible or through reference to the inadequacy of written description to capture the experience. Virtuosos such as Archilei and the castrato Gualfreducci, versed in singing *alla napoletana*—the style of embellishment particularly associated with Roman and Neapolitan musicians—were especially valued and sought after by the Medici. Indeed, Giulio Caccini—who no doubt coached his wife Lucia Caccini for her opening solo in *intermedio* four—was expressly recruited by Grand Duke Cosimo from Rome in 1565 because the duke required a boy soprano with "a beautiful voice and good grace in singing with his *passaggi* in the Neapolitan manner."[15] The solo songs—as notated in the musical publication—were characterized by the kind of extensive embellishment that presumed the singer had *dispositione di voce,* a sure end to evocation of the marvelous.

But the executant—whether painter, writer, or musician—had to have more than just the ability to render ideas with extraordinary clarity and precision. Supreme imaginative powers were needed, as demonstrated by Vasari's account of Leonardo's conglomerative "monster." A term commonly employed for this attribute was *ingegno,* which described the artist's imaginative capacity to invent or fashion the new.[16] The notion of *ingegno* variously suggested imagination, inventiveness, or wit. By the turn of the seventeenth century, the term began to circulate more widely in literary circles, especially among G. B. Marino and his contemporaries, who regarded *ingegno* as a poetic faculty par excellence.[17] In the sixteenth century, references to the artist's ability to inspire wonder through *ingegno* are frequently encountered in descriptions of theatrical performances, most often in regard to the artist-engineer who produced the stage scenery and machinery. In 1589, Buontalenti's *ingegno* was not confined to the stage but according to Rossi extended to the set-up and decorations for the entire theater.[18] Rossi's lengthy account of the theater's *apparato* (decorations) includes this seemingly peripheral description of a painting depicting, among other things, a bear cub and its mother. The subject matter metaphorically illustrates the creative process of the artist, whose *ingegno* enabled the transition from indeterminate matter to creative form:

> In the opening of the said *gradi,* near the doorway on the right, there was a painting in *chiaroscuro* representing Invention, painted by its maker [the artist] in the following way. [There was] a beautiful woman with the wings of mercury over her ears, and a she-bear at her feet, and the she-bear was licking a little bear cub that she had just given birth to, and she was cleaning him perfectly. Because as everyone knows, when the bear gives birth, it is difficult to know what [exactly] it is she gives birth to, but she turns them, by licking them, to her own shape. And the said artificer wanted to demonstrate that from *inventione,* beauty is always born, so he also put at the opposite entry way a figure, also of *chiaroscuro,* and of the same size, which was made to represent Beauty.[19]

Rossi praised Buontalenti more directly when it came to the question of the artist's stage machinery. His most fulsome praise—which explicitly links Buontalenti's *ingegno* with the notion of *meraviglia*—comes at the very end of his account of the theater's *apparato:*

> [T]he architect [Buontalenti] has managed to produce most abundant inventions, so that with a variety of machines that ascend and descend from heaven, and that go through the air and come out from under the stage, and with very frequent changes of scenery, he can show *il vivo suo ingegno* [his liveliness of invention], and at the same time can bring to the people of the audience both *meraviglia* and *diletto* [delight].[20]

As was characteristic of official Florentine *descrizioni* in general, the musicians whose imaginative powers produced the aural delights are never mentioned by name, although poets and composers are routinely noted.[21] (Rossi's description focuses, as was typical, on visual aspects of the characters that individual performers portray, emphasizing the significance of costume designs and attributes.) In unofficial accounts, descriptions of seemingly superhuman performances rarely distinguish technical skill from imaginative prowess, with the two often subsumed beneath a rhetoric of the ineffable. We do know from other sources, however, that a number of the soloists involved in the *Pellegrina intermedi* were renowned for their imaginative abilities.[22] Praising Archilei in the preface to his *Euridice,* Peri refers to Archilei's use of various ornaments "that her *vivezza dell'ingegno* (liveliness of invention) can devise at any time."[23] This was high praise for a female singer; in suggesting imagination, inventiveness, and initiative, *ingegno* was considered an inherently masculine attribute.[24]

Archilei's singing was frequently described as unsurpassed or exceptional during her day; as a singer, she was evidently also valued as one of a very few singers who possessed such extraordinary skill.[25] Rarity—whether with regard to items of material culture or to the singing voice—was also considered a source of *meraviglia*. Solo songs in fact made up a relatively small proportion of the musical numbers in the *intermedi* (and Archilei performed two of the four), but they were strategically placed to produce maximum effect. The scope and variety of musical resources employed for the *intermedi*—from solo voice accompanied by a single string instrument to multi-choir ensembles supported by a diverse array of instrumental forces—also helped to generate *meraviglia*. By the same token, the variety of musical genres employed in the *intermedi*—both "old" and "new" styles—gestured toward the interest in encyclopedism that characterized the age. The concept of variety, though evidently somewhat problematic in theory, was the modus operandi of the *intermedi* (see chapter 3, section entitled "*La varietà e l'unità*").

Novelty or variety—which manifested itself in the interludes through the juxtaposition of the unusually large or small (in terms of musical resources and their cumulative effect)—was also a central aesthetic tenet of contemporaneous museum culture. Indeed, the curiosity cabinet or *teatro di natura* (theater of nature) freely intermixed artificial and natural phenomena of all shapes and sizes in provocative ways that induced wonder and curiosity on the part of the viewer, with the gallery of the Medici dukes at Florence being no exception. Ferdinando himself was an avid collector; during his time as cardinal in Rome he had benefited from the dissolution of collections of antiquities by Counter-Reformation popes, which he transferred to the Uffizi upon his investiture as grand duke.[26] As accounts of his wedding festivities attest, the occasion gave the duke an ideal opportunity to open his gallery doors, but only to specially invited guests.[27]

The spectacle of theater was perhaps the medium best suited to the production of *meraviglia* because of the temporal nature of performance. The wonder evoked through the introduction of surprising or unexpected effects was particularly efficacious. Throughout his account Rossi emphasizes the rapidity of scenic shifts that left the audience two paces behind, as it were, as they mentally adjusted to new and surprising effects. While Rossi's account is clearly that of an insider (and was written *before* he was able to witness the audience's reaction), foreign eyewitness accounts such as those of the German visitor Barthold von Gadenstedt or the anonymous French observer confirm the immediacy and unexpected quality of scenic maneuvers.[28]

An aesthetic of wonder also underpinned the propensity for introducing strange or threatening qualities into the visual landscape during the *Pellegrina intermedi;* like Leonardo's "monster," these elements were intended to surprise and terrify, complementing the interludes' capacity to elicit *diletto.* The didactic function of the monstrous is dealt with elsewhere;[29] what I am interested in here is the general nature of these representations and their relationship to broader cultural practices. *Intermedi* three and four are characterized by the inclusion of monstrous episodes, which, according to eyewitness accounts, both terrified and horrified the audience. Gadenstedt describes the infernal scene of *intermedio* four:

> After this cloud disappeared, the scene changed again, and glowed gruesomely, like fiery flames. And indeed, soon the ground also opened below, out of which blazed a mass of flames, and one could see into it, as if into a glowing furnace, or into Hell, as it was intended to represent Hell. Soon, out of this, the devil appeared, made horribly large and gruesome, with open jaws, monstrous body, and disgusting hands. In his bosom there were many small devils, dressed like him, who sprang from his bosom, [and] danced around him. These [same] took numerous small boys and girls, who were as naked as they came from their mothers' wombs, ordered to do this, running around on [the] stage, and pushed many of them in the devil's jaws, who swallowed them, [and] threw many of them into Hell. Out from under him, thirty-six musicians appear from the halves of the scene, dressed as frightfully as the Furias infernales, the hellish goddesses, are depicted, [and] sit down on chairs which rose up from the ground [in a ring] around the devil. . . . [30]

Gadenstedt's description is characteristic of other accounts of the same scene. But what are we to make of these seemingly exaggerated responses, at least from our current perspective whereby the polytechnics of the film industry produce spectacular effects that quickly lose their efficacy? In our culture of cinematic special effects, where advances in technology are rapidly superseded, a scene such as this quickly becomes commonplace. Yet one has only to remember the account of terrified viewers dodging the approaching locomotive during the screening of the Lumière brothers' first silent film, "La Sortie des usines Lumière." That an audience would respond in this manner reminds us of the special nature of these musico-theatrical extravaganzas at Florence; to be sure, smaller-scale theatrical performances took place at court on a regular basis, but they did not warrant the almost yearlong preparations granted to the *Pellegrina intermedi* nor demonstrate the extensive use of new, advanced technologies.

To summarize, the manifestation of wonder in the *intermedi* reflected the aesthetic's broader cultural currency, at the same time as the intensity of the experience made it "one of a kind." The penchant for the marvelous in general, then, helps to account for the success of the *Pellegrina intermedi* in performance. The *Pellegrina intermedi* were distinguished by the specific ways in which *meraviglia* was exerted through the theatrical medium, its intersection with the ideals of absolutism, and the extent of its efficacy vis-à-vis the spectator-auditor. To address these issues, we first need to explore the Aristotelian conception of wonder as didactic, and consider a competing and influential theory of wonderment promulgated by the distinguished Neoplatonist Francesco Patrizi.

Francesco Patrizi and the Experience of Wonder

During the Renaissance, the Aristotelian conception of *meraviglia,* with its emphasis on the didactic component of the aesthetic, was widespread. To perhaps oversimplify what was hardly a monolithic concept: wonder invoked a sense of the incomprehensible that in turn generated curiosity or desire for knowledge. Drawing on the work of Marvin T. Herrick, Peter Platt has shown that Renaissance writers such as Francesco Robortello, Antonio Minturno, and Jacopo Mazzoni adopted a broadly Aristotelian conception of wonder whereby confusion (or incomprehensibility) was subject to rational scrutiny and thereby ultimately dissipated, in a move Platt has described as the "drive to domesticate the marvelous."[31]

This process of "domestication" played out, for example, in the context of the early modern museum that Paula Findlen has described as "the principal site in which the process of demystification occurred."[32] Findlen also argues that "collecting was not just a recreational practice for sixteenth- and seventeenth-century virtuosi, but also a precise mechanism for transforming knowledge into power."[33] The association between the marvelous and containment (or normalization) was thus infused with the political. I will later suggest that the *Pellegrina* interludes, on one level, enacted their own kind of containment and concomitant didacticism that speaks to the profound political implications of the genre (see below, this chapter, "Structural Underpinnings: Order Restored"). On the other hand, I contend that the Aristotelian propensity for "exercising the understanding" cannot fully explain the cultural work of the *intermedi*. As I will later argue, there was a kind of meta-didacticism at work in the *intermedi* that did not function through demystification, but rather operated through a carefully orchestrated process of mystification, which was integrally tied to the projection of the prince-as-god.[34] In order to track this process, we need first to explore an important anti-Aristotelian conception of wonder that has significant implications for understanding the *Pellegrina* interludes.

In practice, it appears that the Aristotelian notion of wonder, with its emphasis on consequent demystification, was not all pervasive.[35] Yet with one major exception, in theoretical literature there were few challenges to the Aristotelian model of wonder. Strikingly, the most vehement challenge to Aristotle's system came from the (then) Ferrara-based Neoplatonist Francesco Patrizi, whose work coincides with the years leading up to the preparations and performances of the *Pellegrina intermedi*. Patrizi rejected Aristotle's concept of mimesis as the central principle of aesthetic judgment, replacing it with his conception of *meraviglia,* to which he believed all poetry should aspire.[36] He completed his book on wonder, *La deca ammirabile,* in 1587,[37] a work that had been preceded in 1586 by *La deca disputata,* his most sustained attack on the notion of Aristotelian imitation. Both volumes were part of his mammoth treatise on poetics, *Della poetica.* Many of Patrizi's ideas were likely well known to those involved in creating the *Pellegrina intermedi,* particularly to the poet G. B. Strozzi and to Giovanni de' Bardi, who created the interludes' *invenzioni* (plots).

The friendship between Patrizi and Bardi extended back at least to the early 1580s.[38] The two men were united in their effort to defend Lodovico Ariosto's epic poem *Orlando furioso* against the attacks of Camillo Pellegrino.[39] Bardi invited Patrizi to write *Parere in difesa dell' Ariosto,* which he subsequently dedicated to Bardi.[40] Most interesting, Bardi delivered a lecture on February 24, 1583, before the Florentine Accademia degli Alterati defending *Orlando furioso* from the criticisms of Pellegrino that centered on Ariosto's abandonment of Aristotelian unity in favor of *varietà* (variety).[41] As we see in chapter 3, Bardi (using Rossi as mouthpiece) broached the very same issue in regard to the interludes for both *L'amico fido* (1586) and *La pellegrina* (1589).[42]

In his book *Art and Power,* Roy Strong groups Patrizi with other utopian visionaries who understood the state as one element of a magical cosmology, and suggests that the intellectual framework constructed by such occult philosophers provided "a thought-context into which late Renaissance festivals would seem to naturally fit, both in the sense of the ideas they purvey and in their cultivation of mystical monarchy."[43] Although Strong does not go on to develop a connection between Patrizi and aspects of Medicean state- or stagecraft, it is evident that Patrizi's ideas provide a specific thought-context for the aesthetic and political aims of the *Pellegrina intermedi*. I have already noted that Patrizi and his works were well known to Bardi, who had a significant role in defining the conceptual framework for the *intermedi*. Further, in Patrizi's conception of wonder, the reluctance to privilege the intellect resonated with a broader humanist worldview that tempered deference to classical authority with insights gleaned from practical experience.[44] This "new cultural relativism,"[45] as Gary Tomlinson has described it, is particularly relevant to an understanding of the projection and experience of wonder that took place within the performance context of the Uffizi theater.

Patrizi envisioned wonder as a special faculty of the mind that mediated between thought and feeling, that did not demand, and, indeed, actively resisted ultimate resolution through rational explanation:

> [T]he *potenza ammirativa* (power of wonder) is neither knowledge, nor affection, but separate from them both and communicating between them both; and that, placed on the border between them, it is able to unleash and infuse, by its movement, quickly up to knowledge and down to affection. But knowledge being the part contrary in a certain way to affection, it does not seem that it is possible to say that movements of the mind . . . descend to their opposite, neither do movements of the affection ascend to the mind. . . . One is able therefore to say that the *potenza ammirativa* among these two powers is almost an Euripo [a place where the eddy of tides meet together] with the tide running to and fro from reason to affection.[46]

A closely related passage from the same chapter of *La deca ammirabile* mirrors the spectator's experience of the *intermedi* as described by Rossi in his *Descrizione* and as described in unofficial accounts:

> Therefore something new and sudden and unexpected that appears in front of us, makes a movement in our soul, almost contradictory in itself of believing and not believing. Of believing because one sees that the thing exists; and of not believing because it is unexpected, and new, and not before by us either known, or thought, or believed to be possible.[47]

We have already noted that multi-media spectacle was the art form par excellence for producing unexpected or surprising effects. Here Patrizi introduces the seemingly contradictory notion of "believing and not believing," that is, the wondrous state that thrived on an absence of epistemological certainty, nicely exemplified by spectators' frequent expressions of disbelief in the face of apparently impossible aural and visual maneuvers.

Longinus was a chief influence on Patrizi's views on wonder. As Platt has noted, both Longinus and Patrizi "advocated a poetical form of fragmentary, scattered bursts that, on account of their wonder-full and incredible nature, had the power to take the audience 'out of themselves.'"[48] Similarly, the modus operandi of the *intermedi*—with its emphasis on variety over unity— corresponded on a larger scale to the "fragmentary, scattered bursts" of Patrizian-Longinian (rather than Aristotelian) poetics. The *Pellegrina intermedi* seem designed to discombobulate, to transport the audience "out of

themselves." (One may recall Giuliano Giraldi's comments in his funeral oration for Duke Ferdinando regarding the apparent inconceivability of these
spectacles to even the most seasoned of experts.)[49] As such, the interludes fit
a Patrizian-Longinian aesthetic, depending for their efficacy on a degree
of mystification that paralleled the emergent trend toward mystical monarchy.[50]

Hidden Meanings / Hidden Music

On a broader level, the allegorical and technological "mysteries" of the *intermedi* participated in and extended traditions concerned with the significance
of hidden meanings. Mythological imagery and emblems were central to Florentine festival, but they required deciphering and, therefore, as Mario Biagioli notes, "differentiated social groups and reinforced social hierarchies by
controlling access to meaning."[51] While degrees of understanding provided a
means of differentiation, it is also true that even those involved with the entertainment's production found the *intermedi*, in all their complexity, difficult to decipher.[52] In essence, even the most erudite audience member was
engaged in a quest for knowledge that was not entirely within reach, as Giraldi's comments confirm (see chapter 1, section entitled "The Duke as Theatrical Arbiter"). In this respect, Rossi's encyclopedic description of the event
promised a kind of post-performance "emblematic translation" that nevertheless engaged the reader in an unending process of "unknowing."[53] For Michel
de Certeau this is the historical moment when the term mystical "marks the
point of intersection between the endless description of the visible and the
naming of a hidden essential."[54] The hidden organizes the social network,
thereby binding together the participants (whether keepers or seekers of the
secret) in strategic relations.[55] In addition, partial revelation of meaning—"an
inner reality half concealed and half revealed by outer reality"—was in keeping with the Neoplatonic dimension of the entertainment.[56] In this regard, I
would argue that the emblematic quality of the visual imagery was intended
as talismanic or magical.[57]

The significance of magic and hidden meanings in the *intermedi* is in
step with the vision of a hermetic universe envisioned by Patrizi and by Florentine Neoplatonists from the time of Ficino. The latter's influence pervaded
court entertainment such as *intermedi* throughout the sixteenth century,[58]
and his ideas on sound and music are especially important for understanding
the occult dimension of the *Pellegrina* performances. While Rossi's *Descrizione* mirrors general notions about the primacy of the sense of sight (given
authority by Aristotle), some writers, including Aquinas, ranked hearing
above sight, because it was believed that through sound the word of God was

perceived.[59] Accordingly, Ficino privileged the sense of hearing. As animate material that was mobile and flexible, Ficino considered sound to be similar to, or the same as, a disembodied spirit.[60] Sound, or more specifically, celestial music, was central to a hermetic conception of the cosmos, in which "musical harmony, through its numbers and proportions" had "marvelous power to stabilize, to move, and to influence the spirit, mind, and body."[61] Celestial music was believed to be an audible expression of the planets' passage through the heavens; the music produced by these planetary motions therefore determined the outcome of earthly events. It was also believed that the imitation of cosmic harmony on earth could transport celestial influence to the earthly realm.

Tomlinson has addressed the Ficinian notion of imitation, relating it to musical mimesis: "Imitation, in Ficino's view . . . seized and captured things. It struck up profound resonances, active affinities, among the thing imitated, the imitation, its maker, and its perceiver. . . . For Ficino musical imitation, as indeed imitation in general, was a provocative force; for us it has come to be merely evocative."[62] Ficino grants special power to musical mimesis and, as already noted, links "the spirit and music by virtue of their similar motion and airy substance."[63] Tomlinson is here following D. P. Walker's reading of Ficino, explaining how music's similarity to *spiritus*—the light and airy substance that mediated between body and soul—might account for music's potent effect on the listener.[64] The invisible constitution of *both* music and *spiritus* is self-evident, although the perception of music often involves "the sight of sound."[65] One could go on to argue, however, that invisible music has an even more profound connection to Ficino's *spiritus* because of the *absence* of "the sight of sound." In addition, the (invisible) echos heard in interludes one and five are a form of duplication that resonate with the fundamental logic underlying Ficinian Neoplatonism: the network of sympathies and correspondences that connect the physical and metaphysical worlds. For Ficino, music's articulation of this relationship was even more powerful than that of the visual symbol. Further—and this is where Tomlinson's reading of Ficino diverges from that of D. P. Walker and others—"Ficino spoke of music reaching the body, the spirit, the soul, and even the soul's highest faculty, the mind, *by virtue of its motion, not its verbal meanings.*"[66] Thus, for Ficino, music's force did not depend on an inextricable association with words.

Tomlinson's rethinking of Ficino's musical magic has important implications for understanding the *Pellegrina* interludes creators' apparent willingness to allow pure sound, rather than text, to determine performative efficacy. As I demonstrate at length in part 2 of this study, the *meraviglia* that the music evoked in the perceiver was not contingent on the spectator-auditor's comprehension of the songs' texts.[67] This conception seems to fly in the face of the musical humanists whose writings were transmitted through the documents of the Camerata. If we are willing to accept the deep influence that Ficinian Neoplatonism exerted on Florentine court *intermedi*,[68] however, it may now be possible to understand why the entertainment's directive elite allowed *effetti meravigliosi* of the musical kind—"emblems" of a profound metaphysical significance—to override considerations of textual clarity in the context of the *Pellegrina* performances. (I explore the issue of text audibility, or lack thereof, in light of pragmatic considerations in chapter 3.)[69] To judge from eyewitness accounts, the *meraviglia* evoked through "invisible" music, especially echo effects, was perhaps the most potent actualization of occult influence.[70]

The Duke as Neoplatonic Magus

As Thomas Greene has noted, the courts of rulers had, for centuries, been understood as nuclei of magical power;[71] in 1280, the Italian political writer Fra Tolomeo stressed that kings contained "special divine influence and a participation greater than that of ordinary men in the Absolute Being."[72] Yet the Medici principate was a relatively new creation in comparison with long-standing centers of monarchical rule; indeed, Florence did not have the kind of venerated monarchical system that existed in France or England. But as Samuel Berner has shown, the divine-right theory of kingship was filtering into Medici-generated written propaganda as well as receiving attention in various arts including court *intermedi*.[73] As we have also seen, the occult or magical dimension of Florentine court spectacle became especially pronounced in the latter half of the sixteenth century, at the very moment when divine right theories began to infiltrate official discourse. From a visual perspective, the occult dimension was signaled, most notably, by a heavenly descent that represented the transmission of celestial harmony to earth; thus, the prologic opening of the first *Pellegrina intermedio* represented Harmony of the Spheres descending to earth. But the word "represents" diminishes what Neoplatonists understood as a profoundly significant gesture. As Greene has explained, the descent actualized that which, "according to Ficinian metaphysics[,] it was invisibly bringing about."[74]

It is now but a small step to connect the magical musical performance with the Neoplatonic Magus who presided over the production. While Buontalenti—the "architect" of magic—was inconspicuously ensconced in his control booth cut into the *gradi* (the tiered seating area that surrounded the sides and back of the theater), Duke Ferdinando and his entourage were conspicuously positioned on their *catafalco*—literally, their own stage—acting in a performance of their own.[75] Spectators would have noticed the size of the ducal platform as they entered the theater; it dominated the Uffizi by its sheer size, taking up more than half the theater's width, between the two sides of the *gradi*.[76] For the performances of Bardi's *L'amico fido* in 1586, the box (of the then duke, Francesco I) was centrally located in the orchestra at a height of 22 inches and 57 feet from the front of the stage. Interestingly, in 1589 the ducal box remained in the orchestra area but was moved further toward the back of the hall.[77] While the re-placement of the box may have been designed to enhance the ducal party's vision of the stage action,[78] Ferdinando would have been less easily visible to the majority of male spectators in the stalls at the premiere performance, who presumably had their backs to him for most of the production:[79] here is an image of Ferdinando physically presiding over both his invited guests and the performance on the stage that took place, through his initiative, in seemingly effortless fashion.[80] The repositioning of the platform for the *Pellegrina* performances situated the ducal party in closer proximity to the small balcony above the main entrance (behind which was a hidden room) reserved for the musicians who produced the miraculous off-stage sound effects. That these mysterious effects issued forth from a place very close to the duke's person seems no accident; in fact, the set-up presages and closely parallels later musical practices established by Ferdinando at Santa Felicita. We now take a small diversion in order to examine more ritualized musical practices of a similar type instigated by Duke Ferdinando.

From 1602, and likely earlier, the performances of the Offices during Holy Week established by Ferdinando at the Pitti parish church of Santa Felicita (and Santa Niccola, if the Medici were at Pisa) involved polychoral music: the music of one (or sometimes two) "choirs" would emanate from the raised corridor attached to the church, usually in response to music visibly performed in the main part of the church.[81] The corridor was in fact part of Vasari's 1565 building project that eventually linked the Palazzo Vecchio to the Pitti Palace.[82] From the beginning, a portion of the corridor had been attached to the Pitti parish church of Santa Felicita and a loggia was constructed to support the corridor on the church's façade. From 1565—the same year as the corridor's completion—Santa Felicita became closely linked with the regular religious ceremonies of the Medici. In 1589, Ferdinando commissioned Buontalenti to enlarge the part of the corridor attached to the church by creating a small private room above the two chapels at the front of the church opening out to a balcony that offered an unimpaired view of the church's interior. Here, the Medici could attend religious ceremonies unobserved yet hear and see those below who faced the front of the church and had little or no visual access to the ducal party. The godlike presence of the Medici—situated as they were, on a parallel axis to (but *above*) the high altar—must have sent a subtle message to parishioners regarding the nature of Medicean power that was at once omniscient, yet elusive. Those subjects worshiping at Santa Felicita may have wondered whether Duke Ferdinando was physically present in the corridor, a possibly disconcerting and unsettling consideration. In part, this was the point. While Ferdinando might very well have chosen to worship within a private chapel, this semi-public but potentially "invisible display" demonstrated the consistent religiosity of the Medici family in the wake of the Council of Trent[83] at the same time that an impression of distant, yet all-knowing (all-seeing), mysteriousness was projected.[84]

Surprise facilitated *meraviglia* at these religious observances. It would have been impossible for the auditor to predict exactly when the invisible choir or choirs would interject, or to know exactly which musical forces were involved during any given service or throughout the course of a given "performance." Further, as Suzanne Cusick has pointed out, there was an aura of mysteriousness present through the use of women's voices, which were *always* produced from the corridor, and never (visibly) from the main church.[85] For our purposes, it is important to note that the Medici and their musicians were literally situated in the same location—the small room attached to the corridor above the main entrance of Santa Felicita—giving the impression that music literally issued forth from the Medicean body.

In the *Pellegrina* performances, the off-stage location situated in close proximity to the duke was primarily utilized for echo effects, specifically the echo that responded to Archilei for the concluding section of "Dalle più alte sfere" (*intermedio* one) and the double-echo that reiterated each of Peri's concluding phrases in "Dunque fra torbide onde" (*intermedio* five).[86] The off-stage musicians functioned, therefore, as "stand-ins" for Duke Ferdinando. As makers of "invisible" music they were best able to articulate the occult dimension of Ficinian Neoplatonism. Emanating from a place close to his physical body, the entertainment's creators may have wanted to give the impression that it was the duke's bodily presence that actualized music's occult power.[87]

Structural Underpinnings: Order Restored

Despite attempts to fragment the spectator-auditor's subjectivity through the effects of *meraviglia,* on a deep structural level there was a strong push toward resolution and containment in the *Pellegrina* interludes, as if, indeed, a god-like master plan governed the experience of the whole. This trajectory of containment seems all the more powerful because it was projected on a subliminal level.

Peter Platt has demonstrated how a similar trajectory was at work in the English masque. He explains this structural principle by noting that it "allow[ed] the royal center both to inspire awe through spectacle and to reassure the spectators that, by the end, nothing is left unresolved." For Platt the "movement toward containment is . . . important to the inscription of the monarch's power because the king is shown taming the potential threat to reason and order that the marvelous often brings with it."[88] During the *Pellegrina intermedi,* a subliminal process of containment, whereby certain tensions were created and subsequently resolved, paralleled the more overt demonstrations of wonder's effects. A trajectory of order followed by confusion which is finally transformed into restorative order is projected across the six *intermedi,* as well as enacted at the more localized level of individual *intermedi.* That the spectator recognized the broad trajectory at some level is clear. Gadenstedt, for example, noticed the return in *intermedio* six to the scenic apparatus and character types of *intermedio* one.[89] Similarly, the Ferrarese ambassador Gigliolo stated: "In the last *intermedio* then we saw Paradise open again, full, as before, of musical concerts, and clouds with choirs appeared as before, that kept singing and playing without stopping and all descended on the stage. . . ."[90] As James Saslow notes, the opening of the first and last *intermedi* intentionally mirrored each another in order to frame the entertainment with a symmetrical visual structure.[91] The point of the symmetry, of course, was to reestablish (as well as reinforce and amplify) the cosmic and political harmony enacted during *intermedio* one.

Several of the internal *intermedi,* especially numbers three and four, involved some form of conflict that seems to have been intended, by way of contrast and tension, to drive home a final resolution of restorative order in *intermedio* six. In *intermedio* three a threat to order was enacted by the serpent-dragon who was subsequently vanquished in battle by Apollo; the *intermedio* concluded with a victory dance and song, and was thus self-contained in the sense of its inherently restorative trajectory. But in *intermedio* four, the concluding Hell scene—by all accounts the most horrifying scene of the entire set of *intermedi*—seems to have left many spectators with a sense of irresolution, thus heightening the celebratory order that finally prevailed at the conclusion of the entire set. Indeed, the finale of the sixth and final *intermedio* enacted its own (self-contained) tensions through its dialogic musical structure, but the potentially disruptive force—in this case, the female voice—was ultimately subsumed by the larger (male) chorus in order to conclusively establish order and patriarchal control (see chapter 8). Thus, music (and not just visual components) were used to project a sense of containment and resolution by the interludes' directive elite, particularly the finale's composer-choreographer Emilio de' Cavalieri.

CHAPTER THREE

Court *Intermedi* at Florence

Definitions and Controversies

IN 1611 JOHN FLORIO defined the *intermedio* as "the musike that is, or shewes that are[,] betweene the acts of a play."[1] Florio's definition pinpoints the genre's interludic function but is also suggestive of music's centrality to the *intermedio*. From their courtly beginnings in late fifteenth-century Ferrara and continuing through the sixteenth century, one type of *intermedio*—the *intermedio non apparente*—consisted of "invisible" music that emanated from behind the play's scenic apparatus, thus serving to mark off one act of the play from the next. By contrast, the *intermedi apparenti* from the early period were sometimes pantomimical (with action and dance determined by the styles and rhythmic qualities of the music) or could consist of vocal music performed by a costumed singer or singers. *Intermedi apparenti* served an analogous function to the secular interpolations heard between the acts of fifteenth-century miracle plays, and to the sung, danced, and mimed entertainments performed between the courses of court banquets.[2]

Several commentators theorized the resemblance of *intermedi* to the Greek chorus. The declaration added to the printed edition of the comedy *Il granchio* (1566), with *intermedi* by Bernardo de Nerli, stressed the interludes' relationship to "the chorus of the ancient fables of the Greeks," arguing that "as the *intermedi* correspond to the *canzoni* sung by the chorus, and as these were [placed] neither before, nor after the fable, but only sung in the middle of it, it seems reasonable that the *intermedi* . . . should take place only between one act and the other."[3] Yet despite emphasizing a classical model, Nerli evidently felt pressed to justify the modern inclusion of a sung madrigal both before and after the comedy. These madrigals, according to Nerli, were not *intermedi,* but were "added to the four intermedi . . . to avoid a departure from custom, as well as to please the theatre . . . accustomed to seeing something before and after the comedy."[4] For Nerli, then, one senses the importance of adhering to the perceived dictates of classical tradition at the same time as he acknowledges the necessity of satisfying current taste. While the classical ideal might be theorized through the written word, in the context of performance pragmatic concerns and tastes prevailed. Negotiating these competing tensions was an essential part of staging *intermedi*. Indeed, the conflicting opinions raised in regard to the function of *intermedi* were symptomatic of broader tensions in literary and humanist circles involving deference to classical sources and authorities. Liberal humanists tended to adopt a dialectical approach that integrated the insights gleaned from practical experience, while at the same time fulfilling the practical needs of their patrons.

Despite tensions between theory and practice, some *intermedi* did function in the manner of the Greek chorus by commenting on the action of the play. Early examples include the *canzone* written by Niccolò Machiavelli for his *La Clizia* and *La Mandragola*. Regarding a performance of the latter that was to take place in Faenza during carnival of 1526, Machiavelli communicates to his host that the singer Barbara Salutati (La Barbara) "has offered to come with her singers to provide the chorus between the acts."[5] Pirrotta has commented upon Machiavelli's instinctive reference to Greek chorus, and the lack of any need to explain the term's use.[6] Often, however, theorists felt compelled to advocate that interludes *should* resonate with the material of the play to which they were attached, probably because they frequently did not. For example, in 1562 G. G. Trissino complained that the action of the *intermedi* could be so different that "another comedy is made, an inconvenience that does not allow one to enjoy the doctrine of the comedy."[7] Late in the century Angelo Ingegneri suggested that, in comedies and pastorals, *intermedi,* "however similar or dissimilar that they may be to the play . . . always enrich the spectacle and delight the spectators." He believed that choruses should be reserved only for tragedies.[8]

Literary critics differed, then, regarding the relationship between *intermedi* and the ancient chorus. Some purposefully invoked the term chorus as a means of legitimizing *intermedi*[9]—that most unruly of genres. Even more frequently, though, *intermedi* were discussed in terms of their ability to enhance spectacle, delight the audience, and provide relief for the mind from the intellectual task of following the play. Thus, *intermedi* were often implicitly associated with sensual experience, because they were envisaged as counterpoint to the spectator's moral and intellectual engagement with the play. Because the senses were understood to constitute bodily experience, there was a clear analogic relationship between the body's connection to the *intermedi* and the mind's relationship to the play. Though expressed in less explicit terms by sixteenth-century literary critics, the anxiety surrounding interludes' increased tendency to upstage the play they were ostensibly intended to support paralleled anxieties regarding music's sensual and seductive quality, an aspect that was frequently understood as threatening and thereby in need of containment. It is hardly coincidental that music, in some form or other, was the common denominator of almost all *intermedi,* regardless of whether they were visually perceived, and regardless of whether they related directly to the plays with which they were performed. In addition, the emphasis on the body in *intermedi,* particularly through the frequent incorporation of dance, in some ways feminized the genre, making it suspect, especially when women were involved in the dancing.

On a more overt level, literary critics frequently stressed the function of *intermedi* to help mark the passage of time in a play. De' Sommi articulated the interlude's function in this regard with particular clarity:

> I say that comedies at least need musical interludes, both to give some re-
> freshment to the spectator's minds and to grant the poet . . . that interval to
> give proportion to his play, because every one of these interludes, though
> brief, may serve for the course of four, six, or eight hours. However long the
> comedy may be, it must never last more than four hours, yet the action often
> spreads over an entire day and also sometimes half of another; and that no
> actors appear on the stage [during this period] makes this effect [the fic-
> tional passing of time] more efficacious.[10]

As Pirrotta has shown, the Florentine *intermedi* for Landi's play *Il commodo* (1539) were especially successful with regard to marking the fictional passage of time. He describes their effect—which was essentially to produce a sense of time compressed—as one of "temporal perspective."[11] The progress through different times of the day that occurred in Landi's play was rein-forced by the conceptual themes and stage settings of the accompanying *in-termedi.*[12] Thus, in the *intermedio* before the play's prologue, Dawn appeared in the sky from the east; through the course of the entertainment the sun made its appropriate passage across the stage, while the interludes' characters and their designated activities were governed by the sun's progress. Thus, in the third *intermedio,* "Silenus [a satyr]—described by Vergil in his Sixth Eclogue as found sleeping in a cave at noon by Mnasyllus and Chromis and by the very beautiful Aegle—showed us that, as in the comedy, it was noon. Awakened by them, and being begged to sing . . . he began sweetly to play and to sing ["Ò begli Anni del Oro"] . . ."[13] (CD tracks 1–3). The sun finally set and disappeared at the end of act 5; appropriately, Night appeared in the following *intermedio* "sweetly singing to the accompaniment of four trombones."[14]

While highlighting the role of the 1539 interludes as markers of time, Pir-rotta seems less enthusiastic about their lack of adherence to "rules" regarding unity of place and frame.[15] This unity refers to the classical tradition of em-ploying the same group of characters after each act to comment on the story

(mirroring the Greek chorus). In fact, Florentine court *intermedi* rarely fulfilled this function because such restrictions were largely antithetical to a
crucial formal consideration that helped ensure their success in performance:
variety. As time went on, Florentine *intermedi* also abandoned any regard for
"temporal perspective." As I will demonstrate in chapter 4, by 1589 the *intermedi* no longer helped delineate the passage of time in the play; instead, the
intermedi established their own means of delineating time, one that was entirely self-regulating and largely unrelated to the progress of time in the play.

"The wondrous show, alas, of the *intermedi*!"

Pirrotta chose the above phrase—drawn from Anton Francesco Grazzini's
well-known madrigal "Comedy complaining about the intermedi"—as title
to the fifth chapter of his now classic book *Music and Theatre from Poliziano
to Monteverdi.* Grazzini's humorous critique of the *intermedi,* in which he la-
ments the genre's favor with audiences, was echoed by a number of literary
critics during the sixteenth century.[16] Moreover, Grazzini's contention that
"once intermedi were made to serve the comedy, but now comedies are made
to serve the intermedi" is a commonly cited remark about the genre in recent
criticism.[17]

   In one respect, the reasoning behind Pirrotta's choice of title—for a chapter largely devoted to *intermedi* at Florence—is self-evident. The court *intermedi* produced at Florence were occasional pieces for royal weddings and other
state occasions in which "all the stops were pulled out"; in other words, they
were wondrous in every respect, but their wonder was partly dependent upon
their infrequent occurrence—perhaps once or twice every generation.[18] Pirrotta made the useful distinction between these special *intermedi,* which he
described as aulic, or courtly, and the more common and less elaborate nonaulic *intermedi.*[19] In Pirrotta's chapter title, though, the inclusion of "alas" not
only refers to Grazzini's admittedly tongue-in-cheek critique of the *intermedi,*
but also seems to reflect the author's own views regarding the genre's propensity for the wondrous at the expense of unity of place and frame. While Pirrotta's chapter provides a very useful overview of *intermedi* produced at
Florence, his narrative is punctuated throughout by an over-arching concern
about unity, and this concern appears to inform the often very slim thematic
connections he makes between *intermedi* in a given set and a seeming dismay
about a lack of unity. Of the 1586 *intermedi* for *L'amico fido,*[20] which are treated
toward the end of Pirrotta's chronological survey, he states: "The only theme
that the 1586 intermedi all had in common was that of glorifying the bridal
couple." As if to somehow redeem this deficiency, he goes on to present a
progressive trajectory that unites the tradition of court *intermedi*: "All the

themes and characters from previous *intermedi* were called on to help achieve this—of course, with new variations and improvements."[21]

It is true that there was disagreement among sixteenth-century critics regarding the form and function of *intermedi* and that much of this disagreement revolved around whether the interludes had usurped their perceived classical function. The question of unity of theme was in fact dealt with at length by Bastiano de' Rossi in his 1586 description for the *intermedi* for *L'amico fido*. I discuss the relevant portion of Rossi's 1586 *Descrizione* in some detail below, as it presages the author's much abbreviated comments on the same issue in his 1589 description. My point here is to suggest that the emphasis in recent scholarship on unity, though in some ways relevant, mainly reflects current aesthetic preferences and tastes. One can trace these preferences back through the Anglo-Germanic scholarly lineage to Aby Warburg's seminal work on the *Pellegrina* interludes from 1895,[22] and of course the concept of unity has long dominated aesthetic criticism within the discipline of musicology (which itself has been heavily influenced by Germanic scholarship in the humanities). Similarly, recent scholarship has often ignored the importance of variety as a key structural element of court *intermedi,* not only because the concept is easily cast as antithetical to unity but also because variety enhances performative efficacy, which in turn weakens the elevated status of "the work" as a creative endeavor unpolluted by the demands of its audience.

La varietà e l'unità

In 1586, Rossi addressed the qualities of variety and unity at length, which may account for the more cursory treatment of these subject categories in his 1589 *Descrizione.* Because of the close proximity of these two sets of *intermedi,* and also because of the involvement of Bardi, Buontalenti, and Rossi in both productions, a consideration of Rossi's more extensive comments from 1586 may shed light on the issues as addressed in 1589. As official commentator, Rossi was not only the mouthpiece for the Medici but also the "spokesperson" for Buontalenti and especially Bardi, who conceived of the interludes' *invenzioni.* In 1586, Rossi (and by extension, Bardi) is far more deferent to the reader (whose criticism he clearly hopes to assuage) than he would be three years later. He essentially addresses the aficionados, the "wise and educated readers," whom he flatters by stating that it would be presumptive of him to explicate the *invenzioni* of the *intermedi,* "as if these readers, by themselves, were not sufficient to understand such things and to discern them easily."[23] From our perspective, Rossi's comments are somewhat ironic since few in the audience probably understood the complex content of the *intermedi,* and his thoughts stand in stark contrast to those of Giraldi (which admittedly were written upon Ferdinando's death),[24] who regarded the inconceivability of these spectacles as an asset. By way of contrast, Rossi indicates his concern for the connoisseurs who may have critiqued Bardi's choices regarding the form and content of the *intermedi*. Further, in the interest of deflecting criticism, Rossi wants to demonstrate that Bardi is aware of the issues at stake involving unity and variety. Having sufficiently "softened" the aficionados by praising their acumen, Rossi proceeds as follows:

> [A]nd let us tell the state of mind of the poet [Bardi] when, at the beginning, he was trying to find the *favola* for the representation of the said *intermedi*, because it was this [his state of mind] to devise it with a single thread, and for the six representations that he needed to have to come from that [one thread]. But it was judged very proper to the idea that one had specifically in the present show, that before anything else, we should attend to variety; so that it was necessary, in this respect, to lose unity somewhat, and consequently the esteem that can be gained through it. And seeing that it was necessary to have his composition with many different heads, he put himself in the frame of mind wishing to put in every possible way in the variety and disunion, the aforementioned unity, and it was done because all the graces, that in this *intermedi* he feigns, that are done to the mortals, they all appear to be done because of this most happy union [wedding].[25]

Contrary to his earlier statement, Rossi goes on to briefly explicate the six *intermedi*, explaining how each one was individually related to the occasion of the Medici-d'Este wedding for which they were staged.[26] He concludes his summary by reiterating that "in this manner . . . our gentle poet [Bardi] has from such disunity, managed to fashion entire unity."[27] It was apparently these statements that led Aby Warburg to characterize Bardi as the figure who fought against the "pompous baroque" nature of the *intermedi*. Warburg praised Bardi for the assiduity of his attempt to maintain unity in the face of considerable opposition, not least from the "capricious and unnatural combinations" of the interludes' designers, presumably first and foremost Buontalenti.[28] In addition, Warburg and others have emphasized the pressure exerted on Bardi by the Florentine court itself (using the above-cited excerpt as the only apparent evidence). Thus, Bardi is posited as the purist who resented the Florentine court's interference, with the implication that, had arrangements been left to Bardi and Rossi, unity would have prevailed: "For Bardi . . . to be found still, in 1589, inspiring florid Intermedi . . . may at first sight seem strange and even undignified. It was works of just this kind, so highly appreciated in court circles for their 'variety,' that formed the main hindrance to the emergence of any dramatic art and music based on psychology and unity."[29] One can easily see that more is at stake here than Bardi's (apparently conflicted) involvement with the *Pellegrina* interludes.

Indeed, it is also possible to interpret Bardi's role in the interludes as follows. As creator of the Pellegrina *invenzioni,* Bardi balanced an idealized (Aristotelian) classical model vis-à-vis unity (acceptable to the connoisseurs) with the practical demands of producing an efficacious performance at (and for) the Medici court for an audience made up primarily of foreigners and non-specialists. In the accounts of both 1586 and 1589 Rossi alluded to such pragmatic concerns and, as we have seen, prefaced discussion of variety by referring to the performance at hand: "But it was judged very proper to the idea that one had specifically *in the present show,* that *before anything else,* we should attend to variety [italics mine]." Similarly, in 1589 Rossi's remarks on the same question are preceded by a reference to the intended audience.

> And in order to do so [bring wonder and delight to the audience] it didn't seem to him to be appropriate to have a *favola* with only one thread, judging that the listeners will have enough work just following the plot of the comedy. And besides that, if he had taken only one plot, he would have been forced to show and follow continuously just that plot which, in doing this, one can always find something good and something bad. It would have tied the hands of the author [Bardi], and to the aficionados it didn't seem to him that he would have been showing anything new.[30]

Interestingly, in 1589 we find that Rossi and Bardi are still concerned with potential criticism from the connoisseurs, but their tone is much more matter-of-fact, indeed pragmatic, regarding the apparent necessity for unity in which "one can always find something good and something bad." Indeed, Rossi's language emphasizes the restrictive nature of adopting "only one plot," implying that Bardi's creativity would have been compromised—his hands would have been tied—if "forced" to follow only one thread. In 1589, then, the Rossi-Bardi team argues for the necessity of variety to their endeavor.

Once again, it seems important to emphasize that the kind of tensions that Rossi and Bardi were negotiating were not peculiar to the *intermedi* but symptomatic of broader humanistic tendencies, in which insights gathered from practical experience were acknowledged (and put into practice) to varying extents. Consider, for example, comments made by Bernardo Tasso regarding his romance *L'Amadigi* (1542): "In the beginning I had decided to make it one unified action . . . and on this basis I composed ten books; but then it occurred to me that it did not have that *variety* that customarily gives *delight* and is desired in this century, already attuned to Romance; and I understood then that Ariosto [i.e., in *Orlando furioso*] neither accidentally nor for want of knowledge of the art (as some say) but with the greatest judgment *accommodated himself to the taste of the present century* and arranged his work in this way. . . . I have followed this example, which I find more beguiling and delightful."[31] As noted in chapter 2, both Bardi and Patrizi participated in the lively debate regarding Ariosto's *Orlando furioso,* defending the poem. That the *intermedi* embodied the extremes of what today might be considered both populist (read: capitulatory) and "high art" aspirations might also account for the implicit desire in recent criticism to recuperate the genre by emphasizing the concept of unity. But these seemingly twin poles—variety and unity—also indicate that the *intermedi* could be experienced in the same way as many multi-media performances are today: that is, in a variety of ways, that could encompass the visceral or sensual levels and/or the thought-provoking conceptions that sometimes underlie such representations.[32]

The Problem of Musical Humanism

If one opens any music history book that even begins to broach the subject of the *Pellegrina* interludes, one will learn that a central concern of these entertainments, as revealed by their subject matter, was the power of music. Indeed, most (but not all) of the six interludes in some way engage with the notion of music's powerful effects. Yet despite all of Rossi's ruminations on the question of unity, nowhere does he explicitly state that the "power of music" was the thread that bound Bardi's *invenzioni* together. Why, then, are the *Pellegrina* interludes frequently described in this way? Grouping the interludes' plots under this thematic heading may have proven useful for past studies, but the overwhelming weight given to this perspective seems to reflect a need to frame "the work" in unifying terms. After all, the 1589 *intermedi* mark a pivotal moment in the music historical canon. Further, framing the *Pellegrina* interludes in this way helps to compensate for another inconvenient fact: that the music heard during the performances, especially the solo songs, does not appear to embody the text-based aesthetic of musical humanists, particularly those participating in the circle of Bardi, who himself played a pivotal role in the conception of the *intermedi,* and whose ideas influenced the "birth of opera."[33] If the solo songs do not meet the aesthetic ideals promulgated by Bardi's camerata, they also do not support the dramatic ideals of the birth-of-opera narrative.

The music of the *Pellegrina* interludes has at times been criticized for its artificiality or sterility, perhaps by way of implicit contrast to the richer palette of "heartfelt" emotions generated in contexts less closely associated with courtly display. Warren Kirkendale, for example, describes the solo music as "inexpressive," as "almost caricatures in their excessive artificiality," apparently finding the music devoid of feeling. By contrast, other scholars have taken pains to identify stylistic features of particular pieces that *can* be reconciled with the stated aims of the musical humanists.[34] Evidently, the songs do not always provide the modern-day auditor with a satisfying listening experience by comparison, one assumes, with early opera or chamber monody. Yet neither approach (finding the interludes' music "inexpressive" or situating the music within a humanist program) has helped us to understand *if* and *how* the music was meaningful to the audience who experienced performances in the Uffizi theater during May 1589.

A central concern has been the question of "excessive" passagework and lack of text audibility. Discussing the solo music in general, Kirkendale has stated that the "unrelieved long melismas, often on insignificant words and thus not motivated by the meaning, render the text unintelligible (anticipating Bellini or Donizetti)."[35] Indeed, it is true that many spectators were at a loss to fully understand the words of the sung music. This matter may have been of some concern to those who created the *Pellegrina intermedi*. Some three years earlier, Rossi had addressed the issue in his *Descrizione* for Bardi's play *L'amico fido* (for which Bardi had composed music for the sixth *intermedio*). Rossi stated that Bardi

> immediately turned to the musical part, in which he principally wished that the pomp and the finesse of his poem should resplend, so that he wanted that harmony to come out, most copiously, most full, most varied, most sweet, and most artful, above every other [harmony], and at the same time (which is something that is thought to be almost impossible) that it [the music] would be most clear and the words easy to understand, and the connoisseurs will also be able to judge this for themselves through the publication.[36]

Curiously, the concern with text clarity emphasized by Rossi here is entirely absent from the equivalent passage in 1589.[37] In the account above, Rossi does not explain why it was "thought to be almost impossible" for "the words [to be] easy to understand." In all likelihood, he was implying that pragmatic concerns regarding the performance would pose obstacles in this respect: the difficulty of producing music in the large and cavernous Uffizi theater (as opposed to more intimate settings, such as the rooms of Bardi's *palazzo*) and the frequent use of instruments to double voices or provide elaborate "continuo" accompaniment would be obvious factors, aside from the extensive employment of *passaggi* in solo songs. Because of this concern for textual clarity, Rossi specified that the music *in notated form* would be sufficient proof of composers' intent that the words be easily understood, and in doing so tried to forestall any complaints on this point. Indeed, a brief report regarding the *Pellegrina intermedi* sent by Michele Priuli to Cardinal Montalto in Rome (dated May 6) voiced this very complaint: there were "very beautiful and weighty *concerti,* and so many musicians and instruments that one did not even understand the words of the music."[38] It is also clear from the numerous misidentifications of characters and misunderstandings of the "plots" in a number of unofficial accounts that in many instances the audience not only missed visual cues but confused textual ones, even though the gods sometimes identified themselves during the course of their solo song or were identified by other characters. Evidently, many in the audience either did not hear the sung words or could not understand them.

Despite the unintelligible words, the solo songs were nevertheless effective in performance, and this fact poses a direct challenge to one of the key precepts on which musicologists' understanding of this pivotal historical moment has been based: the conception that the efficacy of late Renaissance Italian music lay in the expression (and assumed intelligibility) of a verbal text. What is problematic is that this perspective was propounded in official music-theoretical writings of musicians such as Bardi, Caccini, and Cavalieri, who, as a result of their connection to the Florentine court, were intimately involved with the *Pellegrina* production.[39] Thus, key documents that have continued to inform our understanding of the musical aesthetic of this "transitional" period have been used, unconsciously or not, as the critical lens through which to assess the solo songs, when the testament of unofficial accounts, the practical realities of the performance conditions, and close readings of Rossi's two descriptions suggest that the music's efficacy did *not* in fact rely on comprehension of the songs' texts. Regarding the latter, Rossi—as mouthpiece for Bardi—indirectly indicates as much by way of his reference (cited above) to the "almost impossible" task of making the words clear and "easy to understand."[40] Text clarity is not dismissed, however, but deflected to the printed (not performative) medium, which could be assessed by connoisseurs outside of the performance context. Rossi's comments also suggest that Bardi was keenly aware of the pragmatic concerns regarding the performance at hand, and the necessity of ensuring an efficacious outcome. As Anthony Grafton and others have pointed out, the success of the humanists depended on the relevance of their activities to the practical needs of their patrons.[41] While some of the interludes' music does not appear to fit the model for "good singing" as outlined in treatises by Bardi and others, the music's aesthetic resonates with a more broadly construed conception of humanism that entertained a dialectic between classical authority and the insights gained from practical experience. Indeed, as complement to classical erudition, the humanist propensity for the sensual and experiential paved the way for an aesthetic of *meraviglia* crucial to the *intermedi*. Part 2 of this study identifies those musical devices associated with *meraviglia* and how they functioned in the performance context of the Uffizi theater.

The Performances in the Uffizi Theater

> And when the designer [Buontalenti] had from the poet [Bardi] particular and very detailed information, and having seen and considered the importance of the plot, and having with himself very diligently examined the number and the excellence of the artisans that he needed in order to complete it to perfection, because an infinite number of these things were needed; so having in a great hurry procured [those artisans], and with wonderful judgment and wisdom having assigned each to his task, he [Buontalenti] began to work in the room [the Uffizi theater] that . . . was built by Grand Duke Cosimo specifically to recite, of which the length . . . is 95 *braccia,* the width 35 *braccia,* and the height 24 *braccia;* and the floor is inclined two and one eighth *braccia* from the lowest to the highest.[42]

Thus, Rossi describes the process whereby Buontalenti began the task of adorning the Uffizi theater for the performances of the *Pellegrina* interludes. Plans for a ceremonial space in the Uffizi had been in progress since 1572, some two years prior to Duke Cosimo's death, but it was Duke Francesco who fully developed the space to become the permanent indoor theater that was utilized for the wedding of Virginia de' Medici to Cesare d'Este in 1586. The dimensions that Rossi cites roughly correspond to a hall with a height of 45 feet, width of 65 feet, and a length of 180 feet. A backstage area (of approximately 48 feet) left an area of approximately 130 feet for the auditorium proper (including the stage area).[43] The floor of the auditorium sloped from the back to the front of the hall (at an incline of four feet or so), allowing those positioned in the stalls an unimpaired view of the stage. Various commentators refer to this advantageous set-up, including Pavoni, who states: "In the middle of the room were all the men seated on benches, accommodated in a way that those at the back were able to see as well as those at the front."[44] Both contemporaneous treatises and recent scholarship tend to emphasize the place of the monarch in this scheme, whereby the ruler was positioned in what James Saslow has described as "the one seat in the axially-planned auditorium where the 3–D illusion 'worked'"—that is, on the ducal party's raised platform.[45] Though single-point perspective was clearly designed to favor the eye of the absolutist ruler, here I would like to emphasize instead the way in which the set-up of the auditorium encouraged the male audience members present at the premiere to partially share the duke's vision. As Pavoni's account indicates, the stalls (with their frontal view of the stage) were reserved for the men at the premiere; the women were seated in the *gradi,* the tiered seating area that hugged the sides of the auditorium. As such, the noblewomen in the *gradi* did not have direct visual access to the stage. Indeed, Rossi emphasizes the decorative function of the bejeweled noblewomen who were objects of admiration for the noblemen positioned in the stalls. Saslow develops Rossi's assumption here: "the viewers are male, the women around them merely part of the spectacle."[46]

While the noblewomen in the *gradi* were positioned in a way that did not allow them to share the duke's visual perspective, the grand-ducal party positioned on their *catafalco* consisted of both male and female royalty. I have already discussed the significance of the positioning of the *catafalco* at the back of the hall, in close proximity to the musicians' balcony mentioned by Rossi.[47] A small room with a grated window opened out on to the balcony allowing off-stage musicians inside the room visual access and, more important, sonic access to the auditorium. A surviving drawing by Buontalenti (plate 3) gives some idea of the set-up, showing the musicians' balcony and the grated window of the small room. The singers would have sung from behind the grate, thus remaining out of view from the audience. (Although Rossi specifically mentions a balcony reserved for musicians, no other accounts mention the musicians' visibility, thereby suggesting that they were positioned in the connecting room, hidden from view.)[48] In this respect I disagree with the hypothesis of Annamaria Testaverde Matteini, who argues that the musicians were likely "bumped" at the last minute to allow the invited cardinals to use this incognito viewing space because the windows of the above *galleria* had been covered with cloth, as ordered by Duke Ferdinando.[49] During the period leading up to the performances, the duke was actively showing guests the *meraviglie* contained in his *galleria,* so it is likely that he did not want guests touring the gallery to observe the preparations and rehearsals that were taking place in the theater below. There is no reason why the cloth might not have been moved aside for the performances. Indeed, ten days later on April 22 there is a note in the *Memoriale* suggesting that the *galleria* was indeed to function as a viewing area with "box seats," as it were.[50] Not only was there a large contingent of cardinals present for the festivities (very few of whom could have gained an adequate view from the lone grated window), but a dispatch by ambassador Gigliolo to the Duke of Ferrara (April 29, 1589, cited in chapter 1) indicates that all the cardinals and other guests who were present on April 24 attended the dress rehearsal with Duke Ferdinando.[51]

While the seating arrangements and date of the premiere performance (Tuesday, May 2) are corroborated by various sources,[52] there is some ambiguity surrounding the dates of the other four performances and the composition of the audience at those entertainments. As M. A. Katritzky has also pointed out, it is striking that for a set of performances for which there is so much surviving information, there is still uncertainty about such basic information.[53] I will begin to address the confusion by citing the remarks of the French eyewitness, regarding each of the five performances. Although there are a few obvious inaccuracies, the Frenchman is the only commentator to attempt to summarize the sequence of performances, and hence his general outline and impressions are all the more relevant:

> In order to make this music, the grand duke had searched for all the most skillful men in Italy, and thus the comedy was completed. And it was staged five times: the first in order to rehearse it, the second, at which I was present, for the arrival of the grand duchess. On that day the ladies of Florence were very finely arrayed with an infinity of jewelry. The third time [the comedy was staged] for the Florentine and foreign gentlemen who had come for the wedding, the fourth for the common people and courtiers of Florence. On that day the Venetian and Genoese ambassadors [were present], who had come to the grand duke to congratulate him on his marriage. I came in with them. And the fifth time [was for] the arrival of the Spanish ambassador, who arrived after the wedding for the same reason as the other ambassadors.[54]

As one might note, the Frenchman's reference to the second performance was probably the May 2 premiere, which he himself attended. The new duchess was present, as were numerous noblewomen; his reference to the "infinity of jewelry" worn by the noblewomen concurs with Rossi's emphasis on the same observation. The Frenchman's references to the fourth and fifth performances are also generally in line with other sources. The fourth performance (on May 15 again with the play *La pellegrina*) was apparently held for the Venetian (and Genoese) ambassadors; the Venetian ambassador Michele Contarini had missed the premiere performance, arriving on May 6.[55] The fifth and final performance took place on June 9 for the arrival of the Spanish ambassador, as the Frenchman states.[56]

That at least one performance was held for the Florentine citizenry is confirmed by the May 3 entry in the *Memoriale,* which implies that the public's admission was a last minute decision:

> His Highness definitely wants the comedy repeated on Friday, and we can also invite our friends. [His Highness] wants the repeat performance on Monday to be very polished at that time, and Her Highness the grand duchess and all the nobles will return and a short comedy will be staged. . . .[57]

This entry in the *Memoriale* raises questions of the dating of the second and third performances of the interludes that have already been addressed by

Saslow and Testaverde Matteini. According to several sources, these two internal performances took place on Saturday May 6 (with the Compagnia dei Gelosi performing *La cingana* with Vittoria Piissimi as lead actress)[58] and on the following Saturday, May 13 (again with the Gelosi troupe but on this occasion with Isabella Andreini performing *La pazzia d'Isabella*).[59] While Pavoni insists that there were no performances on Good Friday (May 5),[60] the May 3 entry and successive annotations in the *Memoriale* suggest that there was in fact a performance on that day.[61] I agree with Saslow that there was likely no May 13 performance, in light of the supporting sources that transmit what are perhaps the least reliable dates (Pavoni and Settimani). In my own reading of the sources I propose that there were probably performances on both May 5 and May 6; the latter date is confirmed by Gigliolo, the Ferrarese ambassador (a commentator not considered by Saslow). It is also quite likely, as Saslow has already suggested, that there may have been more than the five performances that are usually cited in the relevant scholarship.

More important, various sources offer at least some indication of the make-up of the audience at these performances. As the above-cited entry in the *Memoriale* indicates, friends of the cast and staff were given a short-notice opportunity to attend the May 5 performance; it may have been a private affair in light of its occurrence on Good Friday,[62] and because a performance immediately following the premiere would have given the producers a more comfortable opportunity to fine-tune any logistical problems. As the Frenchman notes, various classes of Florentine society were invited to attend, and these audience members more closely connected to the performance and the Florentine court may have been more interested in the identities of the performers themselves than in their allegorical significance.[63] (Even Gadenstedt, a foreigner unfamiliar with local musicians, pays special attention to the role of particular singers—not just their mythological identities—in several of the *intermedi*.) As far as the Medici were concerned, however, the most important guests to impress were the nearly 2,800 non-Florentines who attended the wedding,[64] hence the scheduling of extra performances for the late arrival of various foreign dignitaries.

The Commentaries of Spectator-Auditors

While little is known about the lives of individual commentators (as one might expect), their accounts of the *Pellegrina* interludes reflect the aesthetic concerns and interests of the aristocracy in general. Most commentators appear to have attended the premiere performance of the *Pellegrina* interludes on May 2, and therefore briefly mention the comedy *La Pellegrina* that was performed on that occasion.[65] At least two writers appear to have witnessed more than one performance.[66] Each of the unofficial commentators brings distinctive observations filtered through their own knowledge base and tastes, but these tastes also reflect those of commentators' aristocratic patrons, many of whom were unable to attend the festivities in person, and thus for whom most of the published accounts were written. The author of the anonymous publication *Li artificiosi* states:

> [A]nd if the comedy was beautiful, the interludes were very beautiful, and of greater importance [than the comedy] because they were full of almost unbelievable artifice. And because they were such [so beautiful] it appeared to me that I should inform Your Highness so that you can at least enjoy with your mind's eye what you have not seen in person. Therefore, Your Highness should know that at the beginning of the comedy, they started the *intermedi* below.[67]

This account, published in Rome, provides no indication of exactly to whom the description is addressed, although we might eliminate a member of the Roman clergy due to the mode of address.[68] Instead, the author and addressee appear to have had connections with Florence, as evidenced by the reference to Christine of Lorraine as "nostra padrona" in the preface (dated May 2, 1589). A Florentine connection is perhaps further reinforced by the fact that in this description, by way of contrast to every other unofficial account, the basic characters and scene types are identified "correctly" in each *intermedio*. It is therefore possible that the author was relying on some "insider" knowledge as well as his own distinctive observations.

The account by Simone Cavallino, who was from the town of Viterbo, located some sixty miles north of Rome, is dedicated "All'Illustriss. & Reverendiss. Sig. Patriarca Alessandrino, Caetano." The dedicatee must have been Camillo Caetani (1552–1602), who was appointed to the position of Patriarch of Alexandria in August 1588.[69] Camillo's higher-ranking older brother Cardinal Enrico Caetani had earlier held the position; he became Patriarch in July 1585 and later in the same year Pope Sixtus V elevated him to the rank of cardinal.[70] Camillo was papal legate at Madrid to Philip II of Spain from 1592 to 1599, although his aspirations for cardinal were never realized.

Camillo Caetani's interest in the Florentine festivities must have been partly due to his association with Duke Ferdinando while the latter was cardinal in Rome. From 1573 to 1588 Ferdinando was cardinal protector of the confraternity of SS. Trinità, of which Camillo was a member.[71] In 1583 or 1584 the confraternity hired Luca Marenzio, who was recruited some five years later to compose music for the *Pellegrina* interludes. Cavallino's relatively brief account of the interludes that he wrote for Camillo is distinguished by its attention to music, demonstrating that the author had more than a passing acquaintance with musical styles and forms. (He was the only commentator to identify the entertainment's concluding number as a *ballo alla francese,* for example.) Cavallino's attention to musical details obviously reflected the interests of his patron whose appreciation of music spanned both sacred and secular genres. Indeed, Marenzio's *Secondo libro delle villanelle* (1585) was dedicated to Camillo; the dedication, written by Attilio Gualtieri, describes Camillo as one who is knowledgeable "of this very noble profession of music." Other dedications to Camillo in publications of vocal music attest to his interest in secular genres.[72]

Regarding the remaining published descriptions, less information is known about the authors and dedicatees. The dedicatees of Giuseppe Pavoni's extensive *Diario* were the Bolognese patricians Giasone and Pompeo Vizani. (In the early 1590s Giasone Vizani was involved in negotiations to bring the Carracci brothers to Rome to work for Cardinal Odoardo Farnese.)[73] Little is known of Pavoni himself, however.[74] The anonymous account *Li sontuosissimi,* with its emphasis on the Ferrarese wedding guests and especially the activities of Cesare d'Este, appears to have been written with the Ferrarese court in mind, even though Duke Alfonso d'Este was sent a copy of Rossi's detailed *Descrizione* by his ambassador to Florence on May 13.[75] Two anonymous French publications, *Discours de la magnifique réception* and *Discours veritable du marriage,* contain scant information regarding the *Pellegrina* interludes.[76] The latter source contains a short list identifying some of the scenic highlights, in addition to mentioning the entertainment's seven-hour duration, although it was quite usual for a play with interludes to last for six or seven hours.[77] Understandably, one of the main foci of these two French descriptions is the entrance and coronation of Christine of Lorraine.

Barthold von Gadenstedt and an anonymous Frenchman were eyewitnesses to the festivities, and reported their experiences in manuscript diaries. Both attended the premiere performance on May 2, although the Frenchman mentions that he also attended a second performance. W. F. Kümmel provides some background regarding Gadenstedt: he was from a noble family and, after finishing his studies in 1587, took an educational trip to Italy, also visiting Sicily and Malta, before eventually returning home in August of 1589. Kümmel suggests that Gadenstedt appears to have written down his impressions of the *Pellegrina* interludes immediately, and did not revise them or try to work them into conformity with other sources.[78] We must keep in mind, however, that even eyewitness accounts such as Gadenstedt's are never pure or unmediated but reflect the observer's interests and a selective slice of that which was seen and heard. In this respect, Gadenstedt's account demonstrates a particular affinity for and knowledge of Italian music, as well as an interest in dance.

The anonymous Frenchman seems to have pursued topics of interest beyond the moment of performance, outside of the theater itself. He clearly indicates that he discussed perceived ambiguities with other audience members, possibly during the interim between the two performances that he witnessed. For example, after the sorceress's exit in *intermedio* four there was confusion regarding the identity of the "large number of people" suspended in the air (the fire demons). The Frenchman notes that "[m]ost of the spectators thought that they were angels, in that their clothes and ornaments appeared as if they were meant to represent them, but they were mistaken, because I was assured that they were intended as demons, which this woman [the sorceress] had earlier called forth."[79] Thus, the Frenchman appears to have had access to more "authoritative" sources; the assurance that he was given as to characters' significance and identity appears not to have come from a pamphlet that may have circulated, but rather from a personal communication with someone who was either part of, or had connections with, the production team. In addition, the Frenchman's reference to "[m]ost of the spectators" indicates that not only he himself but many audience members were involved in discussing impressions of what they had witnessed. This comment points to the complex nature of individual sources as well as to the nature of the relationship between some sources.

The manuscript description of the *Pellegrina* interludes by an anonymous Bavarian commentator is more or less a verbatim translation into German of the anonymous publication *Li sontuosissimi*. (The Bavarian at times incorporates some Italian words that are derived from the print, further suggesting that he had direct access to the Italian source.) Other sources, however, represent a complex mixture of what appear to be personal observations and information that was evidently attained outside of the performance context, sometimes at a later date. For example, there are short sections of Pavoni's *Diario* that appear to draw on Rossi's *Descrizione,* such as Pavoni's description of the second *intermedio* where the wording is almost identical to Rossi's. At the same time, there is valuable information in Pavoni's account and that of others, especially regarding music, which does not appear in Rossi's description. (An important instance is the information regarding the echo effects in *intermedi* one and five.) As previously mentioned, Rossi's *Descrizione* was completed before the premiere performance, and therefore does not reflect late changes to the production in performance; but his account was also not issued until eleven days after the May 2 premiere. When Rossi's print did appear it seems likely that Pavoni used the official publication to fill in certain gaps in his own account. In general, the unofficial commentators did not attempt to bring their own accounts into complete uniformity with Rossi's.

Unofficial accounts also demonstrate an interest in other audience members' perceptions of the performance. In other words, the commentators' attention was not only focused on the action on stage, but also on those who surrounded them in the theater. (Rossi also attends to audience response, but in his case it is of course an *anticipated response,* because the performances had not yet taken place.) In *intermedio* six, for example, Cavallino reports on the audience's impetus to gather up the "great abundance of gold rain" that had descended from on high, thereby intuiting a sense of the physicality of the audience's engagement. The Frenchman is the only commentator who explicitly identifies the attendees of the five performances in terms of gender, social class, and national identity (see above, "The Performances in the Uffizi Theater"). But he is also keenly attentive to the reactions of the audience at the performances he attended; while several commentators acknowledge the fear they experienced while witnessing the hell scene of *intermedio* four, the Frenchman indicates that he perceived the audience as a whole to be horrified by this scene.

What the unofficial accounts reveal in general is commentators' active engagement with the performative experience, both on and off the stage and inside and outside of the theater. Spectator-auditors were not merely passive recipients of an awe-inspiring spectacle, but were engaged in a complex dialectical process whereby past experience and future projections of an intended readership were brought to bear on what they heard and saw in the performance context of the Uffizi theater. Thus, in written accounts, multiple meanings emerge: some reify the tenets of a nascent absolutism while others suggest that the ephemeral act of performance was registered by momentary glances, not an all-consuming gaze.[80]

PART TWO
Readings

The
Pellegrina
Interludes
in/as
Performance

CHAPTER FOUR

Marshalling *meraviglia*

Manipulating Time, Delineating Space
(*Intermedio* One)

Views of time and space are especially revealing of the dominant attitudes of a particular culture, precisely because they are rarely conscious and because they are expressed in practice more often than in texts.[1]

In this chapter I demonstrate how the experience of witnessing the first of the *Pellegrina* interludes was integrally tied to the spectator-auditor's experience of time and space. Visual and aural media worked in tandem to (re)organize and, at times, confuse these fundamental frames of reference. Spatial perception was frequently delimited by musical (as well as visual) means, while the experience of sound through time was often tempered by visual perception. "Confusing" perceivers' senses in this manner was designed to induce an almost dreamlike state, whereby the lines demarcating reality and artifice begin to blur. Such performative effects served the interests of nascent absolutism, and participated in a more general campaign to posit Medicean representation as a "mystery of state." In this chapter, I interpret the first *intermedio* within a relatively straightforward framework, demonstrating how sound serviced performative absolutism. Judging from the length and detail of the unofficial accounts, the performance of the first interlude immediately attracted the undivided attention of the spectator-auditor (most especially during the opening number).[2] In addition, I use the implications of these spectator accounts to trace certain fault lines in the edifice of absolutism, which in turn reveal more ambiguous readings that undermine the seemingly monolithic, unidirectional nature of power. Before examining these ideas as they play out in performance, I will first consider the tensions inherent in Rossi's official account of the first *intermedio*.

Rossi's quasi-encyclopedic account of the first *intermedio* makes performative efficacy difficult to gauge. Not only was Rossi attempting to convey a sense of the immediacy of a performance that had not yet taken place, he was also trying to strike a delicate balance between, on the one hand, a justification of the performance's authenticity through deference to the appropriate classical sources for the interlude's subject matter and, on the other hand, a rationalization of the creative input of the interlude's *trovatore* (inventor), Giovanni de' Bardi. Indeed, the lengths that Rossi goes to underline ancient precedent is perhaps an indication of the extent to which original sources were refashioned in order to ensure performative efficacy. The very opening of Rossi's account of this *intermedio* is revealing:

> In this *intermedio* the celestial Sirens were represented, guided by Harmony, of which Plato makes mention in his books of the Republic. . . . And because in the same place one finds written that each of the above mentioned Sirens sits on the circle, or circumference of the spheres, and going around the circumference sends out a single pitch loud and clear, making a consonant Harmony; and because Plato says that from all of the Sirens a single consonant Harmony is born, and that Harmony by its nature always goes in front of those that sing, the poet [Giovanni de' Bardi] put forth Harmony on the stage as an escort to the Sirens. And because Plato in another place of the same books of the Republic states that the Dorian Harmony is the best of all the harmonies, and also Aristotle in his Republic [*sic*] confirms it,[3] and furthermore states that all agree that Dorian Harmony is solid and virile and properly speaking has some strength [its own character], it pleased him [Bardi] to show us the Dorian Harmony. . . .[4]

As Rossi makes clear in his description, the subject matter—specifically Harmony and the celestial Sirens—is drawn from Plato's *Republic*. Rossi stresses Plato's reference to the *single* harmony produced by the collective Sirens, perhaps because Bardi had decided to employ a solo singer, rather than a group of Sirens, to open the entertainment. Rossi further justifies this choice by deferring to a natural law of sound: because "harmony *by its nature* always goes in front of those that sing [i.e., the Sirens], the poet [Bardi] put forth Harmony on the stage as an escort to the Sirens" (italics mine). One can surely argue that sound's mobile and flexible nature allows it a certain detachment from its visible source,[5] but there seems to be more at stake here for Rossi and his colleagues.

An examination of Plato's account of the myth of Er reveals that the focus is not on Harmony per se, but rather on those who create Harmony: Necessity with her spindle and the Sirens. In fact, Bardi reserves Necessity and the Sirens for the second part of this *intermedio*. In addition, he takes two distinctive Platonic ideas and fuses them into a single conception by depicting Harmony of the universe specifically as Dorian Harmony because, as Rossi states, it "is the best of all the harmonies," thus justifying Bardi's creative reworking of the source material. For Plato, Dorian music was associated with the regimented order of Spartan troops, while for Aristotle its effect was to produce a "moderate and settled temper."[6] In theory, at least, Bardi's decision to stage Dorian Harmony was an appropriate choice for an entertainment of state. Ironically, though, the song that Dorian Harmony sang—"Dalle più alte sfere" (From the highest spheres) (CD tracks 4–7)—was in the mixolydian mode rather than the dorian, another indication that classical authority and performative efficacy did not necessarily go hand in hand.

There appear to be other, more pragmatic, reasons for Bardi's musical and staging decisions (not articulated in Rossi's account) that were integrally connected to the interlude's success in performance. First, Dorian Harmony's lone appearance and her solo song[7]—functioning as prologue—served as a visual and sonic foil to that which followed: the polychoral dialogue of the Sirens. The affective force of the *Pellegrina intermedi* in general relied on surprising or unexpected scenic and sonic juxtapositions, and the first *intermedio* functioned as a microcosm of the entire set. Second, Bardi's decision allowed the Florentine court to display, from the outset, the singular virtuosity of their prima donna, the renowned Vittoria Archilei. Notes in Seriacopi's *Memoriale* suggest that Duke Ferdinando was especially invested in Archilei's involvement in the interlude because the work is referred to as "the *intermedio primo* of Vittoria [Archilei]."[8] The casting of a female singer, and her appearance for the very opening number of the performance, was no casual decision. The rival court of Ferrara was widely known for its "secret music," with the female singers from that court largely restricted to more private settings. Yet the Florentine court on the important occasion of this Medici wedding went out of their way to stage their female singers in the large Uffizi theater in especially prominent ways. For audience members from neighboring courts who may have recognized the voice of Archilei—albeit a relatively select group—her appearance in and of itself may have been a source of wonderment. Those from Ferrara and other closely associated courts would have likely interpreted Archilei's appearance as a form of courtly one-upmanship:[9] instead of relying on the hearsay of a privileged few who witnessed the singing of women in private—admittedly an effective strategy that created its own mystique—the Florentines displayed their female singers in the court's most public of venues.

In the performance that was open to the Florentine citizenry and the friends of those involved in the production,[10] Archilei's appearance would have signified quite differently. The infrequent presence of Florentine patricians at court probably meant that they too felt privileged to hear the singing of the court's undisputed prima donna. The friends of Archilei's colleagues may have had little interest in Archilei's allegorical significance, more interested perhaps in the expertise of the singer herself. The singer as musician (rather than allegorical figure) was a point of curiosity for the German eyewitness, Gadenstedt, who attempted to track Archilei's appearance in subsequent interludes. Non-Florentines, however, appear to have been concerned with generalized impressions of the singer's sonic/visual presentation.[11] In this respect, the affective quality of Archilei's song "Dalle più alte sfere" was partly due, in Richard Leppert's words, to "the sight of sound."[12] But few in the audience actually recognized the singer as Dorian Harmony, nor did they understand her sung text, despite her self-identifying pronouncement—"I, Harmony, come [down] to you, O mortals"—during the course of her song.

Eyewitness accounts of the performances suggest that Archilei's song was meaningful, but that its efficacy was not dependent on word-for-word comprehension of her song's text.[13] A frequent point of comment concerned the affective quality of Archilei's voice. Gadenstedt noted, for example, that the singer "began to sing so sweetly at the same time 'beating' on the lute, so that everyone said that it was impossible that a human voice could be so sweet, [and] also so moved all the spectators with her singing that they just could not describe it."[14]

It might be tempting to dismiss entirely the remarks of Gadenstedt and others who emphasize the ineffable sweetness of the singer's voice as poetic cliché or as part of a broader phenomenon that Lorenzo Bianconi has described as the "cult of ineffability" (of which it undoubtedly was).[15] It is important to remember, however, that Archilei was versed in singing "alla napoletana," enabling her to perform exceedingly florid embellishment with great velocity. As a female soprano she could sing elaborate passagework in the upper reaches of the soprano range with ease, thus projecting an impression of superhuman virtuosity.[16] In the broadest sense, then, the affective quality of Archilei's song in performance was also due to her extraordinary facility as an exponent of Neapolitan-style singing. The intricate and endlessly varied passagework that we see on the printed page (see plate 4) was likely experienced in performance in terms of broad affective gestures that were delineated sectionally. Indeed, through affective sectional shifts and increasingly demanding, spectacular passagework, the song has impressed modern commentators by exuding an overarching impression of gathering momentum. The florid passagework that characterizes what some have assumed to be the song's final section—beginning with the second statement of the words "Qual voi" (CD track 6)—has been perceived as the most technically demanding and aurally breathtaking of the piece, to judge from recent recordings.

While Archilei's song would appear—on the printed page—to gather momentum as it proceeds, the song's forward-moving trajectory was counterbalanced in the 1589 performances by the visual perception of the singer on a slowly descending cloud (see plate 5).[17] Rossi describes the proposed visual dimension of the scene thus:

> When the curtains fell one immediately saw a cloud appear in the sky, and on earth, at the front of the stage, a little Doric temple of rustic stone [replaced in performances by a rocky cave]. A woman in the cloud that came little by little to the earth was playing a lute and singing. . . . And while the above-mentioned cloud descended to earth little by little, and having under it some sunbeams, it seemed that by following them [the sun beams], it gradually, as it moved, covered the sun.[18]

Almost all descriptions—eyewitness and otherwise—also stress the barely perceptible nature of the descent, leaving spectators at a loss as to exactly how the cloud moved as it gradually descended from the Heavens.[19] This impression, to which the creators of the *intermedi* had given special attention,[20] was part of the wonder and the theatrical game, of course, and resonated with the Patrizian concept of incomprehensibility. My point here, however, is to suggest that the combined effect of the aural and visual media would have produced a sense of time suspended—of time standing still—rather than projecting an impression of gathering momentum. This impression would have been fortified by the necessarily limited physical motion of Archilei as she sang to her lute;[21] indeed, the technique required for singing such elaborate passagework required the singer to remain as physically motionless as possible.[22] The floating, translucent quality of Archilei's passagework was reinforced by the flexible accompaniment of plucked-string instruments that included the singer's own "leuto grosso" and two chitarroni played from behind the scenes.[23] The newly "invented" chitarrone—with its extension neck facilitating a strong and extensive bass range—was able to create a variegated textural support for the singer's extended "windings of the voice" in the upper range. The exclusion of a bowed bass instrument for accompaniment here was crucial because not only did the absence of such a sonority reduce treble/bass polarity, but it also helped to defuse the momentum of tonal directionality. Thus, the sonority produced a sense of groundlessness, allowing the ethereal quality of Archilei's passagework to freely swirl, while her body remained largely motionless.[24]

Thus, the overarching purpose of this opening emblematic tableau—the singer's mesmerizingly incremental descent—was to initiate the spectator into the magical world of the *intermedi,* providing a "psychic displacement from the ordinary"[25] that would prepare the perceiver for the new and unexpected sonic and visual shifts that followed. That the spectator experienced the event on a quasi-religious or mystical level is suggested by the terms used to describe the sound quality of Archilei's voice. The notion of incomprehensibility was commonly associated with the mysteries of the Christian faith, and the frequency with which words such as *stupefare* (to stun, render senseless) and *meraviglia* occur in written accounts suggest the dreamlike, otherworldly quality of the experience. Thus, while Archilei was not recognized as a personification of Harmony, her music and visual presentation produced the intended effect.

The ethereal connotations of Archilei's performance are perhaps most clearly revealed by the perception of the singer as an angel or goddess (rather than as Dorian Harmony). Cavallino attributed this perception to both her visual appearance and her sonorous singing style.[26] The most obvious cue for many spectators was the singer's iconic status as she descended from the Heavens, a perception that was intentionally fortified by producer Emilio de' Cavalieri at rehearsal when he ordered the enlargement of Archilei's cloud so that it surrounded her from above (as well as below) to produce an almost halo-like effect.[27] In this manner, the opening of the first *intermedio* mimicked the kind of spectacular scenic effects utilized for decades in larger Florentine churches for the performance of sacred representations, familiar to Florentines and distinguished visitors alike.[28] The mechanical devices installed as permanent fixtures in some churches enabled angels and other celestial beings to hover in mid-air or enact spectacular descents on important occasions.[29] But in the artificially generated environment of the closed court theater, Archilei's spatial descent was a powerful metaphor for Medici control: with their stage crew literally pulling the invisible strings of wonder, the Medici attempted to actualize their godlike power.

Archilei's descent also had profound philosophical significance, as suggested by Bardi's song text and the emblematic quality of the visual imagery.[30] Because emblems were considered talismanic, some spectators may have understood the descent to indicate what was being brought about invisibly. Thus, the singer's descent functioned in performance as a kind of choreographic magic, whereby cosmic harmony was brought to earth. The duke himself (and the producers of the entertainment) may have interpreted the spectator's awe-struck response as proof of the performance's magical efficacy.

The Mysterious Source of Sound

With these considerations in mind, I will now discuss the significance of the concluding section of Archilei's song. It has long been assumed that the musical print included two possible endings, a more florid and extensive "first ending" and a shorter "second ending" with echo effects (see plate 4; the "second ending" begins with the decorated initial). I previously alluded to the so-called first ending that concluded with increasingly dynamic passagework on the text "strong Hercules" (CD track 6). The shorter "second ending," which sets the same text (CD track 7), is characterized by repeated melodic cells and reiterated syllables in the text, suggesting that the second of each musical cell was performed as an echo. In recent recordings of the song, the echo ending has either been omitted or the endings as they appear in the musical print have been reversed. Either solution allows what appears to be the more vocally spectacular ending to conclude the piece.[31] But several accounts, including one from an eyewitness, confirm that the echo ending concluded the premiere performance in the Uffizi theater.[32] A manuscript description by an anonymous Frenchman who attended the premiere outlines the details:

> In front of the stage, which is very large and high, there were two cloths that covered the entire stage. When they wished to begin, all of a sudden the first, which was red, fell to the ground. The second [cloth], which was like sky blue, remained, right in the middle of which appeared a lady who was seated in a cloud holding a lute in her hand. [She] sang and little by little descended to the stage, where she immediately disappeared. She played and sang so well that everyone admired her, and at the end of her song there was heard an echo that responded to her, which seemed to be quite far away from the stage, a mile or more.[33]

The account of Giuseppe Pavoni confirms the description by the anonymous Frenchman:

> There were two cloths covering the front of the stage. The first one which went down was red; the perspective was then seen, although it was still covered by another cloth that was blue, in the middle of which was a woman who was seated on a cloud, and with a lute began to play and sing a madrigal very sweetly. And thus playing and singing she came, being lowered down little by little, hiding herself among certain rocks, and finishing the madrigal among those rocks with an echo so wonderful that it seemed like its bouncing back was a mile away.[34]

Additionally, Pavoni's account refers to the "certi scogli" (certain rocks) into which Archilei disappeared at the conclusion of her cloud-borne descent, and from whence she concluded her madrigal. The final echo section was thus performed out of the audience's sight, and Pavoni confirms its wondrous effect.

I comment here on the several disorienting (and thus *meraviglia*-inspiring) surprises that many audience members likely experienced at this moment in the performance. Many in the audience probably assumed that Archilei's

song had concluded with her spectacular final flourishes and her disappearance into the "certain rocks." The music that was sung out of eyesight began
in a more sustained, lyrical style with the text "And you, new Minerva"—
referencing Christine of Lorraine, the new duchess of Florence (CD track 7;
plate 4), beginning at the decorated initial.[35] The opening three notes would
have naturally incorporated a gradual crescendo, as the musical line slowly
ascended by step to support a largely syllabic setting of the text. (In order to
enhance this effect, our recording omits the continuo part for the singer's first
note in this section.) In 1589, the audience was likely caught off guard by the
singer's gradually emerging disembodied voice. And, no sooner had Archilei
concluded this short lyrical phrase than she began a rapidly articulated ascending motive on the next portion of text—"and strong Hercules"—that
was echoed, according to spectators, from a considerable distance. From what
is known of the theater's setup it seems likely that Archilei's echo was rendered by a singer stationed at the back of the hall (out of sight) in or behind
the balcony above the main entrance, a position that would explain the emphasis in both descriptions on the considerable distance from which the echo
seemed to originate.[36] For the auditor, the challenge and pleasure of the experience inhered simultaneously in the initial confusion engendered by the echo
and in the attempt to describe the auditory experience—if only to suggest
that the echo appeared to emanate from "quite far away from the stage, a mile
or so." Notice that the auditor did not definitively locate the echo's source. To
do so would have destroyed the novelty of the auditory sensation; thus, for
meraviglia to be efficacious, knowledge, in the Patrizian conception, must remain partial.

   In this final echo section, the auditor may not have understood the
broken syllables of the words "forte Alcide" (strong Hercules), which referred to Duke Ferdinando himself:[37] each syllable was treated in melis-
matic fashion and then echoed. But the text's conceit was surely demonstrated
in the performance space by the musical effect. The duke's pseudonym
"strong Hercules" resounded back and forth from the stage to the far
reaches of the hall, with sound actively expanding the limits of the (on-
stage) theatrical space, and transcending the bounds of the singer's body
now hidden from the audience's view. Thus, sense of space, so frequently
associated with visual perception, was actively defined by aural means. In
other words, the auditor-spectator's experience of *meraviglia*—so frequently
attached to visual perception—was here produced through the absence of
"the sight of sound." One political reading can be advanced: through sound,
"strong Hercules" commanded the far reaches of the theatrical space, projecting an idealized vision of Medicean expansion and control, yet the
source of sound and the means through which it was produced eluded those

Plate 1.

Assault on two fortresses, with Grand Duke Ferdinando I at left, by Jacques Callot.
New York, The Metropolitan Museum of Art, Bequest of Edwin de T. Bechtel,
1957 (57.650.363(13)). Image © The Metropolitan Museum of Art.

2402

Plate 4.

The two "endings" for "Dalle più alte sfere" as presented in the canto partbook of
Intermedii et concerti, 6. Vienna, Österreichische Nationalbibliothek,
Musiksammlung, S.A.78.B.48, by permission.

n: I

In capo sette fiore sopra le treccie e afineintoa nestein tutto di lionato, et adorna d'uel dalti color che campeggino col lionato in mano l'arpe. sopra una nuvola asedere

Plate 5.

Costume design by Buontalenti for Vittoria Archilei in the role of Doric Harmony for *intermedio* one. I:Fn, Palatina C.B.3.53, vol. II, c. 11r. By permission of the Ministero per i Beni e le Attività Culturali della Repubblica Italiana and the Biblioteca Nazionale Centrale, Florence. Further reproduction of the image by any means is prohibited.

Plate 8.

Composite stage design for *intermedio* two by Epifanio d'Alfiano, showing the Pierides at audience right, the Muses at audience left, and the Hamadryads (wood nymphs) in the central panel. New York, The Metropolitan Museum of Art, Harris Brisbane Dick Fund, 1931 (31.72.5(14)). Image © The Metropolitan Museum of Art.

Plate 9. *(facing)*

Seating plan and costume designs for the Hamadryads for *intermedio* two by Buontalenti. I:Fn, Palatina C.B.3.53, vol. II, cc. 30v–31r. By permission of the Ministero per i Beni e le Attività Culturali della Repubblica Italiana and the Biblioteca Nazionale Centrale, Florence. Further reproduction of the image by any means is prohibited.

Plate 10.

Costume design for the Pierides by Buontalenti. I:Fn, Palatina C.B.3.53, vol. II, c. 9. By permission of the Ministero per i Beni e le Attività Culturali della Repubblica Italiana and the Biblioteca Nazionale Centrale, Florence. Further reproduction of the image by any means is prohibited

Plate 11.

Costume design for the Muses by Buontalenti. I:Fn, Palatina C.B.3.53, vol. II, c. 8. By permission of the Ministero per i Beni e le Attività Culturali della Repubblica Italiana and the Biblioteca Nazionale Centrale, Florence. Further reproduction of the image by any means is prohibited.

Plate 12.

Stage scene for *intermedio* three by Carracci with the serpent-dragon at the center and
Apollo (a puppet) descending from on high. New York, The Metropolitan Museum of Art,
Harris Brisbane Dick Fund, 1926, (26.70.4(33)). Image © The Metropolitan Museum of Art.

Plate 13.

Apollo's costume design for *intermedio* three by Buontalenti. The dancer Agostino played the role of Apollo. I:Fn, Palatina C.B.3.53, vol. II, c. 1r. By permission of the Ministero per i Beni e le Attività Culturali della Repubblica Italiana and the Biblioteca Nazionale Centrale, Florence. Further reproduction of the image by any means is prohibited.

Plate 14.

Costume design for a Delphic couple for *intermedio* three by Buontalenti. Antonio Naldi
played the figure on the right. I:Fn, Palatina C.B.3.53, vol. II, c. 16r. By permission of the
Ministero per i Beni e le Attività Culturali della Repubblica Italiana and the Biblioteca Nazionale
Centrale, Florence. Further reproduction of the image by any means is prohibited.

Plate 15.

Costume design for a Delphic couple for *intermedio* three by Buontalenti. The figure on the
left was played by Margherita della Scala, and the figure on the right was likely played by
Lucia Caccini. I:Fn, Palatina C.B.3.53, vol. II, c. 20r. By permission of the Ministero per i Beni e le
Attività Culturali della Repubblica Italiana and the Biblioteca Nazionale Centrale, Florence.
Further reproduction of the image by any means is prohibited.

Plate 16.

Stage design for *intermedio* four by Buontalenti. Lucia Caccini played the sorceress on high in her chariot. Réunion des Musées Nationaux / Art Resource, NY.

Plate 17.

Stage design for *intermedio* four by d'Alfiano with the emergent Lucifer at center.
New York, The Metropolitan Museum of Art, Harris Brisbane Dick Fund, 1931 (31.72.5(13)).
Image © The Metropolitan Museum of Art.

Plate 18.

Preparatory sketch for Lucifer in *intermedio* four by Ludovico Cigoli. Florence, Gabinetto Disegni e Stampe degli Uffizi, 2402A. By permission of the Ministero per i Beni e le Attività Culturali. Further reproduction of the image by any means is prohibited.

Plate 19.

Costume design for sea nymphs in *intermedio* five by Buontalenti. The name of Margherita della
Scala is first among the performers' names listed below. I:Fn, Palatina C.B.3.53, vol. II, c. 10r.
By permission of the Ministero per i Beni e le Attività Culturali della Repubblica Italiana and
the Biblioteca Nazionale Centrale, Florence. Further reproduction of the image by any
means is prohibited.

Plate 20.

Composite stage design for *intermedio* five by d'Alfiano with Anfitrite
(played by Vittoria Archilei) positioned at the center on her mother-of-pearl shell.
New York, The Metropolitan Museum of Art, Harris Brisbane Dick Fund,
1931 (31.72.5(15)). Image © The Metropolitan Museum of Art.

Plate 22.

Naumachia in the courtyard of the Palazzo Pitti by Orazio Scarabelli, c. 1589. New York,
The Metropolitan Museum of Art, Harris Brisbane Dick Fund, 1931 (31.72.5(11)).
Image © The Metropolitan Museum of Art.

perta figura ua uestita tutta di Rosso cð fondo doro. sðtto efasa   La uesta di questa figura intora, e grande.

Alione,   N 16 — Jacopo Peri Zazzerino

Plate 23.

Costume design by Buontalenti for Jacopo Peri in the role of Arion (holding a harp) for
intermedio five. I:Fn, Palatina C.B.3.53, vol. II, c. 6r. By permission of the Ministero per i
Beni e le Attività Culturali della Repubblica Italiana and the Biblioteca Nazionale Centrale,
Florence. Further reproduction of the image by any means is prohibited.

Plate 24.

Costume design for Arion (or Apollo?) holding a six-string viol with a lira da braccio-style peg box. Museo Horne no. 5812, Gabinetto Disegni e Stampe degli Uffizi. By permission of the Ministero per i Beni e le Attività Culturali. Further reproduction of the image by any means is prohibited.

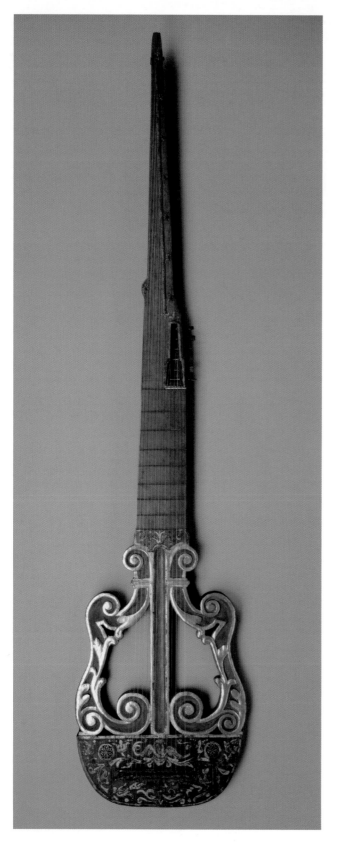

Plate 26.

Theatrical chitarrone.
Museo Civico Medievale,
Bologna. Inv. 1745,
by permission.

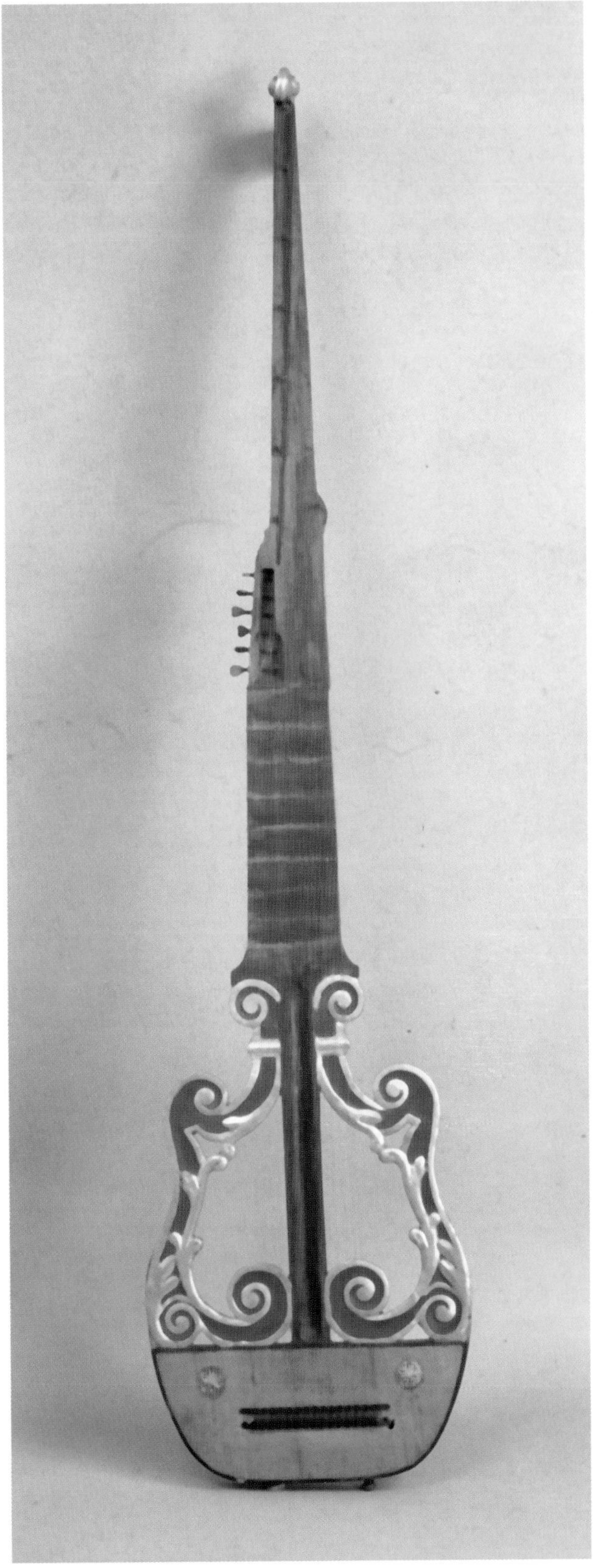

Plate 27.

Stage setting for *intermedio* six by d'Alfiano showing the "golden rain"
observed by commentators who witnessed the performances. New York,
The Metropolitan Museum of Art, Harris Brisbane Dick Fund, 1931 (31.72.5(16)).
Image © The Metropolitan Museum of Art.

Stage design for *intermedio* six by Buontalenti showing the Graces descending on the central cloud. London, V&A Images / Victoria and Albert Museum, no. E.1189–1931, by permission.

BALLO
DELL'VLTIMO INTERMEDIO.

Qᴠᴇꜱᴛᴏ diſegno ci ha da rappreſentare il Palco : & i numeri rappreſentano le perſone, il qual ſegno, ò freggio, come ſi chiami, che è dietro a' numeri hanno hauer uolte le ſpalle; coſi ſeguirà ſtando in Scena, et in ciaſcuna attione, che nel preſente Ballo s'interuenga.

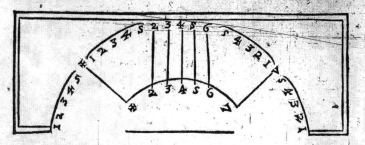

Rɪᴛʀᴏᴜᴀɴᴅᴏꜱɪ tutti in ſu la Scena come ſi dimoſtra ſi laſcierà paſſar dodici pauſe e di poi .1.7. che ſon ſegnati paſſeráno auanti con due ſeguiti, & alla fine di quei ſi trouerano in Luna come qui ſopra ſi uede. Auuertendo, che i Vinti che reſtano ſtaran no fermi, e dipoi i Sette, daranno principio al preſente Ballo.

Qᴠᴇꜱᴛᴏ Ballo ſarà principiato da Sette Perſone; cioè da Quattro Dame, e Tre Huomini, lequali ſaráno queſte le Dame .1.3.5.7. e queſti .2.4.6. gli Huomini, & iɴſieme col pie ſiniſtro faranno la Riuerenza, & à man ſiniſtra le continenze, e una Riuerenza à man ſiniſtra, e .2. cangi co'l pie ſiniſtro, & uno ſeguito trangato auanti, & uno in dietro, e dipoi tutti in ruota à man ſiniſtra col pie ſiniſtro quattro ſpezzate, & altre quattro ſcorſe ritornando al ſuo luogo, e ſubito gli Huomini un trabocchetto auanti ſu'l pie ſiniſtro, & uno in dietro ſu'l deſtro, & una ſcorſa di un ſeguito barattandoſi i luoghi ; & il ſimile faranno le Dame.

ᴋᴋ   Le

Plate 29.

Choreography diagram and beginning of written description for the final *ballo* "O che nuovo miracolo" from *intermedio* six, from the *nono* partbook of *Intermedii et concerti,* 21. Vienna, Österreichische Nationalbibliothek, Musiksammlung, S.A.78.B.48, by permission.

who might try to track its origins. In other words, pure sound, as emblem of Medicean political power, was elevated to the level of a "mystery of state."

Echo's Rocky Cave: An Alternative Reading

Yet, Archilei's echo ending can also be seen to destabilize the monolithic conception that the above reading assumes. As the following reading shows, the nature of absolutism admits a contradiction and concomitant ambiguity, as can a woman's voice. While the creators of the interlude intended Archilei to represent Dorian Harmony, unofficial accounts of the final echo ending suggest that an Ovidian conception of Echo was also envisaged. Originally (according to Rossi), a set with a recognizable vista of Rome was to begin the entire entertainment, in an attempt to confuse the spectator: the audience would assume from the realistic set that the comedy, not an *intermedio,* would begin the entertainment. Archilei would then have appeared on her cloud, with the Roman scene remaining as a backdrop in perspective, producing an unusual confluence of what were, by the 1580s, discrete elements of the entertainment: the comedy and the interludes. The Roman scene would then have disappeared along with Archilei at the end of her song, to reveal paradise full of clouds (a continuation of *intermedio* one), and the audience would only discover after the end of the interlude that the setting for the comedy was in fact Pisa, not Rome.

This elaborate scheme did not materialize—although it would have been appropriate for the Roman singer Archilei, sometimes known as La Romanina, to have sung in front of a scene of Rome, and the city carried many other connotations in Medicean mythology (see chapter 1, section entitled "Shoring Up Dynastic Prerogative: Precedent and Continuity"). Instead, as we know, Archilei sang against a flat blue curtain, and it was only at the very end of her song, when the echo section began, that any stage setting is mentioned in unofficial sources. According to several sources, Archilei disappeared into some kind of rocky structure (which superseded the Doric temple mentioned by Rossi, itself part of the (defunct) Roman scene).[38] As noted above, Pavoni referred to "certain rocks," although the anonymous author of *Li sontuosissimi* is somewhat more confident in his description, stressing the intentionality that he perceived on the part of the creators:

> [A]nd little by little, almost without the audience noticing it, she comes down [while] singing, and thus hides herself among various rocks *that were built for that purpose,* and suddenly the curtain disappeared in an incredible way [italics mine]. . . .[39]

The "rocks" mentioned in both descriptions must refer to the "canonical domain" of Echo following her rejection by Narcissus in the Ovidian story—the rocky cave that became her final retreat.[40] In this place, pining away for Narcissus, her flesh eventually withered away, leaving only bones, and then eventually only her voice. The "various rocks" of the *intermedio* signal an Ovidian conception and thus raise questions about the nature of language—a language that is fragmented and displaced by the use of echo. Indeed, Echo had lost her capacity for full expression even before the cave became her dwelling. Juno, aware that Echo's "idle chatter" was preventing her from catching Jove in his dalliance with a mountain nymph, prevented Echo from annunciating anything more than the ends of phrases.[41] Later, when she pursues Narcissus, Echo cleverly employs fragmentary repetition in an attempt to capture Narcissus's attention. Ovid's Echo tended to elicit negative connotations in mythographic commentators, in part because of her fragmentation of the anterior voice and her capacity to deconstruct words and manipulate meaning. How did these qualities signify within the context of the *intermedio*?

That the creators of the *intermedio* intended to evoke the Echo of Ovid's story is clear; that audience members found her rocky cave difficult to identify is also clear, but easy enough to explain: "hiding herself among certain rocks," only the back, not the opening, of Echo's cave could be displayed (for Archilei herself to remain unseen), thus obscuring the defining element of the structure. A multiplicity of meanings attended this final gesture. From the perspective of the interlude's creators, what happened to Dorian Harmony when Archilei literally disappeared and instead signified Echo through her disembodied voice? A complementary version of Echo's story, recounted by Longus and taken up in somewhat different form by Macrobius, provides a compelling connection to Harmony of the Spheres. In both stories, Echo is associated with Pan. In Longus's story, Pan, envying Echo's musical expertise and angered by her exclusively female-centered music-making, infects the shepherds with madness so that they tear her limb from limb dispersing her body across the earth; the dismemberment is transformed into vocal fragmentation, as the scattered limbs imitate their surroundings. Imitation and fragmentation are thus central to both Longus's and Ovid's accounts of Echo. Macrobius takes up Echo's connection with Pan, although their association is apparently less violent. Because Echo is married to Pan, inventor of the seven-reed musical pipe (and thus creator of seven-fold planetary music), Macrobius allegorizes Echo as Harmony of the Spheres; because she is invisible, Echo becomes an appropriate symbol for heavenly harmony, which also cannot be perceived by the sense of sight. Though the signifying element in the Florentine *intermedio* was an Ovidian one—Echo's rocky cave—the association between Harmony and Echo probably existed in the minds of the interludes' creators. The connection is made apparent in the section on Echo in Vincenzo Cartari's 1571 emblem book, which is known to have influenced conceptions for several interludes, including the first.[42]

In the context of the *intermedio,* then, what else might Echo have to "say" through her fragmented language about the nature of power? Regarding the reenvisioning of silenced or nearly silenced Ovidian women by Renaissance male poets, Ann Rosalind Jones notes that they "displaced the male violence and guilt and the female linguistic loss . . . into purified pastoral settings and reworked them into occasions for rhetorical virtuosity." On the other hand, female writers reconfigured Ovid's transformations through "processes of emphatic identification," thereby signaling women's alliances, and "[r]esisting contemporary injunctions to silence and modesty."[43] As previously mentioned, the lyrical musical line that sets "new Minerva" (referencing the new duchess) is entirely intact (CD track 7, opening); it is only with the words "strong Hercules" that Echo holds sway. While Archilei, as prima donna, was in one sense a "stand-in" for the duke, actualizing his prowess through her musical virtuosity, as a female singer her status was somewhat more ambiguous, or at least open to interpretation. As a woman, she must have been aware of the various implications of Ovid's stories, and may have even been aware of the ways in which the tales had been rewritten from a female point of view. I have argued elsewhere that, although "Dalle più alte sfere" has conflicting attributions to two male composers (one of whom was her husband), Archilei likely composed the work; at the very least, the lavish embellishment she employed that essentially "makes" the song was her own devising.[44] That said, Archilei's very presence on the stage as a singing woman usurped the patriarchal injunction limiting women's vocality and, by extension, their sexuality. Ironically, while Archilei herself enacted Echo's fate in her rocky cave, it was the duke's name that was the subject of her fragmented discourse that she herself (very likely) constructed. If, as Norman Bryson argues, the gaze "seeks to confine what is always on the point of escaping or slipping out of bounds,"[45] then the first *intermedio* stages the failure of the gaze, with the echo ending ultimately subverting Archilei's mesmerizing descent, and replacing it with an absent body and a voice that cannot sustain itself. Ultimately, though, it was up to spectator-auditors, both women and men, to determine the voice's meaning, even if that meaning was little more than a subliminal resonance from a half-remembered myth.

Music and Text

As I suggested earlier, the affective power of this scene did not ultimately rest on the audience's comprehension of Archilei's sung text. This is not to imply, however, that there was little attention to text setting in "Dalle più alte sfere," even within the parameters of Neapolitan-style florid singing.[46] Indeed, throughout the song there is a basic strategy of repeating each short portion of text. In the opening of the piece, for example, the first phrase is sung in a comparatively unembellished manner, but is then repeated with a more elaborate musical setting (see example 4.1, mm. 1–7 and 7–15; CD track 4). In several instances the meaning of the text is represented in musical terms by the use of word painting, as in the rising melodic gestures on "più alte" (highest) at the opening (mm. 2–4) and with the text repetition beginning at m. 8. In example 4.2 the vocal line's undulating figures (at mm. 52–59; part of CD track 5) are clearly intended to depict the "battendo l'ali" (beating wings) of the winged messenger who has "come all the way up to the sky" to deliver the news of the Medici wedding. The stepwise rising bass line accompanying the repetition of the text strengthens this interpretation by depicting the messenger's Heaven-bound ascent (see example 4.2, mm. 51–53). By consulting the musical print—as Bardi no doubt hoped the connoisseurs would do—one sees that the text setting in this song is quite considered, and characteristic of a similar kind of attention bestowed on the other solo songs of the *intermedi*. But in the performance context there is no doubt that some, if not all, of these music-text subtleties were missed by most audience members.

Sound in Motion

> And thus it was, that once the scene disappeared, they saw the whole starry sky with such a splendor lighting it up that you would have said that this was the moonlight. And the scene instead of houses (that reasonably one should expect to see)[47] was full of clouds so similar to real clouds that people were wondering if these clouds wouldn't go up in the sky to bring us rain. And while we were looking at such a thing, we saw four clouds moving on the stage and on these clouds were the previously mentioned Sirens. . . . [48]

From the producer's perspective (and perhaps that of Duke Ferdinando himself), Harmony's magical descent had literally brought Paradise to earth; the scene, as Rossi describes it, was "full of clouds," and the engraving of the scene by Agostino Carracci (plate 6) confirms that clouds filled the entire stage from top to bottom.[49] While the prologue's "action" was thus integral to the scene that followed, it also provided a striking visual contrast, although Rossi only hints at the means through which the dramatic visual shift was put into effect. His reference to "the wonders that this scene [the prologue] was hiding" is confirmed by other accounts that refer to the swift removal of the blue cloth that served as Harmony's

Example 4.1. Vittoria (and Antonio?) Archilei, "Dalle più alte sfere," mm. 1–15 (from *intermedio* one)

Example 4.2. Vittoria (and Antonio?) Archilei, "Dalle più alte sfere," mm. 50–59 (from *intermedio* one)

backdrop to reveal "the open paradise."[50] The first appearance of the actual perspective was clearly a striking moment for the spectator, following Archilei's iconic descent against a (flat) backdrop. In one anonymous account, the author notes that "suddenly the curtain disappeared in an incredible way, and in an instant the open perspective appeared and remained in the Heavens."[51] The wonder was enhanced by the increase in personnel and sonic forces: fifteen or sixteen richly clad Sirens were distributed on four clouds situated on the stage floor, which was intended to serve as the lower portion of the Heavens. (In plate 6 one only sees twelve Sirens divided into two groups; plate 7 shows the elaborate costume design for the third Siren, Mercury, played by Lucia Caccini.) The revelation of heaven as *paradiso* confirmed assumptions that the audience had already made with regard to Archilei: despite the scene's Platonic elements emphasized by Rossi, the spectators believed that they were witnessing a vision of a Christian paradise, with the Sirens situated in the Heavens, much like angels.[52] Duke Ferdinando was not only godlike, then, but aligned with a specifically Christian god.

The focus of almost all of the brief, impressionistic accounts of this scene is the Sirens' cloud-borne *ascent* from the stage floor to the (upper) Heavens, while singing (with no mention of an initial descent). The Siren's ascent, then, directly mirrored Archilei's spectacular descent, and for the spectator this seemingly rudimentary stage action was the defining moment of the first *intermedio*.[53] I say "seemingly rudimentary" because, as I have already suggested, this dynamically charged vertical movement had profound philosophical (not to mention political) implications that were likely understood by the spectator on an intuitive level. If the complexity of the specific allusions eluded them—Rossi's multi-page explanation of the Sirens' costumes and attributes being a case in point—it is arguable that the effect the spectacle exerted on the senses was understood as evidence of its magical efficacy. And, of course, the "letting down and pulling up [that] took place so skillfully," as Gadenstedt described it, was to remain part of the "mystery of state."

If the Sirens' ascent was perceived as a counterpart to Archilei's initial descent, then in essence the entire *intermedio* centered around a relationship between those above and those below. That relationship was suggestive of the easily traversable distance between the two spheres. The union of the upper and lower realms of the cosmos signified on another level. The texts of the various musical numbers express in an overtly political way that which was most clearly impressed on the spectator's mind through visual imagery and sound: the joining together of Heaven and Earth—symbolically representative of the (heavenly) Medici and their (earthly) subjects, allies, and even potential rivals—to praise and affirm the union of the houses of Medici and Lorraine.

If the Sirens' ascent was noted with interest by many of those in attendance, it is important to remember that the *intermedio* proper (as opposed to Archilei's prologic opening) in fact consisted of a series of musical numbers (all composed by Malvezzi). In unofficial reports individual pieces are not described by title, and sometimes remain unremarked upon; yet even in the briefest of reports it is the perception of theatrical space or place, albeit stationary or mobile "space," that helped define and frame selected musical numbers in the mind of the spectator.[54] In other words, the interlude's visual cues helped focus musical attention, singling out particular numbers and blurring distinctions between others. During the heightened experience of performance, then, the spectator-auditor engaged in a process of mental (musical) "editing" that shaped the meaning of the event and ensured the performance's memorability through visceral experience.[55] In unofficial written accounts this process amounted to an abridged version of performance, which nonetheless represented the perceiver's *experience* of the *intermedi*.[56] The meaning-making process was thus a dialectical one, conceived and executed by the Medici and their representatives, but shaped and tailored by the spectator-auditor.

Unofficial commentators experienced the *intermedio* proper not as a set of musically discrete numbers, but as a scenic-sonic conglomerate whose affective force lay partly in the additive or cumulative nature of the musical forces involved. Almost all accounts stress the last impressions of the scene—citing the sheer number of singers and musicians involved at the conclusion—although at the heart of the scene lay the Sirens' memorable ascent. Indeed, aspects of musical style, form, and instrumentation encouraged such conflations, as the *intermedio* pushed toward its climactic conclusion. In this regard, each of Malvezzi's consecutive settings is masterfully paced in order to maximize the cumulative effect of stylistic and formal distinctions between pieces.

The opening madrigal sung and played by the Sirens—"Noi, che cantando" (We, by singing)—is set in eight parts divided into two choirs. As previously noted, the Sirens were deployed on clouds on the stage floor. Carracci's engraving (plate 6) shows that the Sirens were equally disposed on either side of the stage, suggesting, along with the indications in Malvezzi's print, that the piece was performed in polychoral fashion. Thus, the initial sonic focus of the *intermedio* proper appears to be the stage floor where Archilei had concluded her cloud-borne descent. But instead of an echo that resounded from the back of the hall in response to Archilei's centrally located (but disembodied) voice, the Sirens' polychoral madrigal expanded the sonic space outward, toward either side of the stage. While four Sirens on each side sang one on a part, the remaining Sirens on each side accompanied them with a variety of bowed and plucked string instruments specified by Malvezzi. The tone color and texture of the "accompanying" instruments were more or less equivalent in each group, with the resultant polychoral soundscape playing on shifting articulations of musical "space" rather than timbral distinctions. The use of (sustaining) bowed instruments to reinforce the highest and lowest voices in each choir—specifically lire and bass viols—accentuated the textural contrast with Archilei's preceding solo. In addition, groups of gesticulating instrumentalists would have been clearly visible to the audience now, in contrast to the lone, seemingly stationary, singer-lutenist who opened the entertainment.

"Noi, che cantando" began with the full complement of voices and instruments in homophonic fashion as the Sirens exclaim their cosmic function: "We, whose singing makes the celestial spheres sweetly turn around. . . ." Though largely homophonic, the opening phrases are lightly embellished with madrigalisms on appropriate words such as "cantando" (singing) and "rotar" (turn around). Chorus II sings the second phrase alone, with the quinto part (the highest voice of chorus II) rhythmically set off from the lower voices at the beginning and end of the phrase, helping to propel the music forward (example 4.3, mm. 10–15). Pragmatic considerations specific to the theatrical context demanded largely homophonic settings for these bigger concerted numbers. But Malvezzi's artful syncopations and his tendency to intersperse homophonic passages with short polyphonic sections of staggered, imitative entries must have helped to maintain interest. In performance, only the connoisseurs would likely have been cognizant of these smaller musical details, while the average auditor would have experienced a general sense of the piece's rhythmic vitality and propulsion as a sum total of these smaller musical gestures. With a similar objective in mind, no doubt, Malvezzi shifts to triple meter early on in the piece (and back again to duple time another eight bars later), marking an important textual division (see example 4.3, m. 21ff). While the change to dance-like triple meter is entirely appropriate to the celebratory nature of the accompanying text, it also serves to jolt the listener away from the piece's opening subject matter. The Neoplatonic significance of the Sirens is quickly passed over in order to focus attention on the celebration at hand, with its inherent political implication: "On this happy day, leaving Paradise, we sing the greater wonders of a beautiful soul and a beautiful face." In other words, the triple meter shift (21 bars into the piece) is an important means of signifying the change of focus from the Sirens to the royal couple themselves, and for obvious reasons the text is declaimed in the most straightforwardly homophonic manner yet encountered (see example 4.3, mm. 21–24).

On an overtly cognitive level, the listener's interest in "Noi, che cantando" probably lay first and foremost in the polychoral affect. The piece proceeds with alternating choirs, though significant words or short phrases, such as "Meraviglie più alte" (the greatest wonders), are allotted to the full complement of singers and instrumentalists. As we would expect, the piece concludes with both choirs participating simultaneously, with a number of the musical lines fanning out in stepwise contrary motion to suggest a built-in concluding crescendo. While the end of the piece is thus clearly signaled through purely musical means, Rossi's account of the rapidly evolving stage action that follows is suggestive of the ways in which the musical numbers of the *intermedio* proper tended to elide in the spectator's mind:

After they [the Sirens] were done singing, the Heavens opened in three places, and with incredible speed, three clouds appeared in those openings. In the middle [cloud] was the goddess Necessity with the Fates, and in the other [two clouds] were the seven Planets and Astraea. . . . When the sky opened, in it [the sky] and on earth one began to hear such a sweet, and perhaps never before heard melody that it appeared to be from Paradise.[57]

Rossi undoubtedly referred here to the first instrumental piece of the *intermedio*—a six-part sinfonia. Though the sinfonia is not mentioned in unofficial accounts, the carefully choreographed visual transformations that took place

Example 4.3. Cristofano Malvezzi, "Noi, che cantando," mm. 10–24 (from *intermedio* one)

Example 4.3. continued

Example 4.3. continued

in front of the spectators likely helped to create the illusion that discrete musical numbers were seamless. (By way of contrast, the shift from the prologue
to the *intermedio* proper was evoked through the dramatic revelation of a
previously undisclosed scene, and thus served to sharply differentiate in the
mind of the spectator Archilei's solo from the music that followed.)

The *nono* partbook of *Intermedii et concerti* indicates that the instruments
used for the sinfonia included the string instruments already played by the
Sirens, as well as a vast array of additional bowed and plucked strings in the
Heavens—including viols, lutes, cittern, psaltery, and mandola—plus a wind
band consisting of four trombones, a cornetto, and a transverse flute. A total
of twenty-eight instrumentalists were involved.[58] Thus, Malvezzi's sinfonia

continues the chain of shifting sonic configurations that characterized the *intermedio* as a whole.

We now come to the aforementioned centerpiece of the *intermedio:* an immense dialogue between the Fates on high (assisted by the Planets) and the Sirens singing on their ascending clouds. The dialogue opens, however, not with the singing of the Fates (as Rossi indicates) but, as Malvezzi notes, with a "madrigaletto," sung by "un putto di ottima voce." Last minute changes appear to account for the fact that a solo voice sang three brief verses to initiate the dialogue and the Sirens' Heavenward ascent: "Most sweet Sirens / Turn toward the sky, and meanwhile / Singing, let us make a contest on the sweetest song."[59] Notwithstanding the introduction of an accompanied solo voice following such a rich instrumental sinfonia, the brevity of the piece was such that it was mentioned only in passing in one of the many unofficial accounts.[60]

What characterized the more extensive portion of the dialogue "A voi reali amanti" (To you, royal lovers)—enacted between those in the Heavens and the Sirens below—was the visual and aural perception of sound in motion produced by the Sirens' incremental ascent while singing and playing. This moment is mentioned in every single unofficial account. As we have already seen, at the opening of the *intermedio* proper the Sirens were spatially divided into two groups on either side of the stage, but the timbral and textural effect produced by each group was essentially identical. Here, the Sirens combined to form a single unit (situated on the stage floor) pitted against the contrasting sonorities produced by those in the Heavens.[61] Not only did the ascent play out as a satisfying counterpart to Harmony's initial descent, it also reinforced the Neoplatonic undertones of the scene. The account by the anonymous Frenchman hints at why the stage action was so impressive:

> After having played for a long time, little by little the clouds returned and rose again into the sky and disappeared in an instant. . . . All this was done with such artifice that there did not appear to be anything [e.g., ropes, etc.] anywhere.[62]

This vertical maneuver involved not one, but several clouds with more than a dozen musicians disposed thereon. That the Frenchman could not detect any of the ropes or pulleys that made the ascent possible must have contributed to his experience of *meraviglia,* though the mere mention of such apparatus indicates a certain distancing on his part. By the time the Sirens reached the (upper) Heavens the entire stage area—stage left and right, and the upper and lower realms, with everything in between—had been sonically stamped, as it were. Indeed, the entire theater had been marked by sound—most dramatically, perhaps, by Archilei's echo emanating from the far reaches of the hall. There only remained a concluding climax with all forces symbolically joined together, both musically and spatially.

The final number of the *intermedio*—"Coppia gentil d'avenurosi amanti" (Noble pair of fortunate lovers)—was an unambiguous encomium for the royal couple. But for the first time, the text introduces the kind of erotic imagery that will punctuate the set of *intermedi* as a whole and be brought to a climax in the concluding dance-song or *ballo* of the sixth *intermedio*.[63] In "Coppia gentil" Heaven and Earth rejoice and "play" with "amoroso zelo" (amorous zeal) on behalf of the royal couple. But in the finale of *intermedio* six, the text's erotic content was directed toward the royal pair, with the resultant dance-song exemplifying (through both auditory and visual means) the anticipated erotic relationship of the royal couple themselves. Here, however, all that was needed to conclude the *intermedio* was a very short, culminating piece that drew the performers together to present a unified expression of celebration. The brevity of the piece was no doubt intentional. After all, the entire cast was now (finally) situated in the Heavens, and the wonder generated by the visual and sonic display of this first *intermedio* was complete.

CHAPTER FIVE

Scenic Metamorphosis and Musical Warfare
(*Intermedi* Two and Three)

> Having changed the scenery, some of these [scenic elements] appear that had grotesque elements and figures; and the floor of the stage opens [and] great Mount Parnassus, which was more than eight *braccia* high, appears full of men that sing and play. In an instant, part of the scenery turned, opening itself out like a wardrobe of two large grottos as high as the mountain. And [the grottos] were almost contiguous with the mountain, [and] nine musicians appear on each grotto, among which are two women who sometimes sang alone [and sometimes] were united with the music all together. At the end, then, the grottos close up, and disappear; then the mountain returns to the earth in the same manner, and after it disappears, the scenery [*prospettiva*] is removed, and we are left with the scene.[1]

This anonymous Italian description of the second *intermedio* makes no mention of the singing contest between the Pierides and the Muses—drawn from book five of Ovid's *Metamorphoses*—that formed the subject matter of the second *intermedio*.[2] What characterizes most unofficial accounts—of which this anonymous account is one of the most detailed examples[3]—is the emphasis on scenic metamorphosis. In addition, accounts of *intermedio* two tend to be more descriptive in tone, with an emphasis on reportage rather than the rhetoric of *meraviglia*. It appears that spectators were less impressed by the appearance of Mount Parnassus from beneath the stage floor than Rossi and his colleagues had anticipated. Rossi's account, however, explains why he believed the spectator would be awestruck:

> [A]nd in the middle of the grass of this garden, began to arise—that is, on the stage—the tip of a mountain, and little by little it grew to the height of twelve *braccia*, [so] that one could say it almost seemed like a miracle because the stage on its highest part was not taller than five *braccia*.[4]

The feat seemed miraculous because with a stage only five *braccia* high, the spectator was left to wonder how the extra seven *braccia* of scenery emerging from beneath the stage floor had been accommodated, allowing Mount Parnassus to rise to a height of twelve *braccia*. (In fact the mountain had telescoping sections that enabled its transformative ascent to take place in front of the eyes of the spectator.)

As we know, Rossi's descriptions of scenic maneuvers (and occasionally of sound effects) anticipated the audience's response before the first performance in the Uffizi theater actually took place. In his description of the same scene—in which he sets up the context for Mount Parnassus's ascent—Rossi goes to great lengths to describe how the perceiver was entertained both visually and aurally:

> Among those fruits one could see in the garden . . . various animals . . . and on the fruit trees were many little birds, which could almost be believed to be alive, and real, especially because one could hear that they were so pleasingly feigning their song behind the scenery, that it seemed like there was an infinity of nightingales and other little birds that were singing beautifully, that had appeared here and were competing as if they came to audition, to see which one among them with his song could make the most sweet and the most beautiful harmony, with which [harmony] the listeners were also entertained, while they were admiring the garden.[5]

Ironically, this is one of only a few passages where Rossi engages with (assumed) audience reception of the aural dimension in some detail, yet these sound effects are not mentioned in any other source. They may, therefore, never have materialized or were not striking enough to warrant the kind of attention that Rossi had anticipated. As positioned in the narrative, however, Rossi's description of the birds that "were competing as if they came to audition" presaged the singing contest that formed the subject of the *intermedio*.

But to return to our opening description of Mount Parnassus: the actual scenic transformations that the unidentified commentator described reveal an interest, albeit subtle, in the mechanics of how scenic maneuvers were put into effect, and the debate about these mechanics continues to this day. Referring to the two large grottos that would subsequently open out, the anonymous writer mentions that instantaneously *voltata parte della prospettiva* ("part of the scenery turned"). By using the word *prospettiva* in this context the writer is referring to the scenic apparatus on the side stage areas, not the backdrop. More importantly, the use of the word *voltata* implies that the mechanisms used were ones that literally turned—possibly *periaktoi*—in Saslow's description, "triangular or quadrilateral vertical shafts, their faces each painted with a different scene, that could be pivoted on a central axis to present successive faces to the audience. . . ."[6] An alternative mechanism was the use of sliding flat wings that were pushed onto the stage from the side, facilitated by the use of grooves in the stage floor.[7] Although there has been considerable debate as to which method was used, or whether the two were used in combination,[8] it is striking that unofficial sources (especially those in Italian) are lightly peppered with words that suggest the use of a turning mechanism,[9] again, reinforcing the observational quality of these accounts, and the desire to describe the entertainment with precision. The word *voltata* is employed in the anonymous source (cited above) by way of reference to the grottos that flanked Mount Parnassus in *intermedio* two.[10] A more compelling reference in the same source opens the description of the sixth and final *intermedio* with "[v]oltandosi al solito la scena" (the scene turning itself *as usual*), possibly suggesting that the turning was not an isolated occurrence, but was a characteristic element of the interludes in general.[11] Several of the even briefer unofficial accounts also expose the visual and technological acuity of the spectator-auditor—somewhat removed, that is, from the spell of Medici-generated *meraviglia*. The prose in these accounts of *intermedio* two is characterized by an almost matter-of-fact tone that merely states the sequence of "events" as they took place on the stage. Further, some accounts, while acknowledging the ingenuity involved in making realistic set pieces, reveal the spectator's understanding that the sets were indeed labored over and did not magically materialize, even if their effect during performance was miraculous.[12]

Flux and Transformation

Visual shifts and transformations were a consistent feature of the alternation between the acts of the play and the six interludes. The theme of metamorphosis was central to the conception of the second *intermedio,* however, as the derivation of the interlude's *invenzione* (from Ovid) attests. The singing contest between the Pierides (the daughters of Pierus, King of Emathia in Macedonia) and the Muses (the daughters of Mmemosyne, goddesses of literature and the arts) resulted in the transformation of the losers (the Pierides) into magpies that croaked and hopped around the stage. The stage design from 1592 by d'Alfiano (plate 8) represents an amalgam of two parts of the scene—the hopping magpies are clearly visible at the front of stage right and left, while behind them on stage right the Pierides—pre-transformation—are ensconced in their grotto. The Muses are similarly positioned in their complementary grotto on stage left, with the competition judges—the Hamadryads or wood nymphs—draped across the central region of Mount Parnassus. Yet few accounts mention the hopping magpies at the conclusion of the scene;[13] rather, most accounts, like that of Gadenstedt, conclude by describing a kind of "reverse" metamorphosis of the opening: "After this music was executed, the high mountain [Mount Parnassus] subsided again, and the two little mountains [grottos] also turned around again, [and] the scene changed [as if] into houses again, and [they] played the second act [of the comedy]."[14] In other words, as far as most commentators were concerned the central focus of attention was on large-scale scenic metamorphoses.

The elaborate costume designs that Rossi describes (appendix 1c) are not mentioned in unofficial sources either, though they too would have contributed to the spectator's overall experience of flux and transformation. All the costumes were characterized by the incorporation of flowing veils. Regarding the Hamadryad nymphs, Rossi notes:

> The headdress was very fine and beautiful and all of them [the Hamadryads] had blond braids that were falling on their shoulders, and certain veils with gold and silver and many colors and as long as their dress, hanging from their abovementioned hairstyle. And those veils, because they were puffing up with every little bit of breeze, were making the noble dress rich, and more magnificent, and more adorned.[15]

Although a sense of orderliness characterized the seating plan for the Hamadryads as depicted by Buontalenti (plate 9),[16] the swirling veils as well as the variety of stances of each Hamadryad must have contributed to an overall impression of movement and perhaps even instability—a far cry from the stasis that characterized the prologue of *intermedio* one. In addition, Rossi remarks on the *drapi cangianti* (changeable or shimmering quality of [some Hamadryad] costumes), a quality that also characterized the relucent veils of the Pierides.[17] The costume designs for the Pierides and Muses (plates 10 and 11, respectively) seem intended to evoke a similar sense of movement and changeability, although the subtleties and distinctions of dress between the two groups described by Rossi (and intended to delineate character) appear to have gone all but unnoticed in the performances.

"Clothes Make the Man [or Woman]"

Though details of the Pierides' and Muses' costumes are not highlighted in unofficial accounts, the language used to describe the apparel in Rossi's description is infused with the kind of contemporary gender ideologies that undergirded the interludes as a whole, from both conceptual (i.e., tacitly authorial) and perceptual (i.e., audience oriented) bases.[18] Rossi states that the Pierides

> had ornamented that noble dress, *to show their vanity and pride,* with veils of many colors, in a beautiful fashion, and magnificent. From the noblest

hairstyle—which was lascivious and full of shining jewels, and of pearls—fell a shimmering and large veil that with different folds went all the way down to the bottom of their dress. . . . In sum, it was a wanton, and superior, and gorgeous dress but rich *beyond moderation* [italics mine].[19]

Rossi employs derivations of the verb *lascivare* (to live lasciviously) no fewer than three times throughout his short description of the Pierides costumes.[20] The term *lascivo* was implicitly gendered, suggesting that which was wanton, thus implicitly "womanish."[21] By way of contrast, the dress of the Muses, though rich, was described as *semplice, e onesto* (simple and honest).[22] So, too, the hairstyle of the Muses was *semplice* "but resplendent with gold and jewels, and from their hair was hanging a veil *but in a much more modest manner* [than the Pierides] (italics mine)."[23] The Muses, therefore, by way of contrast to the Pierides, were honest (chaste) women.

In their sung text, the Pierides expressed their superiority over two of classical antiquity's all-time "greats"—the musicians Arion and Apollo (CD tracks 10 and 11; for the text see appendix 6). The Pierides' text reified their common characterization as boastful and immoderate, aspects of their nature reflected in Rossi's detailed description of their dress. With this in mind, one should recall that during this period clothes were considered to "make the man" (or woman, as the case may be), not only marking social and gender distinctions but also encapsulating the notion that outward behavior or appearance could transform inner subjectivity. The Pierides' inappropriate vocality and concomitant lack of sexual decorum determined their ultimate fate, a transformation into croaking magpies hopping about the stage. Denied both beauty of voice and physical demeanor they must now—according to Rossi's narrative—"hide from the eyes of everyone else,"[24] their pride and vanity appropriately vanquished. The wording in the accounts of Pavoni and the anonymous Frenchman is even more suggestive: having overstepped the appropriate gender boundaries for women by publicly declaring their vocal superiority—an arena reserved for men, or those women deemed chaste by men—they must now, shamed and acquiescent, hide themselves from the very sight or presence of *hommes* or *huomini,* that is, men specifically.[25] In essence, women— perceived as loquacious and lascivious—must be removed from sight (and sound) in order to signal the necessity of chastity and acquiescence to patriarchal rule, an implication unlikely to have been lost on Christine of Lorraine herself. Ironically, the *actual* presence of women's voices on the stage was a risk that Duke Ferdinando and his directive elite must have considered ultimately advantageous when such messages could be expressed within the "plots" themselves.

The final triumph—at least in Rossi's imaginings—is the (un-staged) victory of the chaste Muses over the dangerous, fish-like Sirens. Although the Sirens play no part in this *intermedio,* Rossi unexpectedly introduces these seductive songstresses at the end of his account: the Muses "were crowned with feathers of different colors,[26] because that is the way the ancient poets were imagining them; not so much for the victory obtained over the daughters of Piero, but rather for the victory that they had over the Sirens."[27] Rossi's unexpected reference to the fish-like Sirens reminds us that the specter of the Siren—who epitomized the dangerous woman—was never far from the surface, both in the minds of the *Pellegrina* interludes' creators and that of the spectator-auditor, a point I elaborate further in chapter 7.

Vere e finte donne (Real and Feigned Women)

Intermedio two was the only interlude to consist entirely of female mythological characters. Yet despite Rossi's careful differentiation among the female mythological figures, in unofficial accounts the three groups were only distinguished as distinct entities because of their positioning on the stage, on either the centrally located Mount Parnassus or one of the two flanking grottos. Both Gadenstedt and the author of one of the anonymous Italian descriptions set the middle group (of Hamadryad nymphs) apart, with the latter describing them as goddesses, and Gadenstedt, somewhat closer to the mythological mark, as nymphs.[28] The pastoral setting probably prompted the association here; the Frenchman described all three groups generically as nymphs.[29] In these three sources, the commentators recognized the mythological gender of the characters, although in other instances some or all of the various on-stage constituents were simply described as *musici* (musicians).[30]

Interestingly, the account that is most explicit vis-à-vis gender gets it right, at least as far as actual cast members were concerned (as opposed to their mythological portrayals). In *Li artificiosi* (cited at the chapter's opening), Mount Parnassus "appears full of *huomini* (men) that sing and play" and among the presumably male *musici* "were *due donne* (two women) who sometimes sang alone [and sometimes] were united with the music all together." The author seems to be commenting on the gender of the performers here, most notably the involvement of two women singers in a mixed ensemble; as such, there appears to be an implicit (and ultimately correct) assumption that the rest of the cast, though portraying female mythological characters, consisted of cross-dressed male musicians. The exception was the involvement of the two female singers—likely the sisters Isabella and Lucia Pellizzari[31]—who, along with their brother, sang the interlude's opening madrigal.[32] Malvezzi's *nono* partbook states that the madrigal—Luca Marenzio's "Belle ne fe natura" (Nature made us beautiful)—"was sung in an exquisite and artful manner by two young women who serve the most serene Duke of Mantua with more than average envy from those who love such noble virtue, and by a young boy, their brother, accompanied by the sound of a harp and two lire."[33] The Pellizzari sisters were members of Duke Vincenzo Gonzaga's *concerto di donne,* and thus were *virtuose* (female virtuosos). Their inclusion in the *intermedio* appears to have been a last-minute decision; neither their song nor their short scene is mentioned by Rossi, but evidently some spectators noticed the involvement of *vere donne.*[34] The apparently last-minute incorporation of the Pellizzari sisters testifies to the interest in highlighting female sopranos, although their very short scene had little chance of upstaging the later appearance of the Florentine court's *concerto di donne* whose extended musical number was reserved for the grand finale of the entertainment.[35]

The emphasis on high female voices in "Belle ne fe natura" was likely reinforced by the way in which the accompanying instruments were utilized. Although lire da braccio could support the singing voice with chordal accompaniment, the instruments could also function melodically, and it is in this capacity that we have utilized the instrument in our recording (CD tracks 8 and 9); the lire double the highest two voices (which have identical ranges) note for note. An equally suitable choice would have been to use the instruments as harmonic support,[36] but the advantage of doubling gives clarity and prominence to the parts originally sung by the Pellizzari sisters, and avoids a "muddier" texture. As sustaining instruments, the two lire also emphasize the equality between the upper two voices, a dimension given special prominence at the opening of the second part of the song (CD track 9) where all three parts enter in imitation (at the unison), initiated by the two lire-supported voices. If performed well, the lire and voices blend so closely at this moment that the attentive listener has the impression that voice and instrument have become one. After the conclusion of this imitative phrase—in which the Hamadryads refer to the upcoming "hard and bitter [singing] contest" between the Pierides and the Muses—the three voices blend in homophonic fashion, demonstrating their beauty and concomitant harmonic perfection, attributes which according to Rinuccini's text qualify them as judges. (For full text and translation see appendix 6.)

The other instrument mentioned by Malvezzi in connection with "Belle ne fe natura" is the harp. It is unlikely that the harp doubled the lowest voice note for note; it would have been more effectively used in the large Uffizi theater in quasi-continuo style, fleshing out the harmonic implications of the three-part texture. Because the low notes articulated by the harp decay relatively quickly, little support is given to the lowest voice's pitches;[37] rather, a more diffuse but transparent texture is articulated. These nuanced decisions about scoring further contribute to the predominance of the two female sopranos with their supporting lire, and attest to the spotlighting of female soloists in the entertainment as a whole.

Marenzio's Theatrical Madrigals

Luca Marenzio composed all the music for *intermedio* two. Like *intermedio* one (in which the music of Malvezzi predominated), this interlude relied for its sonic efficacy, in part, on the gradual increase of vocal and instrumental forces as the interlude progressed as well as on bold contrasts of sonority. Unofficial sources pay very little attention to the aural dimension; however, Cavallino's exceedingly brief reference to the music emphasizes sonority.[38] Further, several spectator-auditors referred to the combinations of the various constituent groups of musicians, an indication that they understood the music's progression as additive and, in some instances, as dialogic.[39]

A notable contrast in musical forces followed the Pellizzari family's trio. The Pierides sang "Chi dal delfino aita" (He [who sang] to the dolphin for help)—their competition piece—in which they boast of their superior vocal skill with a six-part madrigal with one voice to a part (CD tracks 10 and 11; the full text is in appendix 6). The vocal ranges are evenly distributed, so there is little or no "dueting" between the upper two voices, by way of contrast to "Belle ne fe natura."[40] Sung in 1589 by all male voices (in our recording the three highest voices are sung by women), the song's sound is rich and full, qualities reinforced by the madrigal's predominantly low range and the prevalence of foundation instruments: Malvezzi indicates that the instrumental ensemble consisted of bass lute, chitarrone, and bass viol.[41] Although Marenzio's style in this madrigal and the one that follows has been criticized for its apparent "neutrality,"[42] I suggest that the effectiveness of these theatrical madrigals is better assessed within the context of music making in the large Uffizi theater for which they were composed. It is well known that intricate polyphony was not conducive to the theatrical space, so it seems somewhat unproductive to compare these works with Marenzio's "best expressive [non-theatrical] madrigals,"[43] with the latter posited as benchmarks. An implicit assumption of this approach is that expressive potential is evaluated, first and foremost, at the level of part writing (and closely related musical parameters), because contrapuntal craft is most closely tied to meaningful expression vis-à-vis text setting. One must ask, however, whose notion of musical expression we are exploring, and whether the idea of musical expression, as frequently construed today, is even useful here. In James Chater's translation of Marco Bizzarini's monograph on Marenzio, the author identifies key components—sonority and echo—that may have contributed to the performative efficacy of Marenzio's "Chi dal delfino aita" and the madrigal that followed it, "Se nelle voci nostre" (If our voices display). Yet Bizzarini's conception of these two works is far from approving: "It would be futile to seek a qualitative difference between the Pierides' singing and that of the Muses [i.e., the madrigals "Chi dal delfino aita" and "Se nelle voci nostre," respectively]. For each, Marenzio adopts a 'neutral' style, without paying particular heed to the text's semantic aspects, since the musical expression is almost entirely assigned to the climax in sonority and the technique of echo. This music, as Pirrotta has pointed out, 'lacks a poetic afflatus and can only succeed in concealing the emptiness of the plot behind a display of decorative devices'. . . ."[44]

I will sidestep Bizzarini's citation of Pirrotta's designation of the music's function as (merely) "decorative." Instead, I will confine my comments to Bizzarini's remarks regarding the futility of comparing the music of the Pierides and Muses. In chapter 4 I demonstrated how the spectator-auditor frequently missed textual cues and that an understanding of music-text relationships for the interludes *in general* was not crucial for the performances' success in the context of the Uffizi theater. Yet I also demonstrated how nuances of textual meaning were often reflected in the musical settings, even though in most cases the average audience member was likely oblivious or only perceived the more generalized effect of what were in fact an accumulation of smaller-scale musical details related to the text's meaning. I approach Marenzio's madrigals for *intermedio* two in the same way. Bizzarini is correct in suggesting that the "climax in sonority and the technique of echo" were central considerations in the composition of these works; the technique of echo was apparently not perceived as such in the performances, however—a point to which I will return. Regarding "Chi dal delfino aita" (CD tracks 10 and 11), I have already mentioned the importance of sonority, not merely its cumulative effect (in relation to "Belle ne fe natura," CD tracks 8 and 9), but also the ways in which the instruments and voices played key roles in creating distinctive tone colors and textures. In addition, the two madrigals sung by the Pierides and the Muses deserve to be compared because it is clear that in his text settings Marenzio was responding to a general textual conceit: that the Muses' song was superior to that of the Pierides.[45] In this respect, it is notable that the texture of "Chi dal delfino aita" is generally homogeneous in style, but one can also pinpoint changes in musical texture that are a direct response to the text. For example, when the Pierides allude to Apollo, and specifically to his "lost consort" (Euridice), Marenzio adopts a low-range homophonic texture (with the canto and quinto parts leaping down a fifth and fourth, respectively) that contrasts with the preceding flourish in the canto part highlighting the reference to the sound of Apollo's *cetra* (see example 5.1, mm. 13–20). Then, in the middle of m. 20 the canto leaps back up to d to articulate a gradual descent, paralleled by other voices distributed in various configurations, in order to demonstrate Apollo's literal descent to the underworld (example 5.1, mm. 20–27), with striking suspensions at mm. 23–24. This phrase concludes on the downbeat of m. 27, but a rapid shift in mood occurs on the downbeat of the next measure (CD track 11), prompted by the Pierides' exclamation "Non però" (But no!). Marenzio divides the six voices into two groups that stagger their entries so that the listener not only notices the text repetition, but also the forcefulness with which the Pierides assert their superiority (mm. 28–29). The Pierides are responding to the fact that *their* music is more melodious than that of Apollo—hence the necessity for abrupt shifts of texture and range after they so ably demonstrate the musical prowess of this classical poet-musician.

Despite the attention to text setting in the Pierides' madrigal, it is evident that Marenzio intended the Muses' "Se nelle voci nostre" to be the superior song in every respect. However, the actual text sung by the Muses is suitably humble, attributing any possible "sweet accents" to the "gracious gift of Heaven," a far cry from the audacious claims of the Pierides (for the text of the opening of the Muses' madrigal see appendix 6). As Bizzarini points out, the Muses' madrigal involves an increase in forces: the number of voices is augmented to twelve, although the number of accompanying instruments remains the same. The twelve voices are divided into two choirs, but the piece begins with *coro* one alone (CD track 12). Comparatively speaking, the opening music incorporates a degree of harmonic and contrapuntal complexity not previously encountered in either *intermedi* one or two. The opening employs only four of the six singers from *coro* one—the three highest-range voices with a supporting bass voice. After a relatively static opening for the second phrase (example 5.2, mm. 7–9), with the words "dolcezz' accenti o suono" (sweet accents or sound), the singers' parts diverge to create a series of dissonances and resolutions (beginning at m. 11) that only finally resolve on the downbeat of m. 17. With the phrase that follows—"e gratioso dono" (and gracious gift)—Marenzio reduces the texture further to three parts (the lowest of the "highest" voices is dropped) and creates momentum by introducing a homorhythmic figure in shorter note values (upbeat to mm. 18–19), with the canto part delayed by a quarter note at the opening to help emphasize the contrast with the mostly passing tone dissonances that precede this passage. While a measure-by-measure analysis of the entire madrigal is not possible here, we can observe that Marenzio's command of (at times extreme) textural and rhythmic contrasts could hardly be described as bland or neutral; the exchanges between the two choirs are carefully wrought to maximize sonic

Example 5.1. Luca Marenzio, "Chi dal delfino aita," mm. 12–34 (from *intermedio* two)

Example 5.1. continued

clarity and incorporate passages of contrapuntal complexity that would have been appropriate and effective within the performance space of the Uffizi theater.

After the initial statement by *coro* one, the Muses call upon the (Hamadryad) nymphs to judge which choir is "più soave" (most sweet). The words "Hor voi" (now you) presented in homophonic fashion by the full complement of voices from *coro* one are "echoed" by *coro* two, thereby beginning a section of musical "call and response" between the two choirs, although the actual text sung by each choir is the same. Malvezzi's reference to the "voices of one and the other choir" seems to have occasioned an assumption that the technique of echo was fundamental to this madrigal as well as the following one.[46] While the polychoral nature of both "Se nelle voci nostre" and the final madrigal "O figlie di Piero" (O daughters of Piero) is clearly apparent on the printed page, there is no evidence in the unofficial sources that auditors perceived the style as incorporating echo per se, or even polychoral elements. The lack of spatial differentiation between the choirs—augmented to three for "O figlie di Piero"—seems to have made the polychoral dimension of these madrigals less crucial to the overall performative affect. From all accounts, the Pierides, Muses, and Hamadryad nymphs maintained their (initial and distinct) positions on the stage.[47] The

Example 5.2. Luca Marenzio, "Se nelle voci nostre," mm. 7–20 (from *intermedio* two)

spatial dimension, so crucial to *intermedio* one, seems purposefully constricted here. As mentioned, most unofficial commentators ignore the aural dimension almost completely in their accounts, and the descriptions of this *intermedio* in general are comparatively brief; certainly there are no mention of echo effects.

On a meta-structural level, *intermedio* two prepared the spectator for the disruption of the pastoral landscape that would take place in *intermedio* three (and the further disintegration that transformed the landscape into hell in *intermedio* four). Thus, while an articulation of spatial authority through music set the stage in *intermedio* one, disruption must follow in order for the Christian prince to ultimately (re)assert authority over the forces of evil. Only by way of credible threat can the absolutist ruler fully demonstrate his capacity to harness and/or vanquish sinister forces. In this regard, *intermedio* two articulated the ease with which change could occur. At the most obvious level instability was signaled by the emphasis on scenic metamorphoses, with the fluid and shimmering quality of costume elements bolstering the larger-scale effect. Thus, the second *intermedio* functioned in a transitional fashion, preparing the audience for a tangible demonstration—that is, actualization—of the prince's encounter with, and victory over, evil forces. In *intermedio* three the "battle" would be presented in the form of Apollo's encounter with the serpent-dragon.

The Cavallino Factor

[I]n the blink of an eye one did not see [the city of] Pisa anymore, but three alpine mountains, all three [of them] full of sonorous music.

A good number of shepherds and nymphs came forth from both sides [of the stage]. While [they were] dallying and dancing together, a serpent came out to disturb them, but Apollo, being in that place, killed it, having cast many arrows. Thus, the entire chorus of nymphs and shepherds demonstrated a sign of great joy with diverse songs, and gave many thanks to Apollo. And thus [while] singing, playing, and dancing the three mountains [i.e., Mount Parnassus and the two grottos] disappeared and one saw, once again, [the city of] Pisa, which ended the second [*sic*] *intermedio*.[48]

Cavallino conflated aspects of interludes two and three in his report. At the conclusion of his description of *intermedio* three, he reported the return of the major scenic constituents of *intermedio* two: the recurrence of the "three mountains" constituted a kind of visual framing that, in Cavallino's mind, bound the two interludes together. For Cavallino the second *intermedio* began with the appearance of "three alpine mountains" and concluded with their disappearance. Between these bookends, the "nymphs and shepherds" (couples dressed as Delphians, according to Rossi) took the stage, along with Apollo (who slayed the serpent-dragon).

Cavallino's account has been criticized because it appears to indicate that he was clearly "clueless" as to what was *really* going on, by mixing up the order and number of interludes.[49] There were good reasons, in fact, for Cavallino's confusions which, revealingly, are paralleled in other unofficial accounts, particularly the eyewitness ones. Sandwiched between the *meraviglia*-inspiring first interlude and the hell scene that formed the climactic center-piece of the set, *intermedio* two did not command the same degree of heightened attention in performance.[50] Not only was the second interlude less memorable, but Cavallino appears to have blurred the boundaries between interludes two and three precisely because there were a number of common-alities between them. Both interludes incorporated elements of the pastoral, and concluded with rousing finales in which the entire cast participated. Al-though the second act of the comedy separated the two *intermedi*, from a vi-sual standpoint, *intermedio* three picked up where *intermedio* two left off, with a leafy outdoor scene. One might also consider the difficulty of precise retention in light of the spectacle's seven-hour duration.[51]

Intermedio Three: The Pastoral Disrupted

After the second act [had] ended, the scenery changed into the shape of a cheerful forest, most skillfully and delicately painted with various shady trees and bushes. Thirty-six musicians entered the space, dressed in a variety of ways, with all sorts of instruments, and on them played several dances of unusual types, composed to grace the comedy. Of these thirty-six musi-cians, eighteen were divided off on each side, who danced facing each other, and on each side two exceptionally famous dance-masters were appointed to them, who led the dance, by dancing the best. From below, from out of the ground, came a horrible, gruesome, large monster or animal in the shape of a great dragon, [that] spewed out fire, had large wings, with which it made a large clamor, [and] ugly claws on its feet, and it [the monster] presented itself very horridly. It rushed towards the musicians and dancers with opened jaws, just as if it wanted to devour them.[52]

The disruption of the (natural) pastoral landscape described here by Gadenst-edt was effected by the introduction of its antithesis: the unnatural and the monstrous. One of the anonymous Italian commentators described the serpent-dragon (see plate 12) as "un mostro horrendo."[53] Direct translation does not do justice to the potential implications of his description. Florio de-fines the noun *móstro* as "a monster, a misshapen creature, any thing against the course of nature, a monstrous signe, a strange sight."[54] Florio's definition of the adjective *horrendo* heightens the sense of that which was deformed and unnatural: "horrible, frightfull, grizelie, gastly, uglie, hideous, dreadful, strange."[55] The monster appears to have been intended as an amalgam of both a serpent and dragon. The element of monstrosity was thus suggested by the conglomerative nature of the beast; although the classical myth derived from Julius Polux involved a python, Rossi's *Descrizione* utilizes the terms dragon and serpent interchangeably and Agostino Carracci's depiction of the fiend (plate 12) illustrates wings and a large, coiled tail.

Little wonder that the monster was mentioned in all the unofficial accounts; in a word, the visual impression of the beast was wondrous. The sight of it invoked not only "the shock of the unfamiliar" but all that was "thrilling, potentially dangerous, momentarily immobilizing, charged at once with desire, ignorance, and fear. . . ." Stephen Greenblatt elaborates: "[B]y definition wonder is the instinctive recognition of difference, the sign of a heightened attention . . . in the face of the new."[56] Greenblatt's definition is strikingly reminiscent of Patrizi's conception of wonder (see chapter 2, section entitled "Francesco Patrizi and the Experience of Wonder"). The heightened (audience) attention that the beast commanded, in part because of its monstrous appearance, was intensified by the beast's actions, especially by its potential to devour. Rossi's account provided the most detailed description of the monster, of course, making pointed reference to the creature's vast mouth, with its three rows of teeth and flaming tongue.[57] Several unofficial accounts, including that of Gadenstedt above, refer to the monster's mouth and the sounds and/or substances it emitted. The Frenchman speaks of the serpent that "spewed fire onto the stage through his mouth, nose, and ears, with very frightful howls."[58] Likewise, one anonymous Italian commentator referred to "a great bellowing dragon, hurling enough fire to break the circle of the shepherds and nymphs [Delphic couples]."[59] Although the serpent-dragon was ultimately vanquished in this *intermedio* and order was temporarily restored, the depiction of voracious monstrosity presages two important themes that would be revisited with more intensity in *intermedio* four: in the context of Hell, the spectator-auditor witnessed the monstrosity of Hell's various inhabitants, including Lucifer, whose three jaws (on each of his three heads) executed the souls in Hell by devouring them alive. While the serpent-dragon in *intermedio* three only *suggested* this possibility (Apollo intervened), in *intermedio* four the audience actually witnessed the representation of Lucifer consuming small naked bodies (played by young boys).

Musical Warfare: The Power of Music and Dance

The emergence of the serpent-dragon in this *intermedio* interrupted the communal singing and dancing of the Delphic couples. (Most unofficial commentators referred to the couples as nymphs and shepherds—confirming a pastoral association—or simply as women and men.) Malvezzi's publication includes just one song—"Qui di carne si sfama" (Here, gorging himself on flesh)—for the opening of the *intermedio,* although a number of accounts indicate that there was probably more music involved before the monster's appearance.[60] In light of the text of the madrigal—in which the Delphians expressed their fear of the monster and implored Jove for aid—it seems likely that their singing was preceded by dance music intended to establish the opening mood suggested by the scene's "cheerful forest" with "shady trees."

In Marenzio's setting of "Qui di carne si sfama" Jove was invoked for the first time in the set of interludes. The Delphians sang: "But where is the fierce monster[?] / Perhaps Jove has heard our weeping."[61] According to Rossi's account, directly following this question the monster reared its head from the cave. The timing of this action seems to be confirmed by Marenzio's setting of the madrigal such that all singers and instrumentalists rested simultaneously, presumably in reaction to the serpent-dragon's sudden and frightening appearance.[62] The Delphians responded by singing: "O Father or King of Heaven [Jove] / Turn your piteous eyes / To unhappy Delos. / Who demands your help, and weeps and wails."[63] Bizzarini has singled out this moment in the song by equating it with Marenzio's "best expressive madrigals."[64] The words "our weeping" and "weeps and wails" were given special treatment when the largely homophonic setting shifted into a contrapuntal texture filled with suspensions to exemplify the texts' meaning. But it is the appeal to Jove in conjunction with this striking text setting that is of particular interest here. As we will see, Jove was invoked again in *intermedio* four by the sorceress, and finally appeared on stage in *intermedio* six to sing a brief solo (CD track 28), actualizing the transference of heavenly grace to the earthly realm. Thus, the mention of Jove in *intermedio* three initiated a Neoplatonic thread that was given fuller expression (and musical explication) in subsequent *intermedi.*[65]

Although the Delphians invoked Jove, it was actually Apollo who came to their rescue to offer temporary relief, that is, to conclude the third *intermedio* with a sense of joyous resolution before the hell scene ensued in *intermedio* four. Apollonian imagery had long been connected with the Medici court, and Ferdinando continued to cultivate this association.[66] In unofficial accounts only Cavallino and Pavoni identified Apollo (see plate 13),[67] although the Frenchman and the anonymous author of *Li artificiosi* singled out one participant as having a central role in the battle with the serpent-dragon.[68] Conversely, in several accounts, including that of the Bavarian attendee, the emphasis was not on Apollo but on the participation of four expert dancers (of which Apollo, played by the dancer Agostino, was likely one):

> The scene is turned around once, and thirty-six musicians enter with un-
> usual [musical] inventions and [with] four dancers. And while they are just
> singing, out of a cave, or hole, emerges a gruesome monster, which the danc-
> ers and musicians kill with their singing. Thereafter a magnificent dance is
> held, to music.[69]

Likewise, Gadenstedt's account focused on the participation of four dancers who fought the monster.[70] The two German accounts (and one Italian
account) that highlighted the participation of the dancers are not necessarily incongruous with the other accounts that focus on the involvement of
Apollo. As a group, they demonstrate how various viewers who witnessed
the same scene could come away with quite different impressions of what
had transpired in the scene.[71] As I have already noted, the various back-
grounds and interests that each perceiver brought to the performance influenced the impressions formed. Gadenstedt, for example, had a special
interest in the dance masters involved in the *intermedi* as a whole; thus, his
attention was directed toward the participation of the expert dancers in
this scene. Likewise, in the finale of *intermedio* six he nowhere mentioned
the participation of the guitar-playing ladies highlighted by other commentators, but instead focused on the involvement of the male dancers
whose purpose was, in his opinion, to demonstrate "their mastery and
skill."[72]

But to return to the Bavarian's account (which was based on an Italian
source): the most striking and succinct comment concerned the monster that
"the dancers and musicians kill with their singing." That the aural dimension
was considered the primary means through which the monster was vanquished says much about the perception (possibly shared by others in the audience) regarding "the power of music" in this scene. We do not know the
exact nature of the music that accompanied the battle because it was omitted
from the musical publication, but Rossi's extensive description of the five-part
battle accompanied by music and dance provides some indication. That the
intent, musically speaking, was to imitate the ancient modes with "modern
music" has of course already been commented on by other scholars.[73] That
the music was demonstrably effective in performance has not been so exten-
sively addressed. Although Rossi indicated that the intention was to give
"greatest delight to the spectators" (and he preemptively indicated that the
scene fulfilled this function),[74] the music seems to have provided more than
diletto: in essence, it was perceived as deadly.

As one might expect, Gadenstedt's account of the battle focused more on
the dance, was more thorough, and indicated that he perceived distinctive
segments of the dance:

In the meantime, the dancers approached the animal, jumped around this animal with great agility, fought with the same, finally pierced the same, so that it fell to the ground, twisting this way and that, and fell dead with a great clatter, back into the hole out of which it had emerged. Thereafter, the dancers performed yet another dance of joy, [and they] exited from the place [stage] again.[75]

In general, Gadenstedt's account acknowledged several of the five parts of the dance explicated by Rossi, although Rossi referred only to Apollo's involvement. First, the scene was surveyed; second, Apollo danced and leapt around the serpent (at a distance) to demonstrate his contempt; third, the serpent was confronted (again with dancing and leaping) and was pierced with arrows until overcome; fourth, a victory dance was performed; and fifth, once the serpent had been removed out of sight, a final, graceful dance was performed to acknowledge the freedom of the Delphians.[76]

Women's Voices Incognito

Perhaps because of his focus on dance, Gadenstedt did not mention the singing at the end of the *intermedio* that was at least casually mentioned in a number of other unofficial accounts. In the musical publication there are two final madrigals; according to Rossi, before the execution of the fifth part of the dance the madrigal "O valoroso Dio" (O valorous God) was sung (CD tracks 13–15; example 5.3). Although not singled out by commentators, the madrigal is worth discussing because of its stylistic idiom, which was associated with women's voices. Bizzarini noticed the unusual scoring of the madrigal in Marenzio's oeuvre, pointing out that the use of soprano clef for the three highest voices is exceptional. Further, he notes that the style of the madrigal is characteristic of the pieces commissioned of Alessandro Striggio by Francesco de' Medici that were themselves designed to imitate the madrigals for three sopranos written by Luzzasco Luzzaschi for the Ferrarese court's *concerto di donne*.[77] In other words, the emphasis on three high voices in "O valoroso Dio," with a (texted) bass part mainly functioning as foundational support, points to the literal use of women's voices, although Bizzarini speculates that the singers were possibly boys, apparently because of Rossi's reference to the involvement of "two pairs of men" in the scene.[78]

According to Rossi, after the serpent was slain, the two couples who had watched the fight from the wood came forward to ascertain that the monster was dead. Satisfied that the serpent had indeed been vanquished, they began to sing the victory song "O valoroso Dio" (CD tracks 13–15; for full text and translation see appendix 6). Aside from a brief snatch of imitation on "O Dio"

Example 5.3. Luca Marenzio, "O valoroso Dio" (from *intermedio* three)

Example 5.3. continued

Example 5.3. continued

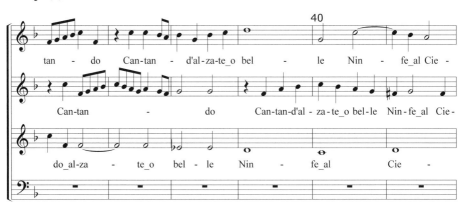

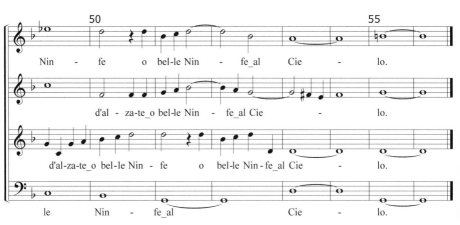

(example 5.3, m. 6) and a short phrase that mirrors the rhythmic profile of the three upper voices (m. 12), the bass voice serves for the remainder of the madrigal as a kind of "vocal continuo."[79] On a number of occasions the bass voice is completely silent (mm. 17–18, 26–27, and 36–42), thus further emphasizing the soprano voices. The reentry of the bass voice at m. 19 (CD track 14) for a short homophonic passage that refers to "l'horribil fera" (the grizzly wild beast) helps to support the striking E flat in the canto part at m. 22 for "horribil" and the cadential suspension in the *quinto* part in m. 24.

The equality of the three soprano voices is especially highlighted at the beginning of their imitative entries at the unison with appropriate melismas on the word "Cantando" (singing), while the bass part functions as harmonic support sustaining the root of the chord (F) in various octaves (example 5.3, mm. 33–35; CD track 15). In m. 36 the bass drops out, and soprano three (notated in the *settimo* partbook) serves as harmonic foundation (mm. 36–42), leaving the melodic interest to sopranos one and two. An identical imitative figure (raised a step) begins the concluding section at m. 43, with the three sopranos entering in successive order, mirroring their first statement. Here, however, the bass reenters and maintains its "continuo" function through the end of the madrigal (mm. 43–56), sustaining whole notes that are finally extended to breves (mm. 51–56). During this final section all three sopranos are free to articulate florid melismas, and soprano one likely added further embellishment (not represented in the publication) in the final measures of the song.

There is no record in Malvezzi's publication indicating exactly who sang the madrigal, although he tells us that it was sung by four voices, one voice on a part. Rossi states that the piece was sung by "due coppie di quegli huomini" (two pairs of those [same] men).[80] He appears to be referring back to the Delphian couples who opened the *intermedio* lamenting the threat of the serpent-dragon, before the creature was finally slain. Yet each Delphian couple consisted of a "man" and a "woman," as Rossi's earlier statements and the designations on Buontalenti's costume designs attest. (Perhaps the reference to male couples was a slip on Rossi's part, as the female Delphians were predominantly played by male actor-musicians.) Plate 14 shows one of the female Delphians who was played by the chitarrone player Antonio Naldi, also known as Bardella (as the annotation above the costume indicates). Another costume design (plate 15) clearly refers to Margherita (della Scala), who performed as a female Delphian. Furthermore, we can be almost certain that Lucia Caccini was also involved in the cast, most likely as Margherita's "male" partner (the cast note above is somewhat ambiguous) or as the female partner in another couple.[81]

Thus, with at least two female sopranos among the cast of Delphians, one would conclude that they sang the upper voices of "O valoroso Dio," a madrigal characterized by stylistic writing for high female voices. Although there was no logistical reason preventing Vittoria Archilei from being the third member of the soprano trio (she is not otherwise involved elsewhere in the *intermedio*), her name is not listed on any of the costume designs. Her involvement may have been precluded by her status as prima donna and her close connection with Duke Ferdinando.[82] Lucia Caccini, on the other hand, was utilized in less auspicious parts. She played a male celestial siren with the more specific planetary attributes of Mercury in *intermedio* one (while her male colleague Jacopo Peri was a siren with the attributes of Venus). If Archilei was not involved, then it is probable that a male alto or the castrato Onofrio Gualdreducci sang the third soprano part; indeed, we can deduce that Gualfreducci was involved in the scene as a male Delphian.[83] In light of the accompanying instruments specified by Malvezzi—lira da braccio and harp—I believe that the bass part would have been sung. Although both harp and lira likely functioned in a quasi-continuo fashion, neither instrument was designed to provide a "true" or sustaining bass line. The plucked harp, with its decay, would not have provided a strong foundation, particularly for the final section of the madrigal (mm. 22–28) where sustained notes were required. Although the lira would certainly have provided some chordal support, it was not an appropriate instrument to play the bass line as written, in contrast to a bass viola da gamba, for example (which in any case was not specified for this number).

In the large-scale ensemble numbers of the *Pellegrina* interludes which involved both men and women characters, the bulk of the female roles were played by cross-dressed men. That these roles were not publicized in *Intermedii et concerti* is not surprising; Malvezzi did not typically identify the singers in ensemble numbers when there was more than one singer per part. But as Delphians, Lucia and Margherita participated in both the larger ensemble numbers and as soloists in the quartet of singers for "O valoroso Dio." Given the unusual nature of women singers' involvement in such a public performance, perhaps Malvezzi did not want to highlight the participation of a cross-dressed woman. In every other instance where female singers are mentioned by name in *Intermedii et concerti,* they are performing the parts of female characters, and usually quite prominent ones. Though the musical style of "O valoroso Dio" called for women's voices, they performed "incognito," as it were. Finally, however, Lucia and Margherita were integrated back into the larger group of Delphians. After Apollo completed the fifth and final part of his dance, the female singers joined their male colleagues to sing the joyous victory song "O mille volte e mille" (A thousand times, and a thousand) to conclude the *intermedio.*

CHAPTER SIX

Diabolical Bodies and Monstrous Machines

A Cautionary Tale (*Intermedio* Four)

ACCORDING TO MOST COMMENTATORS, *intermedio* four was the most horrifying and shocking of the entire set of interludes. It culminated in a Dantesque
hell scene that left the auditor-spectator with a sense of irresolution and un-
ease, prompting several commentators to summarily conclude their accounts
with comments like those of Gadenstedt: "This was certainly an ingenious
intermedio, but moreover very frightening to watch."[1] The German's remarks
nonetheless register his capacity to critically assess the skill and imagination of
the interlude's creators, but it was the fear the performance evoked that elicited
his more visceral reaction. The vision of hell and its inhabitants, which was the
source of such horror, was the only scene in the entire entertainment that commentators consistently identified with complete accuracy. The *intermedio*
began, however, in a somewhat more ambiguous fashion with the arrival of a
sorceress, a figure that was perhaps most familiar to Florentines who had witnessed similar spectacles at previous marriage celebrations. I begin by demonstrating how such an opening inspired wonder through mechanical ingenuity.
I will then speculate upon more subliminal associations that may have been
evoked, especially for Florentine audience members.

Rossi's account states that the fourth *intermedio* opened with a sorceress whose purpose was to invoke the fire demons, who would foretell the
coming of the Golden Age. Rossi does not attempt to justify the sorceress's
appearance by citing the relevant classical sources, as he does, for example,
for the opening of *intermedio* one, when Harmony appears. He merely
states: "In this *intermedio,* a woman—represented by the poet [Bardi] as a
sorceress—appeared above [in] a fine chariot of gold and gems before the
scene was changed."[2] In other words, while the scene from the previous act
of the comedy was still visible the chariot-borne sorceress appeared from on
high, a point to which I will return, because many commentators observed
the interruption. What also garnered attention was the fact that spectators

were unable to see how the chariot traversed the air to the center of the stage, while still remaining close to the Heavens: "Without changing the perspective, a sorceress's chariot appears in the air, pulled by two dragons, a wondrous thing because one was not able to see by what means it moved."[3] Buontalenti and his workmen had done their job well. The wonder was compounded by the subsequent appearance of a large red cloud: in this instance, too, some spectators marveled at "how the machine was able to be in the air without seeing how it was guided, and how it was able to hold so many people."[4] Thus, the most immediately compelling facet of the scene for many spectators was the hidden technology that enabled seemingly impossible staging feats.

Rossi's description does not stress the affective quality of the music in this scene, which complemented the mechanical feats of the engineers, but other accounts do. Particularly striking, given his text's relative brevity, is Cavallino, who begins by announcing: "The fourth *intermedio* gave no less amazement to the eye than wonder to the ear. . . ." suggesting that the visual and aural components of the scene were on equal footing in their capacity to evoke the wondrous.[5] Regarding the sorceress's song in particular, Cavallino notes: "[T]here was a woman who sang alone, and in such a manner that all ears were attentive [in order] to listen to her."[6]

The song to which Cavallino referred was composed by Giulio Caccini and sung by his first wife, Lucia Caccini.

Io che dal ciel cader farei la luna	I, who could make the moon fall from the heavens,
A voi, ch'in alto sete,	To you who are on high
E tutt'il ciel vedet'e voi commando	And see all of heaven, I command you:
Ditene quando il sommo eterno giove	Tell us when the almighty, eternal Jove
Dal ciel in terra ogni sua gratia piove.[7]	Will pour down his every grace from the heavens to the earth.

As the utterance of a sorceress, both the singer's delivery and the music her husband notated seems to have been designed to suggest the sorceress's spellbinding powers. Producing the latter may have been a difficult task for a composer such as Giulio Caccini, whose own reluctance to employ a consistently florid vocal style—a sure-fire technique for evoking the marvelous—is well known. In many ways, Caccini's compositional strategy is typical of his style, with *passaggi* almost invariably falling on the penultimate syllable of a

Example 6.1. Giulio Caccini, "Io che dal ciel cader" (from *intermedio* four)

Example 6.1. continued

phrase (see example 6.1; CD tracks 16–19).[8] The sonic impression of invoca-
tion would have been produced by the declamatory fashion in which Lucia
Caccini, as sorceress, first summoned the demons—hence the speech-like setting and repetition (with slight embellishment) on the words "Io" (I) and "a
voi" (to you) (see example 6.1, mm. 1–4 and upbeat to mm. 11–12; CD track
16). The text repetitions here emphasize the sorceress's attempt to contact her

demonic cohorts; to the less savvy auditor-spectator, the emphasis on "I" and "you" in the text would have at least conveyed the intensity of the singer's relationship with certain unknown, but potentially powerful, deities.[9]

In general, the setting conforms to Giulio Caccini's views on correct text setting. However, the use of passagework is extensive, and does not always appear to be prompted by the meaning of individual words. For the listener, the wondrous experience was likely evoked through the mounting complexity of the passagework in the first half of the poem, with each successive phrase outdoing the last, culminating on "commando" (I command [you]) (upbeat to mm. 21–25; CD track 17).[10] This strategy included the use of *passaggi* on syllables of words that did not call for any special treatment: see, for example, the *passaggi* on "sete" (you are) (mm. 14–15) and, later in the song, on "quando" (when) (mm. 28–29). The dramatic timing of Lucia's silences between phrases would have likely created a sense of expectation in the listener and along with a commanding delivery might explain Cavallino's emphasis on the audience's attentive ears. On two occasions—at m. 26 and m. 33—the continuo is silent in conjunction with the voice. These dramatic pauses would have given the sorceress's listeners a moment to absorb both her spellbinding virtuosity and the implications of her demands. In this sense, too, Lucia's song could make a powerful impression, without the auditor necessarily attaining word-for-word comprehension. Finally, it is the suggestion of Jove's power to pour down his grace that prompts her concluding flourish, with the dotted-rhythm figure "painting" the word "piove" (mm. 36–39; CD track 19).

During key moments in the song the intricacy of the passagework may have become the central object of the auditor's attention, to the exclusion of all else. There is an aesthetic parallel here between the song as it may have been experienced in performance and Rossi's explanation of the visual aesthetic that dominated the *intermedi* at the meta-level. Various comments by Rossi in his *Descrizione* (supported by the testimony of unofficial accounts) suggest that part of the experience of *meraviglia* involved the trumping of one wonder by the next—to the extent that it was possible to forget almost immediately what one had witnessed only moments before.[11] To enhance this trumping effect, lighting could be designed so that it became difficult for the eye to rest on certain visual components of the scene.[12] The point appears to have been to keep the perceiver "off balance," in a state of instability so that the experience of each *intermedio* and the performance as a whole were seemingly always just beyond the spectator's grasp. Similarly, Caccini's solo song demonstrates how each phrase of passagework could outdo the last (by potentially nullifying the impression of the previous one), either through increased complexity over the course of the song or through a striking stylistic shift. By the same token, however, it was impossible for the creators to reliably predict how each auditor would perceive the song; the music's momentary quality as it unraveled through time could be posited as the aural equivalent of unruly glances, rather than an all-consuming gaze, that structured live performance. As such, the attention that the singer literally commanded disappeared as her florid *passaggi* evaporated and new modes of delivery were adopted throughout the course of the song. In addition, musico-theatrical performance was unpredictable in and of itself, because various media, while sometimes working in tandem, could also compete for the perceiver's attention.

Dangerous Women and Monstrous Beasts

Let us now look more closely at the sorceress's visual representation. Though Rossi does not explain why Bardi chose a sorceress to open the *intermedio,* he does provide a quite detailed description of her demeanor, which is reminiscent of the sorceresses or witches of previous Florentine court *intermedi:*[13]

> Disheveled and barefoot, her hair splayed out over her shoulders and enveloped her. [She] had a proud countenance, a beautiful face, [and was] dressed in green velvet, [with] a long blue veil on her head that went down almost to her feet. In her right hand [was] a whip, and with the other [hand] she restrained two fierce, horrible, and frightening dragons, with great wings of many colors and full of mirrors [to reflect the light]. [The dragons were] sometimes shooting out fire from their mouths, and [with] tongues hanging out, it seemed such a lifelike imitation that they were panting from the endeavor of the task [of pulling the chariot].[14]

Because Buontalenti's pictorial representation of the sorceress (see plate 16) is part of a composite design that conflates the major elements of the entire *intermedio,* it only gives us a distant view of her visual appearance and we do not get a sense of how her disruptive entrance occurred in temporal sequence. Nevertheless, one is able to see the sorceress's bare legs and at least one uncovered arm prominently displayed, an atypical sight for a woman on stage at court (or elsewhere, for that matter).[15] The impression of movement and perhaps dishevelment is suggested by her billowing veil, an aspect that is enhanced in Epifanio d'Alfiano's later engraving (see plate 17). Rossi uses the word "scinta" to describe her, which literally means without belt or ungirded.

The sorceress traversed the Heavens from one side of the stage to the other, stopping midway to invoke the fire demons with her song. As the second of three interludes that opened with a soloist, there was clearly a novelty value to her entrance, which attempted to demonstrate yet another form of mastery over the physical environment through seemingly magical means.[16] At the same time, it would have been entirely inappropriate, in symbolic terms, for the sorceress to initiate a descent (as Harmony had done), in light of her potentially threatening and diabolical qualities. Rossi's repeated references to the sorceress's whip, which she used to control her panting dragons, is suggestive of the power that she was designed to wield.[17] On the other hand, only a few commentators aside from Rossi identified her as a *maga* (sorceress)—others referred to her as Juno (a figure commonly associated with previous Florentine duchesses) or merely as *una donna*—although it is arguable that the figure's diabolical potential became apparent as the *intermedio* unfolded.

Almost all commentators noticed how the chariot-borne figure, by entering the scene before the previous act of the comedy had finished, effectively disrupted the traditional demarcation between comedy and interlude.[18] For those audience members who did recognize the figure as a sorceress and noticed her intrusive entrance, the singer's appearance might have prompted more subliminal associations, especially in light of the hell scene that followed. We might begin to understand these associations by considering the figure of the sorceress or witch in the popular imagination and in archetypal visual representations of the period, as well as in previous Florentine court entertainments. Ten years earlier in 1579 a sorceress and a five-headed dragon appeared as part of an entertainment held in the Pitti courtyard for the wedding of Francesco de' Medici and Bianca Cappello.[19] The dragon had bird-like feet and a scorpion's tail and spat fire from its mouth; as for the sorceress, there was no mistaking her loose, unruly, flying hair, which was a common reference to sexual licentiousness.[20] Though the word *maga* rather than *stregha* (witch) was employed, the figure had witch-like attributes and associations.[21] The scene unambiguously referenced the sorceress-witch's diabolical sexual power: she rode her bizarre beast, quite literally representing the monstrous.[22]

Charles Zika has pointed out that almost all visual images of witches during this period "depict witches as riding rather than flying . . . even if it might be through the air."[23] According to Zika, representations of the riding witch drew on a long tradition of wild rides, but by the early sixteenth century the witch as rider was established as a "fundamental feature of literary accounts of the witches' repertoire of evil"; more specifically, the rides were associated with inappropriate sexual pleasure in both literary accounts and visual depictions.[24] A related image that was widespread during the sixteenth century was that of a powerful woman who used her wiles to subjugate men. The most popular depiction of this sort was that of Phyllis with whip in hand riding atop a bridled Aristotle—positioned on hands and knees in beast-like fashion—with the implication that the philosopher's weakness had made him subject to Phyllis's control and sexual domination.[25] Other classic images depicted witches engaged in sexual activity, either with each other or with their dragon-like beast. As such, witches were not only portrayed as inverting the "natural order," but also imagined (and evidently feared) as mistresses of their own sexuality. In light of their perceived sexual independence, witches were commonly believed to cause impotence in men.[26] The popularity of such beliefs during this period seems to reflect increased anxiety about social, moral, and sexual disorder,[27] particularly with regard to the disruptive potential of women. Further, historians have connected the emergence of early modern absolutism with the increasing number of witch trials, although, as Stuart Clark has cautioned, the relationship was not simply one of cause and effect.[28]

In the fourth *intermedio* the sorceress appears to be a somewhat "cleaned-up" version of the archetypal witch; she may not have literally ridden her dragons but she was certainly depicted as controlling them. Her dragons bear a striking resemblance to the monstrous serpent-dragon that Apollo had vanquished in the previous *intermedio*,[29] implying that the earlier threat to "natural" order had not been entirely eviscerated. The visual cues associated with her female figure (the whip, her bare limbs, splayed hair, and general dishevelment), interpreted through the lens of the hell scene that followed, are suggestive of the dangers (and consequences) of women's unbridled sexual power. It is telling that Rossi's description of the hell scene emphasizes semi-naked or naked female nonreproductive bodies that are depicted as deformed and monstrous. In the context of the fourth *intermedio* and the wedding celebrations more generally, the sorceress as a figure of disruption stood in direct opposition to the socially sanctioned marriage for which the entertainment was staged. The *intermedi* were intended to celebrate and symbolically facilitate the fertility of the presumed virgin bride, whose "contained" sexuality would be "released" with the hope of producing a Medici male heir. On a subliminal level, then, the sorceress's presence in conjunction with the subsequent hell scene served a deep structural and didactic function in the *intermedi* as a whole: not only were the consequences of sociosexual disobedience depicted in an especially graphic form in the hell scene, but the restorative order that prevailed in the final *intermedio* was strengthened by the threat to order in *intermedio* four. As such, princely authority was enacted through the literal vanquishing of the worst of all evils: the devil and his entourage. That the Medici progeny was envisaged as Christ-like at the conclusion of the entire set of interludes provided a fitting antithesis to the horrors of hell.

Heaven and Hell

The oppositional nature of hell and heaven, with the Medici aligned of course with the latter, made a decidedly unambiguous statement; by the end of the entertainment, audience members likely made the mental connection. Yet the appearance of a sorceress at the opening of *intermedio* four was somewhat ambiguous from an interpretive standpoint: some commentators picked up on visual cues that marked her as diabolical, while others perhaps experienced her incantation as powerful but ultimately innocuous. Likewise, the fire demons summoned by the sorceress provoked differing reactions among spectators. The Frenchman's account is one of the most interesting: he notes that most of the spectators believed angels were being represented on the stage, but he "was assured that they were intended as demons."[30] Even Rossi alluded to the confusion here by stating that "they seemed to be like angels from paradise," despite their fire-like hair and predominantly red costumes.[31] For obvious reasons, a number of commentators refrained from identifying figures in the scene, merely noting the appearance of a large group of musicians suspended in a cloud. (Here, the *effects* of technology could be wonder enough.) Of all the descriptions, Gadenstedt's provides the most detailed information regarding music's function in the evocation of wonder:

> [T]he chariot was followed by a large closed cloud, in which music was made.[32] When the cloud also [like the chariot] arrived in the middle of the stage, it stood still, both sides divided apart, [and] inside sat twenty-four musicians making music. When this had taken place, the cloud closed up again; the musicians, however, continued to make music, left concealed, as if it came from afar in the clouds; [it was] delightful to hear. Meanwhile it gradually went away, right up to the other side, and disappeared there [just] like the chariot. These two pieces were very skillfully done, so that no one could recognize how it would ever be possible that something like this could be staged, or [how] something like this could have taken place so publicly in the open air.[33]

Rossi doesn't mention that music emanated from the closed cloud as it made its progress toward, and later away from, the center of the stage, but clearly this is another instance of "invisible" music contributing to a *meraviglia*-inspiring effect. When the cloud opened at center-stage, singing and gesticulating musicians were suddenly seen inside. The instrumental ensemble was dominated by chord-playing string instruments—both plucked and bowed— which likely played pseudo-continuo parts, rather than doubling the voice parts as written.[34] As such, the resultant soundscape of the demon's song—"Hor che le due grand'alme" (Now that these two great souls)—would have been full and resplendent, a fitting tribute to the "two great souls"—Ferdinando and Christine—to whom the song referred.

Let us now return to the more ambiguous features of this scene in order to understand how seemingly disparate interpretations coexisted among the commentators. The ambiguity stemmed, in part, from the erudite choice of subject matter. Rossi explains that the sorceress "summoned the demons from the most pure region of the air," referring to those demons closest to the moon, and of purest heat—they were, in effect, good (as opposed to bad) demons. In Neoplatonic cosmology the good demons were understood as part of an interrelated hierarchy of powers. As members of the spirit world, the good fire demons, like angels, were positioned at the top of the hierarchy. In this scheme, influence descended from the spirit world, first to the heavenly realm of stars and planets, which in turn influenced the outcome of earthly affairs, including physical changes.[35] The sorceress's song text articulates exactly this three-tiered Neoplatonic conception of the cosmos: she calls upon *spiritus* (the fire demons) to tap into the planetary realm (Jove) in order to determine when Jove's influence (in the form of *piove*) will be transmitted to earth.[36] In the early modern period, Jove had come to be associated with the cultivation of good government and the magical arts; as such he was the appropriate figure to bring about the "marriage" of heaven and earth. At the same time, Jove's assumed attributes paralleled the projection of Ferdinando as Magus, with the implication that the prince's magical powers would bring prosperity to Florence through just and stable government. Upon becoming duke in 1588, Ferdinando had chosen the emblem of a swarm of bees with the motto *Majestate tantum*—"By dignity alone"—to signify that his rule would be fair and just, enabling the citizenry to accumulate wealth as bees do honey.[37]

Jove does not actually appear in this scene, however; the Neoplatonic chain of influence was only finally effected in the concluding *intermedio* when Jove appeared in the heavens to announce the celebration of the joining of heaven and earth. For now, Bardi was content to personify the spirit world through the good demons. The risk, however, was that good demons might be mistaken for bad demons; in other words, that natural magic might be mistaken for demonic magic.[38] Rossi, and likely also Bardi, seemed to have been aware of this risk, making the distinction clear to those who would read their commentary. Rossi carefully distinguishes between the demons of the "gross air" (who would be closer to the surface of the earth) and those of "the most pure region," and he continually reminds the reader that the fire demons are his subject.[39]

Understandably, the intricacies of Neoplatonic cosmology appear to have been lost on most audience members. For the spectator, confusion may have been compounded by the hell scene that followed, because of an instinctual correlation between "red" musicians (fire demons) in a "burning cloud" and the burning fires that represented hell. Rossi began his description of the Dantesque hell scene as follows:

> After the [fire demons'] cloud closed again and disappeared, in an instant the scene was completely covered in caves, boulders, and nooks and crannies, and full of fires, and of burning fires, and it seemed that, moving in the air, the fires were sending their smoke up to Heaven. After the scene was completely covered with this horror, the stage floor opened, and we saw a much worse horror, because in opening itself, it opened Hell, and we saw coming out of there two groups of furies and frightful devils. But even though they were as such [i.e., frightful], they appeared here with humble and pained expressions and it seemed that they had abandoned their pride because of fear.[40]

Rossi's point here is to depict the creatures of hell—the devils and furies—as already vanquished.[41] According to Rossi the terrifying nature of their appearance, which he later goes on to describe in great detail, did not hide the fact that they themselves were humbled and fearful. In other words, the prediction made by the fire demons—that all evil and lamentation would be banished—was already partially fulfilled.

Rossi's extensive description of hell's inhabitants includes a vivid depiction of two of the furies. (Bardi was a Dante scholar, and descriptive details in Rossi's account closely replicate parts of the *Inferno*.) Nudity, deformity, and monstrosity are general themes, but the furies in particular—with their "dried-up," nonlactating breasts and serpent-like coils covering various body parts—present a particularly striking image of female sterility and gender confusion:

> In the first group there were two furies, with a dress pulled tight around them, which looked like they were naked, with a complexion that was smoky and burnt. Their hands and face were dirty with blood, and they had big dried-up breasts, dirty, long, and drooping, and among those there was entwined about them a serpent with many coils. The serpent-like hair which they [the furies] often and angrily shook, because it was coming down on their face, and similarly around their waists there were serpents of great quantity, and in different positions they were all over their bodies, and they were covering their private parts. On the right hand they had four ugly and deformed devils with paws like eagles [i.e., like talons] and their hands similar to paws.[42]

One needs to remember that the spectator would have "taken in" the scene—as a complex panorama of hell—over a relatively short amount of time. Thus, the main "action" constitutes the focal point of comment in most of the shorter and eyewitness accounts. Charonte—ferrying souls across the river Styx—is identified by some, but almost all commentators described with horror the small, naked children (representing the souls) who were being devoured by Lucifer, himself a gruesome three-headed monster.[43] Some of the souls escaped Lucifer's grip but were quickly caught and delivered back into one of his three mouths.

One of the most graphic and detailed descriptions that gives a sense of the scene as perceived through the eyes of the spectator is that of the anonymous Frenchman:[44]

> [A]nd the stage at once changed shape, and mountains, caverns, fires, and flames appeared, and [the scene] represented hell with two groups of devils,[45] some of whom had their face and hands stained with blood, and snakes around their head and arms. Hell was represented completely on fire,[46] which lasted for quite a long time on the stage, and in hell many souls were being tortured, who were represented by thirty-five or forty entirely nude children, of ages nine, ten, and twelve years old. Lucifer was at the center of Hell, who half showed himself, with a large head of three faces, holding souls in the mouth of each of these, [and] the devils took souls from one side and the other, and carried them to Lucifer. As he devoured one, two others escaped from him, who were caught again by the devils and carried [back] to Lucifer, who immediately devoured them. Charonte with his boat ferried and referried the souls [across the river], and the whole thing was represented so well that it horrified the people [audience].[47]

The Frenchman noticed details of Lucifer's appearance that coincide with Rossi's account (which in turn correspond with Dante): in particular, he notes the half-emergent Lucifer with his three faces,[48] indicating, as an antithesis of the Trinity, his status as anti-Christ. Although such details are not a feature of every account, the scene was depicted in such a way that none could mistake the monstrous figure of Lucifer, who appeared to evoke a combination of curiosity, revulsion, and fear; in other words, he evoked the cognitive and bodily shock and awe that was fundamental to an experience of *meraviglia*. That Bardi clearly had the wondrous in mind here is suggested by the passage from Dante from which Rossi's description of the three-headed Lucifer is derived:

> When I saw three faces in his head,
> how great a marvel it appeared to me!
> One was in front, and was fiery red;
>
> The other two were joined to it upon
> the middle of the shoulder on each side,
> and joined above at the crest:
>
> And the right face was something between white and yellow;
> the left face was like the color
> of those who live along the banks of the Nile.[49]

An earlier portion of Dante's description clarifies why the representation of Lucifer from only the chest up was so efficacious. His enormity and monstrosity—only half emergent—left it to the imagination of the fearful spectator to wonder how vast the rest of him would be.[50] An early sketch by Ludovico Cigoli (plate 18) shows the division between Lucifer's upper and lower body; only the section from the chest up was revealed to the audience.

As the French commentator reminds us, however, not everything was left to the spectator's imagination. The physical violence that was enacted on the stage—especially the pain inflicted on the small, naked children—brought a heightened awareness of the body not only to the stage but to the bodies of audience members themselves. As Cynthia Marshall has demonstrated, in the context of early modern theater, "the representation of physical pain calls attention to bodiliness in a complex way . . . extend[ing] the sense or sensation of suffering to viewers, whose sympathetic bodies might accordingly feel imagined pain."[51] Through vicarious visceral response, the perceiver was made aware of his or her own bodily vulnerability. The means of inflicting pain and death—by being eaten alive—suggested to the audience that the body's integrity was easily violated; indeed, human flesh was reduced to devil's food. Rossi helps account for the efficacy of the scene by stressing Buontalenti's creative impetus in regard to Lucifer's masticating jaws:

> [W]ith no less skill by the one who made this [Buontalenti], a soul had been put in every mouth of Lucifer, and those mouths were made to move [i.e., chew] in a manner that appeared as if the architect [Buontalenti] had wanted to compete in showing it [on the stage] with the poet [Dante] who describes it. . . .[52]

According to Foucault's model of monarchical power, the aim of public torture was "to make an example, not only by making people aware that the slightest offence was likely to be punished, but by arousing feelings of terror by the spectacle of power letting its anger fall upon the guilty person[s]. . . ."[53] The spectacle of the body in pain does not represent, but presents, or, in my reading, actualizes, the monarch's power, exalting and strengthening that power "by its visible manifestations."[54] In Mark Franko's reading of Foucault, "power is force performed," and "its efficacy derives from the visibility of its impact on [suffering] bodies."[55]

To experience horror or fear while witnessing this scene would have entailed a temporary shutting down or paralysis of the cognitive faculties. In the early modern period, affections or passions were understood and experienced as the interrelation of bodily effects and mental states, with equilibrium maintained by the correct balance of bodily or humoral fluids. When

experiencing fear, the humoral fluids were believed to become disordered, flee-
ing bodily extremities and collecting in the heart—today one might think or
speak of blood racing to a pounding heart—leaving the mind confused and
the body unable to act.[56] If the Frenchman was correct in identifying the audience's "horreur" at the hell scene, it is likely that he was describing a bodily
demeanor which reflected the confused state of the (internal) humors. As
Katherine Rowe has noted, the Latin derivation of the word "horror" meant
"visible roughness of surface,"[57] which points to the physical expression of fear
on the body's surface—whether expressed by the face or through other body
language.

For what was clearly the entertainment's most shocking scene, it appears
that silence, or the familiar (and likely unnoticed) sound of machines at
work,[58] accompanied the hell scene as it metamorphosized on the stage. In
this respect, the scene functioned much like the calculated use of silence in
contemporary film: the audible horrors of hell were left to the spectator's own
vivid imagination, prompting her to plumb the depths of her own worst fears.
Because of the descriptive nature of Rossi's account and his tendency to move
back and forth between description and "action," the account does not give
us a clear impression of a sequence of "events."[59] But eyewitness and other
reports confirm that the hell scene *concluded* with the singing of the furies
and devils.[60] Thus, the scene began with the spectator contemplating the horrors of hell with a sonic backdrop of silence.

Melancholy Madrigals: A Tale to Remember

The *intermedio* concluded with the furies and devils singing Giovanni de'
Bardi's setting of "Miseri habitator" (with text by G. B. Strozzi):

Miseri habitator del cieco Averno	Miserable inhabitants of black hell,
Giù nel dolente regno	Down in this sorrowful realm
Null'altro scenderà ch'invidia, e sdegno:	Nothing else will descend but envy and scorn:
Sarà l'horror, sara'l tormento eterno,	The horror and the torment will be eternal.
Duro carcer inferno;	Cruel prison of hell,
A te non più verrà la gente morta,	The dead will come to you no more,
Chiudi in eterno la tartarea porta.[61]	Close forever the gates of hell!

The complexity of Strozzi's text derives from the implication that hell will have no further victims, except for those who are envious and scornful (of the Medici?)—for them the gates of hell *are* still open, and the horrors will be eternal. In this respect, hell is not closed and remote but exists instead as a contained (and controlled) realm reserved for those who—like the pitiful inhabitants on the stage—are judged envious and scornful. In other words, hell is now under the command of a greater power aligned with the celestial realm: the Medici themselves. With the Medici reign as subtext, Strozzi's poem suggests that it is they who will decide (both metaphorically and literally) who will and will not "go to hell."

Though the complex implications of Strozzi's song text likely eluded most, the affective, melancholic quality of Bardi's musical setting is mentioned in almost every account. Gadenstedt states, for example, that "these pieces [however] were composed very dolefully, pitiably and melancholically, as if they [the furies] were half crying. They were doleful to hear."[62] Likewise, an anonymous author notes that the furies "labored with very beautiful, but melancholy madrigals,"[63] thereby stressing the physical effort of the furies' melancholic music making by reference to "the sight of sound." The sense of effortlessness, or *sprezzatura,* that seemed to characterize much of the interludes' musicking is here appropriately inverted in order to reference the basest form of music making—that which required bodily labor—a far cry from the invisible music of the celestial spheres.

That Bardi's actual music was perceived as somehow unusual is suggested by Pavoni's comments:

> In the middle the devils that were seated on the aforementioned rocks made beautiful but sorrowful music—perhaps in order [to express] pain at their unhappiness—which [music] had such sad conceits that did not resemble any other, that grieves and torments. And while this was taking place, they [the devils], the rocks and caves, with the inferno, disappeared, returning the scene to its previous beauty.[64]

Pavoni's remarks point to a singularity of musical style and execution: though Bardi's music was "read" unambiguously as melancholic, according to Pavoni it "did not resemble any other [music]" of melancholic ilk. Certainly, within the context of the *Pellegrina intermedi* and the fourth *intermedio* in particular, the composition distinguished itself in terms of style, range, timbre, and instrumentation. Bardi developed this music—his only contribution to the entertainment as composer—from the experiments and discussions that grew out of his own camerata in the early 1580s. Such music may have been perceived as unusual, especially by non-Florentines. The theories of Bardi's camerata were of a local, specialist nature at this time and would not have been familiar to the general spectator during the performance. Nevertheless, Bardi's music appears to have been particularly effective in projecting melancholy.

The vocal range and chosen instrumentation of "Miseri habitator" helped to establish the general mood of lamentation. Gone was the colorful continuo band that accompanied the singing of the cloud-borne demons. Instead, the four lowest voices of Bardi's five-voice setting (see example 6.2) were reinforced by the sustained sounds of viols and trombones, with the low-range canto part doubled by a lira da braccio that may have thickened the texture by providing chordal support as well. The combination of trombones and viols (with an absence of soprano wind instruments) was by now firmly established as the standard consort to accompany infernal scenes in Florentine court *intermedi*.[65] The addition of the lira da braccio, in less frequent use by 1589, would have enhanced the consort's somber sonority. In keeping with Bardi's aesthetic, the song is largely syllabic, the range is limited, and he is careful to articulate each line of text as an independent unit (by frequent use of rests) in order to ensure clarity of text expression. The piece is in G Dorian mode, but the song avoids cadencing in G until the conclusion of the final line of text (example 6.2, mm. 46–47), where the sense of closure coincides with the words "Close forever the doors of hell!" The music and text of the concluding tercet is then repeated verbatim, producing a cross relation (B natural and B flat) between the alto and tenor voices (mm. 47–48). The oscillation of tonal centers from phrase to phrase, coupled with unsettling harmonic juxtapositions between phrases projected a sense of melancholic uncertainty among hell's inhabitants.[66] Note the disjunct harmonic movement at the beginnings and endings of phrases, particularly at mm. 7–8 (from D major to C major), mm. 18–19 (A minor to G minor), and mm. 39–40 (A major to F major), with the latter producing a chromatic shift in the alto part. For those souls—who had evidently lost their direction and were trapped in "blind Hell"—the torments of the underworld were unpredictable and could go on indefinitely, hence the lack of tonal predictability at both the micro- and macro-level of the music. Bardi also introduced subtle word painting to emphasize this chaos and dramatize the pain experienced by hell's inhabitants. For example, his setting of the final line of the first quatrain—"The horror and the torment will be eternal"—shifts to the hard system (from m. 21). A prepared suspension is here preceded by a leap in the canto part to the highest note of the setting in order to expressively mark the word "tormento" (mm. 22–23). By augmenting or "drawing out" the note values in the lowest four voices from mm. 23–26, Bardi momentarily evokes a sense of stasis at the end of the phrase, suggestive of hell's "eternal torment." These musical details, though hardly perceived on a cognitive level by Pavoni and others, coalesced to create the overarching melancholic

Example 6.2. Giovanni de' Bardi, "Miseri habitator" (from *intermedio* four)

Example 6.2. continued

Example 6.2. continued

Example 6.2. continued

effect that audience members experienced, and probably contributed to the impression of "difference" articulated by Pavoni.

The spectators' accounts suggest that the scene ended with the sounds of the furies and devils—howling and moaning—as they slowly sank to the depths of hell (through trap doors in the stage floor). After his compelling description of the visual horror of the scene (see above), the Frenchman concluded his account of the interlude with the following observations, mentioned almost as an afterthought:

> There were also some rocks on which were devils who sang and made some howls and very sad lamentations. And little by little all of hell disappeared, as if everything had withdrawn into the ground, because afterwards the stage changed to another setting.[67]

The visual impression of the scene was thus mirrored by the audible impression of howling gradually swallowed up or subsumed, as the furies and devils slowly disappeared beneath the stage floor.

After the horrors of the hell scene, the purpose of Bardi's concluding music was perhaps to arouse and then purge the spectator of melancholy, that bodily humor caused by an excess of black bile. Pavoni speculated that the reason for the sorrowful concluding music was possibly a vehicle for the devils to express "pain at their unhappiness." But did the spectator know exactly *why* the devils where unhappy? The suggestion in both Rossi's account and Bardi's song—that the devils were mourning their loss of hell's future victims—is not mentioned elsewhere. While such nuanced questions of textual meaning might have been too subtle for the spectator to grasp, one can return to the perceiver's experience of sight and sound: the furies and devils were gruesome and frightening to watch, yet their final sonic characterization—their concluding lament—suggested that they themselves had succumbed to a power greater than their own. The spectator appears to have understood this much. In fact, the outcome articulated here characterized the *intermedio* as a whole: in essence, the forces of "good" (Ferdinando and Christine) and "evil" (the inhabitants of hell) were pitted against each other, with "good" prevailing. As Stuart Clark has argued, this kind of juxtaposition provided an especially effective means of articulating political ideals, whether the context was the court theater or the court's trial-room: "The proposal that demonic power could be nullified by the authority of the godly ruler . . . made witchcraft prosecutions a critical test of political legitimacy. . . . [D]emons and witches became the perfect antagonists of those who claimed power by divine right, since their defeat could only result from *supernatural,* not physical superiority [italics mine]."[68] Lucifer—as anti-Christ—was the logical opponent of the Christian prince, although it was his cohort of furies and devils who were demonstrably vanquished at the end of the *intermedio.* And it was primarily Bardi's music that sealed that defeat, and by extension the prince's supernatural superiority. Indeed, the apparent contradiction between the furies' initially frightening appearance (and their torturous acts) and the eventual revelation of their melancholic disposition only enhanced the perception of the Christian conqueror's strength.

As a whole, the fourth *intermedio* in performance communicated a concomitant message about the nature of Medicean power that was perhaps
more subtle but thereby more unsettling. While on a surface level Lucifer
and his attendants represented the antithesis of the celestial sphere within
which Ferdinando and Christine were continually positioned during the
course of the entertainment, on another level the audience would have recognized that the Medici controlled the representation, be it diabolical or
otherwise. With the ingenuity of men such as Buontalenti in their service,
the Medici could present wonders that not only elicited delight but also horror in the audience; as such, the genuine fear that this *intermedio* evoked was
an indication of what the Medici were ultimately capable. Their power was
not only benign but, when called for, could be diabolical, causing bodily
harm and painful death. In this sense, the hell scene functioned as a cau-
tionary tale, especially for the women in the audience—most notably Christine herself. The figure of the disheveled sorceress would have been a sinister
reminder of the importance of her submission to patriarchal order—submission
that was considered crucial to dynastic potency and security.

CHAPTER SEVEN

Singing the Marvelous
(*Intermedio* Five)

The Siren's Song

[I]n the blink of an eye [the scene] became a tempestuous sea [with] hard rocks and waves that appeared so natural, that everyone was stupefied by looking at them, because they made that foam that one is accustomed to [see] with the real sea. In the middle of the above-mentioned waves appeared a very beautiful siren—with nine of her prisoners—with such a sweet singing that it would not have been anything to wonder about if it had put to sleep and softened every hard heart; then after singing for a good amount of time, she disappeared. . . . [1]

Cavallino's description of the opening of *intermedio* five pays particular attention to the perceived effect that the first solo song had on audience members. For Cavallino, the singer—who we know was Vittoria Archilei[2]— portrayed a siren whose song had the power to move the audience by softening their hearts and lulling them to sleep as the legendary Sirens had done to the sailors of antiquity. Indeed, in Cavallino's mind the song had already achieved its intended effect, because the singer was accompanied by "nine of her prisoners," whose hearts she had already captured with her "sweet singing."

Cavallino was not the only commentator who identified the singer as a siren.[3] In the eyewitness account by Gadenstedt the soloist is similarly described:

Out of this sea, in the middle, lifted up fairly high, one saw the aforementioned woman, who could sing so well, clad like a Siren, below like a fish,[4] above like a beautiful maiden with long delicate blond hair, towards whom came twelve Sirens out of each half of the sea. They sat somewhat lower, also in similar dress, sung together very delightfully, after which they sank into the sea.[5]

Noting a similarity in dress between the solo singer and the other participants,[6] Gadenstedt naturally assumed that they too were Sirens.

Yet Bardi and his collaborators obviously went to some lengths to ensure that the feathered Sirens introduced in *intermedio* one—the "good" Sirens who moved the spheres—would not be mistaken for the potentially dangerous fish-like Sirens. In his description of a celestial siren from *intermedio* one, Rossi was careful to describe her lower extremities:

> Her little light blue shoes were adorned with jewels, cameos, little masks, and threads of silver and gold. Contrary to the wicked Sirens, whose lower parts are ugly and deformed, the poet [Bardi] had taken heed to make these [Sirens] all perfection in beauty.[7]

It is clear that the creators of the *Pellegrina* interludes wanted to avoid any possible connection with the so-called wicked Sirens.[8] It is likely that any connotation suggesting music's power as a destructive force was purposefully avoided especially—perhaps, because of the presence of "real" women singing in the theater. Gadenstedt, for one, was interested in the singer herself, not just her presumed mythological character, noting that he "saw the aforementioned woman, who could sing so well." Female singers were frequently likened to Sirens during this period, but there was often confusion surrounding the nature of their power—did it lead men from earthly desire to ultimate destruction or to a higher spiritual plane?[9] What seems like a straightforward dichotomy may not have been so clear cut in reality, as the anxiety surrounding Rossi's reference to the "wicked Sirens" suggests.[10] It is therefore somewhat ironic that the singer who opened the fifth *intermedio*—Vittoria Archilei—was perceived as a siren by several observers, a testament to the prevalent image of the siren in the popular imagination.

But in the minds of those who created the *intermedio,* Archilei was intended to represent Anfitrite, Queen of the Sea, surrounded by sea nymphs and tritons (for a sea nymph costume see plate 19). By all accounts, the scene was visually stunning: emerging from a trapdoor in the middle of the stage floor amid the simulated waves, Archilei—positioned in a large mother-of-pearl shell—gradually rose above the sea to a height of five *braccia,* according to Rossi (plate 20).[11] Having emerged from her watery kingdom to salute Duke Ferdinando and his bride, she sang:

Io che l'onde raffreno	I, who still the waves
A mio talento, e son del mar	According to my will, and am
Regina,	Queen of the Sea,
A cui s'attera, e'inchina	Before whom bows down in
	reverence

Ogni nume, ch'al mar alberga in seno	Every divinity who dwells in the bosom of the sea:
Ad inchinarmi, ò Regi Sposi vegno,	To bow down to you, O royal pair, I come
Fin dal profondo del mio vasto regno.[12]	From the depths of my vast realm.

Music on the Printed Page

What, then, was the nature of Archilei's song of which Cavallino, Gadenst-edt, and others make mention? The song, "Io che l'onde raffreno," as presented in the official five-part setting by Cristofano Malvezzi (example 7.1), is only a skeleton of what was apparently sung in performance. In Malvezzi's setting, rests occur simultaneously in all voices after every line of text, with a few exceptions.[13] Malvezzi repeats the text of the opening and closing lines in his setting, following the same pattern. Typically, the final syllable of each poetic line concludes with a whole note followed by a half note rest that accentuates the impression of self-contained musical phrases.

On the printed page, Malvezzi's setting conforms in several fundamental respects to the "new" style of composition propounded by Vincenzo Galilei and endorsed by Bardi. Tim Carter has summarized Galilei's approach and has demonstrated how Bardi's five-part madrigal "Miseri habitator" (from *intermedio* four; example 6.2) is in keeping with these "new" ideals.[14] With regard to Malvezzi's setting of "Io che l'onde raffreno" (example 7.1), we find striking similarities of approach. Both Bardi and Malvezzi consistently used half-note rests to separate each line text, and both settings are largely homophonic. Ensuring that the poetic line remained intact and arranging the rhythms so that they were in conformity with the natural accentuations of the text were considered important means of ensuring text comprehensibility, a point that Bardi stressed in his *Discorso . . . sopra la musica anticha e'l cantar bene*.[15] Although Malvezzi's setting does not exhibit some of the other features favored by Galilei—such as entirely root-position harmonies or disjunct harmonic progressions (Bardi uses the later to help articulate line divisions)[16]—Malvezzi is evidently concerned with setting the text with almost simplistic clarity, a clarity especially apparent from a glance at the publication's canto part.[17]

For reasons that can only be speculated upon, Malvezzi did not provide an embellished version of the canto part in the official print to serve as an indication of what the soloist sang in performance, as he had for several of the other solo songs. Because Cavalieri had given Malvezzi the task of overseeing the publication of the entire set of interludes,[18] it has been suggested that the partbook format Malvezzi chose for this piece—with all five voices texted—provided an opportunity for the composer to promote the performance of his own composition by adopting the typical (utilitarian) format of the period,[19] allowing for a variety of performance options. Although there may be some truth to this theory, the publication had a limited run of 116 copies,[20] and thus the music was not widely disseminated. While the commemorative aspect of the publication did not preclude its use for practical music making, in general the print does not lend itself to practical usage.[21] So why did Malvezzi choose this particular notation style and format? The composer himself tells us that Vittoria Archilei, the Florentine court's prima donna, sang the piece as a solo "maravigliosamente," implying that she embellished the canto part with at least some passagework.[22] If we consider the possibility that Malvezzi may not have had a notated source detailing Archilei's embellishments (as he evidently did for her song "Dalle più alte sfere") or chose not to include one, then Malvezzi may have decided to convey an entirely different musical aesthetic through the medium of print. It is striking how closely Malvezzi's song mirrors Bardi's "Miseri habitator" in terms of the strict usage of rests between phrases and its consistently homophonic texture. While it is true that most of the ensemble music of the interludes is homophonically oriented, none of that music is as consistent in this respect as that of Malvezzi and Bardi. Similarly, the use of parallel rests in all voices to divide the poetic line is nowhere more consistently applied than in these two pieces. Interestingly, in each of the partbooks, Malvezzi's piece follows Bardi's.[23] With the commemorative function of the publication in mind, Malvezzi (as compiler and editor) may have wanted to demonstrate his familiarity with the text-based aesthetic espoused in Florentine musical circles and exemplified by Bardi's "Miseri habitator," which he knew would appear on the page directly preceding his own composition.

Music in Performance

The visual similarities of the pieces by Malvezzi and Bardi on the printed page end just there. In performance, the likely melodic diminution devised by Archilei within Malvezzi's clearly marked-off phrases would have produced discrete "snapshots" of musical wonder. (Bardi's song was sung more or less as written by five voices doubled by instruments.)[24] In addition, by way of contrast with several of the other solos songs in the *intermedi*—in which the complexity of the passagework generally increased as the songs progressed—the effect of "Io che l'onde raffreno" in performance seems to have been somewhat different. If we follow Cavallino's impressions (which are, indeed, the most detailed we have), the hypnotic quality of the song must have called for a completely different approach that relied only partly on the singer's ability to articulate intricate passagework, but relied more fully on the singer's *ingegno*—an imaginative capacity to invent or fashion the new. Several musicians, including her *Pellegrina* colleague, Jacopo Peri, attest that Archilei was adept at such performative "inventions." In Peri's words, Archilei was the singer

> who has always made my music worthy of her singing, and adorns it not only with those *gruppi* and those long windings of the voice, [both] simple and double, that her *vivezza dell'ingegno* [liveliness of invention] can devise at any time—more to obey the usage of our time than because she regards the beauty and force of our singing to rely upon them—but also of those pleasantries and beauties that one is not able to write, and if written, cannot be learnt from the written [examples].[25]

As we have seen, Peri used the term *ingegno* to describe Archilei's imaginative acumen, a masculine attribute connoting imagination, inventiveness, and initiative,[26] and highly prized in both the literary and visual arts spheres.[27] Peri's reference to the singer's *vivezza dell'ingegno* occurs in the context of her capacity to improvise various types of ornamentation, but Peri remarks on the current vogue for *passaggi*. Of course, as a Florentine court musician Archilei's livelihood depended on her ability to execute such passagework with brilliance and precision, as she did in "Dalle più alte sfere" for the opening of the production. Yet Peri suggests that Archilei herself did not believe that "the beauty and power" of singing relied solely upon such techniques. Indeed, the "vaghezze e leggiadrie" (pleasantries and beauties) that Peri went on to mention do not necessarily refer to ornamentation, as has sometimes been assumed.[28] It is more likely that "vaghezze e leggiadrie" refer to other expressive devices for which singers from these circles were renowned and, as Peri points out, "cannot be learnt from the written [examples]."

Comments by Vincenzo Giustiniani—describing the singing of the ladies from the closely related courts of Mantua and Ferrara—will serve to outline some of the expressive effects to which Peri may have been referring. Giustiniani mentions the use of well-placed *passaggi*, but continues by describing more subtle effects:

> Moreover, by moderating or increasing the voice, loud or soft, making it light or heavy, according to the sections [of a particular song], now drawing it out, now dividing it with the accompaniment of a sweet interrupted sigh, now stretching passages out, well followed, detached, now *gruppi*, now leaps, now long *trilli*, now brief [*trilli*], and now with sweet *passaggi* sung softly . . . and with many other particular artifices and observations that will be of note to people more experienced than myself.[29]

Omitted from the excerpt above are references to appropriate physical demeanor, particularly with regard to the body (trunk), hands, and parts of the
face. It is difficult to know to what extent Vittoria might have employed more
subtle physical gestures in her performance of "Io che l'onde raffreno" in the
large Uffizi theater; initially, she had to negotiate the rising movement of her
machine with lute in hand.[30] The mother-of-pearl shell on which she was
perched was intentionally tossed about by the waves,[31] but presumably the
waves subsided as she sang her opening line, "Io che l'onde raffreno."

It seems clear, though, that the subtleties of Archilei's expressive
arsenal—her "pleasantries and beauties"—must have accounted, in part, for
the song's efficacy in performance.[32] Indeed, the song did not require a pronounced teleology (such as increasingly complex passagework) in order to
evoke a sense of wonder in the auditor. On the contrary, each self-contained
phrase directed attention to the "pleasantries and beauties" of the musical
moment rather than a large-scale progression. By taking seriously Cavallino's
remark regarding the power of the siren's song to elicit a sleep-induced state,
and also considering the consistent musical "space" between each phrase of
text in Malvezzi's print, it is possible to create an effective rendition of the
song (CD tracks 20–22). The instrumentation that Malvezzi specified for this
number—chitarrone, lute, and lirone[33]—is crucial in this regard. The chordal
nature of the bowed lirone could create a wash of sound, articulating a sense
of spatial depth and breath appropriate to the song's poetic conceit. Despite
the "spaces" between the singer's finely nuanced phrases, the sustained chords
supplied by the lirone could provide a full and rich textural support, as a
complement to the punctuating articulations of the lute-family instruments
(whose chords ultimately decay). In our recording, we have chosen to use the
bass lute[34] in conjunction with the chitarrone in order to best support the
singer's chosen *passaggi* in the higher range,[35] although the singer's arrangement spans both the upper and lower tessiture. Utilizing a range of well over
two octaves—instead of the narrower range in Malvezzi's print—allows for a
breadth of expression that reflects both the text's general conceit as well as
more specific nuances of textual meaning.[36]

The song begins with two statements of the opening line "I, who still the
waves" (example 7.1, mm. 1–12; CD track 20, opening). The following discussion, though referencing the measure numbers in the "plain" version (example
7.1), largely focuses on the embellished rendition created for the accompanying
listening example (CD tracks 20–22).[37] For the first statement we follow the
contour of Malvezzi's canto part exactly (see example 7.1, mm. 1–6), but with
the repetition (mm. 7–12) we lightly "paint" the words "l'onde" (the waves).
The limited range of a fifth, along with the frequent half and whole notes,
produces a mild sense of stasis appropriate to the text's sense. Each phrase end-

Example 7.1. Cristofano Malvezzi, "Io che l'onde raffreno" (from *intermedio* five)

Example 7.1. continued

Example 7.1. continued

ing is marked off with a typical cadential formula in the continuo that projects a sense of self-contained phrases. As Anfitrite fully proclaims her powers and status—"According to my will, and am Queen of the Sea"—more direction in the musical line ensues (both in Malvezzi's print and in our embellished version), and we add a final, dramatic flourish on "Regina" (Queen). Still, a sense of calm pervades the following section (example 7.1, mm. 21–32; CD track 21), despite the undulating *fioriture* on "mar" (sea) and typical cadential *passaggi* at the end of the section on the word "seno" (breast). More difficult to capture with the written word are "those pleasantries and beauties that one is not able to write [in musical notation]." The auditor will have to listen carefully for the subtle modulations in vocal production, for the legato passages followed by well-accented ones, and the ever-changing *trilli*. The latter are especially apparent through the phrase "inchina / Ogni nume" (bow [down to] every divinity), one of the few places where Malvezzi moves through the end of the poetic line without pause to express the full sense of the text. One of the more strikingly expressive *trilli* in our recording occurs at the carefully placed deceptive cadence on "nume" where a *trillo* in the lower range produces a sense of hushed reverence at the mention of divine power. The third section (mm. 33–56; CD track 22) gathers momentum even from the start of the first phrase—"To bow down to you, O royal pair, I come"—as the singer moves into the upper voice range, with striking embellishment on "sposi," drawing attention to the royal couple. A descending octave leap followed by a stepwise ascent begins the first statement of the final line of text—"From the depths of my vast realm"—presaging the spatial conceit (and the extremities of vocal range) that will characterize this final portion of the song. On "profondo" (depth) our singer begins an appropriate *descent,* largely mirroring the contour of the line in Malvezzi's print, but with the enhancement of "pleasantries and beauties." The bass line (mm. 43–48) is also generally downward-moving. With the repetition of the text the singer leaps down an octave to low G to begin a wide-ranging ascent, culminating at the top end of her range on a high B amid a plethora of *passaggi* on "regno" (realm). Until this moment, the harmonic implications of the accompaniment (implied by Malvezzi's five-part setting) have been relatively simple, consisting mainly of root-position chords with a smattering of first inversions, largely paralleling the rhythmic contour of Malvezzi's "simple" canto part. In the final phrase, the continuo group articulates a series of alternating root and first inversion chords changing on the quarter note above a rising bass line (shown in Malvezzi's setting, mm. 50–52) that mirrors the vocalist's ascent in order to convey Anfitrite's emergence from the ocean's depths. Both melody and accompaniment articulate a keen sense of movement and direction, by way of contrast to the sleep-inducing stasis that pervades the song's first two sections as Anfitrite stills the ocean's waves.

The final musical effect, then, is to produce a sense of spatial breadth that mirrors the spatial implications of the "vast realm" (i.e., the ocean's depths) from which Anfitrite has risen. Though Malvezzi's setting clearly indicates the spatial theme through the descending and ascending melodic lines in both the canto and bass parts, in our recording we have amplified that effect through the use of wide-ranging *passaggi*. Nevertheless, it is only a small step to connect elements of Malvezzi's "simple" setting and aspects of his suggested instrumentation to the immediate cultural milieu for which the song was written. The "vast realm" articulated in Malvezzi's setting coupled with the textural capabilities of the accompanying instruments, most particularly the lirone's ability to articulate a sense of breadth, might be seen to reflect Ferdinando's own aspirations for the expansion of his dominion, especially through control of the sea. In fact, Rinuccini's text projects a vision of Medicean dynastic superiority through the figure of Anfitrite—who herself maintains jurisdiction over the ocean—"bow[ing] down" to the family whose seafaring ventures were well known. (It is also easy to see how Cavallino's impression of being lulled to sleep by a siren's song is not entirely incongruent with the surface level conceit of the scene's creators: to represent the goddess Anfitrite calming the stormy sea as homage to the royal couple.)

During Ferdinando's reign, the Tuscan naval fleet established itself as one of the foremost on the Mediterranean sea, defeating a Turkish fleet in 1608. The posthumous series of engravings by Callot commemorating Ferdinando's accomplishments, and commissioned by his then widow Christine of Lorraine, emphasize the precision and sophistication of the duke's fleet during combat (see plate 21). Ferdinando's nautical ambitions, which included expansion into foreign territories, were apparent through artistic display from the outset of his reign. A naumachia, one of the featured entertainments of his 1589 wedding celebrations, was a novel addition to Medicean festivities. Although such spectacles were probably familiar to Christine from Valois festivals, the technology marshaled to flood the Pitti Palace courtyard without the use of existing water sources was new.[38] For the 1589 naumachia, seventeen boats with Christian crews (each with eight to ten men on board) were pitted against a Turkish flagship and fourteen Turks manning the citadel that, after successive assaults, was claimed by Christian forces (see plate 22).[39]

A maritime theme continued throughout the course of the *intermedio*. The multi-sectional piece that followed "Io che l'onde raffreno"—"E noi con questa bella diva" (And we [too], with this beautiful goddess)—involved Archilei as both soloist and ensemble member in several sections. Hence, several commentators conflated the two opening pieces in their accounts,[40] while one observer noted that the singing and playing took place for a considerable amount of time.[41] The anonymous author of *Li artificiosi* was especially observant with regard to the sequence of musical "events," however, mentioning the soloist (whom he described as the (sea-nymph Thetis) "singing solo to the lute," which was followed by "twelve maritime men [*sic*] who sang and played in the company of the said nymph. . . ."[42]

"E noi con questa bella diva" is a five-voice madrigal by Malvezzi in five sections, with the beginning, central, and concluding sections (CD tracks 23, 25, and 27) sung by the sea nymphs. The instrumentation specified for these sections was lush; it was built upon the continuo group utilized for "Io che l'onde raffreno," with the addition of bass and tenor viols, harp, and two lutes.[43] The latter instruments provided "upper-range" continuo possibilities that balanced the "lower-range" continuo group accompanying Archilei's solo. The overall effect of the voices and accompaniment appears to have been warm yet stately, almost as if the intention was to surround the auditor with the sonic equivalent of the warmth, security, and pomposity provided by a luxurious fur coat.[44] The text of these choral/instrumental sections (see appendix 6) traced a progression that began with Anfitrite's nymphs' salute to the royal couple (CD track 23), the nymphs' prediction that the fame of the Medici progeny would spread from one Pole to the other (CD track 25), and a final reference to the restoration of a Golden Age by virtue of the royal union (CD track 27). The music's rich timbral and textural qualities thus mirrored the positive progression of the text, concluding with a projection of Medicean dynastic security. The central reference to Medici progeny and global fame is worth citing in full, as it encapsulates the central concerns of the wedding that were communicated throughout the course of the entertainment most effectively through aural and visual media. The nymphs sing: "That one foresees, issuing from you, / A famous offspring / That will adorn [the earth] from one Pole to the other." In this section the chorus shifts to triple meter (CD track 25), by way of contrast to the preceding two duple meter sections (CD tracks 23 and 24). A dance-like triple meter (or a triple subdivision of the beat) was often utilized to represent the royal couple, and in this case it referred to their literal union, intended to produce the hoped-for Medici (male) heir.[45] The same kind of metric shifts (and concomitant meanings) were played out in their most complex form in the entertainment's final *ballo,* "O che nuovo miracolo."

The central choral/instrumental section sung and played by the nymphs is flanked by two sections in which the voice of Anfitrite is highlighted (CD tracks 24 and 26). Malvezzi does not specify instrumentation for these two sections. For the first of the two (CD track 24), Malvezzi tells us that Anfitrite (Archilei) sang solo;[46] thus, the five-part texted version of this section in the surviving partbooks was not performed as written. We have thus realized the chordal implications of Malvezzi's setting in our recording using the "low-range" continuo group—chitarrone, bass lute, and lirone—for accompaniment. For the second of these two internal sections (CD track 26)—which was sung as a trio—Malvezzi indicates that the singers were Archilei, her husband Antonio, and Margherita (della Scala).[47] This section provides the starkest contrast of all, immediately following the expansive triple meter section referencing Medici progeny. The text hails the Medici as those who would "rid the world / of the cruel, wicked serpent / whose desire grows, the more he continues to have [in his possession]."[48] The shift back to duple meter, the incisive rhythmic profile, and the hard, biting quality that can be rendered with the precise declamation of words such as "discacciar," "crudo," and "rio" all contribute to the section's strong character.[49] Aspects of the musical setting can be seen to reflect both the desire (and assumed capability) of the Medici to expunge their enemy *and* the dangerous voracity of the serpent itself. Like the hell scene in *intermedio* four, a credible threat is invoked in order to heighten the impression of a return to a Golden Age. At the most basic level, the text and music function by way of juxtaposition with the surrounding choral sections proclaiming Medici hegemony. The piece's concluding choral section reinforces that proclamation through musical repetition of the text (CD track 27): "Thus the happiness / of a former age will return / by your benevolence, O esteemed royal couple."

"With the Admirable Attention of the Listeners": Arion's Echoes

The sinfonia that followed separated *intermedio* five into two distinct parts.[50] Although this sinfonia was not mentioned in unofficial accounts, the scene that it accompanied clearly set off the second part in the minds of most commentators. The second part of the *intermedio* continued the aquatic theme, but the focus now became that most legendary of Greek poet-musicians, Arion. Although Rossi's account includes a description of the scene's basic "plot," he brushes over the musical details; indeed, he identifies neither the poet nor composer of Arion's song and the poem he provides does not correspond with that contained in Malvezzi's print.[51] It seems that preparations for the musical part of this *intermedio* may have been in a state of flux when Rossi prepared his text, or that a last-minute change occurred.[52] Nevertheless, Arion's song was a great success in performance, as eyewitness and other accounts illustrate. Pavoni's provides considerable detail about the sonic and visual components of the scene:

> Then on another side of the sea appeared a galley all covered in gold with perhaps 25 people inside, which, because of the churning of the rough sea, went around four or five times, with such agility that one could not have seen a better [display] in the real sea. Finally [the galley] stopped with its

bow towards the princes, and lowered the sails in respect; then playing a
harp Turrerino [Arion] sang a very beautiful madrigal in the manner of an
echo, to which two other echoes responded with different voices, the one
after the other, [and] it appeared that their voices issued from caves or deep
caverns. While Turrerino sang very sweetly thus, the sailors, having become
envious of his virtue, hurled themselves against him with knives in order to
kill him. But he, having realized this, threw himself into the sea, whereupon
a dolphin, who had stopped there, drawn by the harmony and by such sweet
singing, stirred to compassion by such a virtuoso, took him on his back and
carried him unharmed to the shore.[53]

The double-echo that responded to Arion was a key point of interest for
several commentators, but before addressing its significance I will first attend to Pavoni's reference to the singer's self-accompaniment on the harp.
Many accounts attest that solo songs (particularly those by Archilei and
Caccini that opened interludes one, four, and five) were self-accompanied
by the singer on a lute[54] even if, as we learn from the *Memoriale*, Archilei's
lute was decorated to look like a sea shell in *intermedio* five.[55] Regarding
Peri's solo, an entry in the *Memoriale* states that a harp was to be made for
Peri from papier-mâché, apparently because of the necessity of hurling himself overboard onto the dolphin after his song.[56] This could imply that Peri
actually mimed his accompaniment, rather than playing a functional instrument. In the costume design by Buontalenti (plate 23) the singer poses
with harp in hand; however, Buontalenti's costume design for Archilei as
Dorian Harmony also depicts her with a harp (plate 5), although it is un-
questionable that in performance she held and likely played a lute (hence
Gadenstedt's reference to her "beating" on the instrument). In other words,
the instruments represented in costume designs were not always those used
in performance. In fact, in another costume design that may also have been
for Arion, the figure holds what appears to be six-string viol, with a flat
lute-like bridge, and lira da braccio-style peg box, with the latter feature
hinting at classical allusions (plate 24).[57] While Pavoni's and the Frenchman's accounts of the performance mention Peri playing a harp, Malvezzi
(an eyewitness, admittedly writing two years after the fact) tells us that Peri
accompanied himself on a chitarrone. As a performer-composer, Malvezzi
is clearly more interested in documenting functional instruments, unlike
Bardi and Buontalenti who conceived of the scenes (and instruments utilized therein) in mythic terms. One should acknowledge, however, the
practical desire to fuse conceptions of "ancient" instruments with their
"modern" counterparts, and thus the use of hybrid instruments in performance.[58] Several surviving instruments blend knowledge of "modern" instrument technology with a conception of a "classical" instrument. What

might be described as "theatrical chitarroni"—that combine aspects of the newly "invented" chitarrone (particularly its long extension neck) with an imagined ancient lyre—survive in museums in Vienna (plate 25) and Bologna (plate 26). The instruments are playable and easy to hold; although we cannot be certain they were utilized in 1589, they date from this very period, and are exactly the kind of instrument appropriate for use in a set of *intermedi* dominated by hand-plucked (not keyboard) instruments.[59] It is therefore possible that when Malvezzi refers to soloists playing chitarroni (such as Peri and later Gualfreducci as Jove in *intermedio* six) they may very well have utilized such hybrid instruments.

But let us return to the double-echo mentioned by Pavoni, which was also highlighted in other accounts of the scene (but absent from Rossi's description). The anonymous Frenchman provides further information, stating that "two echoes answered him [Arion], one after the other, so much that one could have said that the echo was from more than two miles [away]; and [so that] it seemed to be far from the stage and from the sea, and as if it came out of a grotto or from a cave."[60] This account agrees with Pavoni's, suggesting that the echo seemed to come from some sort of small enclosed chamber. Perhaps the on-stage scene—a seascape with surrounding rocks and crumbling mountains (from which water apparently issued)—brought to mind the idea of a cavern or cave. Yet the Frenchman indicates that the echo was projected from a considerable distance away from the stage (as he had similarly stressed when describing the echo that responded to Archilei at the end of "Dalle più alte sfere" in *intermedio* one), and this time he exaggerates— suggesting a distance of two miles (not one)—perhaps in response to the double echo. It seems likely, then, that Arion's echoes did not come from behind the stage—which would not have given the impression of sonic "distance" from the original sound source[61]—but rather from the back of the hall, as had been the case in *intermedio* one. The impression of a distant but "enclosed" sound can be explained by the positioning of the singers in the small room attached to the back wall of the theater that opened out onto the balcony for musicians. As before, the singers would have sung from behind the grate, thus remaining out of the audience's field of vision (see plate 3). No commentators mentioned seeing the singers involved; had they been visible there is no doubt that this information would have been incorporated into accounts, because it was part of the "theatrical game" to attempt to understand such mysterious effects. Pavoni notes that the echoes were produced by two separate voices, though other accounts suggest that the voices were not perceived to be emanating from two distinct locations. To produce a double-echo—with the second of the two sonically mirroring the first but at a lower volume—it seems likely that the first echo would have been produced by a singer close to the grate, whereas the second singer would probably have been positioned further back in the room so that the auditory perception in the theater was such that it was perceived as a more distant second echo.

Peri's echo song was in fact the first of its kind to be published, but it seems that the ingenious manner of performing the echo devised by Buontalenti and his crew—producing a mysterious, cavernous sound—was in large part responsible for the sense of *meraviglia* that it evoked in auditors. I suggest that the self-referential or self-reflexive nature of echo itself, coupled with its "invisible" articulation in the Uffizi theater, was a profound demonstration of a belief system bound to Ficinian Neoplatonism, the tradition that had informed Florentine court *intermedi* since their inception. Further, I suggest that it was no accident that the mysterious source of sound was produced from a location close to the duke himself. This was another way in which the duke represented himself as royal Magus: in other words, his physically present body might be understood to be infused with manna—a dynamic, supernatural power that could generate miraculous effects. Yet as discussed in regard to Archilei's echo in *intermedio* one, the fractured nature of the aural component could also be understood to question the authority of the anterior sound source, even though in this case Echo herself was not (invisibly) personified.

By way of contrast to the echo in Archilei's song, which was limited to the song's concluding section, the double-echo that was heard in *intermedio* five was the governing principle that structured the entire piece, thus reinforcing Ann Rosalind Jones's point that echo in the hands of male poets became a vehicle for rhetorical virtuosity. In Arion's song—which was composed, sung, and self-accompanied by the virtuoso Jacopo Peri[62]—the double-echo reiterated Arion's concluding passage at the end of almost every poetic line.[63] Although the poet is unknown, the poem as it appears in the *nono* partbook of Malvezzi's publication reads:

Dunque fra torbide onde	Therefore among the murky waves
Gli ultimi miei sospir mandero fore,	I shall breathe my final sighs.
Ecco gentil con tuoi suavi accenti:	Gentle echo, with your sweet accents
Raddoppia i miei tormenti;	Reiterate my torments;
Hai, lacrime, ahi dolore,	Alas, tears! Alas, pain!
Hai morte troppo acerba e troppo dura.	Alas, death, too bitter and too hard!
Ma deh chi n'assicura:	But who can assure me,
O di Terra o di Cielo	On earth or in the heavens,

Example 7.2. Jacopo Peri, "Dunque fra torbide onde," mm. 27–48 (from *intermedio* five)

Example 7.2. continued

Example 7.2. continued

S'a torto io mi querelo:	If I am wrong to complain?
E s'a ragion mi doglio;	And if my foreboding is justified,
Movetevi a pietà del	Have pity on me in my plight.
mio cordoglio.[64]	

The power of Arion's plaintive yet *meraviglia*-inspiring song ultimately saved the poet-musician from his mutinous crew. After Arion jumped overboard to escape them, a dolphin carried him safely to shore, attracted by his sweet singing. Echoes responded to Arion at most of the line-end cadences, and were also summoned within poetic lines to emphasize dramatic exclamations on the word "hai" (alas) in the first stanza (see example 7.2, mm. 27–37) and "pietà" (pity) in the final line of the second stanza (see example 7.3, mm. 75–77). The wondrousness seems to have been produced, in part, by a projection of musical stasis or immobility as each line or short phrase was iterated twice before the singer could proceed. In this way, the echoes effectively created a perception of time slowing down; and like virtuosity itself, the device was self-referential, calling attention back to the source of sound. (The authority of the sound source may be questionable, however, in light of the fragmentation of the originating

Example 7.3. Jacopo Peri, "Dunque fra torbide onde," mm. 66–86 (from *intermedio* five)

(1) Orig. = C

Example 7.3. continued

Example 7.3. continued

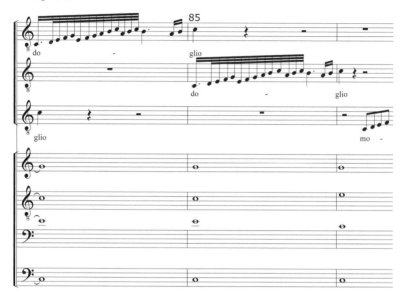

voice.) The song did not provide the listener with a succession of related moments, but rather produced self-contained bursts of wonder with attendant ripple effects produced by the double echoes. Unexpected chordal shifts also contributed to a sense of disjunction between phrases. See, for example, the third-related chord shift in example 7.2 (mm. 46–47), which emphasized Arion's disbelief—with the word "ma" (but)—after contemplating a death that would be "too bitter and too hard." In addition, Peri's song drew on the so-called *bastarda* style in which the soloist not only performed florid passagework in his natural voice range—Peri was a tenor—but expanded the range of available pitches (from both above and below), to incorporate elements of the bass and alto parts that are found in the score in Malvezzi's print.[65] Drawing on the alto voice was particularly appropriate toward the end of the song when Arion's sense of foreboding reaches a peak. In example 7.3 (mm. 66–69) the gradually ascending eighth notes culminating on the high E (at m. 69) on the text "And if my foreboding is justified" reflected Arion's fearfulness and dread by moving the singer's voice into the alto range for elaborate *passaggi*.

The singer's ability to traverse various parts of the ambitus exemplified the kind of Herculean feat that was expected of the virtuoso in this context. The range explored by the singer is roughly two octaves, yet accomplished bass singers at this time were known to sing *bastarda* style with a range of up to three octaves. Indeed, as Richard Wistreich has demonstrated, the bass singer Giulio Cesare Brancaccio, while criticized by connoisseurs for subverting the musical architecture of a piece, could astonish his audience by applying passagework across the entire range of a four-voice madrigal, making porous the boundaries between discrete parts of the musical texture.[66] Similarly, in the 1589 performances, the addition of extensive and wide-ranging passagework in Peri's song drew the listener toward an experience of momentary effects, one that actively worked against a perceived sense of the song's larger design.

The concluding number of the fifth *intermedio*—Malvezzi's "Lieti solcando il Mare" (Happily cutting through the sea)—provides another example of how aural and visual effects might trump even the most ingenious of pieces—Arion's double-echo song. Not withstanding the double echo, Arion's sole accompaniment was his own plucked-string instrument. Juxtaposed against these minimal yet cleverly employed musical forces was a memorable finale in which "all the stops"—both visual and musical—"were pulled out." Pavoni's account, continued from above, provides one of the more detailed descriptions:

> Those on the ship, believing that their companion [Arion] had drowned, seemed to rejoice, and as a sign of this they began to sing and play with trombones, cornetti, dulcians, and other instruments. And [they] put the oars in the waves in order to go around two or three more times in the galley, [and then] took back the route from where they had come before, and in an instant the sea disappeared, and the stage became as it was before.[67]

In this final number the sailors rejoiced at Arion's demise, unaware that he had been taken safely to shore by the dolphin. Unlike most of the other *intermedi,* the concluding scene here did not end with an encomium for the royal couple or a more generalized projection of "good" prevailing over "evil." Most commentators made note of the dolphin carrying Arion to shore, but only a few seem to have been aware of the significance of the final scene, in which Arion's rebellious crew have the last word. Perhaps the exigencies of spectacle demanded a rousing song by Arion's sailors to conclude the scene.

The sonic spectacle appears to have functioned so effectively, in part, because the juxtaposition of disparate musical forces in the finale provided striking contrast with Arion's preceding song. The finale—"Lieti solcando il Mare"—was a seven-part madrigal performed by at least twenty-one sailors, which may indicate that there were three singers per part.[68] Malvezzi mentions that the madrigal was accompanied by the "detti strumenti" (the previously mentioned instruments);[69] one must assume that he refers to the group of plucked and bowed strings employed for the sinfonia. In this context, most of these instruments would have been played continuo style, with the violin likely doubling the canto part. Although not mentioned by Malvezzi, several other sources note the prominent use of wind instruments—such as trombones, cornetti, and dulcians—which may have doubled the vocal lines.[70] The seven vocal/instrumental parts are far from strictly homophonic, with voices often functioning independently (or combining to form small groups) with distinct melodic and rhythmic profiles, creating a relatively dense and (comparatively speaking) complex musical texture. The overall effect of this madrigal's original performance must have been bold and resplendent.

Despite the impressive finale sung by the large contingent of sailors aboard ship, it was the solo songs, both Peri's echo song and Archilei's solo as Anfitrite, which received the lion's share of attention in unofficial sources. It was typical for solo songs positioned at the opening of an *intermedio* to be singled out in reports. (Three of the six interludes began with solo songs.) Even though several spectators conflated Archilei's solo in *intermedio* five with the ensemble madrigal that followed, her singing was still given special attention, most notably by Cavallino, because of her song's siren-like, soporific effect. As we have seen, Gadenstedt also referred to the singer as a siren, but the German commentator distinguished myth from performative reality by referring to the actual singer he believed he had heard earlier in the evening.

Likewise, Gadenstedt draws upon his aesthetic sensibility and critical judgment when referring to Peri's echo song: ". . . after this had finished, the sailor up on the mast, who sang a wonderful tenor, started to sing a solo; he had mastered the right time for coloring [the notes, and] was also enjoyable to listen to."[71] Gadenstedt praises Peri's discretion, likely meaning that his *passaggi* were well placed. It seems that Gadenstedt was aware that in some circles the use of excessive and/or ill-placed passagework was not welcomed. Far from being overwhelmed by *meraviglia,* Gadenstedt was clear-headed enough to give his considered opinion on the merits of Peri's singing. While the song was also "enjoyable" to listen to, Gadenstedt ironically makes no specific mention of the echo effects that had so captivated both Pavoni and the French commentator. If the double echo was a source of *meraviglia* for some, for others it was apparently not all-consuming. By the same token, while the effects of *meraviglia* could be a powerful tool for asserting Medicean supremacy, the spectator-auditor brought to the performance his or her own experiences and interests, which held their own in the face of wondrous and fantastical effects.

CHAPTER EIGHT

"O What New Wonder"

(*Intermedio* Six)

Framing the Festivities: The Heavenly Descent

THE VISUAL STRUCTURE OF THE SIXTH and final *intermedio* mirrored the opening scene in *intermedio* one (just after Harmony's prologue), thus providing the entertainment with a symmetrical frame—a point that was not lost on spectators. Gadenstedt reports, for example, that "the clouds up in the heights again opened up, *as at the beginning of the comedy,* so that one could see into the heaven or paradise, where *then again* numerous musicians in angelic clothing sat making music with all manner of instruments, and singing delightfully to it [italics mine]."[1] As discussed in chapter 2,[2] a broad trajectory of containment and restorative order was projected across the six interludes; in the final *intermedio,* the cosmic (and concomitant political) harmony not witnessed since the opening of the entertainment was finally restored. Even though most mythological intricacies of the return were lost on the audience, the visual symmetry was not, and its attendant meaning was likely understood, at least on a subliminal level.

The idea for the scene was drawn from Plato's *Laws.* Rossi explains:

Jove, having compassion for fatigued and distressed humanity, decided that, in order to give some relief, Apollo, Dionysos, and the Muses [would] take care of this, and he sent them to earth, carrying Harmony and Rhythm, so that, dancing and singing, cheered by such delights, [humanity would] be somewhat revived after so much toil.[3]

Although Plato's general conception was maintained, last-minute changes to the theatrical realization meant that most (but not all) of the musical numbers outlined by Rossi appear to have been exchanged for different pieces. I therefore rely on the order of pieces as they appear in Malvezzi's publication.[4]

At the opening of the *intermedio,* the average spectator-auditor appears not to have sensed a clear distinction between musical numbers, because of the complexity of the visual display. The opening of the *intermedio* involved not one but several consecutive descents by groups of cloud-borne musicians, and in this respect it trumped the opening of *intermedio* one. One will recall that in the first *intermedio,* singer Vittoria Archilei enacted a slow, solo descent before paradise was revealed. The remaining "action" involved the Sirens' ascent from the stage floor to join the Fates and Planets in the upper cosmos before singing a final encomium for the royal couple. In the final *intermedio,* paradise was revealed from the outset, and the descent was amplified by the involvement of a number of celestial contingents. Further, in contradistinction to *intermedio* one, the unification that ultimately took place in *intermedio* six—now between gods and mortals—was enacted on earth, where nymphs and shepherds had gathered.

Cavallino appears to have intuitively understood the symbolic connotations of the physical interaction between the various contingents on the stage. He clearly distinguishes between the clouds "that carried celestial . . . music" and the earthly music of the nymphs and shepherds: "Those blessed ones [those who carried celestial music], having been lowered down, got up and, *having mixed together with the others there,* [italics mine] made many musical choruses. And then they began to do the *balli.*"[5] Most accounts, including Cavallino's, confirm that at least some of the gods alighted from their clouds to interact with the mortals, while other cloud-borne deities, though lowered, may have remained in the air.[6] The general conceit—the bringing of heaven to earth—was evidently communicated.

During this extended final descent and prior to the concluding *ballo,* four musical numbers were performed. The intention of the creators appears to have been to maximize sonic impact. Thus, each successive musical number required more musical resources than the last, ranging from the opening six-part madrigal—"Dal vago e bel sereno" (From the pleasant and clear sky) with one singer per part—to possibly the most ambitious work of the evening, "O fortunato giorno" (O fortunate day), a thirty-part madrigal with two singers on a part (thus with sixty singers total). Just prior to "O fortunato giorno," a brief solo song momentarily interrupted the sonic expansion, but possibly helped to maximize the thirty-part madrigal's ultimate sonic force. This solo song (CD track 28)— "Godi turba mortal"—was composed by Cavalieri for the Pistoian castrato Onofrio Gualfreducci, who accompanied himself on the chitarrone.[7] Gualfreducci represented Jove, who from his summit announced the arrival of song and dance (see appendix 6 for the song's text). Several commentators correctly identified Jove, although none referred to his music making, perhaps because of the relative brevity of the piece.[8] According to the Bavarian commentator:

The scene turns once again, and appears to be nothing but golden tubes [rain]. Thereupon, paradise opens [up] on three sides, and one sees Jove in a cloud, in which he is coming down to the ground, together with two other clouds, and changes himself into a golden shower. With this, the fog disappears, but others come; in this [respect], fifty musicians.[9]

The golden rain is mentioned in every single unofficial account and is clearly depicted in the stage setting by d'Alfiano (see plate 27). Cavallino states that "there was a great abundance of gold rain so that many, believing it was truly raining, moved and wanted to go to collect it,"[10] suggesting the physical engagement of the audience.

What is particularly interesting about the Bavarian's account, however, is the reference to Jove transforming himself into a "golden shower." (In the Italian account from which the German report is derived the author refers to "pioggia d'oro.")[11] The long-anticipated arrival of Jove is referenced in the sorceress's song (at the opening of *intermedio* four) when she finally demands of the fire demons: "Tell me when the almighty, eternal Jove / will pour down his every grace upon the earth [?]" In the final *intermedio*, Jove's grace is represented in tangible form by the golden rain that signifies the ultimate transference of heavenly grace to the Medici realm. Jove's transformation into golden rain derives from the story of Danae, the imprisoned daughter of Acrisius; Jove falls in love with her, and in so doing changes himself into golden rain, thereby making Danae pregnant.[12] Jove, the god of good government and magical arts, had long symbolized the Medici dukes, and as we have already seen, he represented Duke Ferdinando in the *Pellegrina* interludes. As such, the scene symbolized Ferdinando himself, as royal Magus, restoring the Golden Age by impregnating his royal bride with his "golden rain," and thus ensuring dynastic continuity. Further, this transformative moment was the first occasion in the course of the set of interludes in which Ferdinando was mentioned by name; in other words, following Jove's appearance, symbolic allusions to the duke were replaced by direct textual references to "Ferdinando" in the final two musical numbers that concluded the entertainment. The text of the penultimate number—"O fortunato giorno"—is given below.

O fortunato giorno	O fortunate day
Poi che di gioia e speme	Because of joy and hope
Lieta canta la terra e'l ciel insieme[.]	Heaven and earth sing happily together.
Ma quanto sia più adorno:	But even greater adornments will come
Quando sara ritorno	When every royal custom

Per Ferdinando ogni real costume[.]	Will be returned by Ferdinando.
E con eterne piume	And with eternal wings
Da l'uno e l'altro Polo	From one Pole to the other
La fam'andrà col suo gran nome a volo.[13]	Fame will fly with his great name.

"O fortunato giorno" drew on the resources of the entire cast.[14] As we have seen already, the accumulation of musical resources over the course of an *intermedio* was a frequent strategy, but the added complexity of "O fortunato giorno," with thirty individual parts arranged into seven choirs, effectively dispersed the sound, creating an aural equivalent to the bodily "mixing up" or intermingling of characters described by Cavallino in this scene. Exactly how these choirs were arranged on the stage is uncertain. What is clear, however, is that during much of the opening of the piece (see lines 1–3 of the text above) each group functioned sonically as a discrete entity, with overlap between individual choirs only occurring at cadential points, except for a few short sections where the entire ensemble joined forces, most appropriately for the word "insieme" (together). Line four—"But even greater adornments will come"—begins in similar polychoral fashion, with frequent text repetition, as short motives are tossed between the various choirs. However, as the text repetition continues, the overlap between each choral motive becomes progressively tighter, until all choirs resound with tightly staggered entrances of "Per Ferdinando," the first overt reference to the duke.

The final portion of the poem (lines 7–10) is set in a simple homophonic texture (with all voices declaiming the text more or less simultaneously), first by reduced forces and then by the entire cast. A shift to triple meter at the beginning of this final section helps to maintain momentum, but also underscores the text's theme: the implication of movement, specifically flight, is projected as the medium through which Ferdinando's fame will fly "from one Pole to the other." The turn to triple meter parallels the metrical shift that occurs in the fifth *intermedio* when an almost identical conceit is introduced, except that it is Medici progeny, rather than Ferdinando himself, who "will adorn [the earth] from one Pole to the other" (CD track 25). The metaphor of global fame—a literal aim of Ferdinando's that was accomplished through international diplomacy and the cultural exchange facilitated through his expansion of the port of Livorno (see plate 2)—here finds sonic representation with the literal dispersal of multiple musical resources.[15] Not only were the vocal resources split into manifold parts, but "O fortunato giorno" involved the entire instrumental spectrum of available plucked, bowed, and wind instruments.[16] The variety of the tone color, then, was a crucial component of the sonic experience, and one that is not captured by the musical notation, especially in the case of the plucked strings where the players could have articulated their parts in a variety of divergent ways, according to the chordal idiosyncrasies of each type of instrument. The anonymous Frenchman notes that the music was so beautiful that "everyone admired it because of the great number of people who made it and the harmony that was between them, [and because] of the diversity of [musical] instruments."[17]

Music, Memory, and Embodiment

The purpose of the concluding *ballo* from this final *intermedio*—"O che nuovo miracolo" (O what new wonder)—was to bring the entertainment to a high point of excitement through a dynamic interplay of resources that represented the dynastic and physical union of Ferdinando and Christine. As we have seen, veiled allusions to the royal actors were now replaced by overt references; in the final *ballo* the text referenced "proud and happy Ferdinando," "the glory of Medici and Lorraine," and not least the "amorous sport" that would soon take place to ensure the continuity of the Medici line.[18] The *ballo* made explicit the connection between the union of the royal couple and the return of the Golden Age through the gods' gift of music and dance to humankind. Following the descent of the gods to earth to bestow their gifts, the mortals and gods joined together to sing and dance.

The *ballo* or dance-song was structured around a dialogue between the gods and mortals (nymphs and shepherds). Malvezzi's publication indicates that the music of the gods was performed by three of the Florentine court's leading female sopranos—Archilei, Lucia Caccini, and Margherita della Scala.[19] (See appendix 5 for the full text of the *ballo*.) The song's text does not explicitly identify the three singers with specific mythological figures, but I have argued elsewhere that they were likely portraying the three Graces.[20] The text implies that the trio were acting as intermediaries between the principal gods—Jove in particular—and the mortals on earth.[21] This arrangement is reflected in Buontalenti's stage design for the beginning of the scene, which positioned the group of three gods (with a fourth figure just below them) in mid-air between the groups of principal deities above and the mortals below (see plate 28). The characteristic features of the three Graces are displayed in Buontalenti's design: all three appear naked or semi-clad with a loose drape;[22] their stance is one of several traditionally associated with the Graces—the bodies of the two outer Graces are slightly turned from the viewer, while the central Grace is frontally positioned;[23] and their interlocking arms are a direct reference to their participation in the dance.

Malvezzi tells us that the three performers danced, sang, and played musical instruments.[24] I am particularly interested in the kinesthetic quality of the music and the visual effect of the dance as means of ensuring recall by those who attended the entertainment. While printed texts provided one kind of record of the events and were especially useful for those not physically present at the performances, another powerful reminder of the ephemeral performances was the visceral experience itself that the almost 3,000 foreigners who attended the wedding carried home, not only in their minds, but in their bodies. Zakiya Hanafi's description of wonder's effects touches on this specific question of memorability:

> Wonder acts as a sort of trance state, an intermediate state of being in which the ego boundary is more permeable; consciousness of self fades to allow more intense and memorable imprinting of the object onto one's cognitive and memory organs.[25]

I suggest that one of the interludes' most effective modes of dissemination was through aural-kinesthetic memory, particularly in regard to the strategically positioned final *ballo*. The composer and choreographer of the dance, Emilio de' Cavalieri, no doubt hoped that when the spectators finally left the confines of the theater and the city of Florence itself, the duke's *ballo* would remain in their minds and bodies, carried with them to distant lands (or "from one Pole to the other," in the more ambitious language of the official discourse). In fact, the final *ballo* fulfilled this hope when the tune that became variously known as "Ballo del Gran Duca" or "Aria di Fiorenza" became a European "pop standard" around the turn of the century.[26] With this in mind, I suggest that the dance-song's popularity beyond the confines of the court theater was integrally tied to the music's propulsively kinesthetic dimension. For the spectator this "bodily hearing"[27] was heightened by the visual perception of the performers engaged in the corporeal action of the dance, as well as in the physical gestures involved in the playing of musical instruments (a point to which I will return).

Cavalieri's *ballo* consisted of a series of musico-metrical interactions between two groups—a large chorus of nymphs and shepherds and the (abovementioned) three Graces. The various consecutive sections of the *ballo* and the general progression of textual themes are summarized in table 8.1. (See appendix 5 for the text in full.) In section 1 of table 8.1 the musical material is presented in its basic form: the music sung by the trio (example 8.2, mm. 25–54; CD track 29)—thematically and metrically distinct from that of the five-part chorus—directly follows a complete statement of the largely homophonic choral setting (example 8.1, mm. 1–24). In performance, the chorus's

Table 8.1. Diagrammatic representation of Cavalieri/Guidiccioni's *ballo* "O che nuovo miracolo," showing the progression of textual themes and the musical exchange between the chorus and trio of women singers

Section	1	2	3	4	5	6
Ensemble* & Musical Material**	C_1 C_2 C_3 w_4 w_5 w_6	C_1 w_4 C_2 w_5 C_3 w_6	C_1 w_4 C_2 w_5 C_3 w_6	C_1 w_4 C_2 w_5 C_3 w_6	C_1 C_2 C_3	C_4
Meter	6 / 4	4 6 4 6 4 6 / 4 4 4 4 4 4	3 4 3 4 3 4 / 2 4 2 4 2 4	6 3 6 3 6 3 / 4 2 4 2 4 2	4 / 4	6 / 4
Textual Theme	The gods descend bringing song & dance	Return of the Golden Age (implicitly assoc. with Ferdinand's rule)	Ref. to the bride, Christine of Lorraine (erotic imagery-burning flame)	The physical union of Ferdinand & Christine (=progeny)	Florentine prosperity	Celebrate & praise the royal couple

* C = five-part chorus

* w = trio of women (*concerto di donne*)

** 1, 2, 3, etc. = recurring musical material

more stable, weighty, almost plodding duple meter contrasts with the brisk, light, triple dance meter of the trio.[28] This effect is accentuated by the respective musical forces involved: the trio is pitted against the chorus, which comprises the entire cast of some sixty singers, in addition to the instrumentalists. In section 2, Cavalieri maintains the contrasting meters previously assigned to chorus and trio, but increases the tension by dividing up the music into smaller sections or phrases, alternating the music of each respective group with that of the other. The excitement continues to build as the two groups are continually metrically opposed in sections 3 and 4. The opening of section 3 is a particularly striking moment, because for the first time the chorus adopts a more dance-like, forward-moving triple meter, as if finally succumbing to the trio's strongly articulated triple divisions. In the same section, the trio adopts the chorus's defining duple meter, as if to suggest a certain coming together of the respective musical forces. In section 4 the music for *both* chorus and trio articulates a triple subdivision of the beat, although each is distinctive; it is of course no coincidence that during this section the text refers to the physical union of Ferdinando and Christine, and the hoped-for Medici male heir (see appendix 5, lines 41–46).

Susan McClary has suggested that the erotic friction invoked by the rapid repartee in Shakespeare's comedies (expounded by Stephen Greenblatt)[29] might have analogous musical representations.[30] The musical repartee between the (male) chorus and (female) trio in the central sections of Cavalieri's *ballo* would seem to bear out McClary's suggestion.[31] (The chorus, though representing both nymphs and shepherds, were all male singers.) The sexual implications implicit in the physical enactment of Cavalieri's *ballo* were paralleled by the progression of themes in the sung text prepared by Laura Guidiccioni.[32] If one purpose of the *ballo* was to herald the desired Medici heir, the significance of a trio of singing women—the first and only such trio in the entire set of *intermedi*—may have been considered a symbolic means of ensuring procreation. In addition, that the Medici heir was imagined as Christ-like is suggested by aspects of Guidiccioni's poem (appendix 5), which modified a preexisting Christmas text.[33] The miracle birth of the Christ child that was alluded to in the opening line of the Christmas text—"O che nuovo miracolo"—resonated, in the context of the Medici wedding, with the hoped-for Medici progeny, later described as "demigods" (see appendix 5, line 44).

They Sang, Danced, and Played Guitars: But How?

The striking effect of employing a trio of *vere donne* (true women) as the centerpiece of the final *ballo* was enhanced by incorporating the newly introduced Spanish guitar, or *chitarra spagnola* as it became widely known in early

Example 8.1. Emilio de' Cavalieri, "O che nuovo miracolo," mm. 1–24
(from *intermedio* six)

Example 8.1. continued

Example 8.2. Emilio de' Cavalieri, "O che nuovo miracolo," mm. 25–54
(from *intermedio* six)

Example 8.2. continued

seventeenth-century Italy, into the entertainment.[34] Archilei played the "chitarrina alla Spagnola," Caccini the smaller "chitarrina alla Napolettana," and
Della Scala the tambourine.[35] The Spanish guitar was so new to northern Italy
that this is the first record of its existence there;[36] because guitars were not readily available in Florence, Cavalieri had to order them specifically for the occasion from Naples, then a province of the Spanish crown.[37] Like the trio of
singing women, the guitars were reserved until the very final number of the
entire set of *intermedi*. At Florence in 1589, the tone color produced by the
rhythmic articulations of the strummed guitar was new to the courtly sphere,[38]
and primarily associated with the instrument's popular Spanish-Neapolitan
and ultimately New World origins.[39] The physicality of the strumming technique was hardly genteel, and provided a striking contrast to the more refined
and controlled technique of playing required for the lute or chitarrone. The effect produced by the use of complex strumming patterns was almost percussive,
which contributed, along with the tambourine, to the propulsively kinesthetic
quality of the music.[40] The strummed style was perhaps the most effective
means of delineating sectional shifts between duple and triple meter. For those
in the audience, the duple/triple meter shifts would not only have been per-

ceived aurally, but also visually, through the physical actions required of the performers as they strummed up and down across the instruments' strings.

The music sung by the soprano trio and accompanied by guitars was not only characterized by the absence of a bass voice but also by a lack of accompanying bass instrument (CD track 29),[41] thereby providing a striking contrast to the chorus's strongly articulated bass progression.[42] Although the harmonic dimension of the trio's music was outlined by the guitars' chordal function, much of the music was relatively static harmonically. The periods of harmonic stasis coincided with imitative entries at the unison (which were then repeated), producing a circular, almost mesmerizing effect (see example 8.2, especially mm. 25–28 and upbeat to mm. 31–33). The music's lack of "grounding" or support produces a slight impression of suspension, despite the guitar's rhythmic articulations. In this regard, I suggest that the music of the three Graces was designed to convey both their celestial or otherworldly status and the sensual and erotic qualities associated with guitar accompaniment, especially in the hands of female performers.[43] If the orchestration of Cavalieri's *ballo*—particularly the incorporation of guitar-playing women—lent an erotic undercurrent to the performance, the overarching musical form of the *ballo* in conjunction with its text made this intimation explicit.

A detailed choreography of the *ballo* survives (plate 29)[44] and a great deal can be deduced regarding the women's performance in the *ballo* by drawing together the available sources—literary, visual, musical, and choreographic. In a recent article, dance scholar Jennifer Nevile reconstructed the choreography, showing how the dance steps matched the sectional divisions of Cavalieri's music.[45] According to the choreography, seven principal dancers (four women and three men) were positioned center stage in an arc formation that was surrounded by a larger semi-circle of singers and dancers in pastoral dress who represented the mortals (see plate 29). Because of information given in Malvezzi's publication, musicologists (myself included) had assumed that the trio sections of Cavalieri's music (example 8.2, mm. 25–54) were simultaneously sung, played, *and* danced by Archilei, Caccini, and Della Scala, and that this music corresponded to the portions of Cavalieri's choreography involving the above-mentioned principal female dancers.[46] However, by detailed attention to choreographic considerations, Nevile has convincingly demonstrated how the sections of the choreography for the principal female dancers were *not* performed in conjunction with the music sung and played by the three sopranos. Rather, the sections sung by the three ladies were actually danced by the three principal male dancers, while the five-part music for the chorus of nymphs and shepherds (example 8.1, mm. 1–24) was danced by the principal female dancers. The question then remains: Were the three female singers also the principal female dancers?

Nevile has suggested that it was unlikely that the singing ladies danced the parts assigned to the principal female dancers in Cavalieri's choreography. She proposes that the female singers were instead probably part of the larger group of dancers[47]—the nymphs and shepherds—who remain physically inactive until the final sections of the *ballo*. Nevile and other scholars are astute in pointing out that there is a discrepancy between the number of principal female dancers noted in the choreography (four) and the number of singing women mentioned by Malvezzi (three).[48] There are several other inconsistencies among the various descriptive sources regarding the number of female versus male dancers.[49] Regardless of whether there were three or four female dancers, however, the possibility remains that the three singers—Archilei, Caccini, and Della Scala—were three of the principal dancers. I would argue strongly in favor of this possibility. Because the ladies' singing was integral to the piece's visual and sonic conception, it seems logical (for acoustical, visual, and conceptual reasons) that the three ladies were presented as a separate entity in order to highlight their back-and-forth dialogue with the mortals. The ladies would have needed to be prominently placed so that their voices could be heard above the dancing that accompanied their singing and playing. If they were positioned at the back of the stage like most of the nymphs and shepherds, they would have been obscured by the principal dancers who formed the smaller arc in front of them (see plate 29). Further, they needed to be grouped closely together in order to coordinate their performance. It seems most likely, then, that the singing ladies performed as three of the seven prominently positioned principal dancers at front and center of the stage. As such, they would have sung and played instruments in the trio sections to accompany the principal male dancers, and when the chorus of nymphs and shepherds sang, they (along with a possible fourth female dancer) would have danced.

Indeed, several accounts appear to indicate that the principal female dancers were also the female vocalists, and Cavallino's account even makes clear that the singing ladies were involved as the principal dancer-singer-instrumentalists: "they began to do the *balli* in which the beginning was given by three very beautiful women with three shepherds and they made a *ballo alla francese,* and each one of the women had a very beautiful guitar in hand and they sang, and danced, and then all together they leapt and they made diverse *balli.*"[50] Cavallino's account clearly indicates that the principal female dancers were the same dancers who went on to sing and accompany themselves on guitars, the instrument that Malvezzi made a point of mentioning in connection with the women's performance. Another anonymous publication mentions seven principal performers (thus corresponding with the choreography's seven principal dancers) who, after their cloud-borne descent, "came out [on to the stage] and began a *ballo,* which was followed by singing of the women alone, and the reply of the others followed. . . ."[51] The latter source in particular appears to suggest that the women's dancing and singing was done alternately, not simultaneously. Cavallino's account is also of interest because he was the only commentator to explicitly link Cavalieri's *ballo* with the French ballet tradition. Cavallino's reference to a *ballo alla francese* indicates his awareness that an elaborate ballet that was both sung and danced to a specific choreography had its roots in the tradition of the French *ballet de cour.*[52]

Audience Perceptions

While I have argued for the centrality of the singing ladies in the final *ballo*—both from the perspective of those who designed the performance (primarily Cavalieri) as well as from the perspective shared by at least some audience members—there were other spectator-auditors whose interest was evidently focused on the professional male dancers. Gadenstedt, for example, makes no mention of the singing ladies accompanying the dance-masters, but praises the expertise of the professional male dancers,[53] who had previously caught his attention in *intermedio* three. On the other hand, we can surmise that for some audience members—particularly those from Ferrara—the incorporation of the singing ladies would have had special import even though we do not have eyewitness accounts to support their interest.[54]

Indeed, the significance of a trio of singing women within the context of the *ballo*—the first and only such trio in the entire set of *intermedi*—would not have gone unnoticed by the Ferrarese contingent, especially Ercole d'Este and his wife Virginia de' Medici. Beginning with the famed *concerto di donne* in Ferrara in the early 1580s, the establishment of small groups of highly trained female singers at rival northern Italian courts had become widely recognized as a sign of courtly prestige. As singers, the Ferrarese *concerto* performed *in secreta* for a small, select audience in the intimate rooms of the Duchess of Ferrara, a far cry from the circumstances of the Uffizi theater where the Florentine ladies performed.

During the early to mid-1580s the Florentines were captivated by the aura of secrecy surrounding the Ferrarese *concerto,* and engaged in a bit of blatant cultural espionage. Alessandro Striggio was dispatched to Ferrara by his patron, Duke Francesco de' Medici, to listen to and emulate the style of music written for the *concerto* by Luzzasco Luzzaschi. Although Duke Ferdinando did not maintain his brother Francesco's original *concerto,* the new duke showed particular interest in the Ferrara *concerto* during the period leading up to his 1589 wedding. According to Ercole Cortile, Ferrarese ambassador at the Medici court, Ferdinando used composer Luca Marenzio's association with Ferrara to glean information about the Ferrarese *concerto*.[55] It was, thus, a clever artistic, propagandistic ploy by the Florentine court to utilize their singing ladies for the finale of the *Pellegrina* interludes. It seems likely that the three singers were intended to be recognized as *vere donne* (thus provoking associations with the *concerto* at Ferrara),[56] as several commentators identified them as such. An element of courtly one-upmanship was likely involved, a circumstance keenly appreciated by Ferrarese audience members.

The Last Word: Memory and Meaning

> About a hundred people took part in this *intermedio* and later, having varied many times the singing, playing, and dancing, at the end [the words] "Ferdinando, Ferdinando" resounded and thus finished the *ballo,* and the shepherds and nymphs left the stage, and the Heavens closed, ending the *intermedio*.[57]

As the concluding remarks in this anonymous description of the final *intermedio* attest, the last word was praise of Duke Ferdinando. Cavallino's account also confirms that the textual references to Ferdinando in Guidiccioni's text (appendix 5, lines 40 and 66) were heard loud and clear.[58] Though mentioned twice by name in "O che nuovo miracolo" (in addition to the reference in "O fortunato giorno"), it was undoubtedly the triple repetition of "Ferdinando" at the end of the *ballo* that reinforced the message, ensuring the text's audibility. One is struck by the fact that it was only at the very conclusion of the set of *intermedi* that these auditors finally grasped this element of the text; not coincidently, the sung text was the name of the duke himself. Thus, Ferdinando's name was the last sound to reverberate within the Uffizi theater.

Yet as we have seen throughout the *Pellegrina* interludes, the sung texts, along with the arcane symbolism of character and costume, appear to have been the least accessible elements of the entertainment for many spectator-auditors. Rather, the visceral nature of *meraviglia* (produced, very often, through the confluence of visual and aural media) enabled an *experience* that, at times, was indescribable yet unforgettable.[59] The Bavarian commentator concluded his description of the final *intermedio* by referencing both sight and sound: "Seven madrigals [*sic*] are sung to this *intermedio,* and it is indescribable, what a powerful thing it is. One has to see it in order to believe it."[60] The powerful nature of the experience ensured its memorability. Part of that power was linked to the body's experience of *meraviglia* in its various guises, from the "horreur" of the Frenchman who witnessed the hell scene to the physicality that Cavallino described when, during the final *intermedio,* spectator-auditors were moved to rise from their sesats to pick up the golden rain.

As I have demonstrated throughout this study, a number of unofficial commentators indicated that the music was as *meraviglia*-inspiring as the visual media. Gadenstedt, for example, interrupts his account of the concluding *intermedio* to extol the extraordinary nature of the music in general:

> [S]hould someone who does not have much to do or otherwise travels far for the sake of the music (to hear and see such things), he should not regret it because it [the music or performance] is almost [more] like seeing and hearing the work of angels (so to speak) than the work of humans.[61]

Gadenstedt's comments touch on the superhuman, otherworldly experience of witnessing the *Pellegrina* interludes, indicating that, on one level, he was receptive to the absolutist project that I have traced through the course of this study. Characteristically, though, Gadenstedt continues his account in a more pragmatic tone:

> There were said to have been about 150 musicians altogether, and their various [and] different instruments were all simultaneously and harmoniously in fine tune with each other, using the singing voices at the same time. As already partially indicated, these musicians were ordered by the duke of Florence as the most renowned in Italy, and contracted to Florence at great expense. [And] because Italian music was [certainly] much celebrated, all who understand and appreciate music can judge and ponder for themselves what sort of music this was.[62]

Like some other commentators, including the Frenchman, Gadenstedt indicated that he was engaged in post- (and probably pre-) performance discussions with others concerning the production details and music for the spectacle. Ultimately, though, Gadenstedt's comments regarding the music remained indeterminate and unlimited: those auditors with some musical background and knowledge could "judge and ponder for themselves" the nature of the music.

The writings of Gadenstedt and others who experienced the *Pellegrina* interludes indicate that meanings were negotiated through the dialectical interplay of authorial intent (sometimes misunderstood or understood on an intuitive level), the spectator's personal interests and interpretative slant, and the various types of extra-performance communications and exchanges that inevitably took place. Gadenstedt's final comments in his diary regarding his experience of the entertainment demonstrate that personal inquiry could only go so far:

> We would appreciate the opportunity [to see] how this [i.e., the *intermedi*] could have been produced, but it was strictly forbidden to grant anyone permission to see this. This, then, is the description of the comedy, or rather, of the *intermedi* of the comedy.[63]

Not only was Gadenstedt prevented from satisfying his curiosity regarding (presumably) the mechanical workings that produced the interludes' wondrous effects. His final sentence is a recognition that, though it was common practice to refer to the comedy, it was, after all, the *intermedi* that were in his mind (and the minds of other diarists and writers) when he left the Uffizi theater.

Postlude: The Duke's *Ballo*

The music (and not the text) of "O che nuovo miracolo" became a musical emblem for Florence, "spawning numerous progeny throughout Europe," in the words of Warren Kirkendale. It was the chorus's defining bass line and the chordal implications thereof, rather than the music of the Graces, that became widely known throughout Europe. The music of the Graces was not entirely forgotten, however. The prominent guitar parts seem to have led to the inclusion of the variously named "Aria di Fiorenza" or "Ballo del Gran Duca" in nearly every volume of guitar music published over the next seventy years. The harmonic bass progression served as the basis for numerous compositions and was transformed in the process. The latent musical possibilities in the tune's sophisticated musical structure ensured its long life, but due to its unusual length, the twenty-measure progression was frequently modified or simplified, allowing its contours to be retained more easily. Once the tune left the confines of the Uffizi theater it was subject to appropriation, manipulation, and improvisation, becoming, like all repeated bass patterns, a springboard for the virtuosity of composers and performers alike. While musicians and non-musicians may have continued to associate the tune with the city of Florence, its meaning was no longer under the direct control of the Medici family or their representatives. Differing performance contexts, instrumentations, and performers themselves enabled the *ballo* to take on a life of its own.

Appendix 1

Bastiano de' Rossi, *Descrizione* (1589), excerpts

Appendix 1a. *Proemio* (preface), complete. [Rossi, *Descrizione*, 1–6]

[From the second printing (copy in I:Bu); portions in bold highlight the involvement of Cavalieri, omitted from the first printing.]

[**p. 1**] Delle virtù annoverate tra le morali, quella della magnificenza, la qual consiste in ispese grandi, come è l'edificar tempii, e palagi, e altri edifici, che per la lor grandezza paiano diritti all'eternità, ricever forestieri con real pompa, e altre sì fatte cose, fu appo gli antichi sempre in gran pregio: e non solamente vi studiarono, e le Repubbliche, e i Re, ma e gli huomini privati ancora, con ogni lor potere, e con ogni ingegno, si sforzarono, esercitandosi in questa nobil virtù, di lasciar di se a' lor successori eterna, e gloriosa memoria. E di ciò, oltre a' teatri, agli anfiteatri, e all'altre fabbriche, che non pure in Roma, ma in molte altre città d'Italia, e per tutta la provincia dell'Europa, e per l'altre provincie ancora, si veggono infino a' di nostri, ne fanno ampia, e certa testimonianza molti scrittori: mostrando quanto i Greci, e i Romani, e molti altri popoli, non perdonando, ne a spesa, ne a qual si voglia altra cosa, s'affaticassero in ciò: raccontando Plutarco in quell'operetta della gloria degli Ateniesi, che se si fosse venuto al calculo, si sarebbe trovato, essi avere speso più in rappresentazion di tragedie, che nelle guerre contra i Barbari, [**p. 2**] e contra i medesimi Greci, per acquistare imperio, e difender la libertà. E quantunque da alcuni ne fossero agramente ripresi, e morsi, non solo fu mostrato il poco saper di color, che gli riprendevano, ma che eglino (oltre al far nota al Mondo la nobiltà dell'animo loro) il facevan con gran ragione. Quali fossero poi le pubbliche romane magnificenze, le private lo ci dimostrano, poichè per le storie possiam vedere, come Marco Emilio Scauro, huomo privato, quantunque principalissimo cittadino, ardì, per rappresentare alcuni giuochi, e altri spettacoli, fare un teatro di legno, dove capissero ottantamila persone, la cui scena fu di tre ordini: il più basso di marmo, quel di mezzo d'una sorta di vetro non più veduta, e la terza appariva d'oro: e tra le colonne di marmo, che adornavano gli ordini della scena, che furon trecensessanta, mise tremila statue di metallo. Curione, per celebrar l'esequie del padre suo, disiderando di non esser riputato inferior di magnificenza a Scauro, e, per la incomparabile spesa di quel teatro, veggendo di non potere, non avendo, ne tante ricchezze, ne quelle gran dependenze, ch'aveva Scauro, non che superarlo, ma adeguarlo; voltosi allo'ngegno, fece due teatri bilicati su certi perni, che in recitandosi, o commedia, o tragedia, o quel che si fosse, si voltavan l'un l'altro le curvature, perchè non si confondessero i recitanti, poi girando con tutto'l popolo, congiugnevan le corna insieme, e per li gladiatori facevano anfiteatro. Ma lasciando da parte le macchine, e l'altre romane magnificenze, e lo spettacolo, che con tanto numero di fiere, condotte da diverse parti del mondo, fece rappresentare in Roma Pompeo, che fra l'altre dicono, che vi furono uccisi più di cinquecento Lioni; e da queste faccendo ragione, quali fossero le pubbliche, poichè le private eran tali, e venendo al nostro proponimento; diremo, che, tra l'altre provincie dell'Europa, quella della Toscana, e in quella particolarmente la città di Firenze, come per le reliquie de' teatri, e anfiteatri, che fabbricati furono in essa, tuttavia possiamo vedere, ha sempre cosi in pubblico, come in privato, con tutte le forze **[p. 3]** sue, cercato d'imitare le dette venerabili antichità. E oltr'a' detti teatri, e anfiteatri, assai chiaramente lo mostra le pubbliche logge, i tanti maravigliosi tempii edificati da' suoi magnificentissimi cittadini, e ripieni di tante pregiate statue, e d'altri ornamenti nobili, e ricchi, e spezialmente l'eccelso tempio di Santa Maria del Fiore, posto nel mezzo della Città, con l'egregio suo Campanile, che, dagli storici, il campanil del marmo è chiamato, e con la macchina soprumana della sua cupola, la quale, e a gran ragione, e per eccellenza d'architettura, e per ricchezza di fini marmi, e per la incomparabile altezza sua, adeguando in ciò i vicini monti, e lasciando di se sempre nuova maraviglia ne' riguardanti, può anteporsi a qualunque altro edificio, mai stato fatto, o immaginato da qual si voglia piu potente Comune, o Principe, così antico, come moderno. Lasciamo stare il vaghissimo suo paese, le tante ville, e i dilettevoli giardini, che le si veggono intorno, che bene la posson mostrar degna figliuola di tanta madre. E oltr'a ciò, che i suoi cittadini, per le cose dette, e per quanto si son potute estender le forze loro, hanno avuto non meno in pregio la predetta virtù, che s'avessero quegli antichi popoli nominati, e spezialmente quegli della famiglia de' Medici: de' quali, Cosimo il vecchio, quegli che vivo dalla sua patria libera meritò d'esser chiamato padre, di magnificenza fu vero esempio, e gli edifici così pubblici, come privati, apertamente lo manifestano. E non solamente la Toscana, e l'Italia delle magnifiche opere sue, ma infin le città dell'Asia, viva ne riserban la ricordanza. E tanti, e tali furono gli edifici fatti da lui infino da' fondamenti nella sua vita, che a condurgli à perfezione, non bastò un milione, e dugento migliaia di fiorin d'oro: cosa quasi da non credersi, che in quei tempi tanto tesoro, non che in un privato, e sol cittadino, ma in molti Principi, potesse giammai trovarsi. E avendo, oltr'all'altre sue reali magnificenze, lasciato di questa virtù così gloriosa rimembranza a' suoi discendenti; non meno essi in questa, che nell'altre magnifiche operazioni, studiarono d'imitarlo. La qual cosa manifestamente, **[p. 4]** si vide nel torniamento, che in Firenze si fece al tempo del suo nipote Lorenzo, del quale egli, per suo valore, riportò'l pregio: e in quella tanto magnifica, e splendida festa, dove si rappresentò i Magi, che venivan d'Oriente dietro alla stella, la quale fu d'apparato, e d[']altro cotanto nobile, che, come dice lo storico, tenne per più mesi tutta la città ne' lavorii occupata. Delle magnificenze di Lion Decimo, essendo cotanto note, e si può dir fresche nella memoria di ciascheduno, non mi par, che mestier faccia di ragionarne: ne manco, per cagion della brevità, delle suntuose feste di Lorenzo Duca d'Urbino, fatte nella celebrazion delle proprie nozze, quando si congiunse in maritaggio con Madama Maddalena di Francia, della famiglia, illustrissima di Bologna. Ma lasciando da parte questi, e venendo a Cosimo, il primo Granduca di

Toscana, notabile esempio, nell'età nostra, di tal virtù; è maraviglia solo a pensare
con quanta grandezza d'animo ei l'abbracciasse, e ciò chiaramente lo manifestano
i tanti torniamenti, le ricche mascherate, e in tanto gran novero, le reali nozze, le
maravigliose commedie, i nobili, e grandi edifici, infino all'edificar terre da' fondamenti, come Cosmopoli nell'Elba, così detta dal nome suo, la Città del Sole in
Romagna, la fortezza di San Martino in Mugello, e quella al sasso di Simone,
quasi nella cima dell'alpi. Della qual virtù forte innamorato Francesco, secondo
Granduca di Toscana suo primogenito, e seguitando le vestigia paterne, imitò, e
con mascherate, e con tornéi, e con rappresentazion di commedie, e con l'edificare
in contado palagi maravigliosi, e superbi, e cignere d'ampio circuito di forti mura
Livorno, quei così gloriosi fatti. Della imitazion de' quali, non meno invaghito
Ferdinando presente, e terzo Granduca N.S. che si foss'egli, del magnificentissimo
animo suo (oltre alle cose magnificentissimamente operate da lui avanti) ha dato
nella sua assunzione al principato sì fatto saggio, che ben possiamo stimare, che in
qual si voglia magnificenza, non sia per essere inferiore a niun'altro della Serenissima sua famiglia. E volendo pur tuttavia con l'opere mostrare, quanto **[p. 5]** e' sia
amator di questa virtù, oltre all'altre splendide feste, fatte nelle felici sue nozze, le
quali hanno ripieno d'inaudita maraviglia, e stupore, chiunque l'ha rimirate, ha
voluto, per piu onorarle, e magnificarle, fare una rappresentazion di Commedia,
che per bellezza d'apparato, per varietà, e vaghezza di prospettiva, per nobiltà, e
ricchezza d'abiti, che intervengon negli intermedi, per la quantità d'ingegnose, e
superbe macchine, non fosse inferiore ad alcuna, che si sia, per qual si voglia
tempo, recitata in questa città. E ricordandosi con quanta fede, con quanto sapere,
con quanta diligenzia, e con quanta universale soddisfazione, quella, che'l Granduca Francesco, per le nozze del Sign. Don Cesare d'Este, e della Sign. donna Virginia Medici sorella di S. Altezza, fece in Firenze rappresentare, fosse, e dal Poeta
recata a fine, che fu Giovanni de' Bardi de' Conti di Vernio, e dall'Architettore
altresì, che fu Bernardo Buontalenti; Ricordandosi dico del valore di questi due
pellegrini ingegni, e dell'altre cose dette di sopra, e data perciò la cura della 'nvenzione
degl'intermedi al predetto Giovanni **de' Bardi**, e al Buontalenti quella delle macchine, e degl'ingegni, e del fare gli apparati, e le prospettive; **avendo al presente al
suo servigio Emilio de' Cavalieri gentil'huomo romano, nel valor del qual
molto confidava, lo deputò, insieme col predetto Giovanni Bardi, sopra la
presente Commedia, con pienissima autorità,** e **con** libera commission della
spesa; sopra essi, in questo fatto, si riposò. Ricevuto tal carico **ciascun di loro,** e
ragionato, e discorso insieme del modo, e dell'ordine, che per sì gran rappresentazion dovevan tenere, e convenuti, ciascuno si diede à pensare a quanto apparteneva all'uficio suo. E avuto poi l'artefice dal poeta particolare, e minutissima
informazione, e veduta, e considerata l'importanza del fatto, e diligentemente seco
medesimo esaminato, la copia, e l'eccellenza degli artefici, che gli facean di bisogno, per condurlo a perfezione, che numero infinito ne bisognava; fattone con
gran prestezza procaccio, e con ottimo giudicio, e avvedimento ad ognuno asse-
gnato il suo lavorío, cominciò nella **[p. 6]** sala, che, come dicemmo, nella descrizione della di sopra mentovata commedia, à questo uso del recitare, fu dal Granduca

Cosimo fabbricata, la cui lunghezza, che anche di questo v'è menzione, è di braccia 95. di 35. la sua larghezza, e di 24. l'altezza: e due braccia, e un'ottavo pende da imo a sommo il suo pavimento; Cominciò dico l'apparato in questa maniera.

∗   ∗   ∗

[Excerpt from first printing (from p. 5) that omits Cavalieri's involvement completely; (copy in I:Fr). The text in bold was omitted in the second printing.]

E ricordandosi con quanta fede, con quanto sapere, con quanta diligenzia, e con quanta universale soddisfazione quella, che'l Granduca Francesco per le nozze del Sign. Don Cesare d'Este, e della Sign. donna Virginia Medici sorella di S. Altezza, fece in Firenze rappresentare, fosse, e dal Poeta recata a fine, che fu **il Signor** Giovanni de' Bardi de' Conti di Vernio **(delle cui nobili qualità, e virtù, per averne, se non a sufficienza, almeno con diffuso ragionamento favellato nella descrizione della Commedia già recitata, per non offender di nuovo la sua modestia, e per cagion d'esser breve, in questa ne tacerò)** e dall'Architettore altresì, che fu Bernardo Buontalenti, **del sopr'umano ingegno del quale, e per le stesse cagioni, e perchè se l'opera in quella il manifestò, in questa lo potrà maggiormente manifestare, con mi piace, per ora di ragionarne;** Ricordandosi dico del valore di questi due pellegrini ingegni, e dell'altre cose dette di sopra, e data perciò la cura della'nvenzione degl'intermedi al predetto **Signor** Giovanni, e al Buontalenti quella delle macchine, e degl'ingegni, e del fare gli apparati, e le prospettive, e libera commission della spesa, sopra essi, in questo fatto, si riposò. Ricevuto tal carico, **e l'uno, e l'altro di loro, e ragionato** e discorso insieme del modo, e dell'ordine, che per sì gran rappresentazion dovevan tenere, e convenuti, ciascun si diede à pensare a quanto apparteneva all'uficio suo. E avuto poi l'artefice dal poeta particolare. . . .

Appendix 1b. *Intermedio primo.* [Rossi, *Descrizione*, 18–22 (part)]

[p. 18] Ci si rappresentò in questo intermedio le Serene celesti, guidate dall'Armonia, delle quali fa menzion Platone ne' libri della Repub. e due, oltre alle mentovate da lui, secondo l'opinion de' moderni, vi se n'aggiunse, cioè quelle della nona, e decima sfera. E perche nello stesso luogo si truova scritto, che ciascuna delle dette Serene siede sopra il cerchio, o circonferenza, di esse sfere, e gira con essa circonferenza, e girando manda fuora una sola voce distesa, e di tutte se ne fa un'Armonía consonante; il Poeta [Giovanni de' Bardi], poichè Platone vuole, che da tutte ne nasca una consonante, e sola Armonía, e l'Armonía per natura va sempre avanti a color, che cantano, la diede loro per iscorta, e mandolla avanti in iscena. E perchè lo stesso Platone in altro luogo de' medesimi libri della Repub. afferma la Doria di tutte l'altre Armoníe esser la migliore, e Aristotile altresì, pur nella sua Repub. [*sic*] lo conferma, e oltr'a ciò dice, che tutti consentono lei aver dello stabile, e del virile, e propriamente della fortezza, la Doria gli piacque di dimostrarci, e vestilla con abito, che aveva forte intenzione a questo costume: ma degli abiti più di sotto. Cadute le cortine si vide immantenente apparir nel Cielo una nugola, e in terra, avanti alla scena, d'ordine dorico, un tempietto di pietra rustica: in essa nugola una donna, che se ne veniva pian piano in terrra, sonando un liuto, e cantando, oltre a quel del liuto, ch'ella sonava, al suono di gravicembali, chitarroni, e arpi, che eran dentro alla Prospettiva, il madrigal sotto scritto. Allato le sedevano, si dall'una banda, come dall'altra, ma bene alquanto più basse, quasi ad ascoltare il suo canto, tre altre donne, tanto naturalmente, e con tal rilievo dipinte, **[p. 19]** che parean vive. La musica fu d'Emilio de' Cavalieri: le parole del trovatore degl'intermedi [Bardi].

> *Dalle celesti sfere,*
> *Di celesti Sirene amica scorta,*
> *L'Armonia son, ch'à voi vengo, o mortali:*
> *Poscia che fino al Ciel battendo l'ali*
> *L'alta fama n'apporta,*
> *Che mai sì nobil coppia il Sol non vide,*
> *Qual voi nuova Minerva, e forte Alcide.*

E mentre, che la detta nugola scendea'n terra, avendo sotto alquanti raggi solari, pareva, che di mano in man, seguitandogli, dove ell'arrivava, coprisse il Sole. Finito'l canto, finì'l cammino, e si condusse al tempietto, e dentro con la nugola, e con quei raggi solari innanzi, vi si nascose, e con esso sparì, non senza maraviglia di color, che la rimiravano: ne con minor maraviglia si condusse questa nugola in terra, che se n'andasse, perciocchè, non tanto era con la pittura, e con altro contraffatta naturalmente, quanto, che non si potendo in niuna guisa veder donde si reggesse, rassembrava nugola naturale stante nell'aria. E mentre che'l popolo procacciava d'intendere, e di vedere, dove la nugola, e'l tempietto fossero andati, senza quasi avvedersene, in manco tempo, ch'io non l'ho detto, andandosene verso'l Cielo, e quivi ascondendosi, sparì la scena di Roma, la quale anch'ella avrebbe potuto recar non picciola maraviglia, se le maraviglie, ch'ell'ascondeva, e che nel suo partir si lasciò vedere, di tanto gran tratto non s'avesser lasciata dietro la sua, che non si fosse subitamente potuta porre in dimenticanza. E ciò fu, che sparita, videro tutto quanto il Cielo stellato, con un sì fatto splendor, che lo illuminava, che l'aureste detto lume di luna: e la scena tutta in cambio di case (che a buona ragion pareva che si dovesson vedere) piena di nugole, alle vere sí somiglianti, che si dubitò, che non dovesser salire al Cielo a darne una pioggia. E mentre che tal cosa si riguardava, si vide di su la scena muoversi **[p. 20]** quattro nugole, su le quali erano le mentovate Serene, che fecero di se non solamente improvvisa, ma sì bella mostra, e sì graziosa, e con tanta ricchezza, e magnificenza d'abiti, che come di sotto potrà vedersi, eccedevano il verisimile: e cominciarono tanto dolcemente a cantare questo suono in su liuti, e viole, che ben potevano, se la lor vista non gli avesse tenuti desti, con la dolcezza del canto loro, addormentar di profondo sonno, come vere Serene, gli ascoltatori.

> *Noi, che, cantando, le celesti sfere*
> *Dolcemente rotar facciamo intorno,*
> *In così lieto giorno,*
> *Lasciando il Paradiso,*

Meraviglie più altere,
Cantiam d'una bell'alma, e d'un bel viso.

Le parole di questo canto, e gli altri madrigali, che seguono appresso in questo intermedio, furono composizione d'Ottavio Rinuccini giovane gentil'huomo di questa
patria, per molte rare sue qualità ragguardevole, e la Musica di Cristofano Malvezzi
da Lucca Prete, e Maestro di Cappella in questa Città. Cantato, ch'ell'ebbero, immantenente s'aperse il Cielo in tre luoghi, e comparve, con incredibil velocità, a
quell'aperture, tre nugole. In quella del mezzo la Dea della Necessità con le Parche, e
nell'altre i sette Pianeti, e Astrea: e tale fu lo splendore, che vi si vide per entro, e tale
gli abiti degl'Iddei, e degli Eroi che si paoneggiavano in esso Cielo, ricchi d'oro, e di
lucidi abbigliamenti, che potette ben parere ad ognuno, che'l Paradiso s'aprisse, e che
Paradiso fosse divenuto tutto l'Apparato, e la Prospettiva. Aperto il Cielo, in esso, e
in terra cominciò a sentirsi una così dolce, e forse non più udita melodía, che ben
sembrava di Paradiso. Alla quale, oltre a gli strumenti, che sonarono al canto
dell'Armonía, e delle Serene, vi s'aggiunsero del Cielo, tromboni, traverse, e cetere.
Finita la melodía, le Parche, le quali sedevano per [**p. 21**] egual distanza, e toccanti
il fuso, intorno alla madre Necessità nel mezzo del Cielo, e che, come dice Platone,
cantano all'Armonía di quelle Serene, Lachesi le passate, Cloto le presenti, e Atropo
le cose a venire, cominciarono, richiamandole al Cielo, a cantare: e per far più dolce
Armonía, parve al Poeta, che i Pianeti, che sedevano nell'altre aperture del Cielo,
allato à quella del mezzo, cantassero anch'eglino insieme con le tre Parche, e con esso
loro la Madre Necessità. Al qual canto movendosi le Serene in su le lor nugole, e andandosene verso il Cielo, cantando, e faccendo un gentil Dialogo, che fu questo, ri-
spondevan loro a vicenda.

P. Dolcissime Sirene,
   Tornate al Cielo, e'n tanto
   Facciam, cantando, a gara un dolce canto.
S. Non mai tanto splendore
   Vide Argo, Cipro, o Delo.
P. A voi, regali amanti,
   Cediam noi tutti gran Numi del Cielo.
S. Per lei non pur s'infiora,
   Ma di Perle, e rubin s'ingemma Flora.
P. Di puro argento ha l'onde
   Arno, per voi Granduce, e d'or le sponde.
S. Tessiam dunque ghirlande a sì gran Regi,
   E sien di Paradiso i fiori, e i fregi.
P. A lor fronte regal s'intrecci stelle,
S. E Sole, e Luna, e cose alte, e più belle.

Fu veramente cosa mirabile, il vedere andarsene quelle nugole verso il Cielo, quasi
cacciate dal Sole, lasciandosi sotto di mano in man, che salivano, un chiaro splendore. Arrivate le Serene al Cielo su dette nugole, soavemente cantando, finì il dialogo,

e cominciarono tutti insieme, e le Parche, e i Pianeti, ed elleno, in su i mentovati strumenti, novellamente a cantare.

[**p. 22**]

> *Coppia gentil d'avventuro si Amanti,*
> *Per cui non pure il Mondo*
> *Si fa lieto, e giocondo,*
> *E spera aver da voi*
> *Schiera d'invitti, e gloriosi Eroi.*
> *Ma fiammeggiante d'amoroso zelo*
> *Canta, ridendo, e festeggiando'l Cielo.*

Alla fine di questo canto, tutte le sette nugole sparvono, serrossi il Cielo, si dileguaron le stelle, e con esse le nugole, che annebbiavan la Prospettiva, e parve, che esso Cielo fosse tutto alluminato dal Sole.

[An extensive description of the costumes for *intermedio* one follows in Rossi, *Descrizione*, pp. 22–32.]

Appendix 1c. *Intermedio secondo.* [Rossi, *Descrizione*, 37–41]

[**p. 37**] Divenne tutta quanta la scena un vago giardino, che ricoperse in modo le case, che più non si vedeva alcun segno d'esse, e pareva tutto intorniato da verdissimi, e vivi aranci, e da limoni, e da cedri, carichi tutti di vecchi frutti, e di nuovi, e biancheggianti di fiori: e sentendosi l'odore dell'acque nanfe, che si spargean per la scena, faceva quasi credergli naturali, e che procedesse l'odor da essi. Aveva oltr'a ciò in questo giardino, per di molte parti, viali diritti, e belli, coperti da graticolati volti a botte, sopra i quali camminavan diverse piante di verzura, e di viti, che adombravan tutto'l giardino: e alle viti, perchè rappresentava di Primavera, tra i pampani una gran quantità di fiori: appiè delle quali, per quanto era lunga la via, apparivano certe spallierette d'erbe odorifere: e tra le spalliere, per egual distanzia, stavano alcuni vasetti molto ben fatti, pieni qual di persa, qual di sermollino, qual di gelsomini di Catalogna, e quali d'altre odorate erbe, e allegri fiori. In su' crocicchi de' quai viali, surgevano certe cupole, pure anch'elle a graticolato, coperte d'una verzura tutta fiorita, retta da termini messi d'oro: e sotto alle cupole in certe nicchie, statue finte di marmo. E per li quadri poi del giardino, tra gran quantità di diversi frutti, qual fiorito, quale sfiorito, e carico di picciole frutte di poco tempo avanti allegate, apparivano fontane, che da più zampilli, parea, che in aria schizzassero acqua, e tutte adorne di statue, e d'altri ornamenti a fontane convenienti. Lungo le vie appiè di quei pergolati dentro ne' quadri, per tutto pien di rosai, e qual bianco, e qual vermiglio, e quale incarnato, e tra'l vermiglio, e tra lo'ncarnato alcun gelsomino. Le vie, si come il prato, ch'egli avea innanzi, ch'era il pavimento del palco, coperte d'erba [**p. 38**] minutissima, e verde tanto, che parea nera [*sic;* vera], dipinta di fior bianchi, e gialli, e rosseggiante di fragole. Tra quei frutti si vedevan per lo giardino in varie attitudini, vari animali, come lepri, conigli, spinosi, testuggini, e sì fatti: e sopra essi frutti molti uccelletti, i quali poteron credersi vivi, e veri, sentendosi massimamente contraffare dentro alla scena, così piacevolmente il lor canto, che pareva, che una infinità d'Usignuoli, e d'altri uccelletti, che cantano soavemente, fossero quivi compariti, e, gareggiando, venuti in pruova, chi di loro, col suo canto, facesse più dolce, e più soave armonía: con la quale, mentre vagheggiando il giardino, si trattenevan gli ascoltatori; ecco cedere il canto degli uccelletti a una dolcissima melodia di vari strumenti, e cominciare a venir su nel mezzo del prato d'esso giardino, cioè sul palco, la cima d'un monte, e a poco a poco alzarsi infino all'altezza di braccia dodici, che potette si può ben dir quasi parer miracolo, conciosia che'l palco dalla più alta sua parte non eccedesse le cinque braccia. Nel qual monte, tutto coperto d'erbe, e di fiori, sedevano in su certi fioriti seggi, fatti ne massi, sedici Ninfe, che co' vaghi loro abiti l'ornavano di maniera, che pareva, che su quel monte uscente di terra, si fossero raccolte tutte le bellezze di questo mondo. Appiè del qual monte, tra certe grotte, e massi scoscesi si vedevan correr certi acquitrini, come, per li naturali monti, spesse volte veggiamo tra masso, e masso avvenire. E avanti che'l detto monte si fosse condotto sopra'l palco, all'altezza, ch'abbiamo detta, gli comparve due grotte, una dall'una, e l'altra dall'altra banda tutte intorno intorno di spugne, dalle quale uscendo alcune gocciole d'acqua, ed essendo ricoperte in alcuna parte di verde musco, pareva, che l'acqua, che naturalmente da esse suole spruzzare, avesse ciò cagionato. Nell'una di queste grotte a manritta erano le figliuole di Piéro, e nell'altra le nove Muse: e nel mezzo in sul monte stavano le Ninfe Amadriadi: perchè il Poeta ci rappresentò in questo intermedio, la contesa del canto tra esse figliuole di Piéro, e le Muse, e la trasformazione in Piche delle perdenti. Occuparono le figliuole di Piéro, come **[p. 39]** più altiere, e poco delle Muse curanti, il primiero luogo e primiere alla presenza delle Ninfe giudicatrici vollon cantare: e questo, sopra liuti, e viole, fu'l canto loro: composizione d'Ottavio Rinuccini soprannominato, si come i due madrigali seguenti, e Musica di Luca Marenzio della nobil Città di Brescia, del valor del quale in sì nobil'arte, ne rendono viva testimonianza le pubbliche opere sue.

> *Chi dal Delfino aita,*
> *Nelle tempeste sue, cantando, impetra,*
> *E quei ch'al suon di cetra*
> *La perduta consorte*
> *Trae dell'Infernal porte:*
> *Chi pietre, e marmi duri,*
> *Cantando, alletta a formar torri, e muri,*
> *Non però, come noi canta soave.*
> *Che più? Se'l Ciel non have*
> *Si dolce melodia,*
> *Ch'appo'l nostro cantar roca non sia?*

Finito, cominciarono similmente sopra liuti, e viole, a cantare dall'altre parte le Muse.

> *Se nelle voci nostre*
> *Risuona di dolcezza accento, o suono*
> *E grazioso dono*

Del Ciel, da cui procede
Quanto di bello il Mondo intende, e vede.
Or voi di queste Linfe
Abitatrici Ninfe,
Se del nostro cantar diletto avete,
Al Ciel grazie rendete,
E di palme, e d'alloro
Incoronate il più soave coro.

Udito, che le Ninfe ebbero le Muse, con questo canto sopra arpi, lire, lire arciviolate, e soprani di viole sentenziarono in questa guisa.
[**p. 40**]

O figlie di Piéro,
E qual follia v'ingombra?
E 'l vostro canto un'ombra,
Appo sì dolce canto:
A lor si deve il vanto
D'ogni dolcezza: o Cielo, o Terra, o Venti,
Dite s'udiste mai sì dolci accenti.

E tosto, che le Ninfe, con la fine del lor canto ebber giudicato, miracolosamente si vide le donzelle perdenti diventar piche, e, gracchiando, e saltellando su per la scena, nascondersi agli occhi altrui, e in quel tanto sparire il monte, e le grotte, e dileguarsi il giardino. Le Ninfe Amadriadi, che sedevano in sul monte eran sedici, e tutte a i colori del vestito differenti in qualche cosa l'una dall'altra, e ognuna d'esse di più colori: perchè quale fu vestita di turchino, e di rosso, qual di pagonazzo, e di bianco, qual di verde, e di giallo, qual d'azzurro, e ranciato, e qual di drappi cangianti: e tutti i vestimenti di raso. Il cinto, e l'ornamento, che intorno allo scollato avean della vesta, tutto d'oro, e dalla parte dinanzi si chiudeva con una maschera tutta piena di begli smalti, e 'l cinto, e 'l rimanente dell'ornamento di gioie. Erano accincignate, come s'accincigna Diana, e pien di frecce il turcasso al fianco, e l'arco ad armacollo dietro alle spalle, perchè avieno strumenti in mano. L'acconciatura fu vaga, e bella, e a tutte cadevano bionde trecce sopra le spalle, e certi veli d'oro, e d'ariento di più colori, e lunghi quanto la vesta, della detta acconciatura pendeva loro: i quali gonfiando per ogni poco di vento, rendevano quel nobile abito, e ricco, più magnifico, e più adorno. E perchè sono nominate per lo general nome degli arbori, e della quercia spezialmente, come vogliono alcuni antichi scrittori, e che anche nascano con essi, o veramente con essi muoiano, come si vede nella favola d'Erisíttone, nel tagliamento di quella quercia; di fronda di quercia parve al poeta d'inghirlandarle, e l'abito similmente di tronchi, e di foglia [**p. 41**] della stessa quercia era ricamato, e similmente i calzati, oltre all'esser tutti sparsi di ricche gioie.

Le Cantatrici dalla man destra, vestita ognuna d'esse di più colori, qual d'azzurro, giallo, incarnato, e verde, e quale degli altri differenti a' predetti. L'abito di queste donzelle, di raso, come l'abito delle Ninfe, a superbi, e lascivi ricami d'oro, con ornamento, intorno al loro scollato, d'oro, e ricco di gioie, e cinto ricascante lor fino a' piedi, e per artificio, e per ornamento di gioie, di gran valore. Erasi poscia tutto ornato quel nobile abito, per mostrare la lor vanità, e alterezza, di veli di più colori, in belle guise, e superbe. Dalla nobilissima acconciatura, e lasciva, piena di risplendenti gioie, e di perle, cadeva un rilucente, e gran velo, che per diversi stravolgimenti si conduceva al fin della vesta. Avieno certe belle maschere d'oro per ispallacci, e ornate di cerchia d'oro tutte le braccia: in somma un'abito lascivo, superbo, e vano, ma ricco fuor di misura. Rassembravano, come tutte l'una dietro all'altra nate in otto anni, da' quindici a' ventitre. Le Muse furon vestite di color dissimili alle Pieridi, e alle Ninfe, di ricco, ma semplice, e onesto abito. La vesta di sopra di velluto verde, che pendea più tosto all'oscuro, e quella di sotto d'un nobil drappo cangiante incarnato, e bianco, adorno d'un semplice fregio, ma di molta magnificenza. L'acconciature semplici, ma risplendenti d'oro, e di gioie, e da esse pendeva un velo in maniera molto modesta: in mano strumenti, ed erano coronate di penne di più colori, così dagli antichi poeti finte, non tanto per la vittoria ottenuta per le figliuole di Piéro, ma eziandio per quella, ch'ell'ottenner delle Serene. E qui finisce il secondo, e vegniamo ora al terzo intermedio.

Appendix 1d. *Intermedio terzo.* [Rossi, *Descrizione,* 42–48]

[**p. 42**] Sparito il monte, e le grotte, e dileguatesi gracchiando, e saltellando le piche, ritornò la scena al primiero modo, e cominciò'l secondo atto della commedia: e finito, furono ricoperte le case, da querce, da cerri, da castagni, da faggi, e da altri arbori di questa sorta, e tutta la scena diventò bosco. Nel mezzo del bosco una scura, grande, e dirocciata caverna, e le piante, vicine a quella, senza foglia, arsicciate, e guaste dal fuoco. L'altre più lontane, la cui cima parea, che toccasse il Cielo, erano belle, e fresche, e cariche delle frutte, ch'elle producono. Apparita (nuova maraviglia) la selva, si vide dalla sinistra venire nove coppie tra huomini, e donne, in abito quasi alla greca: ma tutti, e per qualche colore, e per gli ornamenti, come diremo poco di sotto, differenti l'un dall'altro in alcuna parte, e al suono di viole, di traverse, e tromboni, cominciarono, giunti in iscena, a cantare.

> *Ebra di sangue in questo oscuro bosco*
> *Giacea pur dianzi la terribil fera,*
> *E l'aria fosca, e nera*
> *Rendea col fiato, e col maligno tosco.*

Le parole di questo, e de' seguenti madrigali dello'ntermedio presente, furono d'Ottavio Rinuccini sopra mentovato, e la Musica del Marenzio. E mentre, che gli usciti in iscena cantavano il madrigal sopraddetto, si vide, dall'altra banda, venire altre nove coppie d'huomini, e donne, e ripigliare, sopra gli stessi strumenti, il canto, dicendo.

> *Qui di carne si sfama*
> *Lo spaventoso serpe: in questo loco*
> [**p. 43**]
> *Vomita fiamma, e foco, e fischia, e rugge:*
> *Qui l'erbe, e i fior distrugge:*

> *Ma dov'è 'l fero mostro?*
> *Forse avrà Giove udito il pianto nostro.*

Ne appena ebber quest'ultime parole mandate fuora, che un serpente, drago d'inestimabil grandezza, dal poeta figurato per lo serpente Pitone, vomitando fuoco, e col fumo d'esso oscurando l'Aria d'intorno, cavò fuori dell'orrida, e tetra caverna il capo. E quasi coperto da quelle arsicciate piante, non vedesse quegli huomini a lui vicini, si stava lisciando al Sole, che bene al Sole si poteva assomigliar lo splendore della così bene allumata scena, e alquanto stato il rimise dentro. Onde i miseri, veduta la cruda fiera, tutti insieme, sopra gli strumenti predetti, con flebile, e mesta voce, cantarono queste parole, pregando Iddio, che volesse liberargli da così acerbo, e strano infortunio.

> *Oh sfortunati noi,*
> *Dunque a saziar la fame*
> *Nati sarem, di questo mostro infame?*
> *O Padre, O Re del Cielo,*
> *Volgi pietosi gli occhi*
> *Allo'nfelice Delo,*
> *Ch'a te sospira, a te piega i ginocchi,*
> *A te dimanda aita, e piange, e plora.*
> *Muovi lampo, e saetta,*
> *A far di lei vendetta,*
> *Contra'l mostro crudel, che la divora.*

E mentre, che durò 'l canto, cavò egli nella stessa guisa due altre volte il capo, e 'l collo della spelonca. E finito, con l'aliacce distese, pieno di rilucenti specchi, e d'uno stran colore tra verde, e nero, e con una smisurata boccaccia aperta, con tre ordini di gran denti, con lingua fuori infocata, fischiando, e fuoco, e tosco vomendo, in vista spaventoso, e crudele, quasi accorto degl'infelici, che erano in quella selva, **[p. 44]** per uccidergli, e divorargli, tutto in un tempo saltò fuor di quella spelonca: ne appena fu allo scoperto, che dal Cielo, venne un'huomo armato d'arco, e saette, che gli soccorse, e per Apollo fu figurato: perciocchè ci volle il Poeta in questo intermedio rappresentar la battaglia Pitica, nella guisa, che c'insegna Giulio Polluce, il quale dice, che in rappresentandosi con l'antica musica questa pugna, si dividea in cinque parti: nella prima rimirava Apollo se 'l luogo era alla battaglia conveniente, nella seconda sfidava 'l serpe, e nella terza, col verso iambico, combatteva: nel qual iambico si contiene ciò che si chiama l'azzannamento, dichiarato poco di sotto. Nella quarta col verso spondéo, con la morte di quel serpente, si rappresentava la vittoria di quello Iddio. E nella quinta, saltando, ballava un'allegro ballo, significante vittoria. Essendo a noi, dalla malvagità, e dalla lunghezza del tempo, tolto il poter così fatte cose rappresentar con que' modi musici antichi, e stimando il poeta, che tal battaglia, rappresentata in iscena, dovesse arrecare, si come fece, sommo diletto agli spettatori, la ci rappresentò con la nostra moderna musica, a tutto suo potere, sforzandosi, come intendentissimo di quest'arte, e d'imitare, e di rassomigliar quell'antica; fece venire Apollo dal Cielo, e con incredibil maraviglia di chiunque lo rimirò: perciocchè con piu prestezza non sarebbe potuto venire un raggio, e venne, quasi miracolo (perciocchè niente si vide, che'l sostenesse) con l'arco in mano, e'l turcasso al fianco pien di saette, e vestito d'un'abito risplendente di tela d'oro, nella guisa, che fu posto nel primo intermedio, tra i sette pianeti in Cielo. E ben vero, che'l detto abito non era tanto infocato, e, perchè fosse destro, e spedito, non circondato da raggi. Arrivato in questa maniera sul palco, alla melodía di viole, di traverse, e di tromboni, cominciò la prima parte della battaglia, che è di riconoscere il campo, e con gran destrezza, ma da lontano, intorno al serpe ballando, acconciamente quel riconoscimento ne dimostrò: e ciò con prestezza fatto, e mostratosi al fier serpente, saltando, e ballandogli intorno, con bello atteggiamento, e gentile, ci [**p. 45**] rappresentò la disfida, e si vide il serpe fischiando, scotendo l'ale, e battendo i denti, accignersi fiero, e con grande orrore alla pugna. Nella terza parte ci mostrò egli, pur tuttavia ballando, e saltando, il combattimento, e frecciando spesso il serpente, e'l serpente lui seguitando: e al suon della melodía ruggendo, e dirugginando i denti, con maravigliosa attitudine, si troncava le saette, ch'egli avea fitte nel dosso, e squarciavasi le ferite, e da esse versava in gran copia il sangue, brutto, e nero, che parea inchiostro: e con urli, e con gemiti spaventevoli, tuttavia mordendosi, e perseguitando chi lo feriva, cadde, e morì. Caduto, e morto, egli tutto lieto, gonfio, e altiero, ballando sopra musica significante vittoria, espresse col ballo felicemente quell'atto di quella lieta alterezza: e ballato si ritirò dal serpente morto, e gli pose il piè dritto, quasi trionfante, sopra la testa. E, ciò fatto, s'accostarono due coppie di quegli huomini, che erano lungo la selva a veder la pugna, quasi non credessero, e volesser chiarirsi del morto drago: e vedendolo in terra, tutto imbrodolato, in uno scuro, e quasi nero lago di sangue, e Apollo, che'l piè gli teneva sopra la testa, cominciarono in allegro tuono, e sopra dolci strumenti, lodando quel Dio, e chiamando i compagni a tanta letizia, a cantare in questa maniera.

> *O valoroso Dio,*
> *O Dio chiaro, e sovrano,*
> *Ecco'l serpente rio*
> *Spoglia giacer della tua invitta mano.*
> *Morta è l'orribil fera,*
> *Venite a schiera a schiera,*
> *Venite, Apollo, e Delo*
> *Cantando alzate, o belle Ninfe al Cielo.*

A quel canto s'accostarono tutti gli altri, che uscirono al principio dello'ntermedio, i quali s'erano ritirati lungo la selva, a veder da lontan la pugna, e andarono a veder con maraviglia il morto serpente, il quale alla fine del canto, fu [**p. 46**] via strascinato, ne più si vide. E sparito il mostro, Apollo, alla solita melodía, festeggia, e balla, e con grazioso atteggiamento della persona, esprime la quinta parte di quella musica, che fu la letizia dell'aver liberato i Delfi da peste sì orribile, ed importuna, com'era quella di quel serpente. Finito il suo ballo, i Delfi, così huomini, come donne, che gli si ritrovavano intorno, cominciarono, ed egli insieme con esso loro, rallegrandosi, e ringraziando Iddio d'una tanta grazia, una carola, cantando, sopra liuti, tromboni, arpi, violini, e cornette, dolcemente queste parole.

O mille volte, e mille
Giorno lieto, e felice:
O fortunate ville,
O fortunati colli, a cui pur lice
Mirar l'orribil'angue
Versar l'anima, e'l sangue,
Che col maligno tosco
Spogliò'l prato di fior, di frondi'l bosco.

E carolando, e cantando, se n'andarono per la medesima via, ond'eran venuti: sparve la selva, e lo'ntermedio finí. E perchè dagli antichi fu finta la battaglia Pitica in Delo, alla presenza de i Delfi, il poeta [Bardi] ci rappresentò quei popoli, che furono tra huomini, e donne diciotto coppie, in abiti tendenti al greco, e de' colori si rimise nella discrezion dell'Artefice [Buontalenti]. E perchè alcuni vogliono, che Delo fosse edificata da Delfo figliuolo di Nettuno, a tutti adattò in mano, o in capo, o nella vesta alcuna cosa marina. La prima copia un bel giovane huomo, e una bella giovane donna: l'huomo con roba di raso azzurro scollata, che gli arrivava a mezza la gamba, con ricami, e frange d'oro dappiè, e tutta l'abbottonatura di botton d'oro: stretta infino alla cintola, da indi in giù al quanto più larga, e due maniche strette, e lunghe quanto la vesta gli pendevano dalle spalle. Sopra aveva un'altra vesticciuola più corta d'Ermisino verdegiallo, [p. 47] con bendoni a ricamo d'oro dappiè. E sopra questa un'altra robetta a mezza la coscia, di raso incarnato con fregio intorno, e dagli spallacci pendevano alcuni bei nappon d'oro, ed era cinto con una cintura di raso rosso, la cui serratura, erano due belle maschere d'oro, che serrando si congiugnevano insieme. In capo una bella, e bionda ricciaia, e in piede i calzari di raso rosso, lavorati a nicchie, e a chiocciolette, e ricamati d'oro, come la vesta. In mano strumenti. La donna il busto di raso turchino a ricamo co' suoi spallacci a bendoni con frange d'oro. La vesta di sotto di raso bianco con un fregio d'oro drappiè, e una sopravvesta di drappo incarnato con bel ricamo: squartata, e le squartature abbottonate con certi riscontri d'oro. Dalla serratura del cinto, che era una testa di marzocco, che avea due risplendenti gioie per occhi, pendevano due veli d'oro, che, serpeggiando, le cadevano con bello ornamento fin quasi a' piedi. L'acconciatura, tutta adorna di branche di corallo, e di veli, e un velo turchino grande sotto la gola, che con amendue i capi, per lo'ntrecciamento passando de' suoi capelli, e dalla parte di dietro cadendole infino a' piedi, faceva suentolando una bella vista.

Nell'altra coppia un'huomo con una vesta lunga di raso azzurro abbottonata infino in terra a riscontri d'oro, e alcune borchie d'oro sopra le spalle: gli spallacci verdi, e le maniche di raso rosso, con ricamo di seta nera, e similmente i calzoni. In capo un turbante a chiocciola, in cima al quale aveva una chioccioletta marina, e nella serratura del cinto due nicchie dentrovi alcune gioie di pregio.

La donna con busto di raso rosso con un pregiato fregio alla fine d'esso. Le si partia dalla scollatura un'ornamento d'oro massiccio, che l'arrivava sotto le poppe.

Gli spallacci bianchi ricamati di seta nera, e le maniche di colore all'arance simile. La vesta lunga, per fino a' piedi, mavì, fregiata a ricamo d'oro, e di seta. Una robetta sopra di raso bianco, a ogni palmo traversata con due liste gialle, che n'avieno una turchina nel mezzo. Il cinto era tutto d'oro, e da una testa di marzocco, che copriva la serratura, pendevano [**p. 48**] alcuni veli di seta, e d'oro, che, con alcune ricascate artificiose, le facean dinanzi un bello ornamento. Al collo un vezzo di grosse perle, e di sotto la gola le si partiva un velo turchino, che andava annodandole con bel gruppo le bionde trecce, le quali faciono una cupola con tre ordini, e in cima una palla, dalla quale surgeva una branca di bel corallo. Un velo d'oro, e'ncarnato le pendeva con belli svolazzii infino in su' piedi, e sopra la fronte le cadevano alcuni ricci piene di perle, e di coralletti. Gli abiti, e gli ornamenti di tutti gli altri, così huomini, come donne, ne di bellezza, ne di ricchezza, ne d'ornamenti, ne d'artificio, ne di splendore, non cedevan punto a' primieri. Ed erano tutte adorne l'acconciature di quelle donne, e similmente le veste, di coralli, di nicchie, di perle, di madreperle, di conchiglie, e d'altre cose marine, e tutte diverse l'una dall'altra. E anche agli huomini, e in capo, e ne' panni sì fatte cose. E tanto, e più vaghi, e più belli fur giudicati, quanto furono differenti d'artificio, e d'ornamento, e tutti simiglianti all'abito greco, che si mostrò veramente l'artefice, che ne fece i disegni, ricchissimo d'invenzione, poichè potette esser tanto vario, e tanto vago nell'unità. Ma passiamo alquanto, perciocchè se particolarmente dovessimo scrivere tutto ciò ch'avieno i personaggi di questo intermedio intorno, allungheremmo troppo'l volume. Faccia ragione il leggitor da' descritti, in che maniera il rimanente fosse vestito: non essendo, come abbiam detto, niun di loro all'altro inferiore in alcuna parte.

Appendix 1e. *Intermedio quarto* [Rossi, *Descrizione*, 49–54]

[**p. 49**] Comparve in questo intermedio, avanti, che si mutasse la prospettiva, sopra un pregiato carro d'oro, e di gemme, una donna figurata dal Poeta per una maga: scinta, e scalza, le chiome sparte sopra le spalle, e avviluppate, d'altiera vista, di viso bella, vestita di velluto verde, un lungo velo azzurro in capo, che l'andava infin quasi a' piedi: nella man destra una sferza, con l'altra frenava due fieri draghi orribili, e spaventosi, con grandi aliacce di più colori, e piene di specchi: e gittando alcuna volta fuoco per bocca, e la lingua tenendo fuori, pareva, sì vivamente eran finti, che, ansando, per la fatica, ciò operassono. Giunto questo carro a mezza la scena, la maga raffrena i draghi, posa la sferza, raccomanda le redini a una palla del carro, prende un liuto, ch'ella v'ha dentro, e a quel suono, e all'armonía di lire grandi, e di bassi, di viole, di liuti, d'un violino, d'arpe doppia, bassi di tromboni, e organi di legno, che sonavano dentro, mentre ch'ella attraversava la scena, cominciò soavemente a cantare, e nel suo canto a chiamare, e costrignere i Démoni della region più pura dell'aria, appellata fuoco, a dire, quando il mondo doveva godere supreme felicità, ed essi vengono in uno stante, e nella più bella forma, e più nobile in una infocata nugola a ubbidire, dicendo nel canto loro, che per questo real maritaggio gli s'apparecchiano. Di questi Démoni, che'l Poeta ci rappresenta, fa menzion

Platone in più luoghi, e dice, che si come la terra, e l'acqua hanno amendune i loro particolari animali, gli ha, e l'aria grossa altresì, e la più pura, infino al concavo della Luna, e che questi tali s'appellan Démoni: la cui natura, si come egli dice, sapientissima, è di rapportar le cose divine agli huomini, si come, e l'umane agl'Iddei. E perchè ciò facciano, [**p. 50**] gli fa il Poeta costrignere da quella Maga, con questo canto.

> *Io, che dal Ciel cader farei la Luna,*
> *A voi, che in alto sete,*
> *E tutto'l Ciel vedete, Eroi, comando,*
> *Ditene quando senza'nvidia alcuna*
> *Il Cielo in Terra ogni sua grazia aduna.*

La Musica di queste parole, e l'ordine della Melodía degli strumenti predetti, fu opera di Giulio Caccini Musico pregiato de' nostri tempi. Le quai parole, si come il rimanente de' madrigali di questo quarto intermedio, furono opera di Giovambatista Strozzi, gentil'huomo ornato di nobili, e belle scienze, del cui pellegrino ingegno, molte opere, e spezialmente di Poesia, cene fanno testimonianza. Cantato ch'ell'ebbe, e riposto nel carro il liuto, ripresa la sferza, e le cavezzine, sferzando i draghi, che sferzati, cominciarono a distender l'ali, scotieno il capo rabbiosamente, e, mordendo il freno, sbuffavan fuoco, mossero il carro, ed ella andò a suo cammino, e si cominciò a vedere una nugola in aria di forma tonda, ma a bozzi, come veggiamo le vere nugole, e pareva un monte di fuoco, senza che segno di creatura umana vi si vedesse: e comparita improvvisamente in iscena: perciocchè (non solo questa, ma niuna altra sospesa macchina di tanto spettacolo) non si vide mai da che fosse retta; infino che non fu nel mezzo di essa scena, si stette chiusa, e arrivata al mezzo s'aperse, e fecesi un semicircolo: ne mi par punto da domandare, ne da scrivere eziandio, se con maraviglia di chi la vide e non solamente potette nascer la maraviglia nel vedere così gran macchina aprirsi in aria, ma nel vederla così carica di persone, vestite d'abito, che per oro, e per artificio risplendevan fuor d'ogni stima, le quali rappresentavano i Démoni, che la Maga col suo canto aveva chiamati, e per l'angelica, e dolce armonía, che in aprendosi, cantando i predetti Démoni al suono degli strumenti detti di sopra, fecion sentire.

[**p. 51**]

> *Or che le due grand'Alme insieme aggiunge*
> *Un saldo amor celeste,*
> *D'ogni alta gioia il Mondo si riveste:*
> *Ogni alma al bene oprar s'accende, e punge:*
> *Volane lunge la cagion del pianto.*
> *Felice eterno canto,*
> *Che più che mai soave in Ciel risuona,*
> *Di sua felicità speranza dona.*

La musica fu del maestro di cappella predetto. I Démoni, che cantavano nella nugola, e perchè si fingevan di quegli, abitanti, come dicemmo, nella region più pura dell'aria chiamata fuoco, vicini al concavo della Luna, il poeta gli fece alati: l'ali finte d'ermisin rosso infocato, spruzzate d'argento, e sotto penne mavì, spruzzate anch'elle pur d'ariento. I capelli assai lunghi, e crespi, d'un colore mischiato d'ariento, e di fuoco, con faccia rilucentissima, e bella: vestiti infino a mezza coscia di teletta d'argento, e rossa, e da mezza coscia al ginocchio di tela d'oro, e di seta verde, e la vesta di sopra sparata a guisa di camicia, e si chiudeva quello sparato da una maschera d'oro, che si conducea fino al petto, daila [*sic;* dalla] quale pendeva un bel fermaglio di gioie. I calzari cilestri a ricamo d'oro, con fregio d'oro su per gamba infino al ginocchio, e alla fine del fregio un camméo: erano alquanto arrovesciati, e'l rovescio di teletta d'argento rossa. In mano strumenti, su' quali, come abbiam detto soavemente cantavano. Ed era questo cosí vago, e ricco loro abito, con l'artificiose ale, e con quella infocata zazzera, di tanto pregio, e splendore, e di cotanta bellezza, che agnoli rassembravan di Paradiso. Richiusa, e sparita la Nugola, la scena in uno stante fu coperta tutta di scogli, d'antri, caverne, piene di fuochi, e di fiamme ardenti, e pareva, che, serpeggiando per l'aria mandassero il fumo al Cielo. Coperta la scena di questo orrore, s'aperse il palco, e uno via molto maggiore ne dimostrò: perche, in aprirsi, aperse l'inferno, e uscinne due schiere di furie, e diavoli spaventosi: ma [**p. 52**] avvegnachè fosser tali, per tutto ciò comparvero quivi in vista sì dolorosa, e dimessa, che pareva, che per paura avessero abbandonata la lor fierezza. Posersi pianamente, e dolenti in su quegli scogli a sedere, e con una musica malinconica, e lamentevole (opera del nostro poeta [Bardi]) cominciarono, cantando, sopra arpi, viole, e cetere, à lamentarsi con tai parole del bene, che n'avevan pronosticato i démoni della Nugola.

> *Miseri abitator del cieco Averno,*
> *Giù nel dolente regno*
> *Null'altro scenderà, che'nvidia, e sdegno:*
> *Sarà l'orror, sarà'l tormento eterno.*
> *Duro carcere inferno,*
> *A te non più verrà la gente morta,*
> *Chiudi in eterno la tartarea porta.*

Nella prima schiera due furie, con un abito tirato, e stretto, finte ignude, di carnagione arsiccia, e affumicata. Avevano le mani, e'l volto imbrodolato di sangue, con poppacce vizze, sporche, lunghe, e cadenti, tra le quali era avviticchiata una serpe, che con diversi giri le circondava. I crini serpentelli, i quali spesso, e rabbiosamente scotevano, perchè serpeggiavan lor su pel viso: e simile intorno alla cintola aggruppati serpenti in gran quantità, che in diverse attitudini trascorrevan per tutto'l corpo, e ricoprivan lor le vergogne. Da man ritta aveano quattro brutti, e deformi Diavoli, con zampe aquiline, e simili le mani alle zampe. L'aliacce grandi, e vestiti d'un drappo di seta a scoglio di serpe, e le cosce nere, e vellute. Si cignevan con due serpenti, e in capo, con una zazzera affumicata, avevano due acute, e terribilissime corna. Allato a questi, due femmine, simili quasi alle dette Furie, ma vestite d'un travisato drappo di seta, bianco, turchino, e giallo, in istrana guisa, e i colori parevano affumicati, così bene in quei drappi eran contraffatti. Non avevan così gran torma di serpi, come le prime, ned eran così deformi, ma anch'elleno, **[p. 53]** e brutte, e orribili più che la morte. Altrettanti, e Diavoli, e Furie a rincontro, differenti, per la varietà de' colori degli abiti, e per la maschera, e per gli strumenti da tormentare: ne di spavento, ne di bruttezza cedevan punto a descritti. L'inferno appariva tutto fuoco, e fiamma, e per quei fuochi, e per quelle fiamme si vedevano infinite anime, tormentate da grandi schiere di Diavoli, che in guisa si studiavano a tormentarle, che pareva bene, che volessero sopra loro, con più rabbia, e più furor, che l'usato, sfogare il conceputo novello sdegno, per lo promesso bene all'umana generazione. All'entrar dell'Inferno si vedeva il vecchio Caronte, con la sua barca, come par che'l dipinga Dante, con barba lunga, e canuta, intorno agli occhi, simili a fuoco, alcune ruote di fiamme, e empieva la barca d'anime, che facevano a gara per imbarcarsi, perchè egli con lo'nfocato remo batteva chi s'adagiava. Per tutto l'Inferno, come è detto, infinite schiere di brutti Diavoli, e d'anime tormentate, e spezialmente intorno a Lucifero: il quale tra quei fuochi, che finti, ve n'erano, e naturali, e tra quegli orrori, che lo circondavano, stava in un lago, a guisa di cerchio, tutto di ghiaccio, e usciva di quello, da mezzo il petto in su, otto braccia. La sua testa aveva tre facce, quella dinanzi, come vuol Dante, vermiglia, quella a man destra tra bianca, e gialla, e la terza nera. Sopra la fronte una brutta cresta, e grande a proporzione. Sotto a ciascuna di queste facce due ali, del color di quelle del Vispistrello, e come se stato fosse vero, e non finto, quelle continuo suolazzava: ne con minor maestría gli era dall'artefice stata messa un'anima in ogni bocca: e quelle bocche in guisa fattegli dimenare, che pareva, che avesse voluto gareggiar nel mostrarlo in fatto, col poeta che lo descrive, il qual dice.

> *Da ogni bocca dirompea co' denti*
> *Un peccatore, a guisa di maciulla,*
> *Si che tre ne facea così dolenti.*

[p. 54]

> *A quel dinanzi il mordere era nulla*
> *Verso'l graffiar, che tal volta la schiena*
> *Rimanea della pelle tutta brulla.*

Era tutto coperto di lunghi velli del colore della filiggine: e mentre ch'e' masticava, due di quell'anime (che erano certi fanciulletti assai destri) gli uscirono, preso il tempo, di bocca, e fuggirsi: ma furono seguitate da due diavolacci, e raggiunte, e l'uno d'essi una ripresa con un forcone, quasi una forcatella di fieno, gliele rimise in bocca con esso: l'altro Diavolo aggrancì l'altra anima con le branche, e perche non arrivava alla bocca, appigliò se alle vellute coste, e sagliendo, ve la rimise: ed egli allora con più rabbia cominciò a strignerle, e maciullarle. Allato a Lucifero da man ritta nel primo luogo era Gerione, che pareva in viso un buon'huomo, e giusto: le branche, i piedi, il fusto dipinto a scoglio di serpente a rotelle, e la coda, come Scorpione, e Plutone, e Satan, due rabbiosi diavoli appresso. Dopo questi Minos con vesta lunga di porpora, ma affumicata, corona reale in capo, e coda lunghissima, che tutto quanto lo ricigneva, e d'orribil vista: e in modo fu contraffatto, che di lui poteva ben dirsi.

> *Stavvi Minòs orribilmente, e ringhia.*

A sinistra, rincontro a questi, erano Arpie, e Centauri, in atto spaventoso, e crudele, e dopo loro il Minotauro, e Cerbero, che mordeva l'anime, che gli stavano a giacere in terra tra i piedi. Per tutto il ghiacciato stagno si vedevano anime, qual col capo in giù gambettare, qual sotterrata infino alla gola, e qual fino al petto, e di qual si vedeva un braccio e di quale una gamba sola. Finito i diavoli, che sedevano in su gli scogli, il lor mesto canto, con urli, e strida lamentevoli, sprofondarono, e similmente Lucifero, e si richiuse lo'nferno, e gli scogli, e gli antri, e le caverne affocate si dileguarono: la scena tornò nella sua primiera bellezza, e lo'ntermedio finì, e cominciò'l quarto atto della Commedia, alla fine del quale, si diede cominciamento al quinto intermedio.

Appendix 1f. *Intermedio quinto.* [Rossi, *Descrizione,* 55–59]

[**p. 55**] La quinta volta la scena si coperse tutta di scogli marittimi, e'l palco divenne Mare ondeggiante, circondato da quegli scogli, che pareano dirocciati monti, tra quali scaturivano vive, e cristalline fontane. Appiè de' quai monti si vedeva per la marina alcune picciole barchettine, intorno agli scogli, le quali lo sfondato della scena allontanava sì dalla vista, che era quasi, come veder da lunge un comodo legno. E mentre ch'elle ondeggiavano per quell'acqua, cominciò a uscir del mare una nicchia del color della madreperla, larga cinque braccia, e tre alta, tirata da due Delfini, che in movendosi à salti (come suol propriamente fare il Delfino, nel mare) odorifera acqua mandavan fuori, la quale pareva, che, notando, avessero preso in bocca. Uscita fuor dell'acqua tutta la nicchia, vi si vide seder su Anfitrite, vestita d'un'abito sì stretto, e sì attillato, e tanto simile al color del la carne, che più ignudo non avrebbe mostrato lo ignudo proprio: una mantellina a armacollo del color dell'acqua del Mare, ricamata a nicchie, e a chiocciolette, e a pesci, e'n capo una magnifica acconciatura, e sopra essa, tra alcune branche di corallo, una corona di madreperla: dalle cui trecce, quasi del color della mantellina, pendevano alcune filze di grosse perle, una delle quali filze le veniva infino a mezza la fronte, e due altre perle agli orecchi. Al collo un vezzo di varie gioie marittime, e alle braccia coralli. I calzaretti, un pesce a scaglie d'argento, ornati, come l'acconciatura, superbamente. E mentre che la nicchia veniva fuso, si vedevano a poco a poco uscir dell'acqua con essa, Tritoni, e Ninfe marine, parte della compagnia di Nettuno. I Tritoni avevano il capo tutto incerfugliato di chiome azzurre, e ghirlanda di canna palustre: dalla qual ghirlanda, [**p. 56**] e cerfugli, quando, cominciarono a uscir su, pioveva loro giù pel viso acqua in quantità, e simile dall'acconciatura alle Ninfe. La coda a' Tritoni, che furono quattordici, e quattordici le Ninfe altresì, era finta di raso turchino a scaglie d'argento. Le Ninfe, fuor chè nella corona, e nella quantità delle perle, in abito simile ad Anfitrite, cominciarono a sonare gli strumenti, ch'elle avevan condotti seco, che erano viole, e lire arciviolate: e Anfitrite, sonando sopra alla nicchia un Liuto, cominciò soavemente a cantare.

> *Io, che l'onde raffreno*
> *A mio talento, e son del Mar Regina,*
> *A cui s'atterra, e'nchina*
> *Ogni Nume, ch'al Mare alberga in seno:*
> *Ad inchinarvi, o regi sposi, vegno,*
> *Fin dal profondo del mio vasto regno.*

Tutti i madrigali di questo quinto intermedio, fuorche'l seguente, del trovatore degl'intermedi, furono d'Ottavio Rinuccini soprannominato: la musica di Cristofano prete già detto. E finito, che Anfitrite ebbe il canto, cominciarono le Ninfe al suono de' detti strumenti a cantare.

> *E noi, con questa bella*
> > *Nostra diva Anfitrite,*
> > *Da' liquidi cristalli,*
> > *Da perle, e da coralli,*
> > *Siamo, a'nchinare a voi, gran regi, uscite.*
> *Godi, coppia reale,*
> > *Poichè d'ardente zelo*
> > *Colmo, t'inchina il Mar, la Terra, e'l Cielo.*
> *Che vede uscir da voi*
> > *Un così chiaro seme,*
> > *Ch'adornerà l'un polo, e l'altro insieme.*
> *E discacciar dal Mondo*
> > *L'ingordo serpe, e rio,*
> > *Cui più sempre d'aver cresce il desio.*

[p. 57]

> *Onde farà ritorno*
> > *La vaga età primiera,*
> > *Vostra mercede, o regia coppia altéra.*

Finito il canto, quei Tritoni diedono nello scherzare, e gettarsi con le man dell'acqua nel viso, e anche a schizzarne con le boccine, e bagnavan le belle Ninfe, le quali si sarieno adirate sicuramente con essi, se un suono di chiarini, e una soave melodía, che loro, e Anfitrite fece con la sua nicchia tuffar nel mare, non le faceva nascondere, e similmente le barchettine, veggendo un legno maggior del loro, feciono alto, e, dando con prestezza de' remi in acqua, si dileguarono. Sparite, e tuttavia sonando i chiarini, comparve in Iscena una galea, bene armata, e ben corredata, con la sua ciurma, alla quale sonavan per l'atroce ferro le gambe, e vogando la facea camminare, con albero, antenne, vele, e áncore, e tutte l'appartenenze, che a bene armato legno s'aspettano: Lunga quindici passi andanti, e alta, e larga a proporzione: si come a proporzione lungo il suo albero. Aveva la poppa brunita d'oro, e, di quaranta persone carica, se ne venne ondeggiando in mezzo la scena, su la quale stette sempre in continuo moto: e quivi giunta, voltò lo sprone verso i Principi, e ammainò le vele per reverenza, e ammainato, si cominciò a sentir cantare, sopra un'Arpe, questo madrigale da un'huomo solo.

> *Ardisci, Ardisci forte,*
>   *Entra in quell'onde torbide, e sonanti:*
>   *O volontaria morte*
>   *Sortirai quivi, e ti torrai davanti*
>   *A questi feri, o, con eterno grido,*
>   *Giugnerai salvo, e glorioso al lido.*

Ci rappresentò il Poeta con questo navilio, la favola d'Arion Citaredo, e poeta lirico, scritta da Plutarco nelle morali. Il quale ricevute lettere da Periandro tiranno de' Corinti, e partendosi con molte ricchezze d'Italia, per andarsene **[p. 58]** a quella volta: e per ventura essendoglisi presentato avanti un navilio Corintio, salitovi sopra, e fatto vela, verso quel luogo si dirizzò. Ed essendo in alto, e i marinari fatto consiglio d'ucciderlo, per torgli le sue ricchezze, gli fu da uno d'essi nascosamente rivelata il lor malvagio pensiero. Impetrò, preso il suo ornamento scenico, di cantare, a guisa del Cigno, il suo funerale, e poscia, per salute sua, della nave, e de' marinari, alcun verso pitico. E ritrovandosi, cantando, a vista della Morea, e'l Sole andando già sotto; i marinari, non volendo più aspettare, allo scelerato fatto s'accinsero. Egli veggendogli venir verso lui, con le coltella in mano per ucciderlo, preso il corso, dalla sponda del legno si gettò in mare. E da' Delfini, per volontà degl'Iddei, perchè quegli scelerati avessero il meritato gastigo, fu salvo condotto al lito. Stava colui, che rappresentava Arione, come vuole il detto Plutarco, sopra la poppa della galea a sedere, in abito di musico, e di poeta all'antica, inghirlandato d'alloro, e la vesta di teletta rossa con fondo d'oro, quasi da Re: in mano una lira fatta a guisa della nostra arpe, su la qual cantò il madrigal soprascritto: e cantato, i marinari andando con le coltella ignude alla volta sua, egli, precipitosamente, così vestito, si gettò in mare, e si vide l'acqua schizzare in alto, nel suo cadere, ed egli stare alquanto a ritornar sopra, portato da un Delfino, che lo conduceva alla riva: e tosto saltato, credendolo i marinari annegato in mare, pieni d'allegrezza, cominciarono, sopra tromboni, cornetti, dolzaini, e fagotti, in questa guisa a cantare.

> *Lieti, cantando, il mare*
>   *Solchiam, compagni fidi, ecco che'l Cielo*
>   *A i nostri bei desir cortese aspira:*
>   *Già, fatto freddo gielo,*
>   *L'infelice Arion l'anima spira,*
>   *Dentro quest'acque: or noi*
>   *Godiam felici de' tesori suoi.*

Stava colui, che comandava il navilio nel mezzo d'esso, **[p. 59]** appoggiato all'albero, con un suo fischio, appiccato con una corda di seta al collo, e fischiando ammae- strava la ciurma: Aveva un bel berretton di raso incarnato, con rovescio turchino, barba bianca, e lunga, una robetta mavì, e un paio di calzoni alla marinesca di raso bianco, e in mano un bastone. Il rimanente de' marinari, tutti con berrettoni in capo, chi rossi, chi azzurri, e chi pagonazzi, e similmente le robette a mezza la coscia, e i calzoni lunghi, e tutti di raso. La sfortunata ciurma, era vestita di bigio, e similmente di raso, e in capo berrettin rossi. Cantando il madrigal sopraddetto, voltarono la prua al disegnato viaggio, e vogando, via camminarono, e sparì, e'l navilio, e l'acqua, e gli scogli, e la scena si ritornò nella prima guisa, e finì il quinto intermedio, e cominciò l'ultimo atto della Commedia: alla fine del quale, si diede immantenente al sesto cominciamento.

Appendix 2

[Anon.], *Li sontuosissimi apparecchi* (1589), title page and *intermedi* description only

LI
SONTUOSISSIMI
APPARECCHI,
TRIONFI, E FESTE,
FATTI NELLE NOZZE
DELLA GRAN DUCHESSA
DI FIORENZA:
Con il nome, et numero de Duchi, Prencipi, Marchesi,
Baroni, et altri gran Personaggi: postovi il modo
del vestire, maniere, et livree.
Et la descrittione de gl'Intermedii rappresentati in
una Comedia nobilissima, recitata da
gl'Intronati Senesi.
Aggiontovi l'ordine, & modo che s'è tenuto nel Coronare
l'Altezza della Serenissima Gran Duchessa.

Stampata in Fiorenza, & in Ferrara per Vittorio Baldini.
Et ristampata in VENETIA Per Lodovico Larduccio. 1589.
Con licenza de' Superiori. Si vendono à S. Lucca.

[Description of the *intermedi* only]

Descrittione de gl'Intermedii rappresentati nella
Comedia recitata da gl'Accademici Intronati,
alla presenza della Gran Duchessa,
& d'altri Prencipi, e Signori.

Si fa una Comedia recitata da Comici Sanesi, detti gli Intronati, chiamata la Pellegrina, nella quale si fanno gli infrascritti Intermedii.

1. Vedesi un stanzone grande tutto dipinto di varii colori à oro, vago, et bellissimo, con sue lumiere, et altre appartenenze, et apparisce con tela rossa, la quale mandata giù, rimane coperta la prospettiva da un'altra tela azzura, nel mezo della quale vi è una sedia, et sopra vi è un'Idra, quale canta sola eccellentissimamente, et a poco a poco quasi non se n'accorgendo il popolo se ne cala cantando, et cosi si perde in varii scogli à ciò fatti, et subito sparita la tela con modo incredibile, et in un tratto se ne sparisce in Cielo, et rimane la prospettiva scoperta, et si vede il Paradiso aperto in tre bande, et quattro nuvole,

che sono in terra, con destro modo se ne vanno cantando in Cielo, et spariscono, et ci si sente varii Madrigali, et Musiche, et in tutto questo intermedio sono 44. Musici à cantare, et sonare, il che seguito subito si volta la Prospettiva tutta, et apparisce la Città di Pisa.

2. Intermedio, si muta di nuovo la prospettiva, et apparisce tutti monti, scogli, e fonti, e nasce un Monte, che viene sotterra, che figura Parnaso, dove le dee in numero di 18. musichi cantano leggiadramente, e cantando un Madrigale subito si volta la prospettiva da due bande, e ne nasce due antri, ne' quali vi sono 12. musici per ciascuno di essi, et tutti insieme fanno un sentire bellissimo con varie musiche, et sinfonie.

3. Intermedio, si muta la prospettiva, et escono fuori 36. musici di varie inventioni con 4. ballettini, et cantano, e nasce di un antro un mostro horrendo, il quale detti ballerini col canto della musica l'ammazzano, il che seguito, si fa un bellissimo ballo in musica, intermedio vago, e bellissimo.

4. Intermedio, si muta la prospettiva, si vede per l'aria passare Giunone in un Trionfo tirata da due animali; e và tanto rasente in Cielo, che non si scorge dove sia appiccata, et arrivata in mezo la Scena canta una donna sola un madrigale bellissimo, e dipoi si parte, e sparita dall'altra banda apparisce una nuvola grandissima, la quale passa con destro modo, et arrivata nel mezo della Scena si apre detta nuvola, e vi sono dentro 22. musici, i quali cantano, e suonano, e dipoi si partono, et subito sparita apparisce l'Inferno, e viene Lucifero mostro bruttissimo, e furie infernali con la fucina di Vulcano, e varii fuochi, lavorati con madrigali bellissimi; ma malenconici.

5. Intermedio, si muta la prospettiva e nasce un mare naturalissimo, nel qual viene una Nicchia, sopravi le Dee Maritime, quali cantano un bellissimo madrigale, e dipoi se ne vanno, et ci apparisce una Nave tutta à oro, con 20. persone sopra, la quale và travagliata dal mare, e si volta con tanta agilità, che pare impossibile à chi la vede, sopra la quale il Turrerino canta solo in un madrigale, e dipoi salta sù un Delfino, che lo stà ad udire, quale lo porta via, et la barca si parte, e questo appare intermedio stupendo.

6. Intermedio, si muta la prospettiva, et apparisce tutte canne d'oro, e si apre il Paradiso in tre bande, e Giove si parte in una nuvola, e insieme con due altre nuvole viene in terra, e si converte in pioggia d'oro, et dette nuvole si consumano, et spariscono, et due altre nuvole rimangono in aria sospese, sopra le quali tutte nuvole sono 50. musici, et in terra apparisce 40. altri musici di varie inventioni, e tutti sono 90. et dipoi tutti all'ultimo insieme cantano, e sonano, et fanno un ballo, che vi sono 4. ballerini, che lo guidano, e in questo intermedio ci si cantano sette madrigali, e la grandezza loro non si può raccontare, et non è capace à chi non la vede il crederla.

Appendix 3

Simone Cavallino, *Le solennissime feste* (1589),
title page and *intermedi* description only

Raccolta di Tutte
LE SOLENNISSIME FESTE
NEL SPONSALITIO
DELLA SERENISSIMA
GRAN DUCHESSA
DI TOSCANA
Fatte in Fiorenza il Mese di Maggio 1589.
Con brevità Raccolte da Simone Cavallino da Viterbo.
All'Illustriss. et Reverendiss. Sig.
Patriarca Alessandrino, Caetano.

In Roma, Appresso Paolo Blado Stampatore Camerale 1589.

[p. 3]

Prima considerando la magnificenza, & grandezza del luogo [the Uffizi theater], ove vi erano da cinquemilia persone in circa tutti rassettati commodissimamente che ogn'uno vedea benissimo. Il loco era ornato di bellissime statue di numero dieci, e di sedici lampioni, ogn'un di quali teneva trenta ò quaranta lumi, & candelieri grossi che ogn'uno sosteneva torce grossissime di numero 18.

Calata la prima tela restò in aria una nube che vi era dentro una Donna da Angiola vestita, che a guisa d'Angiola cantava si sonoro, & con bellissimi concenti che ogn'uno restò maravigliato, & stupido la qual nube, a poco a poco calata sparì, & restò la scena con un Paradiso & Cielo che parea si naturale, essendovi le stelle tanto apparenti, che da ciascheduno erano stimate rubate dall'ottavo Cielo. Il Paradiso era ornato di molto numero di Dei con vestiti superbissimi, & vi erano tre Chori di Musiche tutti tre su le nubi, & quel di mezo cantava prima ove era diversi instrumenti una voce sola, & poi tutto il resto de musici di detta nube, & seguitando le altre rendevano un'armonia si dolce, che rassembrava parte della suavità, che colassù si ode, & durato un pezzo questo, sparì il Cielo, & le nubi, & restò la scena sotto forma d'una Città nomata Pisa.

Atto primo. Scena prima.

Uscì un giovane intermedio nomato, & incontrando una maschera, si scoprì per Donna chiamata comedia, e depoi haver trascorso un pezzo si congiunsero [p. 4] insieme per marito, & moglie. La comedia si chiama la peregrina [*sic*]. Il soggetto della quale è un bellissimo intrico, v'entra un Pedante, qual havendo fatto l'amore con la figlia del suo padrone l'ingravidò, & ella essendosi promessa ad un'altro Gentilhuomo Pisano, per non prenderlo si finse matta, & il Pedante all'ultimo scoperto da un Tedesco suo discepolo fatto dal padre della giovane carcerare, si scoprì fratello di quel Todesco nobilissimo di Vienna.

V'intervenne una giovane Francese in habito di peregrina, che per amor spenta venne in Pisa, & ritrovò che colui à chi la sopradetta del Pedante era promessa, a colui, che cotanto amava & che era stato cagione del suo peregrinaggio, & con bellissimi modi scopertaseli oltre i bellissimi ragionamenti d'amore, & oltre le querele compassionevoli ch'ivi intervennero, ci furno molti e diversi recitanti, come una donna che tenea Camere locande, ove habitava detta peregrina, una serva dell'innamorata del Pedante, lequali ambedui recitorno molto bene, s'intesero passi de roffianesmo, & altre cose, v'intervennero tre servitori i quali discorsero molto bene, e tra gl'altri ragionamenti uno vituperava la fedeltà & l'altro la difendea questo con succintissime parole, e il soggetto della detta Comedia, che il Pedante se pigliò per moglie la figlia del padrone, & il Gentilhuomo Pisano la peregrina, che stava si bella, che era da tutti i riguardanti, e da ciascheduna persona per vera donna, & peregrina giudicata, & vi erano molti che con lascivo occhio la miravano. Narratovi il soggetto della Comedia vi vo[glio] in parte, che non potrei, s'io havessi mille [**p. 5**] lingue, dirvi a pieno il superbo, & bello apparato, del secondo intermedio il quale, in un voltar d'occhio non si vidde piu Pisa, ma tre monti alpestri, tutti tre pieni di musiche sonorissime.

Usciti di due parti un buon numero de pastori, & ninfe, che scherzando & ballando insieme uscì un serpente à disturbarli, ma essendo ivi Appollo, quello ammazzò dipoi haver li tirato molti strali, di che tutto quel Choro di Ninfe, & pastori con canti diversi ferno segno di grand'allegrezza, & resero molte gratie ad Appollo, & cosi cantando sonando, & ballando, sparirno che nessuno vide ove s'andassero, & con essi sparirno anco i tre monti, & si vidde di nuovo Pisa, che fini il secondo [*sic*] intermedio.[1]

Il quarto intermedio non diede meno stupore all'occhio, che maraviglia all'udita [*sic*], poi che persa la vista della Citta di Pisa se vidde tutta la scena piena de nubi, & nell'aria un carro tirato da un drago sopra del quale era una donna che cantava sola, & in tal guisa che tutte l'orecchie eran'attente ad ascoltarla, & sparita quella ne comparse un'altra la quale era ferrata & come fu nel mezo s'aprì & restò con tre parti tutti in musica & quel che rendea piu stupide le genti, era che non si vedea come quella machina potesse star nell'aria senza vedersi come era guidata, & come poteva sostener tante genti, che ivi erano, & cantato che si fu per un pezzo sparì, & ritornò la scena a mostrar Pisa di nuovo.

Il Quinto [*sic;* quatro] intermedio[2] poi si vidde un'inferno con tanto foco, & tante anime, che bollivano, un Plutone si brutto che diede grandissimo spavento stupore a [**p. 6**] riguardanti, grandissimi copia de demonii, & tanti fanciullini ignudi, che quei diavoli gli stratiavano, & davanli a mangiare in bocca de serpenti.

Usciron poi tutti gli dei infernali che da demonii gli era dato il lor tributo, & gli rappresentavano uno di quei fanciulli, apparse un pipalterio, che se aprì il Cielo, &

cosi spari l'inferno, & ritorno Pisa, & come fusse nessun lo può giudicare; con si bello ingegno, & artifitio fu fatto.

Il Sesto [*sic;* cinque] intermedio, non fu men[o] bello che maraviglioso, vedendo ogn'uno una Citta, & una Terra ferme divenire in un voltar d'occhi tempestoso mare & scolgi duri l'onde del quale parevano si naturali, che tutti stupivano in riguardarle, che facevano quelle spume, che suole il vero mare. In mezo di dette onde apparve una bellissima serena con nove suoi prigioni con si dolce canto che senza maraviglia havria fatto adormentare, & ammollire ogni duro cuore, dopò havere un buon pezzo cantato, sparve, & in questo si sentì una sonora tromba rimbonbante non meno che fa nell'istesso mare & così si scoprì una bellissima nave di bella grandezza ove erano da trenta persone in circa, tutti vestiti di habito de marinari ricch[i]ssimi, & vi era ciò che fa di bisogno su la nave come è a dire arbori, vele, sarti, ancore, arteglierie, timone, foconi, & ciò che in quella si ricerca, & navigando per detto mare i marinari cantavano uno de quali volendosi affacciare fuor della nave cadde in mare, & in questo apparve un delfino, & postoselo su le spalle lo ridusse salvo al lito, la nave piu volte voltò per detto mare & alla fine se ne ritornò, & placò il vento, [**p. 7**] & non parve piu mare ma la Citta di Pisa.

Ricco, & superbissimo fu veramente il settimo & ul[ti]mo intermedio, che dopo essersi fatti li sponsalitii, & nozze delli dui recitanti cioè del pedante, & sua padrone, e del Gentilhuomo Pisano con la peregrina Francese. Pisa Citta non si vidde piu, ma in segno di grandissimo festa s'aprì il Cielo, & piobbe in grand'abbondantia pioggia d'oro che molti credendosi che veramente piovesse si mossero per volere andare a raccorne & in questo viddero da sessanta tra Ninfe & Pastori uscir fuora sonando, & cantando, & apertosi il Paradiso di mezo discesero tre bellissime nube, & due altre da un'altra parte, che seco portavano musica celeste, & non terrena, calati giù si levorno quei beati di lasù calati, & mescolatesi insieme con gl'altri che ivi erano si ferno molti chori di musiche, & poi cominciorno a far balli tra quali diedero principio tre bellissime Donne con tre pastori & ferno un ballo alla francese, & le donne ciascheduna di loro havea in mano una chitarra bellissima & cantavano, & ballavano, & poi tutti insieme saltorno & ferno balli diversi, la fine fu che tante voci insieme cantavano viva Ferdinando, viva Ferdinando, Gran Duca di Toscana.

[Cavallino's description of the *Pellegrina* interludes finishes here.]

Appendix 4

[Anon.], *Li artificiosi e dilettevoli intermedii* (1589), title page and *intermedi* description only

LI
ARTIFICIOSI
E DILETTEVOLI
INTERMEDII

Rappresentati nella Comedia fatta per le
Nozze della Serenissima Gran
Duchessa di Toscana.

Dove si descrive minutamente et con bel ordine la varietà d'huomini e di donne per l'aria, il comparir in un istante Monti grotte, draghi, Ninfe, Pastori, Mare, Nave, Furie, et infinite altre cose degne di esser viste et lette.
In Roma, Con Licenza de' Superiori. Appresso Tito e Paulo Diani Fratelli. 1589.
[Description of interludes only; dedication omitted]

Primo Intermedio.

In prima levata la tenda rimane una tela turchina inanzi alla quale è à mezz'aria una nugholetta dove siede l'armonia Celeste che canta sola sul cent[r]o quale sene viene in terra adaggio senza vedersi in che modo, Dipoi levata detta tela turchina apparisce la prospettiva tutta in forma d'aria e nugole e si vede quattro nugolette in terra con quattro huomini per nugola, la quale alla fine dell'intermedio se ne salgono al Cielo adagio senza vedersi in che modo & ancora si apre il Cielo per tre aperture, dove si vede una nugola lungha che si move con deciotto huomini & ancora si vede per dette aperture i cori celesti, dove sono i pianeti e finito detto intermedio apparisce la scena.

Secondo Intermedio.

Mutate le prospettive della Scena ne comparisce certe con grottesche e figure; & aperto il palco apparisce il gran monte di Parnaso pieno di huomini che cantano e sonano, il quale comparito all'altezza di piu d'otto braccia, in un tratto voltata parte della prospettiva si apre à uso di armario due grande grotte alte quanto il monte; è fatta quasi una congiuntione con il monte, vi apparisce nove musici per grotta, fra i quali vi sono due donne, che cantavano alcuna volta sole, e unitosi tutta la musica insieme. Alla fine poi si serrano le grotte, e spariscono: di poi il monte se ne ritorna sotterra con il medesimo ordine, e finito di sparrire, levata la prospettiva resta la Scena.

Terzo Intermedio.

Levata la Scena apparisce la prospettiva in forma d'un gran bosco e per piu strade cominciano à venire sul palco Ninfe e pastori, i quali fatto un bel cerchio cantano, suonano, e danzano, e in questo mentre apertosi il palco dentro à detto cerc[h]io ne esce un gran drago muggiando, il quale buttando assai fuoco rompe il cerchio de pastori e Ninfe, il che visto da uno de pastori uscito del cerchio danzando con freccie ammazza il drago, il quale morto ritornano à lor luoghi e danzando se finisce l'intermedio, e ritorna al solito la Scena rappresentante la Città di Pisa.

Quarto Intermedio.

Senza mutar prospettiva apparisce per l'aria il Carro di una Maga, tirato da due draghi, il quale è mirabile per non vedersi donde possa esser mosso, sul qual carro è la Maga sopradetta, la quale canta su'l leuto sola, ferma nel mezzo. Dipoi passata apparisce una gran nugola rossa tonda, la quale condottasi nel mezzo aprendosi tutta à uso d'armario si vede sedervi per un filo solo deciotto, i quali cantano e sonano, e in questo mezzo mutatosi in un tratto la Scena in prospettiva con fiamme grandi e nere, è in faccia la Citta di Dite, e apertosi il palco apparisce Plutone con suoi seguaci, i quali havevano gran numero di puttini ignudi, che ne facevano stratio à uso d'anime dannate e comparisce le furie infernali cantando e sonando sparisce la nugola rossa, e restato l'Inferno con le furie dette, à poco à poco sene partono, e levate le prospettive resta la Scena.

Quinto Intermedio.

Sparita la Scena, apparisce la prospettiva piena di scogli, & il palco s'apre tutto uscendo fuori acque, le quali apertosi in mezzo esce la Ninfe Tethi fuor dell'acque sedendo sopra una gran nichia cantando sola sul liuto. Essendo uscita detta nicchia circa dua braccia fuori dell'onde mostra da lati due ali di longhezza di diece braccia sopra le quali erano dodeci huomini marini, che cantavano e sonavano in compagnia di detta Ninfa e finito il lor canto si tornorono sotto l'acqua tutti, e tornate l'onde quiete apparì d'un lato della prospettiva la prova d'una gran nave con sue banderole, e seguendo d'uscire detta nave, finita d'apparire si scoperse di longhezza di 14, ò 16. braccia, con il suo albero, sendo nella popa de trombetti i quali sonavano all'uso di marinari, e nella fine della popa era la sua lanterna accesa nella qual nave erano circa trenta persone, che parte attendevano à servitii della nave, & il resto cantavano è sonavano fra i quali, il principale padrone lamentandosi di sua disgratia, solo cantando, li era risposto da Ecco, & alla fine del suo canto buttandosi per disperato in mare, fu ricevuto da un Delfino il quale lo salvò à riva, da poi voltegiando la nave ritornò al luogo d'onde si era partita, e sparita la marina e la prospettiva restò la scena solita.

Sesto, et ultimo Intermedio.

Voltandosi al solito la scena, apparì una prospettiva piena di pioggia d'oro, & aper-tosi il Cielo per le tre bocche, che si aprì la prima volta ne uscì per il mezzo una nugola laquale haveva sopra sette Ninfe, e pastori, fra i quali vi erano dua ale piccole che regevano sei simili pastori e Ninfe la qual nugola calando un poco fu accompag-nata à mezz'aria da dua nugolette, che vi era sopra quattro per nugola similmente ninfe è pastori, & in questo mentre essendo uscito per le strade della scena circa quaranta, fra pastori e Ninfe fermandosi in giro fecero ala alle nugole che si calavano à terra, dove essendo arrivate ne scesero le Ninfe e pastori i quali unitosi insieme fe-cero una mezza Luna d'onde uscitosi li sette che sedevano su la nugola principale principiato un ballo, seguendo di cantare le donne sole, e dall'altri essendoli risposto si unì poi tutta l'armonia che era nel Cielo, & in sul palco una musica à sessanta, & si intervenivono in tutto questo intermedio circa cento persone e doppo haver più volte variato i Canti, e suoni, e balli, alla fine risonando Ferdinando Ferdinando si finì il ballo, e si partirono i Pastori, e Ninfe, e si serrò il Cielo finendo l'intermedio. IL FINE

Appendix 5
Text and translation of Laura Guidiccioni's "O che nuovo miracolo"

From Malvezzi, *Intermedii e concerti, nono*, 19–20

Tutti

O che nuovo miracolo
Ecco ch'in terra scendono
Celeste alto spettacolo
Gli Dei ch'il mondo accendono

5   Ecco Himeneo e Venere,
Co'l pie la terra hor premere.

Tre Donne

Del grande Heroe, che con benigna legge
Hetruria frena e regge
Udito ha Giove in Cielo
10   Il purissimo zelo
E dal suo seggio santo
Manda il ballo, et il canto.

Tutti

Che porti, ò drappel nobile
Ch'orni la terra in mobile.

Tre Donne

15   Portiamo il bello e'l buon ch'in Ciel si serra
Per far al Paradiso ugual la Terra[.]

Tutti

Tornera d'auro il secolo[?]

Tre Donne

Tornera il secol d'oro
E di real costume,
20   Ogni più chiaro lume.

Tutti

Quando verra che fugghino

All

O what new miracle!
Here descending to the earth
in noble, celestial display,
the gods who bring light to the world.

Here Hymen and Venus
now set foot upon the earth.

Three Ladies

Jove in Heaven has heard

of the purity and devotion
of the great hero
whose benign rule governs Etruria,
and from his sacred throne
sends dance and song.

All

What do you bring, o noble crowd,
to adorn the immovable earth?

Three Ladies

We bring beauty and goodness that are stored in Heaven
so that the Earth may be like Paradise.

All

Will the Golden Age return?

Three Ladies

The Golden Age will return,
and royal customs
each more clearly illuminated.

All

When will all things evil

I mali e si distrugghino[?]

Tre Donne
Di questo nuovo sole
Nel subito apparire
25   I gigli e le viole,
Si vedranno fiorire.
Tutti
O felice stagion beata Flora[.]
Tre Donne
Arno ben sarai tu beato a pieno
Per le nozze felici di Loreno.

Tutti
30   O novella d'Amor fiamma lucente:
Tre Donne
Questa e la fiamma ardente
Ch'infiammerà d'Amore
Ancor l'anime spente.
Tutti
Ecco ch'amor e Flora
35   Il Cielo arde e innamora.
Tre Donne
A la sposa reale
Corona trionfale
Tessin Ninfe e Pastori
Dei più leggiadri fiori.
Tutti
40   Ferdinando hor va felice altero;
Tre Donne
La vergine gentil di santo foco

Ard'e si accinge a l'amoroso gioco.

Tutti
Voi Dei scoprite a noi la regia prole.

Tre Donne
Nasceran semidei
45   Che renderan felice
Del mondo ogni pendice.
Tutti
Serbin le glorie i cign'in queste rive

be banished and destroyed?

Three Ladies
As soon as this new sun
appears;
lilies and violets
will then bloom.
All
O happy season, O blessed Flora!
Three Ladies
Arno, you will be fully blessed
By the happy marriage with
Lorraine.
All
O shining new flame of love!
Three Ladies
This is the burning flame
that will inflame with love
even lifeless souls.
All
Behold how Amor and Flora
Inflame the heavens with love.
Three Ladies
For the royal bride
let nymphs and shepherds
weave a triumphal crown
of the loveliest flowers.
All
Ferdinand is now happy and proud.
Three Ladies
The noble virgin burns with holy
ardor
and prepares herself for amorous
sport.
All
O Gods, reveal to us the royal
progeny.
Three Ladies
Demigods shall be born
that will render the world
happy in every place.
All
May the swans on these banks
preserve the glory

	Di Medici e Loreno eterne e vive.	Of Medici and Lorraine for ever.

Tre Donne

Three Ladies

	Le meraviglie nuove	The new wonders
50	Noi narreremo a Giove[.]	we shall relate to Jove.
	Hor te coppia reale,	Now, to you, royal couple,
	Il Ciel rend'immortale.	the heavens give immortality.

Tutti

All

	Le quercie hor mel distillino	Let oak trees drip with honey
	E latte i fiumi corrino	and rivers run with milk.
55	D'amor l'alme sfavillino	Let souls sparkle with love
	E gl'empi vitii aborrino	and abhor wicked vices
	E Clio tessa l'historie,	and Cleo weave the story
	Di cosi eterne glorie	of these eternal glories.
	Guidin vezzosi balli	Let graceful dances lead us
60	Frà queste amene valli	among these pleasant valleys,
	Portin Ninfe e Pastori,	let nymphs and shepherds bring
	Del'arno al Ciel gl'honori	Arno's honors to the sky
	Giove benigno aspiri	let Jove benignly grant
	A i nostri alti desiri	our noble wishes.
65	Cantiam lieti lodando	We sing happily honoring
	Cristiana, e Ferdinando.	Christine and Ferdinand.

Appendix 6
CD information

The Pellegrina Project consists of the following musicians:
> Nina Treadwell, director, chitarrone, five-course guitar
> Susan Judy, soprano
> Samela Beasom, soprano
> Christen Herman, mezzo-soprano
> Dan Plaster, tenor
> William Hanrahan, bass
> Scott Graff, bass
> James Tyler, lute in G, bass lute in D, four-course guitar
> Daniel Zuluaga, chitarrone, lute in G
> Margaret Cohen, double harp
> Robert Mealy, lira da braccio, tenor viol
> Denise Briesé, bass viol, lira viol, tambourine
> David Morris, lirone
> Gregory Squires, recording engineer (Gregory K. Squires Music Production)
> Wayne Hileman, CD editing and compilation

CD Tracks and Musicians

1–3. Francesco Corteccia, "Ò begli Anni del Oro" (*Intermedio* III, 1539)
DP (tenor); DB (lira viol)

4–7. Antonio and Vittoria Archilei, "Dalle più alte sfere" (*Intermedio* I, 1589)
SJ (soprano); SB (soprano echo); NT (chitarrone); DZ (chitarrone); JT (bass lute)

8–9. Luca Marenzio, "Belle ne fe natura" (*Intermedio* II, 1589)
SJ (soprano); SB (soprano); CH (mezzo-soprano); RM (lira da braccio); MC (double harp)

10–11. Marenzio, "Chi dal delfino" (*Intermedio* II, 1589)
SJ (soprano); SB (soprano); CH (mezzo-soprano); DP (tenor); Scott Graff (bass); WH (bass); DB (bass viol); NT (chitarrone); JT (bass lute)

12. Marenzio, "Se nelle voci nostre" (excerpt), (*Intermedio* II, 1589)
SJ (soprano); SB (soprano); CH (mezzo-soprano); WH (bass); DB (bass viol); NT (chitarrone); JT (bass lute)

13–15. Marenzio, "O valoroso dio" (*Intermedio* III, 1589)
   SJ (soprano); SB (soprano); CH (mezzo-soprano); WH (bass); RM (lira da braccio); MC (double harp)
16–19. Giulio Caccini "Io che dal Ciel" (*Intermedio* IV, 1589)
   SJ (soprano); DB (bass viol); NT (chitarrone); JT (bass lute); DM (lirone)
20–22. Cristofano Malvezzi "Io che l'onde raffreno" (*Intermedio* V, 1589)
   SJ (soprano); NT (chitarrone); JT (bass lute); DM (lirone)
23–27. Malvezzi, "E noi con questa bella diva" (*Intermedio* V, 1589)
   SJ (soprano); SB (soprano); CH (mezzo-soprano); DP (tenor); WH (bass); DB (bass viol); NT (chitarrone); JT (lute); DM (lirone); RM (tenor viol); MC (double harp); DZ (lute)
28. Emilio de' Cavalieri, "Godi turba mortal" (*Intermedio* VI, 1589)
   CH (mezzo-soprano); NT (chitarrone)
29. Cavalieri, "O che nuovo miracolo" (excerpt), (*Intermedio* VI, 1589)
   SJ (soprano); SB (soprano); CH (mezzo-soprano); NT (five-course guitar); JT (four-course guitar); DB (tambourine)

CD Song Texts and Translations, with Cue Points

A note on the texts: With the exception of Corteccia's madrigal,[1] the texts below are drawn from the *nono* partbook of *Intermedii et concerti*. Occasionally, the texts differ slightly from those that underlay the music as presented in the various partbooks of *Intermedii et concerti*. In these instances I have adjusted the texts so that they are in conformity with the music on the accompanying CD. (I have also added text repetitions that occur in the music when they effect CD cue points—for example, tracks 6–7.) Otherwise, the punctuation, diacritics, spelling, etc. of the texts as presented in the *nono* partbook have been retained. All translations are my own.

"Ò begli Anni del Oro" (*Intermedio* III, 1539)
Music by Francesco Corteccia; text by G. B. Strozzi, il vecchio
[Sileno]

[1] Ò begli Anni del Oro, ò secol divo:	O beautiful golden years, O heavenly century
Alhor non Rastro, ò Falce, alhor non era	Then there was no rake or sickle; then neither
Visco, ne laccio; et no'l rio ferro, e'l tosco;	birdlime nor snare; and no wicked iron and venom.
Ma sen gia puro latte [2] il fresco rivo;	But the fresh river already flowed with pure milk;
Mel'sudavan' le querce; Ivano à schiera	The oak trees dripped with honey; in groups
Nymfe insieme et Pastori, al chiaro è'l fosco.	Nymphs and shepherds went around together, in daylight and darkness.

[3] Ò begli anni del Or', vedrovvi io mai?
Tornagli ò nuovo Sol, tornagli homai.

O beautiful golden years, will I ever see you?
Bring them back new sun, bring them back soon.

"Dalle più alte sfere" (*Intermedio* I, 1589)
Music by Vittoria (and Antonio?) Archilei; text by Giovanni de' Bardi [Dorian Harmony]

[4] Dalle più alte sfere
Di celeste sirene amica scorta
L'armonia son, ch'a voi vengo, ò mortali,

From the highest spheres,
As friendly escort to the celestial Sirens,
I, Harmony, come [down] to you, O mortals:

[5] Poscia, che fino al Ciel Battendo l'ali
L'alta fama n'apporta,

Because, beating its wings,
Exulted Fame has brought up to Heaven [the news]

Che mai si nobil coppia il sol non vide

That never has the sun seen such a noble couple,

Qual voi nuova Minerva, e forte Alcide.

As you, new Minerva and strong Hercules.

[6] Qual voi nuova Minerva, e forte Alcide.

As you, new Minerva and strong Hercules.

[7] Qual voi nuova Minerva, e forte Alcide.

As you, new Minerva and strong Hercules.

"Belle ne fe natura" (*Intermedio* II, 1589)
Music by Luca Marenzio; text by Ottavio Rinuccini [Hamadryad nymphs]

[8] Belle ne fe natura
E perche all'armonia beltà risponde

Nature made us beautiful,
and because beauty responds to harmony

Vero giuditio d'armonia n'infonde

true judgment in music was instilled in us:

[9] Onde d'acerba e dura
Contesa sian noi di beltà perfette,
A gran sentenza elette.

therefore, in this bitter and hard contest, we, perfect in beauty,
have been elected to cast judgment.

"Chi dal delfino aita" (*Intermedio* II, 1589)
Music by Marenzio; text by Rinuccini [Pierides]

[10] Chi dal delfino aita
Nelle tempeste sue cantando impetra,

He who sang to the dolphin
for help in the stormy sea

E quei ch'al suon di cetra
La perduta consorte

And he who to the sound of the lyre,
rescued his lost consort

Trae dell'infernal porte
[11] Non pero come noi canta soave
Che più s'el ciel non have
Si dolce melodia.
C'appo'l nostro cantar rocca non sia.

from the underworld:
But no! None sing so sweetly as we;

for Heaven itself does not have
such a sweet melody
that by comparison with our song,
would not seem coarse.

"Se nelle voci nostre" (excerpt), (*Intermedio* II, 1589)
Music by Marenzio; text by Rinuccini
[Muses]

[12] Se nelle voci nostre
Risuona di dolcezza accento, o suono
E gratioso dono
Del ciel da cui procede
Quanto di bello il mondo intende e vede[.]

If our voices display
sweetness or phrase or tone,
that is the gracious gift
of Heaven, the fountainhead
of all the beauty that Heaven wills
and sanctions.

"O valoroso Dio" (*Intermedio* III, 1589)
Music by Marenzio; text by Rinuccini
[Delphians]

[13] O valoroso Dio
O Dio chiaro, e sovrano
Ecco'l serpente rio;
Spoglia giacier della tua invitta mano
[14] Morta è l'horribil fera,
Venite a schiera a schiera,
Venite Apollo e Delo
[15] Cantando alzate o belle Ninfe al Ciel.

O valorous God,
O renowned, sovereign God,
behold the wicked serpent,
slain by thine invincible hand.
The grizzly wild beast is dead,
come, gather around,
come, Apollo, and Delphians
Raise your voices, oh beautiful
nymphs, to the heavens.

"Io che dal Ciel" (*Intermedio* IV, 1589)
Music by Giulio Caccini; text by unknown author
[Sorceress]

[16] Io che dal Ciel cader farei la luna

A voi, ch'in alto sete,
[17] E tutt'il ciel vedet'e voi commando

[18] Ditene quando il sommo eterno giove
Dal ciel in terra ogni sua gratia [19] piove.

I, who could make the moon fall
from the heavens,
To you who are on high
And see all of heaven, I command
you:
Tell us when the almighty, eternal
Jove
Will pour down his every grace
from the heavens to the earth.

"Io che l'onde raffreno" (*Intermedio* V, 1589)
Music by Cristofano Malvezzi, with ornamentation by Susan Judy
and Nina Treadwell; text by Rinuccini
[Anfitrite]

[20] Io che l'onde raffreno	I, who still the waves
A mio talento, e son del mar Regina	According to my will, and am Queen of the Sea,
[21] A cui s'attera, e'nchina	Before whom bows down in reverence
Ogni nume, ch'al mar alberga in seno	Every divinity, who dwells in the bosom of the sea:
[22] Ad inchinarmi ò Regi sposi vegno	To bow down to you, O royal pair, I come
Fin dal profondo del mio vasto regno.	From the depths of my vast realm.

"E noi con questa bella diva" (*Intermedio* V, 1589)
Music by Malvezzi; text by Rinuccini
[Sea Nymphs]

[23] E noi con questa bella diva	And we [too], with this beautiful goddess,
Nostra Anfitrite	Our Anfitrite,
Da liquidi cristalli	Have come forth from crystal waters
Di perle e di coralli,	[bedecked] with pearls and coral
Siamo a inchinarc'a voi gran Regi uscite.	to bow down to you, great royalty.
[Anfitrite]	
[24] Godi coppia reale:	Rejoice, royal couple,
Poi che d'ardente zelo;	now that, with ardent zeal,
Lieta t'inchina il Mar la Terra e'l Cielo.	the sea, earth, and sky joyfully bow down to you
[Sea Nymphs]	
[25] Che vede uscir da voi	That one foresees, issuing from you,
Un cosi chiaro seme,	A famous offspring
Ch'adornerà l'un Pole e l'altro insieme.	That will adorn [the earth] from one Pole to the other.
[Anfitrite and two Sea Nymphs]	
[26] E discacciar dal mondo,	And to rid the world
L'ingordo serpe rio;	of the cruel, wicked serpent
Chi di più sempre haver cresce il desio.	whose desire grows, the more he continues to have [in his possession].
[Sea Nymphs]	
[27] Onde fara ritorno	Thus the happiness
La vaga età primiera,	of a former age will return
Vostra mercede o regia coppia altera.	by your benevolence, O esteemed royal couple

"Godi turba mortal" (*Intermedio* **VI, 1589**)
Music by Emilio de' Cavalieri; text by Rinuccini
[Jove]

[28] Godi turba mortal, felice, e lieta,   Rejoice, happy and joyful mortal
                                                  throng,

Godi di tanto dono,   rejoice in such a great gift;
E col canto e col suono: and with song and music
I faticosi tuoi travagli acqueta.   rest from your toilsome travails.

"O che nuovo miracolo" (excerpt), (*Intermedio* **VI, 1589**)
Music by Cavalieri; text by Laura Guidiccioni
[Three Graces]

[29] Del grande Heroe, che con   Of the great hero, who with benign rule
benigna legge
Hetruria frena e regge   governs and reigns over Etruria.
Udito da Giove in Cielo   Jove in heaven has heard
Il purissimo zelo   of [his] most sincere zeal,
E dal suo seggio santo   and from his holy throne
Manda il ballo, e il canto.   sends dance and song.

Notes

Introduction

1. Simone Cavallino was from the town of Viterbo, which was under papal sovereignty during this period. Regarding Cavallino and the dedicatee of his report see chapter 3, section "The Commentaries of Spectator-Auditors."

2. Cavallino's account of the *Pellegrina* interludes is transcribed in appendix 3.

3. Rossi, *Descrizione*. (Unless otherwise indicated, all references to this source refer to Rossi's 1589 publication.)

4. Some accounts, though not official, may have been indirectly sanctioned by the Medici. I use the term "unofficial" loosely to refer to any sources that were not directly commissioned by the Medici court.

5. Pavoni, *Diario*.

6. Saslow, Review of *La place du prince*.

7. Warburg, "I costumi teatrali," 280–81.

8. There are a number of closely related passages in various sources, suggesting the derivative nature (of parts) of some accounts.

9. Rossi's account has its own problems: although it did not appear until after the premiere performance, it does not reflect what appear to be last minute changes to the program.

10. Aside from Rossi's *Descrizione*, I draw on the official musical publication for the event—*Intermedii et concerti*—assembled by composer-performer Cristofano Malvezzi.

11. Sisman, "President's message."

12. Saslow, *Medici Wedding*, 3.

13. See McClary, *Modal Subjectivities*.

14. Malvezzi was charged with the task of preparing the music of the various contributing composers for publication. Although there is no evidence regarding the state of the music as given to Malvezzi, as overseer and arranger he had the task of deciding on the format in which each piece would be presented.

15. Rossi, on the other hand, routinely lists the musical instruments involved in various numbers and includes the song texts of each *intermedio,* but rarely projects an impression of the aesthetic experience of hearing the *intermedi.*

16. As Samuel Berner indicates, divine-right theory was not a fully developed or worked-out theory during the late Cinquecento. "One does not find a book, sermon or oration exclusively devoted to it, where its implications are worked out in detail." See Berner, "Florentine Political Thought," 191–93.

17. Saslow, *Medici Wedding*, 34.

18. Biagioli, *Galileo, Courtier,* 51–52. The phrase "mystery of state" is drawn from Kantorowicz, "Mysteries of State."

19. Donington, *Rise of Opera,* esp. chapter 2 and chapter 5 (pp. 43–48).

20. With regard to the latter, however, Rossi describes only mythological characters, avoiding any mention of the musicians themselves who graced the stage, thereby keeping these details of staging in the mythical realm.

21. Schoenfeldt, *Bodies and Selves,* 11–12.

22. Ibid., 12.

23. See chapter 2, section "The Currency of *meraviglia,*" and Rossi, *Descrizione,* 3 and 19 (appendix 1a and 1b).

24. Franko, "Majestic Drag," 84.

25. Gadenstedt's remarks are cited in full in chapter 8, section "The Last Word: Memory and Meaning."

26. See chapter 4.

27. Bryson, *Vision and Painting,* 87–132.

28. Mark Franko makes the differentiation between (dance) performance and painting in "Figural Inversions," 49n14.

29. Contrary to the official documents, Gadenstedt asserted that the singer who opened the show was also the soloist in *intermedio* four. See Kümmel, "Ein Deutscher," 13, and Katritzky, "Aby Warburg," 241.

30. See especially chapter 5, section "The Cavallino Factor."

31. Saslow, *Medici Wedding,* 9.

1. The Politics of Dynasty

1. See Saslow, *Medici Wedding,* 19, for a calendar of these events.

2. For further background information see Hale, *Florence and the Medici,* Berner, "Florentine Society," Cochraine, *Florence in the Forgotten Centuries,* and Saslow, *Medici Wedding.*

3. Contini, "Aspects of Medicean Diplomacy," 55.

4. On the importance of diplomacy in helping shore up the Medici's dynastic prerogative see ibid.

5. Ibid.

6. Minor and Mitchell, *Renaissance Entertainment,* 18.

7. Brown, "Concepts of Political Economy," 279–93.

8. In addition, Cosimo spent almost half of each year away from the Florentine court, keeping a watchful eye on his territory at large. Satkowski, *Giorgio Vasari,* 29.

9. Berner, "Florentine Patriciate," esp. 12–13. Unlike some other European courts—most notably that of France under Louis XIV a century later—the tactic of the Medici principate was to keep patricians at a distance. As Berner suggests, however, this did not entail "the complete alienation of the patriciate from the court." One of the ways in which the Medici kept powerful members of the aristocracy in check was to create the Order of the Knights of Santo Stefano in 1562. Membership brought with it a heightened sense of social importance (and concomitant separation from other less distinguished social groups) at the same time as it forbade engagement in trade, impeding increased wealth and power on the part of potential patrician rivals.

10. Contini, "Aspects of Medicean Diplomacy," 86. See also Cantini, *Legislazione Toscana,* IV, 304.

11. Cited in Contini, "Aspects of Medicean Diplomacy," 85; see also Fragnito, "Le corti cardinalizie," 23.

12. Berner, "Florentine Society," 212.

13. Ibid., 208. Berner discusses several conflicting contemporary reports regarding Ferdinando's apparent parsimony.

14. For a translation of the grand ducal patent outlining Cavalieri's duties at Florence see Kirkendale, *Cavalieri,* 85–86. As the following portion of the patent indicates, the authority vested in Cavalieri was considerable: "Likewise we also depute the said Emilio [de' Cavalieri] with full authority and superintendence over all of our chapel and music, both of voices, as of every kind of instruments, so that he take particular care of it and be obeyed as ourselves by all of our musicians, being responsible also in this to no one but ourselves." The translation is Kirkendale's.

15. Cited in Contini, "Aspects of Medicean Diplomacy," 86.

16. See Goldthwaite, *Building of Renaissance Florence,* 128, 207–209, 220–21, 249–50, and Burke, *Historical Anthropology,* 134.

17. Rossi, *Descrizione,* 1 and 3 (appendix 1a).

18. Goldthwaite, *Building of Renaissance Florence,* 207–8.

19. "Et queste cose quanto saranno di maggior spesa tanto più lodevoli saranno: perche, nel vero, son proprie di generosi, magnanimi, et ricchi Signori, nimici della brutta avaritia. Questo già viddero gli occhi miei in alcune Scene ordinate dall'intendente Architetto Girolamo Genga, ad instantia del suo padrone Francesco Maria Duca di Urbino, dove io compresi tanta liberalità nel Prencipe, tanto giudicio et arte nell'Architetto. . . ." Serlio, *Tutte l'opere d'architettura,* 51v. For a useful summary of the range of vocabulary utilized to characterize the virtue of *magnificenza* see Burke, *Historical Anthropology,* 133–34.

20. The term *apparato* can refer variously to scenery or any decorative elements associated with a particular entertainment. When an indoor space was involved, the term was often used to refer to the hall's decorations that were specific to a given production.

21. De' Sommi, *Quattro dialoghi,* 61–62: "Piú magnificenza fu quella del signor Duca Guglielmo, a spender tanti migliaia di ducati in quello stupendo aparato, e poi guastarlo subito che se ne fu servito." (Duke Guglielmo's *magnificenza* was even greater by spending so many thousand of ducats on that wondrous set, and then destroying it immediately once it had served its purpose.)

22. Palisca devised the title "Prescriptions for Intermedi" (for Strozzi's otherwise untitled work), which I will henceforth adopt. See Palisca, *Florentine Camerata,* 209. Palisca argues that the work likely dates from c. 1609 (ibid., 212–13).

23. "Ma hoggidì la magnificenza de Principi, e quì particolarm[ent]e in Firenze gli ha tanto aggranditi et innalzati, che 'l fin degli Intermedj mostra che sia il far con le grandezza loro stupir' ciaschendun riguardante. . . ." Palisca, *Florentine Camerata,* 220. The Italian texts are drawn from Palisca; the translations are mine.

24. ". . . non quistionerò se così s'harebbe à fare ò non fare, ma lodando in ciò l'altezza degli animi grandi. . . ." Ibid., 220.

25. Rossi, *Descrizione,* 4–5 (see appendix 1a).

26. The emphasis in Rossi's description is on visual media. Although he provides the texts for the vocal music, and lists instrumentation, he rarely, if ever, mentions specific *effects* generated by aural components in a given scene that are documented in unofficial accounts.

27. See, for example, Strong, *Art and Power,* 126–52, Cox-Rearick, *Dynasty and Destiny,* 3–9, 233–91, and Berner, "Florentine Political Thought."

28. The second arch, for example, served the function of melding the republic and duchy together by representing a series of Medici marriages from both regimes, up to and including that of Duke Ferdinando I.

29. Strong, *Art and Power,* 131.

30. For further analysis of Christine's entry see Strong, *Art and Power,* 129–33. Strong notes the parallels between the entrance of Joanna of Austria, Cosimo's second bride, in 1565 and that of Christine in 1589. The latter was based on the former, but there is a significant shift of emphasis in 1589. According to Strong (*Art and Power,* 132): "The virtues of a good ruler that had formed so substantial a part of the 1565 entry were abandoned in favour of outright apotheosis."

31. See, for example, the account of Christine's entry by a Bavarian commentator in Katritzky, "Aby Warburg," 231–32 and 235–36.

32. Gualterotti, *Descrizione del regale.* The dedication page of book two is dated May 1 (the day after Christine's entry) and the first book is dated June 4. For an overview of the two books and their purposes see Saslow, *Medici Wedding,* 23–24.

33. Saslow suggests that this book was programmatic in function (i.e., intended for use during the festivities), although it was undoubtedly also meant to memorialize the events. Ibid.

34. Rossi, *Descrizione,* 1–6 (*proemio*). See appendix 1a for this and forthcoming references to Rossi's *proemio.*

35. Rossi, *Descrizione,* 1, 3–4. Rossi also uses the concept of magnificence as textual diversion by interpolating a description of Florence's long-standing cathedral, and the effect of wonder that it produced on the viewer. The description is cited at the opening of chapter 2.

36. Rossi, *Descrizione,* 2. Citing Plutarch, Rossi recounts that Athenians spent more money on the staging of tragedies than in the wars against the barbarians. Rossi's aim here was to cite precedent for the outlay of expenses for the current entertainment. Rossi's valuation of theater over war provides an interesting counterpart to the ideas presented in a roughly contemporary discourse by the Florentine writer Francesco Bocchi. In Bocchi's 1581 *Discorso* the notion of *virtù* is embedded in a military model cast in opposition to the decadence of Imperial Rome, which in turn was based, according to Bocchi, on the dubious cultivation of music and the arts in ancient Greece. See Perruccio, ed., *Due scritti,* 85–109, esp. 105–9.

37. Rossi, *Descrizione,* 3.

38. "Crederon gli spettatori, che la Prospettiva, che al cader delle cortine si mostrò loro, nelle quale immantenente riconoscer poteron Roma, quella fosse, dove si doveva rappresentar la Commedia, ne che altra Prospettiva v'avesse, e che fosse nato in Roma quel caso, tanto aveva l'Artefice con l'eccellenza dell'arte, saputo adombrare il vero, e con lo sfondato allontanarne dagli occhi i più nobili, e più superbi edifice antichi, e moderni della sovrana città, e sotto fingervi il palco, dove star dovevano i recitanti, che non solamente quella rappresentò, ma la prospettiva del tutto vera." Rossi, *Descrizione,* 17.

39. Saslow, *Medici Wedding,* 151–52; Rossi, *Descrizione,* 16–17.

40. Geertz, "Religion as a Cultural System," 28.

41. Favorable comparison with Rome was a familiar trope in Medici-generated discourse: ". . . e inchina il suo magnanimo Heroe il Serenissimo Don Ferdinando Gran Duca di Toscana, le cui fabbriche sono di tanta eccellenza, e stupore, che se Roma non avesse altro di maraviglioso, sarebbe non dimeno una delle più belle Città del Mondo." (. . . and bowing to the magnanimous hero, the most glorious Don

Ferdinando Grand Duke of Tuscany, whose buildings are of such excellence, and [cause such] amazement, that if Rome also didn't have wonders, [Florence] would be, no less, one of the most beautiful cities of the world.) Bellaviti, *Panegirico,* 10. See also Vieri, *Compendio,* 313. Barbara Wisch makes the point that not only did festivals and rituals "give an identity to power by mirroring existing social hierarchies and modes of thought" but "they also represented a visionary program for the city and the society in which they took place." See Wisch and Munshower, eds., *Art and Pageantry,* xv.

42. Rossi concludes his description of the opening of the *intermedio* (*Descrizione,* 19) by noting: "And while the people were trying to understand and to see where the cloud and the little temple had gone, almost without noticing, and in less time than it took me to say it, *the scene of Rome went towards the sky,* and hiding itself in that place disappeared. And this again could have created not a little amazement [italics mine]. . . ."

43. In light of the dramatic effect that Rossi anticipated, and the propensity of the spectator-auditor to focus on critical junctures in the performance (especially opening and closing moments), I think we can be certain that the Roman scene as Rossi described it never materialized.

44. Minor and Mitchell, *Renaissance Entertainment,* 223–24.

45. Regarding technological innovations in the intervening years see Strong, *Art and Power,* 135. There are differing views as to whether the Uffizi theater was purpose-built. For each entertainment the theater was entirely decked out anew, although machinery and other stage materials were held in storage. After the conclusion of the *Pellegrina* performances, the beginning of the entry in the *Memoriale* (67v) for June 10 states:

"Debbesi fare quanto appresso per conto della commedia e del salone, secundo la
   volontà et resolucione del signor Emilio de' Cavalieri, cioè:
mandar via tutte le panche a sedere.
Disfare una parte del palco di S.A.S. e levare la montata di detto palco.
Ritochare le pitture de' gradi, il che ha preso a fare Francesco Roselli senza pagha-
   mento.
Levar la tenda rossa e riporla in un cassone.
Tirar su la prospettiva finta fatta [da] Alessandro Pieroni e avvoltarla perchè manco
   pata.
Tirar in mezzo al palco la barcha e tenere chiuso il cancello.
Tirare le nugole e altre machine a luogi loro, legharle di sorte si tenghino senza portar
   pericolo di caschare e si cavino tutti li canapi e si riponghino ne' cassoni, ma prima
   si conttrasegnino tutti con numeri o alfabetti corrispondenti a quelli de' luogi dove
   hanno a stare, per ritrovarli commodamente e presto
Il serpente si riduca nelle stanze della Guardaroba, appichato al palco.
Si faccino stimare li abiti delli intermedii.
Si ordini che ogni mese una volta sia spolverato i gradi, palchi e prospetive e altro. . . ."

(The following needs attention on the stage and in the theater, according to the will and resolution of Emilio de' Cavalieri:

[R]emove all the benches used as seating.
Take down a part of the grand-ducal dais and remove the mounting of the said dais.

The paintings on the *gradi* to be restored, which Francesco Roselli has begun to do without payment.

Remove the red cloth and pack it in a crate.

Pull [off] the fake scenery made by Alessandro Pieroni and roll it up so it would suffer less damage.

Pull the boat [of Arion] into the middle of the stage and lock the gate.

Pull the clouds and other machinery to their places, and tie them up well so that there will be no danger of collapse. All the other materials are to be crated, but beforehand one must assign all [these things] with numbers or letters to correspond to those places [on the stage] where they should be, in order to return them easily and quickly [to the stage].

Take apart the serpent (fastened to the stage) in the rooms of the wardrobe.

Assess the value of the clothes of the *intermedi.*

Let it be ordered that one time every month the *gradi,* stages, scenery, and other [things] be dusted. . . .)

46. Minor and Mitchell, *Renaissance Entertainment.*

47. Harness, *Echoes of Women's Voices,* 23–26. The following discussion is indebted to Harness's observations regarding the significance of the movement of the sun during the performance. I would like to thank her for sharing this information with me before publication of her book.

48. The political implications are also obvious in Francesco Giambullari's description of the paintings. For example, his description of the paintings on the west side of the courtyard begins: "On the other side, on the west, opposite the return of Cosimo [il Vecchio], appeared the auspicious nativity of the Most Illustrious Duke Cosimo, as a new beginning of a happier century." For a translation of Gambullari's text pertaining to these paintings see Minor and Mitchell, *Renaissance Entertainment,* 130–35. For further analysis regarding the significance of the individual paintings see Harness, *Echoes of Women's Voices,* 23–26.

49. Rossi, *Descrizione,* 7–17.

50. Most tellingly, this lack of attention to the hall's iconography characterizes the account of Barthold von Gadenstedt, which elsewhere tends to identify visual imagery (whether correctly or incorrectly) whenever possible. For his comments on the Uffizi theater see Katritzky, "Aby Warburg," 238–39, and Kümmel, "Ein Deutscher," 7. Regarding the hall's decorations, the Bavarian eyewitness account merely states that "Erstlich ist ein herrlich grob zimer mit gold und allerley farben gar lustig aubgemalen. . . ." (Firstly a magnificent large room is very cheerfully decorated with gold and various colors. . . .) Katritzky, "Aby Warburg," 232 and 236. Settimani's brief remarks are also vague, yet give a sense of the hall's all-encompassing richness (see Solerti, *Gli albori* II, 17).

51. The program for the statues was conceived by G. B. Strozzi, and was described at length by Rossi (*Descrizione,* 10–14).

52. By the same token, I would argue that most spectators overlooked the symbolic content of the two statues of long-bearded men spouting water that framed the stage area. Rossi informs us that they were intended to depict the Arno and Moselle rivers (Florence's *impresa,* the lily was held by one of the men), and thus symbolized the union of Tuscany and Lorraine. See Rossi, *Descrizione,* 35.

53. Ibid., 13. I do not wish to underestimate the tremendous amount of thought and attention that went into devising and constructing the décor for the theater. It was of course crucial that Rossi record these details so that they could be transmitted through the medium of print. What I am suggesting is that during performance these details were not experienced as details to be analyzed as such but, rather, were intended to evoke a general impression of wonder and awe, in response to the sumptuousness of the lights, colors, and textures of the whole.

54. Giambullari, *Apparato et feste.*

55. Berner, "Florentine Political Thought," 186.

56. Ibid., 187.

57. Berner, "Florentine Patriciate," 12–13.

58. "Sia certa V. Eccell., . . . che non vidder mai gli occhi miei spettacolo più nobil di questo, che il veder il Gran Duca Ferdinando senza guardia, con poche genti a cavallo e meno a piede, andarsene tutto fangoso per la città, facendo quello ufficio che è vero principe. E come io soglio dire che la più bella fabbrica che facesse il Gran Duca Cosimo fu quella dello sporto al ponte Vecchio per passare col suo corridore a'Pitti, perchè negandogli quel cittadino il passo per sopra la sua casa, non volle valersi della potenza; così veramente lo dico, che non spero di aver a veder il Gran Duca in atto più bello e più pomposo di quello in che per mia ventura mi abbattei quel giorno a vederlo, che mi tirò le lacrime agli occhi; cosi l'assicuro di buona fede, che se la troppa mia timidità non m'avesse ritenuto, sarei dall'infinito affetto che mi sentiva commuovere andato ad abbracciargli e baciargli i piedi." I:Fas, Manoscritti, 130, fs. 173r–176r (letter from Ammirato to Virginio Orsino; November 15, 1589); cited in Aiazzi, *Narrazioni Istoriche,* 29.

59. On the Baldracca theater see Saslow, *Medici Wedding,* 77–78.

60. "Doppo pranso il Sig. Don Cesare fu alla Comedia de' publici et ordinari Istrioni, in luogo assai bello di positura, et più di apparato, fatto fare à posta dal Gran Duca per tale effetto." *Li sontuosissimi,* n.p. (see "Relatione dell'entrata della Gran Duchessa di Fiorenza").

61. The corridor is discussed in Francesco Bocchi's 1591 guidebook to Florence, *Le Bellezze della citta di Fiorenza,* 56–58.

62. The Pitti Palace only became the regular residence of the Medici dukes with Ferdinando's accession in 1587. See Satkowski, "Palazzo Pitti," 338. For the exact route of the aerial corridor see Satkowski, *Vasari's Architecture,* 78.

63. Del Vita, *Giorgio Vasari,* 92.

64. Satkowski, "Palazzo Pitti," 339.

65. See documents cited in Marongiu, "Corridoio vasariano," 94.

66. Satkowski, *Vasari's Architecture,* 92.

67. See, for example, the texts for the 1539 *intermedi* in Minor and Mitchell, *Renaissance Entertainment.*

68. Iain Fenlon has suggested that the fact that Duke Ferdinando used both Bardi and Buontalenti to create the *Pellegrina intermedi* was not just a matter of convenience; both had been involved in the production of the *intermedi* for *L'amico fido* four years earlier for Grand Duke Francesco so were in a position to ensure that the *Pellegrina intermedi* were far superior in every respect. See Fenlon, "Preparations for a Princess," 266.

69. See chapter 2, "The Duke as Neoplatonic Magus."

70. Tim Carter makes the point that it was *intermedi,* not early opera that continued to be the favored genre at Florence during the early decades of the seventeenth century. See Carter, "Florentine Wedding," 93–94.

71. Solerti, *Gli albori,* II, 17.

72. See, for example, the chapter on machines in *Il corago,* which directly links machines with the experience of the supernatural (see esp. p. 116).

73. In the concluding *ballo* from the *Pellegrina intermedi* the royal progeny were described as *semidei (Intermedii et concerti, nono,* 20).

74. On the preparations for the *Pellegrina intermedi* and for the 1589 wedding celebrations in general see Saslow, *Medici Wedding.*

75. Nagler, *Theater Festivals,* 69.

76. By foreign I refer to non-Florentines.

77. On this point see Wisch and Munshower, eds., *Art and Pageantry,* xv.

78. Biagioli, *Galileo, Courtier,* 154ff.

79. On this aspect of travel narratives see Daston and Park, *Wonders,* 63. Another notable correspondence between travel narratives and descriptions of court spectacle is the tendency in each to lament the inadequacy of words to capture the moment.

80. "Come agevolmente avrei mossi i vostri animi a maraviglia, in parlar della splendidezza della sua Corte . . . degl'intertenimenti, degli spettacoli, i quali, benchè sempre non fosser premeditati, sempre però furon grandi, sempre pomposi, sempre maravigliosi, sempre da Rè. Quanto sarebbe stato da dire sopra la pompa, e magnificenza delle sue nozze, . . . I superbi apparati, la pomposa mostra, gli artificiosi divisamenti d'inestimabili arnesi, i maravigliosi spettacoli, i quali non solo superavano l'espettazione universalmente di tutti gli huomini, ma la'mmaginazioni de' più periti, e più savi; non solo non si potevano avanti alla rappresentazione figurar nella mente, ma, rappresentati e rivisti, non si capivano. Era incredibile la spesa, inimmaginabile l'artificio, nobilissime le'nvenzioni, e si colmava la gloria loro, e del Principe, nel confessargli ciascuno, di comune consentimento, maravigliosi, e che altrove, che in Firenze non si vedevano, che altrove che in Firenze non si potevan condurre, ne da altro Principe potevan farsi rappresentare, che dal Granduca." Giraldi, *Delle lode di D. Ferdinando,* 23.

81. Saslow discusses the squabbles between Buontalenti and Seriacopi in which each man, having the "ear" of the Duke, felt that the other might have represented him unfairly. See Saslow, *Medici Wedding,* 93–94 and 99.

82. "Questa mattina il signor Emilio de' Cavalieri m'ha detto havere lettere per parte di S.A.S. sopra il sollecitare tutte le cose concernenti alle festi [*sic*] reali nella venuta della serenissima sposa e per ciò si dia quanto prima principio al viale di legno che si parte dal salone della commedia, passa sopra i tetti e lungho la chiesa di Santo Piero Scheraggi e arriva al salone dipinto dove si ha da fare il banchetto." Seriacopi, *Memoriale,* 21v.; Testaverde Matteini, *L'officina delle nuvole,* 198.

83. See Seriacopi, *Memoriale,* 46r.; Testaverde Matteini, *L'officina delle nuvole,* 228.

84. Seriacopi, *Memoriale,* 25v.; Testaverde Matteini, *L'officina delle nuvole,* 204.

85. Warren Kirkendale (*Cavalieri,* 171) also made this suggestion.

86. "S.A. vuol venire mercoledì et vuol vedere la commedia tutto con li abiti e che si rireciti e con tutti l'ingegni et con l'intermedio primo di Vittoria. De' lumi non si cura, poichè vuole il fresco, sì che si faccia finire quello si puole se si faccia tutto tutto tutto se è possibile, mostrisi questa al provveditore." Seriacopi, *Memoriale,* 42r.; Testaverde Matteini, *L'officina delle nuvole,* 222.

87. "... fra 3 giorni S.A.S. vuole si rifacci la commedia. ...." ("... in three days His Most Serene Highness wants to do the comedy again. ...) Seriacopi, *Memoriale,* 47v.; Testaverde Matteini, *L'officina delle nuvole,* 229.

88. "[P]erche il Gran Duce era occupato in veder provare la Comedia, che si dovrà recitare alla venuta della sposa (dove anco erano tutti li Signori Cardinali et Forastieri, che si trovano) non si puote haver quel giorno. ...." I:MOs, Cancellaria Ducale, Ambasciatori, Firenze, b. 31; see also Ledbetter, "Marenzio," 211.

89. See Rossi, *Descrizione,* 16.

90. Regarding the latter, see chapter 2, section "The Duke as Neoplatonic Magus."

2. The Aesthetic of Wonder

1. Regarding the concept of *magnificenza* see chapter 1, section "Princely Magnificence."

2. Rossi, *Descrizione,* 3 (appendix 1a).

3. Kenseth, *Age of the Marvelous,* 25ff. Portions of the following discussion are indebted to Kenseth's introduction to this volume.

4. On the marvelous in medieval culture see Le Goff, *Medieval Imagination,* 27–44.

5. For a full account of the European experience of wonder in relation to the New World see Greenblatt, *Marvelous Possessions.*

6. It was also now possible to not only suspend clouds, but literally to blow them onto the stage. See Strong, *Art and Power,* 135.

7. Palisca, *Florentine Camerata,* 222–23.

8. The castration of boys before puberty resulted in an extensive tessitura characterized by strength and greater evenness of tone across the entire range.

9. Shearman, *Mannerism.*

10. The story is recounted by Kenseth, *Age of the Marvelous,* 26. The translation is Bull's from Vasari, *Lives,* 258–59 (see Vasari, *Le vite,* IV, 23–24).

11. Kenseth, *Age of the Marvelous,* 26.

12. On this point see Greenlee, "*Dispositione di voce.*"

13. Conforti, *Breve et facile,* 1–iv.

14. Giovanni Bardi, "Discorso mandato a Giulio Caccini detto romano sopra la musica antica, e'l cantar bene": "E mi stomaco quando mi souuiene d'alcuni che hò uditi o, soli, o, accompagnati al libro cantare, non curanti che alcuna delle loro parole compressa sia, et mi ricordo essendo in Roma l'anno 1567 udendo la fama d'un Basso che oltra misura era lodato un giorno andai à udirlo essendo in compagnia con certi uirtuosi forestieri, il quale ci empì di marauiglia, di marauiglia dico, perche non fù mai huomo che hauesse in questo fatto più dote di costui dalla natura: auuenga che ricercaua assai uoci tutte sonore, e dolci così nell'alto, come nel basso, e per lo mezo. ...." (I become nauseated when I recall some singers I have heard, whether solo or accompanied by others, improvising on a choirbook, not caring if any of their words were understood. I remember, when I was in Rome in the year 1567, hearing of the reputation of a famous bass who was praised beyond measure. I went to hear him one day in the company of certain accomplished foreigners. He filled us with wonder—with wonder, I say—because there was never a man who had greater natural gifts than this one, for he could reach a large number of notes—all resonant and sweet—up high as much as in the deepest and middle ranges.) Palisca,

Florentine Camerata, 122–23. The translation is Palisca's. The identity of the bass singer whom Bardi heard in Rome is unknown. It could not have been Giulio Cesare Brancaccio because he was in France at the time; it may have been Alessandro Merlo or "Gio. Andrea napoletano," both of whom were mentioned by Giustiniani as active in Rome during this period. I would like to thank Richard Wistreich for this information.

15. Carter, "Giulio Caccini," 13–17, and Hill, *Roman Monody,* 62–63.

16. Kenseth, *Age of the Marvelous,* 38–39.

17. On the importance of *ingegno* with regard to Marinesque style see Mirollo, *Marino,* esp. 117.

18. Rossi, *Descrizione,* 5 (appendix 1a).

19. "Negli sguanci de' detti gradi, allato alla porta a man ritta, era una gran figura di chiaro oscuro, rappresentante la'nvenzione, così figurata dal buono artefice. Una bella donna con l'alie di Mercurio sopra gli orecchi, e un'orsa a' piedi, che leccava un suo orsacchino, che di poco avea partorito, e lo riduceva à perfezione: perchè, come ognun sa, l'orsa fa i suoi parti si contraffatti, che difficilmente si conosce quel che si sieno, e gli riduce, leccandogli, alla sua forma. E volendo il detto artefice dimostrare, che dalla'nvenzione ne nasce sempre bellezza, le mise nello sguancio rincontro una figura, pure anch'ella di chiaro oscuro, e della stessa grandezza, effigiata in questa guisa per la Beltà." Ibid., 7.

20. "Egli s'è oltr'a ciò ingegnato di far l'Architetto abbondantissimo d'invenzione, acciocchè esso, con quantità di macchine saglienti, e discendenti dal Cielo, passanti per l'aria, e uscenti di sotto'l palco, e con ispessi mutamenti di scena, possa mostrare il vivo suo ingegno, e in un tempo recare al popolo, e maraviglia, e diletto." Ibid., 17.

21. We know the names of the musicians, in this instance, from the ninth partbook of the music publication, *Intermedii et concerti.* While publication of the music for sixteenth-century court *intermedi* was rare, printed *descizioni* for these occasions were ubiquitous.

22. Regarding Peri's ability as a solo singer, see the sources cited in Hitchcock, "Caccini's 'Other' *Nuove musiche,*" 457.

23. Peri's comments regarding Archilei's *ingegno* are cited in chapter 7.

24. Florio, *New World of Words,* 253.

25. Vincenzo Giustiniani (in his *Discorso* of 1628) posits Archilei as the exemplar or model for other Roman singers. From Giustiniani's perspective, we see the performer, rather than the self-proclaimed composer, as the leading exponent of a style that only late in the century found its way into written form. Giustiniani's remarks regarding Archilei occur in the context of a discussion of Roman singers during the period 1571 to 1587. See also Hill, *Roman Monody,* 1:107, and Solerti, *Origini del melodramma,* 109–10.

26. See Strong, *Art and Power,* 128.

27. In this respect, the gesture functioned both to massage the egos of those who were granted special access and to maintain an aura of mystique surrounding the collection. (The same strategy was utilized by Duke Alfonso d'Este of Ferrara in regard to his *musica secreta;* only a select few were invited to witness performances by his singing ladies.) One of the anonymous accounts first published by the Ferrarese ducal printer Vittorio Baldini begins by noting the friendly embrace that Duke Ferdinando gave Cesare d'Este (and by extension the Duke of Ferrara) when he gave Cesare access to his gallery. *Li sontuosissimi,* n.p. (see "Relazione dell'entrata della Gran Duchessa di Fiorenza").

28. For the diary of Barthold von Gadenstedt see Kümmel, "Ein deutscher." For the Frenchman's account see Monga, ed., *Voyage,* 113–16.

29. See the section "Structural Underpinnings: Order Restored" in this chapter, and especially chapters 5 and 6.

30. "Demnach diese wolcke verschwunden hatt sich das perspectiff abermhall verendertt und greulich geschienen wie feurflammenn, wie sich dann auch alsbaltt untten der boden aufgethan daraus feurflammen geslagenn mitt haufen, und mann hatt konnen hienein sheen als in einen gluenden ofen oder in die helle [= Hölle] welchs dann die helle bedeuten sollte. Daraus alsbaltt der teufell schrecklich gros und grausam gemacht, heraus kommen mitt offenem rachen ungeheurem leibe und scheuslichen henden, welchem in seinem bosem etliche kleine teufell gesessenn also angekleidet, die ihm aus dem busem gesprungenn umb ihn herumbgedantzett, dieselben etliche kleine jungen und magdelin gar nackentt wie sie von Mutterleib gekommen und darzu verordnet gewesen und auf dem platz herumb gelaufen, genommen und dem teufell etliche in den rachen gestecket der sie verslungen etliche in die helle geworfenn. Unter diesem gheen herfur aus den halben des perspectifs 36 Musicanten gekleidet schrecklich wie man die furias infernales mhalett die hellischen gottinne, setzen sich uf stuele die von dem boden heraus gekommen rings umb den teufell herumb. . . ." Kümmel, "Ein Deutscher," 14, and Katritzky, "Aby Warburg," 242.

31. Platt, *Reason Diminished,* 3.

32. Findlen, *Possessing Nature,* 22.

33. Ibid., 17–23. See especially Findlen's account of the interpretive power granted naturalist Ulisse Aldrovandi upon the appearance of a large serpent in the countryside near Bologna.

34. See chapter 1, section "Shoring Up Dynastic Prerogative: The Prince as God."

35. See Platt's thesis as outlined in *Reason Diminished.*

36. On Patrizi's rejection of Aristotelian poetics see Aguzzi-Barbagli, "Humanism and Poetics," 134–40.

37. Patrizi is perhaps best known in musicological literature for his views on Greek tragedy—that it was sung throughout as outlined in his *La deca istoriale*—and for his treatise *L'amorosa filosofia* (1577), in which he extols the virtues of the singer Tarquinia Molza.

38. Letters attest to the long-standing friendship between Patrizi and Bardi, particularly those sent by Patrizi to Lorenzo Giacomini Tebalducci and G. B. Strozzi, in which Patrizi mentions Bardi (Patrizi, *Lettere,* esp. 64, 69, 87). Both Strozzi and Bardi collaborated and exchanged their work with Patrizi. Patrizi mentions the exchange of ideas on ancient music that took place between Bardi, Vincenzo Galilei, and himself in his *La deca istoriale.* See Patrizi, *Della poetica,* I, 329–30; 354. There are also interesting resonances between aspects of Bardi's *Discorso* on ancient music and Patrizi's "La deca istoriale" (see Warburg, *Renewal of Pagan Antiquity,* 358, 393n39). On other exchanges and collaborations see Patrizi, *Lettere,* 63n1 and 64–65. Patrizi's work, including the yet unpublished chapter titles of his *Della poetica,* appeared on the agenda of the Accademia degli Alterati at Florence, and were heatedly debated by the Aristotelian contingent, particularly Lorenzo Giacomini (see Hanning, *Of Poetry and Music's Power,* 18).

39. Ariosto's work provoked lively debate throughout the sixteenth century because of the author's disregard for the Aristotelian concept of unity.

40. See Weinberg, *History of Literary Criticism,* vol. 2, 1139.

41. I:Fn Magl. VI, 168, fols. 50–77v. See also Weinberg, *History of Literary Criticism,* vol. 2, 1116, and Patrizi, *Lettere,* 87n3.

42. See chapter 3, section *"La varietà e l'unità."*

43. Strong, *Art and Power,* 73.

44. See chapter 3, sections *"La varietà e l'unità"* and "The Problem of Musical Humanism."

45. Tomlinson, *Monteverdi,* 8.

46. "[L]a . . . potenza ammirativa nè conoscente sia, nè affettuosa, ma da ambedue separata e ad ambedue communicantesi; e che, posta di quelle in sul confino, sia atta a diffondere, e ad infondere, il moto suo tostamente allo 'n sù nelle conoscenti, e allo in giù nelle affettuose. Ma essendo la parte conoscente contraria in certa guisa alla affettuosa, non sembra che dir si possa che i movimenti della mente . . . scendano nella sua contraria, nè i moti dell'affetto salgano alla mente. . . . E si può perciò dire la potenza ammirativa essere tra queste due potenze quasi uno Euripo, per lo quale la marea, dalla ragione agli affetti correndo e ricorrendo." Patrizi, *Della poetica,* II, 361–62 (from book 10, "Che cosa sia la maraviglia").

47. "Per cosa adunque nuova, e subita, e improvvisa, che ci si pari avanti, fa un movimento nell'anima, quasi contrario in sè medesimo, di credere e di non credere. Di credere, perchè la cosa si vede essere; e di non credere, perchè ella è improvvisa, e nuova, e non più da noi stata nè conosciuta, nè pensata, nè creduta poter essere." Ibid., 365.

48. Platt, *Francesco Patrizi,* 393.

49. See chapter 1, section "The Duke as Theatrical Arbiter."

50. See chapter 1, section "Shoring up Dynastic Prerogative: The Prince as God."

51. Biagioli, *Galileo, Courtier,* 112.

52. Agostino Carracci, for example, who was responsible for a number of engravings of the *Pellegrina intermedi,* confused the identity of figures in *intermedio* one. See Palisca, *Florentine Camerata,* 218.

53. It is notable, of course, that while Rossi's description explicates allegorical significance, it gives few hints regarding the technological workings of the *intermedi.*

54. Certeau, *Mystic Fable,* 96.

55. Ibid., 97.

56. Donington, *Rise of Opera,* 26, 64.

57. Donington makes a similar point (ibid., 21), although as the title of his book might suggest, his treatment of pre-operatic theatrical music is teleologically geared toward later styles, culminating in his "Part 2: The Achievement of Opera."

58. Ibid. (esp. chapters 2 and 3), for an overview of Neoplatonism and its influence on sixteenth-century theatrical music.

59. Classen, *Worlds of Sense,* 3.

60. Tomlinson, *Renaissance Magic,* 136.

61. Ficino, as cited in Greene, "Magic and Festivity," 646.

62. Tomlinson, *Renaissance Magic,* 112.

63. Ibid.

64. Ibid., 87. Tomlinson goes on to reevaluate our received understanding of Ficino's views on music and text; his rethinking of Ficino has important implications for this study.

65. The phrase is drawn from the title of Richard Leppert's book of the same name.

66. Tomlinson, *Renaissance Magic,* 114.

67. This was especially evident when echoes were utilized, because of the even greater propensity for splitting up consecutive words, phrases, or syllables.

68. Greene's article, "Festivity and Magic," is an excellent introduction to the subject. In his opening paragraph, however, Greene notes the difficulty of proof; indeed, the very nature of magical influence makes it difficult to prove. Greene states: "Although in practice the presence of occult beliefs in the intentions of a court impresario is not always easy to demonstrate, what we know of the court productions and what we know of the culture that generated them suggest that we should be alert to this potential presence." Greene, "Magic and Festivity," 636.

69. See chapter 3, sections "*La varietà e l'unità*" and "The Problem of Musical Humanism"

70. See especially chapters 4 and 7.

71. Greene, "Magic and Festivity," 637.

72. Bloch, *The Royal Touch,* 76, cited in Greene, "Magic and Festivity," 637.

73. As Berner notes, however, "One does not find a book, sermon or oration exclusively devoted to it [the divine right theory of kingship], where its implications are worked out in detail." See Berner, "Florentine Political Thought," 191–93.

74. The quoted material is drawn from Greene, "Magic and Festivity," 648.

75. The term *catafalco*—used by several commentators—can actually refer to a stage. See Florio, *New World of Words,* 88.

76. Saslow, *Medici Wedding,* 124 and 295n8.

77. "Li Prencipi, e Prencipesse, erano dietro à tutti capo della Salla sopra un Catafalco." (The princes and princesses were behind everyone, at the head of the room, on a raised platform.) See "Ordine della prima Cena" in *Li sontuosissimi,* n.p. See also Pavoni, *Diario,* 14, and Pirrotta, *Li due Orfei,* 298n102. The Ferrarese ambassador Gigliolo also confirms this point: "In capo della sala à basso tutti li Principi, et Principesse a questo modo sopra un palco la Gran Duchessa in mezzo al Gran Duca. . . ." (At the head of the room on the lower level [were] all the princes and princesses in this way on a platform, the grand duchess in the middle with the grand duke. . . .) I:MOs, Cancellaria Ducale, Ambasciatori, Firenze, b. 31 (see also Ledbetter, "Marenzio," 217).

78. It was usual to coordinate the duke's line of vision with the vanishing point of the perspective.

79. To a certain extent, the same can be said for the female observers who, for the premiere performance, were seated in the *gradi.* Few women seated in the *gradi* would have had an easy line of vision toward the duke, although they could have turned their heads less conspicuously than the men seated in the orchestra.

80. Various official texts, including his funeral orations, posited Duke Ferdinando as the presiding Magus of entertainments. Portions of the oration by Giuliano Giraldi are cited in chapter 1, section "The Duke as Theatrical Arbiter." See also Bellaviti, *Panegirico,* 10.

81. I would like to thank Suzanne Cusick for sharing her sources with me regarding musical practices at Santa Felicita and Santa Niccola. They were discussed in her paper "Performance, Performativity, and Politics in Early 1600 Florence" in the conference "Structures of Feeling in Seventeenth-Century Cultural Expression" (Part 4, "Performing Bodies"), University of California, Los Angeles, June 2005.

82. See chapter 1, section "Shoring Up Dynastic Prerogative: The Prince as God."

83. The officially commissioned diary of Tinghi makes a point of regularly mentioning Ferdinando's presence at mass from the corridor, before the duke continued on his way to the Uffizi to attend to affairs of state.

84. I am not suggesting that the Medici were never visible. A stone staircase could enable them to reach the main chapel in order to receive the sacraments.

85. Email communication with Suzanne Cusick (March 18, 2007).

86. Music performed by hidden musicians was not an uncommon occurrence in the interludes, and took various forms. For example, in *intermedio* four a large closed cloud made its way across the upper stage while music emanated from inside (see the account by Gadenstedt cited in chapter 6).

87. What appears to be another version of the print by Pavoni (cited in Pirrotta's *Li due Orfei*) suggests that the auditor in fact associated wondrous music with the duke's actual body. In reference to the echo of Harmony in *intermedio* one, Pirrotta's transcription reads: ". . . e finendo tra quelli il madrigale in un Echo tanto maravigliosa, *che pareva fosse nascosto il re stesso un buon miglio* [italics mine]." The corresponding passage of Pirrotta's book in the Eales translation (on p. 380) is as follows: ". . . and finishing the madrigal from between them [the rocks] with such a marvelous echo effect that it seemed as if the king himself was hidden there in very truth." I have been unable to trace the original source of this citation. However, there are enough distinctions between Pavoni's account as it exists in I:Fn (Palat. 22.B.8.7) and the citations of Pavoni included in Pirrotta's book to suggest that two distinct versions of the publication exist.

88. Platt, *Reason Diminished,* 99.

89. See chapter 8.

90. "Si vide poi nell'ult.° Intermedio aprir di nuovo il Paradiso pieno come p.a de concerti musicali, et comparir medesiman.te nuvole de chori che non facevano che cantar, et sonare, discendendo poi sopra il palco tutti, . . ." I:MOs, Cancelleria Ducale, Ambasciatori, Firenze, b. 31 (Ledbetter, "Marenzio," 217). See also *Li artificiosi* (appendix 4, "Sesto, & ultimo Intermedio.").

91. Saslow, *Medici Wedding,* 241.

3. Court *Intermedi* at Florence

1. Florio, *New World of Words,* 263.

2. For an overview of the various types of *intermedi* see *The New Grove Dictionary of Music and Musicians,* s.v. "intermedio" (by David Nutter), http://www.grovemusic.com/ (accessed March 29, 2007).

3. Cited in Pirrotta, *Music and Theatre,* 174–75.

4. Ibid., 175. For other references regarding the conception of the *intermedio* as Greek chorus see Pirrotta, *Music and Theatre,* 154n57.

5. The letter is cited in Slim, *Gift of Madrigals,* 1:93.

6. Pirrotta, *Music and Theatre,* 153–54.

7. *La 5a et la 6a divisione della poetica* (Venice, 1562), 32. Cited in *New Grove Dictionary,* s.v. "intermedio." Trissino also lamented the inclusion of so many buffoons and jugglers.

8. Ibid.

9. Pirrotta, *Music and Theatre,* 154.

10. De' Sommi, *Quattro dialoghi,* 56: ". . . dico che gl'intermedii di musica almeno, sono neccessarii alle comedie, sí per dar alquanto di refrigerio alle menti de gli spettatori, et sí anco perché il poeta . . . si serve di quello intervallo nel dar proporzione a la sua favola, poscia che ognuno di questi intermedii, benché breve, può servir per lo corso di quattro, sei et otto ore, a tale che, quantunque la comedia, per lunga che sia, non ha da durar mai piú

che quattro ore, spesso se le dà spazio di un giorno intiero, et anco alcuna volta di mezzo un altro; et il non comparire personaggi in scena fa questo effetto con maggiore eficacia."

11. Pirrotta, *Music and Theatre,* 154.

12. Regarding the more overtly political dimension of this particular entertainment see chapter 1, section "Shoring Up Dynastic Prerogative: Precedent and Continuity."

13. "Il Sileno da Virgilio descritto nella VI Egloga sua, trovato al Meriggio da Mnasilo et Chromi, et dalla bellissima Egle, in uno antro à dormire; ci dimostrò, come gia era per la Comedia, l'hora del mez[z]o giorno. Et isvegliato da quelli, come pregato di cantare . . . cominciò soavemente à sonare et cantare ['Ò begli Anni del Oro'] as follows . . . ." Giambullari, *Apparato et feste,* 125. The translation is drawn from Minor and Mitchell, *Renaissance Entertainment,* 297–98. In addition, the twelve shepherds of *intermedio* two call on the sun god to temper summer's heat, while the hunting nymphs of *intermedio* five indicate evening's approach as they sing and walk across the stage on their return from the hunt.

14. Minor and Mitchell, *Renaissance Entertainment,* 342.

15. Pirrotta, *Music and Theatre,* 157.

16. On this point see *New Grove Dictionary,* s.v. "intermedio."

17. See, for example, *New Grove Dictionary,* s.v. "intermedio," Shearman, *Mannerism,* 105, and Pirrotta, *Music and Theatre,* 172.

18. After the 1539 entertainments for the wedding of Cosimo de' Medici and Eleonora of Toledo, the Florentine court did not see such extravagance again until the flurry of theatrical activity that took place more than a generation later, beginning with the *intermedi* for *La confanaria* to celebrate the marriage of Francesco de' Medici and Joanna of Austria in 1565. Regarding the Florentine *intermedi* produced during the 1560s, see Nagler, *Theatre Festivals,* chapters 2 and 3.

19. On the nonaulic *intermedi* and the range of possible resources involved see Harness, "Nonaulic intermedi."

20. Giovanni de' Bardi wrote the comedy.

21. Pirrotta, *Music and Theatre,* 209. Roy Strong's summary of Florentine court *intermedi* is also governed by the question of unity or lack thereof. Ironically, Strong refers to the same set of *intermedi* (those of 1586) as discussed by Pirrotta in terms of their "major innovations in respect of unity of theme." See Strong, *Art and Power,* esp. 135.

22. Warburg, "I costumi teatrali per gli Intermezzi del 1589."

23. "Ma vegniamo oramai à raccontare le maraviglie, e le ricchezze degl'intermedi: le cui invenzioni da quali, o autori, o fondamenti, o ragioni, o allegorie, sieno dal nobile ingegno del Poeta stati ritratti, non mi prenderò cura di scrivere in questo libro: poichè faccendolo temerei biasimo d'ostentazione, in troppo minute cose, e di mala presunzione, contra gl'intendenti, e savi lettori: quasi egli, per se medesimi, a conoscer sì fatte cose non fosser sofficienti, e a scernere agevolmente, se da' comunali raccoglitori di tai soggetti, che per le mani sono a ciascuno, o da nascosi luoghi di pregiati scrittori antichi sien cavati dal trovatore." (But let us now turn to recount the wonders and the wealth of the *intermedi;* I will not actually care to write in this book from which authors, or bases, or reasons, or allegories, the noble *ingegno* of the poet [Bardi] has derived the inventions [ideas] of the *intermedi.* Because by doing this I would be afraid of being accused of ostentation, in showing things that are too detailed, and to show presumption against the wise and educated readers; as if these readers, by themselves, were not sufficient to understand such things and to discern them easily, whether such subjects are taken by the poet either from those anthologies [collections] of such subjects which we see going around in

the hands of everyone [probably emblem books], or from hidden places written by very prized ancient writers.") Rossi, *Descrizione,* 1586, 5v–6r.

24. See chapter 1, section "The Duke as Theatrical Arbiter."

25. "[E] diciamo qual fu l'animo del Poeta, quando, da principio, gli convenne cercar la favola per la rappresentazion de' detti intermedi, che fu questo, di ritrovarla con un sol filo, e poscia far nascer da quella tutte, e sei le rappresentazion, che gli abbisognavano. Ma fu giudicato opportuno alla'ntezione, che s'aveva principalmente nel presente spettacolo, che innanzi ad ogni altra cosa s'attendesse alla varietà: di maniera, che gli fu necessario, per cotal riguardo, perderne l'unità, e per conseguente il pregio, che per essa può guadagnarsi. E veggendo, che il suo componimento esser conveniva di molti capi, si dispose per ogni guisa di voler mettere nella varietà, e disunione la sopraddetta unità, ed egli venuto fatto perciocchè tutte le grazie, che in essi intermedi finge, che vengan fatte a' mortali, tutte appariscono per cagione di questo felicissimo maritaggio." Rossi, *Descrizione,* 1586, 6r.

26. Grand Duke Francesco's half-sister, Virginia de' Medici, married Cesare d'Este.

27. "[E] in questa maniera . . . ha il nostro gentil Poeta, d'una sì fatta disunione, intera cavatane l'unità." Rossi, *Descrizione,* 1586, 6v.

28. Cited in Katritzky, "Aby Warburg," 221.

29. Warburg, *Renewal of Pagan Antiquity,* 351. Following Warburg's lead, Tim Carter (*Jacopo Peri,* 12–13) notes: "[E]vidently by 1586 the [Florentine] court would not tolerate any lessening of the variety of theatrical effects which had become the *intermedio*'s raison-d'être. Rossi clearly sided with his fellow-member of the Crusca [Bardi], just as he was to do in 1589, and both seem to have resented the fact that court tastes should have intruded into their world of academic idealism."

30. "E per ciò fare non gli parve a proposito una favola d'un solo filo, giudicando, che gli uditor non faranno poco, se a quella della commedia staranno attenti. Oltrechè, pigliando una sola favola, era sforzato a mostrare, e a seguir continuamente quel filo, nel quale sempre del buono, e del cattivo par che si truovi: legava le mani all'artefice, e agli scienziati non gli pareva mostrare alcuna cosa di nuovo." Rossi, *Descrizione,* 17.

31. Cited in Shearman, *Mannerism,* 139. The italics are Shearman's.

32. The music videos of Madonna are one example of multi-media performance that can be understood on numerous levels. Many appreciate the commercial appeal of her work without necessarily engaging with the sexual, religious, or political nature of her music.

33. In particular, I refer to aesthetic ideas elaborated by Galilei in his *Dialogo della musica antica, e della moderna.*

34. See Carter, *Jacopo Peri,* 118–21.

35. Kirkendale, *Cavalieri,* 166.

36. "[Bardi] fu incontanente sopra l'opera della musica: nella quale volle principalmente, che risplendesse la pompa, e la finezza del suo poema perciocchè, e copiosissima, pienissima, variissima, dolcissima, e artificiosissima, oltre ad ogni altra, ed insieme (il che s'ha quasi per impossibile) chiarissima, ed agevolissima ad intenderne le parole, volle che riuscisse quell'armonia, come anche di questo, per la pubblicazione, gl'intendenti s'accerteranno." Rossi, *Descrizione,* 1586, 2r. These *intermedi* were apparently never published.

37. "Ma vegniamo oramai a raccontar delle maraviglie degl'Intermedi, ne' quali il facitor d'essi, a tutto suo poter s'è sforzato, che l'operazioni, che si deon far nella favola,

tutte vengan fatte per lor natura: per esempio, che se nello'ntermedio si ballerà, o si can-
terà, la favola lo richiegga: e che'l poeta abbia facultà di far varie sorte di madrigali, e i
Musici sopra essi, con vari strumenti, musiche di consertate varie, e di vari tuoni, al trovato appropriate dello'ntermedio." (But let's turn now to tell about the wonders of the
intermedi, in which the one who made them [Bardi] tried with all his might so that all
the actions that must be done in the fable must all be done according to their nature. For
example, if there is going to be dancing or singing in the *intermedio,* the fable will demand it, and the poet will have a chance to write different types of madrigals, and the
musicians, on these madrigals with varied instruments, and various concerted musics,
and in various tones [modes], [will have a chance to perform things] that would be chosen to be appropriate to the *intermedio.*) Rossi, *Descrizione,* 17.

38. There were "concerti molto belli et gravi, et per la quantità de' musici et di stromenti non s'intendevano ne anco le parolle della musica." Kirkendale lists the source of
this citation as I:Vas, Nunziatura di Firenze 12A/22 (*Cavalieri,* 174n59). This citation
contains an error. The archive is Vatican, Archivio Segreto (I:Rasv), which is sometimes
abbreviated as "Vas," although most commonly "I:Vas" refers to Venice, Archivio di
Stato. My thanks to John Walter Hill, Beth Glixon, and Jonathan Glixon for providing
helpful information that enabled me to locate and consult a copy of the document in
question.

39. See Cavalieri, *Rappresentazione,* and Caccini, *Le nuove musiche.* For Bardi see
Palisca, *Florentine Camerata,* 90–131.

40. On Rossi's role as mouthpiece for Bardi see Saslow, *Medici Wedding,* 29.

41. Grafton and Jardine, *From Humanism to the Humanities,* xiv.

42. Rossi, *Descrizione,* 5–6 (appendix 1a).

43. Rossi, *Descrizione,* 6–7; Saslow, *Medici Wedding,* 78–79.

44. "Nel mezo della Sala vi stava gli huomini tutti à sedere sopra à banche accom-
modate in modo, che tanto vedeva gli ultimi, come li primi." Pavoni, *Diario,* 14. Gadenstedt notes: ". . . in solchem shaall haben viel 1000 pershonen raum haben konnen und
ein jglicher die comoedi fuglich ansehen konnen." (. . . in this hall, many thousands of
people could fit, and everyone was able to watch the comedy properly.") Kümmel, "Ein
Deutscher," 7, and Katritzky, "Aby Warburg," 238.

45. Saslow, Review of *La place du prince,* 148.

46. Rossi, *Descrizione,* 16; Saslow, *Medici Wedding,* 151.

47. See chapter 2, section "The Duke as Neoplatonic Magus."

48. Rossi, *Descrizione,* 7.

49. *Memoriale,* 46r, April 13, 1589; Testaverde Matteini, *L'officina delle nuvole,*
88–89.

50. "Il signor Emilio vorrebbe n. XXIIII sghabelli n.° 24, quali li vuole su in paradiso nelle stanze della galleria." (Signor Emilio [de' Cavalieri] would like xxiiii
stools, 24 in number, and he wants them up in paradise, in the rooms of the *galleria.*)
Memoriale, 50r, April 22, 1589; Testaverde Matteini, *L'officina delle nuvole,* 232. The
term *paradiso* is used in this context to mean "up high." Saslow notes that Cavalieri
uses the term *paradiso* loosely, sometimes referring to the *galleria,* while at other times
indicating the catwalks or the actual heavenly stage setting (*Medici Wedding,* 150 and
301n5).

51. Regarding Gigliolo's dispatch, see chapter 1, section "The Duke as Theatrical
Arbiter." A note in *Li sontuosissimi* ("Ordine della prima Cena") states the following: "Li
cardinali erano in disparte soli sopra quelle de' Prencipi. . . ." (The cardinals were alone

and out of sight above those [places] of the princes. . . .) It is not clear which performance the author was referring to, but most likely he was writing about the premiere performance. The statement does not necessarily mean that the cardinals were in the musicians' room. It is equally plausible that they were watching from the *galleria* windows at the back of the hall.

52. The following lesser known sources, in addition to better known ones, confirm the Tuesday, May 2, premiere performance: *Li sontuosissimi,* n.p. ("Ordine della prima Cena.") and the account of Gadenstedt, the German eyewitness (Katritzky, "Aby Warburg," 238, and Kümmel, "Ein Deutscher").

53. Katritzky, "Aby Warburg," 118.

54. "Pour faire ceste musicque le grand duc avoit recherché tous les plus habiles hommes d'Italie et aussi la commedie fust parachevee; et a esté representee cinq fois: la premiere pour faire l'essay, la seconde, où j'estois, pour la venue de la grand duchesse. Ce jour là y estoient les *done* de Florence fort bien parees avec une infinitté de pierreries. La 3ᵉ fois pour les gentilzhommes florentins et estrangers qui estoient venuz aux nopces, la quatrieme pour le commung peuple et les courtisans de Florence. Ce jour là [y estoient] les embassadeurs des Venitiens et Genevois qui estoient venuz vers le grand duc pour le congratuller en son mariage: je y entray avec eulx; et la cinquieme fois à la venue de l'ambassadeur d'Espagne qui arriva après les nopces pour la mesme raison que les autres ambassadeurs." Monga, *Voyage,* 116.

55. *Memoriale,* 66r; Testaverde Matteini, *L'officina delle nuvole,* 246; see also Saslow, *Medici Wedding,* 162, 302n27. According to Gigliolo: "Hieri [May 15] si tornò à recitare la gran Comedia con gl'Intermedii per farla vedere a l'Amb.re di Venetia, il quale desinò con il Duca. Vi concorse tanto popolo come se forse stata la prima volta che si fosse recitata." (Yesterday the grand comedy was again recited with the *intermedi* in order for the Venetian ambassador to see it, who dined with the duke. So many people flocked there as if it had been the first time it was recited.) I:MOs, Cancellaria Ducale, Ambasciatori, Firenze, b. 31; Ledbetter, "Marenzio," appendix 87. One assumes that by "gran Comedia" Gigliolo refers to Bargagli's *La pellegrina,* as his previous entry regarding the performance of the interludes specifies that the Gelosi troupe recited the comedy.

56. *Memoriale,* 66v; Testaverde Matteini, *L'officina delle nuvole,* 247. Once again, Gigliolo specifies that the "Gran Comedia" was performed.

57. "Venerdì certissimo vuole S.A. si rifaccia la commedia et noi altri potremo mettervi li amici. Lunedì vuole si rifacci poi politissimamente et vi ritornerà S.A.S. la gran duchessa et tutti i signori et si farà una commedia corta. . . ." *Memoriale,* 52v, May 3, 1589; Testaverde Matteini, *L'officina delle nuvole,* 235. The reference to a short comedy indicates that the original comedy, *La pellegrina,* was not performed.

58. Pavoni, *Diario,* 29. Ambassador Gigliolo notes: "Questa sera si fà la Comedia un'altra volta, recitata però dai Comici Gelosi secondo il solito loro, ma con gl'Intermedii dell'altra sera con l'intervento delli Principi, Principesse, Dame, et Cav.ri." (This evening the comedy will be performed another time, recited instead by the Comici Gelosi in their usual way, but with the *intermedi* of the other evening with the involvement of the princes, princesses, ladies, and lords.) I:MOs, Cancellaria Ducale, Ambasciatori, Firenze, b. 31; see also Ledbetter, "Marenzio," appendix 85 (dispatch of May 6).

59. Pavoni, *Diario,* 46, and I:Fas, Manoscritti, filza 130, f. 149r (Settimani, *Memorie*).

60. Pavoni, *Diario,* 29.

61. On this point see Saslow, *Medici Wedding,* 162, and Testaverde Matteini, *L'officina delle nuvole,* 235n294.

62. Franco Berti has also made this suggestion (see Berti, "Alcuni aspetti," 165–66); in addition see Saslow, *Medici Wedding,* 162.

63. Saslow (*Medici Wedding,* 302n28) makes a similar point.

64. Contini, "Aspects of Medicean Diplomacy," 87.

65. The exception is the account by Cavallino which, comparatively speaking, devotes considerable time to also describing the play itself (see appendix 3).

66. The anonymous Frenchman mentions attending a second performance (see this chapter, section "The Performances in the Uffizi Theater). Pavoni appears to have witnessed both the premiere performance and the later performance of the interludes staged in conjunction with *La pazzia d'Isabella.*

67. ". . . & se la comedia è stata bella l'intermedii sono stati bellissimi, e di maggior importanza per esser tutti pieni di arteficii quasi incredibili, & per esser stati tali, mi è parso di farne partecipe à V.S. accio goda almeno con l'occhio della mente quello, che non ha presentialmente visto. Saprà dunque V.S. che nel cominciar la Comedia: si dette principio alli infrascritti intermedii." *Li artificiosi,* dedication, n.p.

68. The publication is addressed to "MOLTO MAGNIFICO / Signor mio osservandiss." The absence of "Reverendissimo" tends to indicate that the author's patron is not a member of the clergy.

69. *Dizionario biografico degli italiani,* XVI: 137. I wish to thank Giulio Ongaro for bringing this to my attention.

70. Ibid., 149.

71. See Bizzarini, *Luca Marenzio,* 61 and 172. See also DeFord, "Marenzio," 536–37.

72. Bizzarini, *Luca Marenzio,* 61n19.

73. See Zapperi, "Summons of the Carracci," 203–4.

74. Regarding Pavoni's commentary in general and his special interest in martial and athletic display see Saslow, *Medici Wedding,* 161ff.

75. "È uscito in istampa il libro che dicchiara l'apparato della comedia, et intermedii vedutisi in queste nozze. . . ." I:MOs, Cancellaria Ducale, Ambasciatori, Firenze, b. 31 (see also Ledbetter, "Marenzio," 122 and appendix 86). Ledbetter first suggested that Ambassador Gigliolo's dispatch of May 13, 1589, referred to the appearance of Rossi's *Descrizione.*

76. Similarly, the anonymous Bolognese publication, *Le ultime feste,* does not discuss the *Pellegrina* interludes, but documents the other types of festivities that occurred during the wedding celebrations, beginning on May 7, 1589 (i.e., after the premiere of the interludes had already taken place).

77. "On a desia ioué une Comedie, où fut representse un spectacle admirable, à sçavoir sept nuees qui passoyent parmy l'air, se haussans & baissans, sans qu'on peut cognoistre comment cela se pouvoit faire, & y avoit de gens au dedans, iusques environ six vingts personnes. ll y avoit des intermedies à sçavoir, un grand Charioit, une navire, & un mont de Parnasse, & deux grottes de montaigne, & dura le ieu sept heures." *Discours veritable du marriage,* 21.

78. Kümmel, "Ein Deutscher," 3.

79. "La pluspart des assistans pensoient que ce fust des anges, d'aultant que leurs habitz et ornemens paraissoient comme s'ilz les eussent voulu representer, mais l'on

s'abusoit, d'autant qu'il me fust asseuré qu'ilz estoient faictz pour demons, lesquelz ceste done avoit auparavant appellé." Monga, *Voyage,* 114.

80. See Bryson's conceptions of the glance and the gaze in *Vision and Painting,* 87–131. Bryson summarizes (on p. 131): "To dissolve the Gaze that returns the body to itself in me-dusal form, we must willingly enter into the partial blindness of the Glance and dispense with the conception of form as con-sideration, as Arrest, and try to conceive of form in-stead in dynamic terms, as matter in process, in the sense of the original, pre-Socratic word for form: *rhuthmos,* rhythm, the impress on matter of the body's internal energy, in the mobility and vibrancy of its somatic rhythms; the body of labour, of material practice."

4. Marshalling *meraviglia*

1. Burke, *Italian Renaissance,* 182.

2. The hell scene from *intermedio* four was also given special emphasis in unoffi-cial accounts.

3. The *Republic* was the work of Plato, so it is likely that Rossi was referring here to Aristotle's *Politics,* book 8, part 6, which discusses the effects of modes. Although Aristo-tle does not say that Dorian is the best of the modes, he does say that the Dorian will give a "moderate and settled temper" in contrast to other modes. I would like to thank Giulio Ongaro for his attention to this point.

4. Rossi, *Descrizione,* 18 (appendix 1b).

5. As the inventor of the *intermedio,* Bardi's task also concerned the problem of personifying an essentially disembodied and (for some) inaudible music—the harmony of the spheres. For Ficino there were two kinds of divine music: one existed entirely in the mind of God; the second was the motions and order of the Heavens, which made a marvelous harmony (Ficino, *Meditations,* 67).

6. Aristotle *Politics,* book 8, part 6.

7. There was also strong precedent for employing a single performer for the pro-logue of such spectacles.

8. Seriacopi, *Memoriale,* c.42r., April 7, 1589; Testaverde Matteini, *L'officina delle nuvole,* 222.

9. The question of which court's *concerto di donne* was superior—Florence or Ferrara—was debated within musical circles at the Florentine court itself by archrivals Giulio Caccini and Emilio de' Cavalieri. See the letter of Ercole Cortile cited in Fenlon, "Preparations for a Princess," 275.

10. See chapter 3, section "The Performances in the Uffizi Theater."

11. None of the foreign diarists mention Archilei by name, although it is evident from several accounts that she was recognized as a female (not male) singer.

12. See appendix 6 for full text and translation of "Dalle più alte sfere." Bardi wrote the song text. See Rossi, *Descrizione,* 19 (appendix 1b). Rossi's version of the text differs slightly from that presented in Malvezzi's print, by beginning thus: "Dalle celesti sfere. . . ." Titles of all song texts are drawn from Malvezzi's *Intermedii et concerti* unless otherwise stated.

13. Despite a lack of word-for-word comprehension, it is evident that in general the audience understood that the songs were alluding to the royal couple. For example, at the opening of his brief description of the *intermedi,* ambassador Gigliolo notes: "Si vede al p.o il Paradiso aperto circondato da nuvole con chori di musica d'ogni sorte, et giovanetti et fanciulle che cantavano canzoni per alludere alli novelli sposi." (At the beginning one

sees paradise open, surrounded by clouds with musical choruses of all sorts, and young women and men who sang songs alluding to the newlyweds.) I:MOs, Cancelleria Ducale, Ambasciatori, Firenze, b. 31; Ledbetter, "Marenzio," 216.

14. "[W]elchs so lieblich angefangen zu singenn zugleich auf der lautten slagende, das Jederman sagte, es where unmueglich das eines menschen stimm so lieblich sein konne, hatt auch aller Zuseher gemhuet also bewegett mitt ihrem singen das darvon nicht zuschreiben." Kümmel, "Ein Deutscher," 8, and Katritzky, "Aby Warburg," 239.

15. Bianconi, *Music in the Seventeenth Century,* 61. As Peter Burke notes, the term "sweet" (*soave, dolce*) was the "most overworked term of praise" as far as music was concerned, although it is difficult to attribute precise meaning. Although he does not draw a parallel, Burke later remarks: "Of all the ways in which Christians have imagined God, two seem particularly characteristic of the period. The emphasis on the sweetness of God . . ." is one of them. Burke, *Italian Renaissance,* 155, 185.

16. Regarding the mechanics of the Neapolitan singing style see chapter 2, section "The Currency of *meraviglia*: Inside and Outside the Theater."

17. In this regard, the actual length of Archilei's song would have been carefully timed to coordinate with her cloud's descent and her eventual disappearance.

18. Rossi, *Descrizione,* 18–19 (appendix 1b).

19. See especially *Li sontuosissimi,* n.p. (appendix 2) and Gadenstedt's account in Katritzky, "Aby Warburg," 239, and Kümmel, "Ein Deutscher," 8.

20. Notes in Seriacopi's logbook reveal the concern to disguise the visible beams and ropes supporting the clouds with cloth and felt: Seriacopi, *Memoriale,* c.25r., February 13, 1589; Testaverde Matteini, *L'officina delle nuvole,* 203.

21. It is also possible that Archilei mimed her accompaniment on the lute, because two chitarrone players backstage also provided support.

22. I would like to thank Richard Wistreich for sharing this information.

23. The humanist influence—specifically the model of the Greek poet declaiming to a stringed instrument—is the important connection. Either plucked-string instrument would have provided appropriate accompaniment, because the tendency was to associate "modern" instruments with those of the ancients. According to Vincenzo Galilei, the harp was essentially the Greek kithara with a slightly different shape and more strings; instruments such as the lute and chitarrone (which literally meant "big kithara") were also thought of in terms of ancient counterparts.

24. The *Pellegrina* interludes were dominated by the use of hand-plucked string instruments that were essentially used as continuo instruments. However, in his address to the reader in *Intermedii et concerti,* Malvezzi mentions the use of three wooden organs in the *concerti.* ("Intervenivano in tutti gli concerti tre Organi di legno dolcissimi due all'unisono, et uno all'ottava bassa.") In the *nono* partbook Malvezzi does not identify specific compositions in which organs were utilized; it is therefore not entirely clear which pieces he considered *concerti.*

25. David Burrows, "On Hearing Things," 189.

26. "[When] the first cloth fell, a cloud remained in the air inside which there was a lady dressed as an angel, who like an angel sang in such a sonorous manner, and with most beautiful accompaniments that everyone remained in wonder and stunned; and that cloud, having descended little by little, disappeared. . . ." Cavallino, 3 (appendix 3). See also Gadenstedt's observations regarding the singer as goddess: Katritzky, "Aby Warburg," 239, and Kümmel, "Ein Deutscher," 7–8.

27. "Crescer la nuvola del primo intermedio che vada più alta della signora Vittoria. . . ." (Enlarge the cloud of the first *intermedio* [so] that it goes higher [above] Signora Vittoria [Archilei]. . . .") Seriacopi, *Memoriale,* c.25r., February 13, 1589; Testaverde Matteini, *L'officina delle nuvole,* 203. See also Saslow, *Medici Wedding,* 99.

28. One of the most memorable Annunciations was staged for the marriage of Prince Francesco de' Medici and Joanna of Austria in 1565 under the dome of Santo Spirito: "Paradise appeared open and full of a stupendous splendour, and in it God the Father sat amidst a multitude of Angels and Cherubim, and told the Angel Gabriel in a beautiful mandorla all full of lights descended slowly to earth, and above him then was a Choir of Angels that descended with him half way then stopped, and the mandorla where the Angel Gabriel was then went slowly by itself to earth." The description (by Domenico Mellini) is cited in Newbigin, *Feste D'oltrano,* 214–15. See also Newbigin, "The Word Made Flesh."

29. See Strong, *Art and Power,* 36. See Hanafi, *Monster in the Machine,* 78 and n. 72, regarding Jesuit scientists' active role in devising mechanical wonders.

30. Emblems were of course also important as memory aids. See Yates, *The Art of Memory.*

31. In Katelijne Van Laethem's recent recording of the song, the echo "ending" has been omitted, while Emma Kirkby's recording reverses the "endings" as they appear in Malvezzi's print. In reversing the endings, Kirkby prefers to conclude the piece with what appears to be the more vocally spectacular ending. Kirkby's performance is found on the Taverner Consort's *Una 'Stravaganza' di Medici;* the rendition by Van Laethem is on the Huelgas Ensemble's recording, *La Pellegrina.*

32. Rossi's account, with its emphasis on the visual dimensions of each scene, does not mention the use of echo effects.

33. "Au devant du theatre, qui est fort grand et hault, y avoit deux toilles qui couvroient tout le theatre. Quand l'on voulust commencer tout à ung instant la première, qui estoit rouge, tomba par terre. La seconde, qui estoit comme azuree, demeura, tout au millieu de laquelle parust une *donna* qui estoit assize dans une nuee tenant ung luct en sa main, laquelle chantoit et peu à peu descendit jusques sur le theatre, dont elle disparut incontinant. Elle jouoit et chantoit si bien que chacun l'admiroit; et sur la fin en son chant fust ouy ung esco qui luy respondoit, lequel paroissoit estre bien loing du theatre d'un mil ou plus." Monga, *Voyage,* 113.

34. "Innanti alla Scena vi erano due tele, che la coprivano. La prima era rossa: la quale mandata giù, rimase la prospettiva pur'anco coperta d'un'altra tela azzurra: nel mezo della quale vi era una donna, che stava à sedere sopra una nuvola, et con un liuto cominciò a sonare, et cantare molto soavemente un madrigale: et cosi sonando, et cantando venne calando giù à poco, à poco nascondendosi in certi scogli, finendo tra quelli il madrigale in un'Echo tanto maraviglioso, che pareva fosse discosto il reflesso un buon miglio." Pavoni, *Diario,* 14–15.

35. Associating the new duchess with the goddess Minerva was fitting in several respects. The warrior goddess was known for perpetuating peace and learning, an appropriate connection in light of the political alliance that was being forged. The union of "strong Hercules" and "new Minerva" thus signified the peace and prosperity that would result from the combined strength of Tuscany and Lorraine. In addition, Minerva was a symbol of chastity, an assumed attribute of the royal bride. Regarding Minerva's attributes, see Wittkower, "Transformations of Minerva," 199.

36. Although Malvezzi's musical print does not include a separate partbook for the echo (which could indicate that Archilei produced her own echo), I am convinced that the echo was indeed rendered by another singer stationed at a considerable distance from Archilei, which is why several of the auditors make a point of mentioning the effect.

37. The figure of Hercules had been associated with the Medici since the fifteenth century, and was claimed as the mythological founder of Florence. For more information see Fiorani, *Marvel of Maps,* 35–41.

38. I would like to thank Deanna Shemek for bringing this distinction to my attention, urging me to consider the mythological figure of Echo, and verbalizing suggestive readings for understanding Echo within the context of the first *intermedio.*

39. *Li sontuosissimi,* n.p. (appendix 2).

40. See Hollander, *Figure of Echo,* especially 6–13.

41. One should note the relationship of both Juno and Jove to Echo in this part of her story. As will be seen, Jove represented Duke Ferdinando throughout the interludes. It is Juno who recognizes Echo's smoke screen of "chatter" that allows Jove to continue his infidelities, and thus it is a female deity who punishes Echo. Although Christine of Lorraine is nowhere identified as Juno in official commentary, the goddess had long been associated with Florentine duchesses, and in fact several unofficial commentators (mistakenly) identify the goddess on a number of occasions (see especially commentaries of *intermedio* four cited in the appendixes).

42. See Cartari, *Le imagini,* 135–37. Regarding other references to Cartari see Ketterer, "Florentine intermedi," 193, 193n3, 201n28

43. Jones, "New Songs," 265–66.

44. Treadwell, "Florentine monody 'alla Romanina,'" 16–18.

45. Bryson, *Vision and Painting,* 93.

46. Bardi evidently anticipated criticism from the connoisseurs in this regard; the issue is addressed in chapter 3: see sections *"La varietà e l'unità"* and "The Problem of Musical Humanism."

47. Rossi is suggesting that the spectator may, at this juncture, have expected the opening scene from the play, which was a view of the city of Pisa.

48. Rossi, *Descrizione,* 19–20 (appendix 1b).

49. Rossi later reiterates this point: ". . . Paradiso fosse divenuto tutto l'Apparato, e la Prospettiva" (ibid., 20). ". . . and the stage and perspective seemed to have become Paradise."

50. See, for example, Monga, *Voyage,* 113; Katritzky, "Aby Warburg," 239, and Kümmel, "Ein Deutscher," 8; Pavoni, *Diario,* 15.

51. See *Li sontuosissimi* (appendix 2). See also the description by the Bavarian commentator (Katritzky, "Aby Warburg," 232 and 236), although it clearly derives from the former account.

52. Kathi Meyer-Baer has pointed out that in the first *intermedio* "Elysium was in heaven . . . [whereas] in Greek mythology it was situated at the end of the world toward the west." See Meyer-Baer, *Music of the Spheres,* 205–207.

53. The parallel is made explicit in the description contained in *Li artificiosi* where both the descent and ascent are described in identical terms. *Li artificiosi,* n.p. (appendix 4).

54. See, for example, the brief account of *intermedio* one in *Li sontuosissimi* (appendix 2), where sound is persistently attached to a specific theatrical space or, similarly, sound is described in motion.

55. This process was also linked to the spectator's perception of time, as I argued earlier with regard to Harmony's mesmerizingly incremental descent.

56. Discussing cultures of print (and especially anthologies) some two centuries later, Leah Price makes analogous observations by remarking that the "anthology trained readers to pace themselves through an unmanageable bulk of print by sensing when to skip and where to linger." See Price, *Rise of the Novel,* 4ff.

57. Rossi, *Descrizione,* 20 (appendix 1b).

58. Although Rossi clearly indicates that all the instruments in Heaven and on Earth initially played the sinfonia together, it is possible from a pragmatic standpoint that each of the groups played the piece separately, as well as together. (We should also recall that any last minute changes are not reflected in Rossi's account.) Howard Brown suggested a scoring that would involve the earthly instruments alone (*Sixteenth-Century Instrumentation,* 110–11n45), and indeed the piece has been successfully recorded with Brown's configuration in mind. In Andrew Parrott's recording with the Taverner Consort the sinfonia is initially played by the earthly instruments, which are supplemented on the repeat by the heavenly forces.

59. "Dolcissime Sirene, / Tornate al Cielo, e'ntanto / Facciam cantando a gara un dolce canto."

60. The only commentator to mention the introduction of the solo voice was Cavallino: "The Paradise was embellished by a great number of Gods with beautiful clothes, and there were three musical choirs, all three on the clouds, and the one in the middle sang first where there were several instruments and one voice." See *Le solennissime,* 3 (appendix 3).

61. The instruments involved are the same as those utilized for the sinfonia; thus, the Heavenly deities play a colorful variety of wind and string instruments.

62. "Après avoir longuement joué, peu à peu les nuees retournerent et remonterent au ciel et disparust à l'instant. . . . Le tout estoit si artificiellement faict qu'il ne paroissoit aucune chose partout." Monga, *Voyage,* 113.

63. There were numerous visual and textual parallels between the first and last *intermedi,* some of which were recognized by spectators.

5. Scenic Metamorphosis and Musical Warfare (*Intermedi* Two and Three)

1. *Li artificiosi,* n.p. (appendix 4, "Secondo Intermedio").

2. The anonymous French eyewitness was one of the only commentators to recognize the presentation of a singing competition, although he had no idea of the identity of the participants or the judges (see Monga, *Voyage,* 113). Like most of the other unofficial accounts of this *intermedio,* the Frenchman's report is relatively perfunctory. (His description of *intermedio* four, for example—involving a sorceress and hell scene—is five times longer than this passage, suggesting his more pronounced engagement with the performance.) Pavoni's account of this *intermedio,* in which he *does* identify the characters involved, appears to be an abbreviated version of Rossi's account. Pavoni's listing of musical instruments replicates Rossi's almost exactly (Pavoni, *Diario,* 16).

3. I exclude Pavoni's account here, as it appears to be primarily drawn from Rossi's account (see above n. 2).

4. Rossi, *Descrizione,* 38 (appendix 1c).

5. Ibid. (appendix 1c).

6. Saslow, *Medici Wedding,* 82–83.

7. Saslow claims this mechanism was used, pointing out that Seriacopi's notebook frequently makes reference to *canali* (grooves) in the stage floor, suggesting the use of sliding flats (*Medici Wedding*, 83).

8. Saslow has summarized the considerable amount of scholarship that supports either one design or the other, or (in one case) both hypotheses. Ibid., 82–83, 284nn17–18. Berti ("Diario di Girolamo Seriacopi," 164–65) has suggested the use of both *periaktoi* and flats, a theory which I support, in light of the additional evidence presented here.

9. Katritzky comes to a similar conclusion when considering the German and anonymous French descriptions in this regard ("Aby Warburg," 218).

10. In *intermedio* two the term is used in reference to the two grottos that turned out—like the doors of a wardrobe—to display the musicians inside. Saslow suggests that the use of mobile grottos in *intermedio* two was a special case, implying that a similar mechanism was probably not used in other *intermedi*. Ibid., 284n18.

11. *Li artificiosi*, n.p. (appendix 4, "Sesto, & ultimo Intermedio."). The author of *Li sontuosissimi* uses similar terminology to describe the appearance of the set of Pisa (for *La pellegrina*) following the first *intermedio*: ". . . subito si volta la Prospettiva tutta, et apparisce la Città di Pisa." ([S]uddenly all of the scenery turns, and the city of Pisa appears.) *Li sontuosissimi*, n.p. (appendix 2). Gadenstedt mentions the same moment, but his wording is more specific: ". . . das prospectiff auf den halben umbgewand. . . ." ([T]he scene turned to the half. . . .) Kümmel, "Ein Deutscher," 10, and Katritzky, "Aby Warburg," 240.

12. For example, the Frenchman ends his account of *intermedio* two by referring to ". . . sources, jardins et fontaines si diligemment faict que l'on n'appercevoit quasi rien." (. . . springs, gardens, and fountains made so cleverly that one could *almost* not notice anything [italics mine].) See Monga, *Voyage*, 113. The mere fact that the Frenchman qualifies his statement suggests that perhaps he noticed some construction details that were not intended for the spectators' eyes.

13. The Frenchman was one of the few commentators to mention the magpies (Monga, *Voyage*, 113). Pavoni's account also mentions the magpies but, as previously mentioned, his account paraphrases Rossi's.

14. "Nach verrichteter Musica hatt sich der hoehe berg wieder hienuntter gelasenn und die 2 kleinen berge auch wieder umbgewendett das perspectif wieder als in heuser mutirt und haben den andern actum agirett." Kümmel, "Ein Deutscher," 10–11, and Katritzky, "Aby Warburg," 240.

15. Rossi, *Descrizione*, 40 (appendix 1c). Veils also characterized the dress of the Pierides and Muses.

16. Gadenstedt makes a point of mentioning the orderly seating arrangements for both the "goddesses" (i.e., Hamadryads) as well as the "musicians" (i.e., Pierides and Muses) on either side of the stage. Katritzky, "Aby Warburg," 240, and Kümmel, "Ein Deutscher," 10.

17. Rossi, *Descrizione*, 40–41 (appendix 1c).

18. The title of this section is drawn from the title of Valerie Hotchkiss's book *Clothes Make the Man: Female Cross Dressing in Medieval Europe*.

19. Rossi, *Descrizione*, 41 (appendix 1c).

20. Ibid.

21. Florio (*New World of Words*, 277) defined *lascivo* as "lascivious, letcherous, lustfull, wanton, womanish."

22. The connotations of the term *onesto* (and its counterpart *disonesto*) were integrally tied to both mind *and* body. See Florio's definition of *honesto* (*New World of Words*, 230).

23. Rossi, *Descrizione*, 41 (appendix 1c).

24. Ibid., 40 (appendix 1c).

25. "À ung instant la pluspart de ces nymphes [*sic*] furent transmuees en pies, lesquelles vindrent sur le theatre chantant et cherchant lieu pour se cacher et tirer de la presence des hommes. . . ." (In an instant most of these nymphs [*sic;* Pierides] were transformed into magpies, who came onto the stage singing and looking for a place in which to hide themselves and to withdraw from the presence of men. . . .) Monga, *Voyage,* 113. See also Pavoni, *Diario,* 16.

26. The feathered headdress of the Muses can be seen in Buontalenti's costume design (see plate 11).

27. Rossi, *Descrizione,* 41 (appendix 1c). Rossi's description of the Muses' triumph over the Pierides and Sirens is close to that of Vincenzo Cartari. See *Fountaine of Ancient Fiction,* n.p.

28. For Gadenstedt's description see Kümmel, "Ein Deutscher," 10, and Katritzky, "Aby Warburg," 240; the Italian description in question is *Li sontuosissimi,* n.p. (appendix 2).

29. Monga, *Voyage,* 113.

30. See the account of the Bavarian commentator who consistently refers to *musici* (Katritzky, "Aby Warburg," 232 and 236–37); see also the account of *intermedio* two in *Li sontuosissimi,* n.p. (appendix 2). Strictly speaking, the term *musici* referred to male musicians, but the usage here does not seem intended as a means of highlighting gender.

31. Concerning the probable participation of the Pellizzari sisters see Fenlon, *Music and Patronage,* 1:128–33. In light of the scoring for high voices, Bizzarini (*Luca Marenzio,* 182) suggests that the madrigal may have been sung by the Florentine *concerto di donne;* however, the information provided by Malvezzi clearly contradicts this assertion (see below n. 35).

32. The song was preceded by an opening sinfonia (Malvezzi, *Intermedii et concerti nono,* 8) that was likely heard as the scenic metamorphosis took place.

33. "Il seguente Madrigale cantorno con esquisita maniera, & arte due giovine, che servono il Serenissimo Duca di Mantova con invidia più che mediocre de gl'amatori di cosi nobil virtù: e da un putto lor fratello accompagnate dal suono di un' Arpa, e due Lire." Ibid.

34. The author of *Li artificiosi* goes on to suggest that the two women had further involvement in the *intermedio.* His comments suggest that they potentially joined the larger group of Hamadryads to sing the interlude's concluding number "O figlie di Piero."

35. It is also notable that Malvezzi, though mentioning the duke of Mantua, omits the names of the Pellizzari singers in the *nono* partbook. If one considers how carefully he documents the names of the Florentine court's female singers, one wonders if this is a purposeful omission.

36. Howard Brown proposed this option in his hypothetical reconstruction of the disposition of voices and instruments for the *Pellegrina* interludes. Brown, *Sixteenth-Century Instrumentation,* 114.

37. In our recording the lowest voice is sung by a mezzo-soprano rather than boy soprano.

38. Cavallino, *Le solennissime feste,* 5 (appendix 3).

39. *Li artificiosi,* n.p. (appendix 4, "Secondo Intermedio."); *Li sontuosissimi,* n.p. (appendix 2); and Gadenstedt (Katritzky, "Aby Warburg," 240, and Kümmel, "Ein Deutscher," 10).

40. The upper end of the canto range is the same in both songs, but in "Chi dal delfino aita" the canto part maintains a lower tessitura overall.

41. Malvezzi, *Intermedii et concerti, nono,* 8: "Era formato il concerto di quest'altro Madrigale di un Leuto grosso, un Chitarrone, un Basso di Viola e sei voci."

42. Bizzarini, *Luca Marenzio,* 184–85.

43. The wording here is drawn from James Chater's translation of Bizzarini (ibid., 185). For further opinion of Marenzio's madrigals as "inexpressive" see Walker (*Musique des intermèdes,* xxvi), who compares them to the *madrigal ordinaire* (ordinary [i.e., nontheatrical] madrigal).

44. Bizzarini, *Luca Marenzio,* 184–85.

45. Barbara Hanning tentatively posits that Marenzio may have attempted to make a distinction between the music of the Pierides and that of the Muses (see Hanning, *Of Poetry and Music's Power,* 10).

46. *"Stravaganza" dei Medici,* 45–47; Bizzarini, *Luca Marenzio,* 184–85. Malvezzi (*Intermedii et concerti, nono,* 8) writes: "Questo che segue similmente era con gli medesimi Strumenti e voci da l'uno e l'altro Coro."

47. Regarding the positioning of the three constituent groups see section above "Flux and Transformation" and plate 8.

48. Cavallino, *Le solennissime feste,* 5 (appendix 3).

49. Saslow, *Medici Wedding,* 167.

50. Indeed, for Cavallino the hell scene—which was only a *part* of *intermedio* four—was evidently so striking that in his mind it constituted an *intermedio* all of its own.

51. The anonymous source *Discours de la magnifique réception* (p. 21) mentions the entertainment's duration.

52. "Nachdem der ander actus sich vollendett hatt sich das perspectiff verendertt in die form eines lustigen waldes gar kunstlich und zierlich mitt mancherlei schachtigen beumen und buschswerk bemhalett Sein auf den platz kommen 36 musicanten auff mancherlei art bekleidett allerlei Instrument habende und darauf spielende etliche dantze sonderlicher artt zur zierung der comoedi gemacht. Von diesen 36 Musicanten sein auf jeder seiten 18 abgetheiltt worden, jegeneinander [gegeneinander] uberr haven gedantzett und sein auf jeder seitten 2 dantzmeisters sonderlich beruemett ihnen zugeordnett gewesenn, die den dantz gefhuerett, in dem die ahm besten gedantzett, ist von untten aus dem bodem heraus ein scheuslich greulich groses monstrum oder Thier in gestalt wie ein groser drache heraus gekommen, [hat] feur ausgespien, hatte grose fittigen, mitt welchen es ein gros gethoene machte, hesliche klauen ahn den fuesen und sich sher schrecklich erzeigett, ist auf die Musicanten und dantzers zugeeilett, gleich als wenn es sie mitt aufgethanem rache verslingen woltte. . . ." Kümmel, "Ein Deutscher," 11–12, and Katritzky, "Aby Warburg," 241.

53. *Li sontuosissimi,* n.p. (appendix 2).

54. Florio, *New World of Words,* 324.

55. Ibid., 230.

56. Greenblatt, *Marvelous Possessions,* 2 and 20.

57. Rossi, *Descrizione,* 43–44 (appendix 1d).

58. "[C]e serpent . . . mestoit sur le theatre du feu par la bouche, nez et oreilles avec des hurlemens fort espouventables. . . ." Monga, *Voyage,* 114.

59. *Li artificiosi,* n.p. (appendix 4, "Terzo Intermedio.")

60. See Gadenstedt's account above, the Frenchman's account (Monga, *Voyage,* 113), Pavoni, *Diario,* 16–17, and Rossi, *Descrizione,* 42 (appendix 1d).

61. "Ma dove'l fero mostro / Forse havrà Giove udito il pianto nostro[.]" Malvezzi, *Intermedii et concerti, nono,* 10.

62. For a more extended discussion of Marenzio's "Qui di carne si sfama" see Pirrotta, *Music and Theatre,* 224–28.

63. "O padre ò Re del Cielo / Volgi pietosi gli occhi; / All'infelice Delo / A te dimanda aita, e piange, e plora[.]" Ibid.

64. Bizzarini, *Luca Marenzio,* 185.

65. See chapter 6 and chapter 8, section "Framing the Festivities: The Heavenly Descent."

66. For a wealth of information see Hanning, "Glorious Apollo."

67. Cavallino, *Le solennissime feste,* 5 (appendix 3) and Pavoni, *Diario,* 17.

68. The Frenchman noted: "alors il descendit du ciel ung homme armé d'un arc et fleches si subtillement qu'il ne fust point apperceu jusques à ce qu'il fust sur le theatre. . . ." ([T]hen a man armed with a bow and arrows descended from the sky so subtly that he was not noticed until he was on the stage. . . .) Monga, *Voyage,* 114. Alternatively, the anonymous author suggested that the main dancer was one of the shepherds [Delphians] who emerged from their circle. *Li artificiosi,* n.p. (appendix 4, "Terzo Intermedio.").

69. "Man verkhort die *prospettiva* aber einmal, und gehn 36. Musici heraus, mit selzamen Inventionen und mit 4. tanzern. Und weil sie nur singen, wechst aus einer hole, oder *antro* ein greilichs *monstrum.* Das bringen die tanzer und Musici mit irem gesang umb. Darnach thuet man ein herrlichen tanz in Musica." Katritzky, "Aby Warburg," 233 and 237. The account in *Li sontuosissimi,* n.p. (appendix 2) is almost identical.

70. Kümmel, "Ein Deutscher," 11–12, and Katritzky, "Aby Warburg," 241. Regarding the participation of four dance masters, see also *Li sontuosissimi,* n.p. (appendix 2).

71. Of course, accounts were adapted after the fact and also conflated with other reports that may have been circulating. (There is also the possibility that the four performances were not identical.) In this instance however, the Frenchman and Gadenstedt, both eyewitnesses to the premiere performance, had quite different impressions of the scene.

72. Katritzky, "Aby Warburg," 243, and Kümmel, "Ein Deutscher," 17.

73. Pirrotta, *Music and Theatre,* 228.

74. Rossi, *Descrizione,* 44 (appendix 1d). By the same token, Apollo's miraculous descent from on high as described by Rossi (see plate 12) seems not to the have caught the attention of any other commentators, save the Frenchman whose description seems somewhat ambiguous (see above, n. 68).

75. "[U]ntter dessen die dentzers [*sic*] sich ahn das Thier gemachtt, mitt groser behendigkeitt umb dis Thier gesprungenn, mitt demselben gekempffett, endlich dasselbe durchstochenn, das es zur erden gefallen, sich hinundwieder geweltzett, und thoett [= tot] wieder in das loch mitt grosem geprassell gefallen, daraus es herauf kham. Darnach habenn die däntzers fur freuden noch einen lustigen dantz gethann sein von dem platz wieder abgewichen. . . ." Kümmel, "Ein Deutscher," 12, and Katritzky, "Aby Warburg," 241.

76. See Rossi, *Descrizione,* 43–45 (appendix 1d).

77. Bizzarini, *Luca Marenzio,* 181–82.

78. Ibid., 182n46.

79. The observation and its wording is Pirrotta's, *Music and Theatre,* 229.

80. Rossi, *Descrizione,* 45 (appendix 1d).

81. The costume design for the latter is reprinted in Saslow, *Medici Wedding,* 228 (plate 46) with notes at 228–29. In this case, too, the cast note is not entirely clear.

82. Vittoria had come to Florence in Ferdinando's entourage, along with Cavalieri, from Rome. Lucia Caccini, on the other hand, had previously been in Francesco de' Medici's employ, and, like a number of Francesco's musicians, had been cut from Ferdinando's payroll.

83. See the costume design for Gualfreducci in Saslow, *Medici Wedding,* 218 (plate 36), with notes at 216–17.

6. Diabolical Bodies and Monstrous Machines

1. "Dieses whar zwar ein kunstreiches Intermedium aber darbeneben sher schrecklich anzusehenn." Kümmel, "Ein Deutscher," 15, and Katritzky, "Aby Warburg," 242.

2. Rossi, *Descrizione,* 49 (appendix 1e).

3. *Li artificiosi,* n.p. "Quarto Intermedio." (appendix 4). See also *Li sontuosissimi,* n.p. "4 Intermedio" (appendix 2) and Monga, *Voyage,* 114. The Bavarian report states: "Man verkhört die *prospettiva* mehr ein mal. Und erscheint in dem lufft Juno in einem Triumphwagen dene 2. thüer ziechen. Und ist so selzam angemacht, das mans nit merckhen oder sechen khan, wo und an weme es seye." (The scene is turned again once more, and Juno [*sic*] appears in the air, in a triumphal carriage [being] drawn by two animals. And it is so strangely attached that one cannot notice or see where, or onto what.) Katritzky, "Aby Warburg," 233 and 237.

4. See Cavallino, *Le solennissime feste,* 5 (appendix 3).

5. Ibid.

6. Ibid.

7. The text and translation are based on versions of the song that survive in two manuscripts (I:Fn, Magl. XIX.66 and B:Bc, ms. 704, pp. 15–16). I have omitted the text repetitions that can be seen in the musical setting (example 6.1) and regularized capitalization at the beginning of each poetic line. The text by G. B. Strozzi provided in Rossi's *Descrizione* differs in some respects from that given in the two manuscripts. Malvezzi's official print omitted Caccini's song as a result of court politics.

8. This was a formula that he put into practice and advocated in print, railing against those singers whose words could not be understood because of the profusion of embellishment.

9. The text of the Caccini song differs from that of the other two solo songs in interludes one and five—"Dalle più alte sfere" and "Io che l'onde raffreno," respectively—because the identity of the character portrayed is not revealed through the text of the song itself.

10. Regarding the wondrousness of Lucia Caccini's singing, the Bavarian commentator states: "Wann nun solche Juno in mitten des *theatri* khombt, da singt ein ainigs weib gar herrlich, darnach zeuchts widerumb darvon, und erscheint auf der anndern seiten ein grosser nebl, der sich, so bald er in die mitl khombt, aufthuet." (Now when such a Juno [*sic*] gets to the middle of the stage, one solitary woman sings most

wonderfully, after which she goes away again, and on the other side a great fog [cloud] appears which, as soon as it reaches the middle, opens up.) Katritzky, "Aby Warburg," 233 and 237.

11. A good example of this strategy is articulated by Rossi when he describes the intended effect of the rapid disappearance of the opening scene of Rome from the first *intermedio* (a scene that in fact never actually materialized in performance): "And, while the crowd was trying to figure out and see where the cloud and the little temple had gone, almost without realizing what was happening, and in less time than it took me to say it, going toward the Heavens and hiding there, the scene with Rome disappeared, which [the scene of Rome] could have caused not a little wonder, if the wonders which it was hiding and that in leaving it revealed, left its own wonder so far behind, that one could immediately forget about it." Rossi, *Descrizione,* 19 (appendix 1b).

12. Regarding the lighting on the costume of the first Siren in *intermedio* one Rossi notes: ". . . e per più farla lieta, e adorna le mise dietro alle spalle un manto di drappo rosso, nel quale, percotendo i lumi, che invisibili nelle nugole furono dall'artefice accomodati, come più di sotto diremo, risplendeva sì fattamente, che non vi si poteva affisare gli occhi." (. . . and to make her more cheerful and adorned, he put on her shoulders a mantle of red cloth which, when struck by the lights (which had been placed in an invisible manner in the clouds by the maker [of the scene] as we will explain later), was shining in such a way that one could not stare at it.) Rossi, *Descrizione,* 23.

13. See, for example, Passignani, *Descrittione dell'intermedii fatti nel felicissimo palazo del Gran Duca Cosimo,* 5–6: "Nel secondo Intermedio comparse Eritone maga, della quale non solo Lucano, ma Dante ancora parlò. Fingevasi questa, donna fatta, cioè da quarant'anni in là, di viso pallido, magro, scapigliata, capellatura nera, canuticcia, coronata d'arcipresso, scalza da un piede, scinta, in mano una verghetta di colore scuro, vestito di bigio." (In the second *intermedio* the sorceress Eritone appeared, of whom not only Lucan, but Dante also spoke. This was portrayed as a mature woman, that is, older then forty, with a pale, thin face, disheveled, with black hair with a little gray, with a crown of cypress, with one bare foot, with a loose dress [lit., without belt], with a little rod of a dark color in her hand, dressed in gray.)

14. Rossi, *Descrizione,* 49 (appendix 1e).

15. In the later engraving of the same scene by Epifanio d'Alfiano the sorceress's legs appear to be covered.

16. Winches and pulleys in the flyloft were supported by a permanent wooden grid that facilitated a complex variety of aerial maneuvers. For more on the machinery see Saslow, *Medici Wedding,* 84–86.

17. The verb "frenare" that Rossi uses can mean "to govern" or "to rule" in addition to the more literal translation of "to bridle."

18. *Li artificiosi,* n.p. (see appendix 4, "Quarto Intermedio."). Pavoni, *Diario,* 17: "Comparve in Scene (ma in aria) avanti, che si mutasse la prospettiva, un carro dorato, ornato di gemme, sopra del quale stava una donna, figurata per una Maga. . . ." (On the stage, but in the air, a golden chariot decorated with gems appeared, before the change of scenery. Inside the chariot was a woman portrayed as a sorceress. . . .) Monga, *Voyage,* 114: "Auparavant que le theatre changea parust ung chariot à quatre roues tiré par deux dragons. . . ." (Before the scene changed, a four-wheeled chariot appeared, pulled by two dragons. . . .)

19. The *sbarra* is discussed in Nagler, *Theater Festivals,* 49–57.

20. Nagler suggests that the sorceress's hair consisted of veils; nevertheless the implication is still one of loose, flying hair. As we saw in relation to Rossi's description of the costumes for the Pierides and Muses (from *intermedio* two), some veils could be perceived as more licentious than others.

21. Earlier Florentine *intermedi* referred to both *magae* and *streghe.* The latter were included in the interludes for Grazzini's comedy *La Gelosia,* first produced in 1550. See Ghisi, *Feste Musicali,* xxiv.

22. The position of riding, as a representation of power, was typically reserved for men. Equestrian statues featuring the prince seated atop his horse and presiding over the Renaissance piazza were emblematic of his authority over his dominion. See Burke, *Eyewitnessing,* 67.

23. Zika, "She-man," 171.

24. Ibid., 172–74.

25. One such depiction is the print by Baldung Grien reproduced in ibid., 180.

26. Couliano, *Eros and Magic,* 152.

27. Regarding the belief that witchcraft caused disruption and chaos see Clark, *Thinking with Demons,* 555–59.

28. Ibid., 553f.

29. On this point see Ketterer, "Florentine intermedi," 201.

30. Pavoni (*Diario,* 18) makes a similar point.

31. Rossi, *Descrizione,* 51 (appendix 1e).

32. The music to which Gadenstedt refers is the sinfonia found in *Intermedii et concerti.* It is mentioned in the *nono* partbook (p. 10) after Malvezzi states: "Qui manca un'aria" (an aria is missing here), referring to the sorceress's song, which is omitted from the publication.

33. Katritzky, "Aby Warburg," 241–42, and Kümmel, "Ein Deutscher," 13–14: "[D]em wagen gefolgett ein grose wolcken zugethan in welcher musicirt ward, wie dieselbe auch oben mitten in die scenam gekommen, ist sie stillgestanden sich auf beiden seiten voneinander gethan, haben darinn 24 Musicanten gesessenn musicirt, wie solchs geschehen, hatt sich die wolcke wieder zugethan, die Musicanten gleichwoll musicirt, welch gar heimlich gelasenn, als wann es von fern in den wolcken where, whar lieblich zuhoerenn, ging inmittels mhelig fortt bis auf die ander seitten, und darselbst wie der wage verschwunden, diese beide stucklin sein gar kunstlich gemachtt gewesenn, dann niemand erkennen konnen, wie es immer mueglich where das solchs kontt regirt werden, oder wie solchs also offentlich in freier lufft hette konnen fortt kommenn."

34. The chord-playing instruments are listed in the *nono* partbook (pp. 10–11) and included lire da braccio, lira viol, alto and bass lutes, chitarrone, psaltery, and harp. With regard to the pseudo-continuo function of these instruments for this song (as opposed to their role in the preceding sinfonia), I disagree with Brown's reading (*Sixteenth-Century Instrumentation,* 121–22).

35. Clark, *Thinking with Demons,* 217.

36. Note that the sorceress refers to the fact that the demons "who are on high see all of heaven" which alludes to this chain of influence, whereby the spirit world oversees and can influence the planetary and stellar worlds. In Rossi's *Descrizione* the hierarchical transmission of influence is not so clearly defined as we see in the sorceress's song. Citing Plato, Rossi posits the demons as intermediary figures that "report divine things to men, and human things to gods" (*Descrizione,* 49; appendix 1e).

37. Young, *Medici,* 346.

38. On the risk of confusion between devils and "good demons" see Clark, *Thinking with Demons*, 219–20.

39. Rossi, *Descrizione,* 49–51 (appendix 1e).

40. Ibid., 51–52 (appendix 1e).

41. The hell scene from the *intermedi* for *L'amico fido* presages this idea; the devils were presented as already vanquished and lamenting their defeat.

42. Rossi, *Descrizione,* 52 (appendix 1e).

43. "[A]nd the stage having opened up, Pluto and his followers appear, who had a great number of naked little boys that they were torturing as if they had been the souls of the damned. . . ." *Li artificiosi,* n.p. (appendix 4, "Quarto Intermedio."). Cavallino refers to "many little naked children who the devils were torturing, and they gave them [the children] to the mouths of serpents to be eaten." Cavallino, *Le solennissime feste,* 5–6 (appendix 3).

44. Gadenstedt's eyewitness account of this scene has already been cited (see chapter 2, section "The Currency of *meraviglia:* Inside and Outside the Theater").

45. The Frenchman's "devils" appear to correspond to the above-cited description by Rossi of the two furies.

46. According to Rossi (*Descrizione,* 53), some of these fires were feigned, while others were real.

47. "[E]t aussi tost le theatre changea de forme et parust des montagnes, cavernes, feuz et flambes et se representa l'enfer avec deux bandes de diables, aucuns desquelz avoient le visage et les mains teinctes de sang et des serpens à l'entour de la teste et des braz. L'enfer fust représenté tout en feu, qui dura assez long temps sur le theatre, et dans l'enfer plusieurs ames qui estoient tourmentees, pour la representation dequoy il y avoit 35 ou 40 ensfans tous nudz de l'a[a]ge de 9, 10 et 12 ans. Lucifer estoit au millieu de l'enfer qui se monstroit à moictié avec une grosse teste à trois faces, tenant des ames en la bouche de chacune d'ycelles; les diables prenoient des ames d'une part et d'autre et les portoient a Lucifer. Comme il en devoroit une, il en eschappa deux autres, lesquelles furent reprises par les diables et portees à Lucifer qui aussi tost les devora. *Caron* avec sa barque passoit et repassoit les ames et le tout si bien representé que cella faisoit horreur au peuple." Monga, *Voyage,* 114–15.

48. Rossi notes that Lucifer, in the context of the fires that surrounded him, was "in a lake, in the shape of a circle, all made of ice, and he was coming out of the lake from the middle of his chest, eight *braccia.* His head had three faces, the one in front—just as Dante says—was red, that one on the right was white and yellow, and the third one was black." Rossi, *Descrizione,* 53 (appendix 1e). Rossi's description is drawn from canto 34 of *The Inferno* (see Dante, *Inferno,* 354).

49. "Oh quanto parve a me gran maraviglia / quando' io vidi tre facce a la sua testa! / L'una dinanzi, e quella era vermiglia; / l'altr' eran due, che s'aggiugnieno a questa / sovresso 'l mezzo di ciascuna spalla, / e sé giugnieno al loco de la cresta: / e la destra parea tra bianca e gialla; / la sinistra a vedere era tal, quali / vegnon di là onde 'l Nilo s'avvalla." Dante, *Inferno,* 354. My translation is adapted from that of Anthony Esolen.

50. "Lo 'mperador del doloroso regno / da mezzo 'l petto uscia fuor de la ghiaccia; / e più con un gigante io mi convegno, / chei giganti non fan con le sue braccia: / vedi oggimai quant' esser dee quel tutto / ch'a così fatta perte si confaccia." (The emperor of the reign of misery / from his chest up emerges from the ice: / I and a giant are more near in stature / Than are a giant and that creature's arm, / and if one limb is so enormous, you can see how vast the rest must be.) Ibid. The translation is by Esolen.

51. Marshall, "Bodies in the Audience," 54.

52. Rossi, *Descrizione*, 53–54 (appendix 1e). Rossi goes on to cite the relevant passage from Dante: "He was chewing up with his teeth / a sinner on every mouth, just like a press, / So that he was making three of them hurt. / To the one in front the biting was nothing / Compared to the scratching, that sometimes his back / Was completely left without skin."

53. Foucault, "Spectacle of the Scaffold," 58.

54. Ibid., 57.

55. Franko, "Figural Inversions," 45.

56. On the relationship of early modern humoral medicine and the language of modern emotion see Schoenfeldt, *Bodies and Selves,* 169–70. Rowe ("Humoral Knowledge," 181–82) treats the relationship between fear, humoral fluids, and the heart.

57. Rowe, "Humoral Knowledge," 182.

58. As Susan McClary reminded me, the sound of the machines would have almost gone unnoticed, in the same way that audiences of so-called silent films mentally edited out the sound of the film as it rolled.

59. Rossi's account is somewhat confusing because near the very opening of his account he indicates that the furies and devils sang, and he provides their song text. A two-and-a-half page description follows, in which he details the horrors of hell. But right at the end of his account he states: "And after the devils who were sitting on the boulders finished their sad song, with sad screeches and screams, they sank, and similarly Lucifer, and Hell was closed again, and the rocks and the caves, and the nooks and crannies on fire disappeared immediately [and] the scene came back to its original beauty. . . ." He thereby suggests that the singing actually came at the very end of the scene, as unofficial sources confirm.

60. Thus, I disagree with Hugh Keyte's assumption (in the CD booklet for "Una 'stravaganza' dei Medici," p. 59) that there was probably no music for the conclusion of the *intermedio*. For accounts that confirm the use of music to conclude rather than open the scene, see the Bavarian report in Katritzky, "Aby Warburg," 233 and 237; Gadenstedt in Katritzky, "Aby Warburg," 242, and Kümmel, "Ein Deutscher," 14–15; Monga, Voyage 115; *Li sontuosissimi,* n.p. ("4 Intermedio"); Pavoni, *Diario,* 19.

61. Malvezzi, *Intermedii et concerti, nono,* 11.

62. "Aber solche stucke wharen gantz kleglich erbermlich und melancholischs componirt, als wenn sie halb weineten, whar kleglich zuhoern." Katritzky, "Aby Warburg," 242, and Kümmel, "Ein Deutscher," 14.

63. *Li sontuosissimi,* n.p. (see appendix 2, "4 Intermedio"). See also the Bavarian report (Katritzky, "Aby Warburg," 233 and 237).

64. "In questo mezo i diavoli, che sedevano su scogli detti dianzi, fecero una bella, ma dogliosa musica, forse per dolore della infelicità loro: la quale haveva concetti tanto mesti, che non simigliavano altro, che affanni, e tormenti. Et in questo mentre, loro, li scogli, et caverne, con l'Inferno sparrirono, ritornando la Scena nella sua prima bellezza." Pavoni, *Diario,* 19.

65. For a summary of past usage of these instruments for infernal scenes in Florentine *intermedi* see Weaver, "Sixteenth-Century Instrumentation," 370–72.

66. For Ficino the melancholic disposition was a response to the loss of the celestial realm. On this point see Schiesari, "Gendering of Melancholia," 240.

67. "Il y avoit aussi des rochers sur lesquelz estoient des diables qui chantoient et faisoient des hurlemens et plainctes fort tristes et peu à peu tout l'enfer disparut comme

si tout [s]e fust retiré dans la terre, car après le theatre changea d'une autre forme." Monga, *Voyage,* 115.

    68. Clark, *Thinking with Demons,* 552.

7. Singing the Marvelous (*Intermedio* Five)

    1. Cavallino, *Le solennissime feste,* 6 (appendix 3).

    2. Malvezzi, *Intermedii et concerti, nono,* 11.

    3. Some spectators merely described a generic goddess or goddesses. See the Bavarian's report in Katritzky, "Aby Warburg," 233 and 237. The Frenchman notes the appearance of a sea goddess, but correctly identifies her companions as (sea) nymphs and tritons (Monga, *Voyage,* 115). Pavoni (*Diario,* 20) is one of the few to identify the singer as Anfitrite.

    4. Gadenstedt is the only observer to mention a distinctive physical similarity between the singer and a siren. If the scene was indeed close to that reproduced in the engraving by d'Alfiano (plate 20), then it seems that Gadenstedt probably mistook the front nib of the shell that splayed out on either side for the typical two-forked tail of a siren. Rossi (*Descrizione,* 55; appendix 1f) emphasizes the singer's nudity: "[When] the niche had completely exited from the water, one saw Anfitrite seated on it, dressed in apparel so tight, and so tailored, and so similar to the color of flesh, that one wouldn't have appeared more nude than if shown nudity itself"—but no other commentator mentions nudity (which they undoubtedly would have, as is evidenced by descriptions of *intermedio* four). The maritime theme most apparent to the audience was described by the Frenchman: in the mother-of-pearl shell there was ". . . une deesse maritime toute couverte de perles et une infinitté de joyaux avec plusieurs branches de corail et une couronne sur la teste." Monga, *Voyage,* 115. (There was ". . . a sea goddess completely covered with pearls and an infinite number of gems, with several branches of coral and a crown on her head.") These aspects concur with both Rossi's account (appendix 1f) and the engraving by d'Alfiano (plate 20).

    5. "Aus diesem mher in der mitten zimlich hoch erhaben, sach [= sah] man das weib, dessen bereits gedachtt welchs so lieblich singen kontt gekleidett wie eine syrenen untten wie ein fischs, oben wie eine schone jungfraue mitt gelben langen zirlichen harenn auf welcher jeden halben 12 syrenen aus dem mher khamen sasen etwas niedriger auch also gekleidett, sungen mitt einander sher lieblich, darnach versunchken sie im mher." Katritzky, "Aby Warburg," 242, and Kümmel, "Ein Deutscher," 15.

    6. Rossi confirms the visual similarity between what was intended to be a representation of Anfitrite with sea nymphs (and tritons). See Rossi, *Descrizione,* 56 (appendix 1f).

    7. "I suoi calzaretti mavì adorni di gioie, di cammei, di mascherini, e di veli d'ariento, e d'oro, avendo il poeta avuto riguardo, contrario alle malvage Serene, che hanno le parti basse brutte, e deformi, di far queste in tutta perfezion di bellezza." Rossi, *Descrizione,* 23.

    8. In the second *intermedio* of 1539, three aquatic Sirens appeared: "Apparsero in un tratto tre Serene ignude, ciascuna con le sue due code minutamente lavorate di scaglie d'argento." (Three nude Sirens appeared in an instant, each with her two tails finely worked with silver scales.") Giambullari, *Apparato et feste,* 111.

    9. See Treadwell, "Restaging the Siren," especially chapter 1.

    10. Even Rossi succumbed to the blurring of boundaries when he referred to the sleep-inducing effect of the (good) Sirens' song in *intermedio* one: "[T]hey began to sing

so sweetly to the sound of lutes and viols, that had not the sight of them held the listeners awake, they might have been able, like true Sirens, with the sweetness of their song, to lull them into a deep sleep." Rossi, *Descrizione,* 20 (appendix 1a).

11. Ibid., 55 (appendix 1a). Almost all reports comment on the singer's emergence from the sea, reporting that she rose to a considerable height. Aside from Rossi's, the most detailed account is that of the Frenchman, who noted that the singer's niche "se leva peu à peu jusques à ce qu'elle fust parvenue de hauteur de quatre braces pour le moings et trois de largeur. . . ." ([The niche] rose up little by little until it reached the height of four 'braces,' at the least, and three in width.) For the full account see Monga, *Voyage,* 115.

12. Malvezzi, *Intermedii et concerti, nono,* 11.

13. There are two exceptions. The composer continues his musical phrase through the end of the third line to conclude the sense of the poetic line, ending with a striking deceptive cadence on "nume" (deity). The penultimate line ends with the usual whole note, although there is no half note rest preceding the first statement of the final line.

14. Carter, *Jacopo Peri,* esp. 115–17.

15. Palisca, *Florentine Camerata,* esp. 121–27.

16. Carter, *Jacopo Peri,* 116–17.

17. Malvezzi, *Intermedii et concerti, canto,* 27. The page is reproduced in Treadwell, "Music of the Gods," 41.

18. See the dedication to the new Duchess of Florence in Malvezzi, *Intermedii et concerti.*

19. See Keyte, *De' Rossi to Malvezzi,* 29–30.

20. Kirkendale, *Cavalieri,* 162.

21. The multiple choir pieces that call for a variety of forces as well as the technical difficulties inherent in the solo songs (that were written for specific virtuosos) suggest that the print would have had limited practical usage outside of the original performance context.

22. Malvezzi, *Intermedii et concerti, nono,* 11.

23. See, for example, Malvezzi, *Intermedii et concerti, canto,* 26–27. In the performances, of course, Bardi's song concluded *intermedio* four while Malvezzi's song did not occur until the opening of the fifth *intermedio,* after the fourth act of the comedy.

24. Bardi's song is analyzed in chapter 6.

25. ". . . la quale ha sempre fatte degne del cantar suo le musiche mie, adornandole non pure di quei gruppi e di quei lunghi giri di voce semplici e doppi, che dalla vivezza dell'ingegno suo son ritrovati ad ogn'hora, più per ubbidire all'uso de' nostri tempi, che perch'ella stimi consistere in essi la bellezza e la forza del nostro cantare, ma anco di quelle e vaghezze e leggiadrie che non si possono scrivere, e scrivendole non s'imparano da gli scritti." Peri, *L'Euridice,* iii–iv.

26. See John Florio's definition in Florio, *New World of Words.*

27. See chapter 2, section "The Currency of *meraviglia*: Inside and Outside the Theater."

28. I have deliberately translated "leggiadrie" as "beauties" rather than using terms such as "graces" or "ornaments," which today are often equated with the idea of embellishment. In the sixteenth century "leggiadrie" did not necessarily suggest ornamentation. I would like to thank Giulio Ongaro for these suggestions.

29. ". . . e di più col moderare e crescere la voce forte o piano, assottigliandola o ingrossandola, che secondo che veniva a' tagli, ora con strascinarla, ora smezzarla, con

l'accompagnamento d'un soave interrotto sospiro, ora tirando passaggi lunghi, seguiti bene, spiccati, ora gruppi, ora a salti, ora con trilli lunghi, ora con brevi, et or con passaggi soavi e cantati piano . . . e con molti altri particolari artifici et osservazioni che saranno a notizia di persone più esperimentate di me." Solerti, *Le origini del melodramma,* 108.

30. Rossi (*Descrizione,* 56) mentions Archilei's self-accompaniment on the lute, as does the anonymous author of *Li artificiosi,* n.p. (see appendix 4, "Quinto Intermedio").

31. See Rossi, *Descrizione,* 55; Pavoni, *Diario,* 20.

32. This song is understandably given less attention in the sources than "Dalle più alte sfere" perhaps because it required more attention on the part of the listener to comprehend performative nuances.

33. Malvezzi, *Intermedii et concerti, nono,* 11.

34. The bass lute was not specified by Malvezzi for this song, but was frequently used in the *intermedi* and was the instrument used for Archilei's self-accompaniment for "Dalle più alte sfere."

35. As Agostino Agazzari pointed out some years later, playing in a low register helps avoid doubling the upper part; it was especially important not to "obscure the excellence of the note itself or of the *passaggio* that the good singer improvises on it." Treitler and Strunk, *Source Readings,* 624.

36. Malvezzi's unembellished canto part only spans one octave. I am indebted to my colleague and friend, soprano Susan Judy, who brought her own *vivezza dell'ingegno* to create our rendition of this song.

37. I am again indebted to Susan Judy, who worked with me to create the embellishments heard on the accompanying recording (CD tracks 20–22).

38. Strong, *Art and Power,* 144.

39. For a full account of the mock nautical battle see Saslow, *Medici Wedding,* 168–69.

40. See, for example, the account by the Bavarian commentator (Katritzky, "Aby Warburg," 233 and 237), and *Li sontuosissimi,* n.p. (appendix 2).

41. See the Frenchman's account (Monga, *Voyage,* 115).

42. *Li artificiosi,* n.p. (appendix 4, "Quinto Intermedio").

43. Malvezzi, *Intermedii et concerti, nono,* 11–12.

44. I would like to thank Mitchell Morris for sharing this vivid impression that captures the sense of "surround sound" that he himself experienced when singing the large ensemble numbers from the *Pellegrina* interludes.

45. See the commentary regarding "Noi che cantando" in chapter 4, section "Sound in Motion."

46. Malvezzi, *Intermedii et concerti, nono,* 12.

47. Ibid. Margherita della Scala was the ward of Vittoria and Antonio Archilei, and later became Giulio Caccini's second wife.

48. It has been suggested that the serpent is a veiled reference to the king of Spain.

49. In order to emphasize these aspects (and because Malvezzi did not clarify which instruments were used) we decided to record this section a cappella.

50. The title of this section comes from Malvezzi, *Intermedii et concerti, nono,* 12: ". . . con mirabile attentione de gli ascoltanti."

51. Malvezzi, *Intermedii et concerti, nono,* 12, and *tenore,* 25–28.

52. Earlier in his description of the fifth *intermedio,* Rossi notes that all the madrigals were the work of Rinuccini and Malvezzi, which appears to indicate that the composer Jacopo Peri was not involved at the time of Rossi's writing (see Rossi, *Descrizione,*

56; appendix 1f). The final number of the *intermedio* "Lieti solcando il Mare" (that follows the song of Arion) was indeed created by the Malvezzi-Rinuccini team.

53. "Da un'altra banda del mare apparve poi una Galera tutta messa à oro, con forsi vinticinque persone dentro: la quale per il travaglio del mare turbato girò sù, e giù quattro, ò cinque volte, con tanta agilità, che nel proprio mare non si haveria potuto veder meglio; finalmente ella si fermò volta con lo sperone verso li Principi, et ammainò le vele per riverenza; poi il Turrerino cantò, sonando un'harpa, un bellissimo madrigale à modo d'un'Echo: al quale dui altri Echi l'un dopò l'altro, con voce diversa rispondevano, che pareva le lor voci uscissero da antri, ò da profonde caverne. Mentre che il Turrerino così dolcemente cantava, i marinari fatti invidiosi della sua virtù, se gli aventarono contra con coltelli per ucciderlo: ma egli di ciò accortosene, si scagliò nel mare; la onde un delfino, che tirato dall'harmonia, e così suave canto si era ivi fermato, mosso à compassione d'un tanto virtuoso, se lo tolse sul dorso, e lo portò salvo al litto." Pavoni, *Diario,* 20–21.

54. See especially the accounts by the Frenchman in Monga, *Voyage,* 113–15.

55. *Memoriale,* 46v, March 9, 1589; Testaverde Matteini, *L'officina delle nuvole,* 205. No commentators mention this decoration, nor do they mention the decoration of instruments in general into which the interludes' creators put considerable effort. Instruments, especially consorts, were frequently decorated to resonate with the theme of a scene.

56. *Memoriale,* 41v, April 7, 1589; Testaverde Matteini, *L'officina delle nuvole,* 222: "Dice il signor Giovanni [de' Bardi] si faccia l'arpe di cartone per il Zazerino [Jacopo Peri] che si ha gettare sul delfino."

57. I would like to thank James Tyler for his comments on the instrument's features in plate 24. For further information regarding the costume design see Saslow, *Medici Wedding,* 240–41.

58. For example, Rossi mentions that Arion had ". . . a lira in hand, made in the manner of *our* harp [italics mine]. . . ." Rossi, *Descrizione,* 58 (appendix 1f).

59. For further information see Goodwin, "Some unusual lutes," 18–19.

60. ". . . lui repondoient deux escoz, l'un après l'autre, tellement que l'on eust dict que l'esco en estoit à plus de deux mil, tant il sembloit estre eslongné du theatre et de la mer et comme s'il fust sorty d'un antre ou d'une caverne." Monga, *Voyage,* 115. See also *Li artificiosi,* n.p. (appendix 4, "Quinto Intermedio.").

61. The so-called back stage area was relatively small. Regarding the dimensions of the Uffizi theater see chapter 3, section "The Performances in the Uffizi Theater."

62. Malvezzi, *Intermedii et concerti, nono,* 12.

63. The opening line of each stanza is not echoed.

64. Malvezzi, *Intermedii et concerti, nono,* 12.

65. Ibid., 13–15.

66. Wistreich, "'Real Basses, Real Men.'"

67. "Quelli della nave credendo che si fosse annegato il compagno, mostrarono di rallegrarsi molto, e per segno di ciò cominciarono con tromboni, cornetti, dolzaini, et altri stromenti à sonare, e cantare; et dato de' remi nell'onde, per due, ò tre altre volte girarono la galea: la qual ripigliò la strada per dove prima era venuta; et in un subito sparve il mare, e ritornò la Scena come stava prima." Pavoni, *Diario,* 21.

68. Rossi mentions forty sailors, but according to Saslow, who has examined the surviving costume designs (*Medici Wedding,* 237), only twenty-one can be accounted for.

69. Malvezzi, *Intermedii et concerti, nono,* 15. The instruments to which Malvezzi refers are violin, chitarrone, bass viol, two lutes, and "un'organo di pivette" (*Intermedii et concerti, nono,* 12).

70. Rossi, *Descrizione,* 58; Pavoni, *Diario,* 21; *Li artificiosi,* n.p. (appendix 4, "Quinto Intermedio."); for the Frenchman's account see Monga, *Voyage,* 115.

71. "... [d]emnach diese aufgehoertt, fing der schifman oben auf dem Mastbaum ein stuck allein zusingen [an], welcher einen herlichen Tenor sang wuste aus der kunst zu rechter zeitt zu coloriren whar auch lustig zuhoeren. ...." Kümmel, "Ein Deutscher," 16, and Katritzky, "Aby Warburg," 243.

8. "O What New Wonder" (*Intermedio* Six)

1. "[T]haten sich die wolcken oben in der hoehe wieder voneinander, wie anfangs der comoedi, das man in den himmell oder paradeis sheen kontt, do dann hinwieder viel Musicanten in Engelendischer kleidung sasenn mitt allerlei Instrumenten musicirende und lieblich darinn singende." Kümmel, "Ein Deutscher," 16, and Katritzky, "Aby Warburg," 234.

2. See chapter 2, section "Structural Underpinnings: Order Restored."

3. "... Giove avendo compassione al legnaggio umano affaticato, e ripien d'affanni, diliberò, per dargli alcun refrigerio, che Apollo, e Bacco, e le Muse, si prendessero eglino questa cura, e mandógli in terra a portare l'Armonía, el Ritmo, acciocchè ballando, e cantando, e con sì fatti diletti rallegrandosi, prendesse dopo le tante fatiche qualche ristoro. ...." Rossi, *Descrizione,* 61. Kirkendale (*Cavalieri,* 169n43) notes that Rossi's wording is very similar to a passage in Patrizi's *La poetica deca istoriale.*

4. On the distinction between Rossi's and Malvezzi's accounts see Brown, *Sixteenth-Century Instrumentation,* 127n69.

5. Cavallino, *Le solennissime feste,* 7 (appendix 3).

6. A careful reading of Cavallino might suggest that the "blessed ones" that alighted might have only included the "two . . . [clouds] from another part [of the heavens] that carried celestial . . . music," not the three clouds he initially mentions. Other accounts are equally ambiguous. What can be asserted is that at least some of the gods did descend all the way down to earth to join with the mortals.

7. Malvezzi, *Intermedii et concerti, nono,* 16. Once again, the score as presented in *Intermedii et concerti* suggests that the piece was arranged for publication. Gualfreducci sang the piece with *passaggi,* but the simple version of his tune lacks shape and distinctive features, indicating that the song was not originally conceived in this manner.

8. The Bavarian commentator identified Jove, as did the anonymous author of *Li sontuosissimi,* n.p. (appendix 2).

9. "Die *prospettiva* verkhört sich noch einmal, und scheint alls wanns lautter guldene gerör weren. Darn thuet sich das Paradeyb auf 3. seiten auf, und man sicht den *Iouem* in einer wolckhen, wie Er sich dann darin, sambt noch 2. anndern wolckhen, herab auf die erden lasset, und sich in ein gulden rögen verendert, damit verzeren sich die nebl, doch khomen anndere, darin 50. Musici." Katritzky, "Aby Warburg," 233 and 237.

10. Cavallino, *Le solennissime feste,* 7 (appendix 3).

11. See *Li sontuosissimi,* n.p. (appendix 2).

12. Vasari recounts the story of the golden rain in his *Ragionamenti,* a dialogue he began in 1558 that explains the paintings he executed for Duke Cosimo in the Palazzo

Vecchio. Regarding the Room of Jove see Vasari, *Le opere,* vol. 8, 62–71, and for the story of the golden rain in particular see p. 68. Vasari also talked "of gifts 'rained down' from heaven" more generally, linking the transmission of divine inspiration to Neoplatonic philosophy. On this point, and the corresponding relationship to the concept of *furor,* see Ruvoldt, *Imagery of Inspiration,* 1–2.

13. Malvezzi, *Intermedii et concerti, nono,* 17.

14. With the exception, however, of the three female *virtuose* highlighted in the concluding number, "O che nuovo miracolo," who were not involved in "O fortunato giorno."

15. Giuliano Giraldi's propagandistic text expounds a similar sentiment regarding Ferdinando's renown in faraway countries (*Delle lode di D. Ferdinando,* 9–10).

16. Malvezzi (*Intermedii et concerti, nono,* 17) refers to "gli primi sopranominati strumenti e tutti gli altri" (the first abovementioned instruments and all the others), thereby indicating that the instruments included all those utilized for the first number of the *intermedio,* "Dal vago e bel sereno," in addition to those used for the second number, "O qual risplende nube." The instruments thus involved were: four lutes, two chitarroni, cittern, mandora, psaltery, five viols, two lire da braccio, lirone, violin, four sackbuts, and two cornetti. Brown (*Sixteenth-Century Instrumentation,* 129–31) has provided a hypothetical scoring for "O fortunato giorno," which is one of several possible solutions.

17. "[C]hacun l'admiroit à cause du grand nombre des personnes qui la faisoient et de l'accord qui estoit entre eux [et] de la diversitté des instrumens." Monga, *Voyage,* 116. Although the Frenchman appears to have been making a statement about the music of this *intermedio* in general, it is likely to have been "O fortunato giorno" or possibly the final number "O che nuovo miracolo" (in which the full complement of voices and instruments were utilized) that most closely epitomized the experience he described.

18. See appendix 5, lines 40, 48, and 42, respectively.

19. Malvezzi, *Intermedii et concerti, nono,* 19.

20. Treadwell, "Performance of Gender."

21. This impression permeates Guidiccioni's entire text but see particularly lines 7–16 and 49–52 (appendix 5).

22. In the Renaissance, both clothed and unclothed Graces were recognized, although the former never became as popular as the naked Graces, which were generally accepted as the classical model. If clothed, as Seneca imagined them (and Botticelli depicted them in *Primavera*), "nothing in them should be bound or restricted. That is why they are clad in ungirdled garments, and these are transparent because benefits want to be seen." The passage quoted, from Seneca's *De beneficiis,* I, iii, 5, is drawn from Wind, *Pagan Mysteries,* 34.

23. For various permutations on this configuration see Wind, *Pagan Mysteries,* 31–38.

24. Malvezzi, *Intermedii et concerti, nono,* 19.

25. Hanafi, *Monster in the Machine,* 192.

26. Regarding the prevalence of the tune see Kirkendale, *L'aria di Fiorenza.*

27. These words are used in the title of Andrew Mead's article "Bodily Hearing: Physiological Metaphors and Musical Understanding."

28. The recording *Una "Stravaganza" dei Medici* makes much of these contrasts.

29. Greenblatt, *Shakespearean Negotiations,* esp. 88f.

30. McClary, "Constructions of Gender," 37.

31. The male chorus that closes the *ballo* in sections 5 and 6 must ultimately contain the repartee.

32. Guidiccioni was an aristocratic poet from Lucca and the only woman to contribute a text to the *Pellegrina intermedi*. She collaborated with Cavalieri on several other musical entertainments: *La disperatione di Fileno, Il Satiro,* and *Il giuoco della Cieca*. See Carter, *Jacopo Peri*, 26n75, 28. As was frequently the case with *balli,* the text was added after the music was composed so that the musical form and dance pattern were not governed by a preexistent text.

33. John Walter Hill has demonstrated the striking resemblance between Guidiccioni's text and a contemporaneous poem concerning the Nativity of Christ preserved in a manuscript in I:Fn, Palatino 251. There is no doubt that the two texts are related, and Hill has convincingly argued that Guidiccioni's text is derived from the religious text. See Hill, "O che nuovo miracolo," 283–322.

34. Indeed, the effect must have been particularly memorable: almost twenty years later in 1608 a similar *ballo* was performed as the finale in the *intermedi* for Michelangelo Buonarroti the younger's play *I giudizio di Paride*. In the 1608 *ballo* six sopranos were showcased, including the original 1589 performers Vittoria Archilei and Margherita della Scala, as well as Settimia and Francesca Caccini (the daughters of Lucia Caccini, the third member of the 1589 trio). Aside from the emphasis on the soprano range, which recalls Cavalieri's *ballo,* both Vittoria Archilei and Francesca Caccini accompanied themselves on guitars. See Carter, "Florentine Wedding," 89–107. For further evidence regarding the influence of Cavalieri's *ballo* on subsequent compositions see Fenlon, "Origins of the Seventeenth-Century Staged *Ballo,*" 13–40.

35. The four-course Neapolitan instrument was generally the smaller of the two types of guitars, but with the diminutive *chitarrina* applied to both guitars, we cannot be certain that the Spanish instrument that Archilei played was larger than Caccini's instrument. Archilei's instrument appears to have been the newer five-course guitar, however.

36. See Kirkendale, *L'aria di Fiorenza,* 48. See also Treadwell, "Chitarra Spagnola," 15–16. The Neapolitan guitar, unlike its Spanish counterpart, was not a new instrument. However, in the context of the *ballo,* and in light of the new interest in chordal sonorities at this time, Lucia Caccini would have undoubtedly employed the new style of strumming that became primarily linked with the Spanish instrument. In this sense, she matched Vittoria Archilei by playing "alla Spagnola" style, thus reinforcing the Spanish association. The earlier repertory for the Neapolitan guitar was closely allied with that of the lute, that is, in the plucked style. This is not to suggest, however, that the earlier Neapolitan guitar was not sometimes strummed. An early mention of the practice can be found in Juan Bermudo, *El libro llamado declaraciòn de instrumentos musicales* (Osuna, 1555), libro segundo, chapter 32. See also Scipione Cerreto, *Della prattica musicale et strumentali* (Naples, 1601), 321. I would like to thank James Tyler for drawing my attention to these sources.

37. Kirkendale, *L'aria di Fiorenza,* 48–49.

38. Although the rhythmic articulations produced on the *chitarra spagnola* would have been a rather novel effect for many members of the audience, for the practitioners themselves the effect was probably not so new. Those involved in the composition and performance of the *ballo,* such as Emilio de' Cavalieri and Vittoria Archilei, were of Roman origin, and therefore almost certainly had long been familiar with this style of playing.

39. By the early seventeenth century the Italians almost invariably described the instrument as the *chitarra spagnola*.

40. These rhythmic strumming patterns, such as the *trillo* and *repicco,* were soon notated in the earliest manuscripts and prints for the instrument. For chronological listings of these sources see Tyler and Sparks, *Guitar and Its Music.* The Italian term *battente* (beating) gives some indication of the more rigorous movements required of the player for the strummed style.

41. Unlike the modern instrument, both the Neapolitan and Spanish guitars used for accompaniment had no bass range, and frequently employed reentrant stringings. For further information see Tyler and Sparks, *Guitar and Its Music.*

42. The chorus's music had a clearly articulated bass and was harmonically progressive, providing a sense of closure in the *ballo* by reiterating the opening music of the piece (see table 8.1, section 5), and then appending a concluding tag (section 6).

43. During this period the *chitarra spagnola* was frequently associated with both the sarabanda and chacona, dances that were characterized by women dancing to guitar and percussion accompaniment. In late sixteenth- and seventeenth-century literary sources the chacona dance was frequently condemned because of its overt sexual connotations. (Surviving texts of the chacona reinforce their irreverent quality; see Hudson, *Passacaglio and Ciaccona,* 5–11.) In 1599 Padre Fray de la Cerda complained of the "indecent costumes of the dancing girls and the obscene effect achieved by movements of the eyes and neck, the tossing of the hair, and the expressions of the face," and in 1615 the chacona was banned because of its "lascivious and impure movements." Provocative dances such as the chacona and sarabanda signified both the danger and excitement of female sexuality, a signification that, at some level, was already established by the mere physical presence of women performing music and dance in a public venue. Lope de Vega made these connections explicit in 1632 when he wrote: "God forgive Vicente Espinel, who brought us this novelty and the five-courses of the guitar . . . with the gestures and lascivious movements of the Chaconas, which bring such offense to the chastity and decorous silence of women." (Cited in Hudson, *Passacaglio and Ciaccona,* 16.) By associating women's chastity with silence, Vega implies that women's musical performance was ineluctably linked with inappropriate behavior and sexual desire.

44. Malvezzi, *Intermedii et concerti, nono,* 21–23.

45. For Nevile's reconstruction see "'O che nuovo miracolo,'" 353–88. For related material see Nevile, "Social Dances of Caroso and Negri," 119–33.

46. Malvezzi, *Intermedii et concerti, nono,* 19. Regarding this assumption see, for example, Treadwell, "Performance of Gender," and Kirkendale, *L'aria di Fiorenza,* 48.

47. Hugh Keyte has also made this suggestion. See *Una "Stravaganza" dei Medici,* CD booklet, 79.

48. See Kirkendale, *L'aria di Fiorenza,* 47n2, and Nevile, "'O che nuovo miracolo,'" 362–63.

49. Gadenstedt notes the participation of four dance masters (Kümmel, "Ein Deutscher," 17, and Katritzky, "Aby Warburg," 243), as does the author of *Li sontuosissimi,* n.p. (appendix 2). Cavallino, on the other hand, mentions three male dancers (shepherds). See Cavallino, *Le solennissime feste,* 7 (appendix 3). Four figures, not three, are depicted on the central cloud in Buontalenti's stage setting, although the upper three figures are clearly grouped together through their participation in the dance.

50. Cavallino, *Le solennissime feste,* 7 (appendix 3).

51. *Li artificiosi,* n.p. (appendix 4, "Sesto, & ultimo Intermedio."). Although he does not mention the resources involved, the Ferrarese ambassador, Girolamo Gigliolo, was struck by the dialogic nature of the *ballo* (as well as by its visual symmetry). "[C]ongiungendosi insieme in una schiera danzando, et rispondendosi del canto gl'uni à gl'altri. . . ." (Coupling together dancing as an orderly multitude, and responding the one to the other in song.)

52. For more on the relationship between Cavalieri's *ballo* and the French ballet de cour tradition see Fenlon, "Seventeenth-Century Staged *Ballo,*" 17, and 39–40.

53. Kümmel, "Ein Deutscher," 17, and Katritzky, "Aby Warburg," 243.

54. The Ferrarese ambassador at Florence, Girolamo Gigliolo, was new to his post and only sent a very brief description of the *intermedi* to Duke Alfonso d'Este of Ferrara.

55. Fenlon, "Preparations for a Princess," 267f.

56. By contrast, in the larger ensemble numbers in which both Lucia Caccini and Margherita della Scala participated, it seems that the recognition of their gender was superfluous because they were merely considered "one of the boys."

57. *Li artificiosi,* n.p. (appendix 4, "Sesto, & ultimo Intermedio").

58. "At the end, many voices sang together 'long live Ferdinando, long live Ferdinando, Grand Duke of Tuscany.'" Cavallino, *Le solennissime feste,* 7 (appendix 3).

59. Greenblatt (*Marvelous Possessions,* 20) makes a similar point: "The expression of wonder stands for all that cannot be understood, that can scarcely be believed. It calls attention to the problem of credibility and at the same time insists upon the undeniability, the exigency of the experience."

60. "Zu disem Intermedio singt man 7. Madrigal. Und ist nit zubeschreiben, was es für ein gewaltig ding. Es khans auch khainer glauben, alls ders sicht." Katritzky, "Aby Warburg," 233 and 237.

61. ". . . [D]er sonst nicht viel zuschaffen oder etwas zuverseumen der Musica zugefallen (wann einer dergleichen hoeren oder solche sachen sehen kontte) viel reisenn es soltte ihm nicht gereuenn, denn es fast Engelischs (also zu reden) als menschslich werk anzusheen, und anzuhoern." Kümmel, "Ein Deutscher," 18–19, and Katritzky, "Aby Warburg," 244.

62. "Der Musicanten sollen in allem bey anderthalb hundertt gewesnn sein, dheren mancherlei und unterschiedene Instrumentt alle mitt einanderr zu gleich fein eintrechtig wharen in einander gestimmett die Musicam vocalem zu gleich mittgebrauchende. Diese Musicanten wie bereits zum theill gedachtt hatte der hertzog vonn Florentz als die beruembtesten in Italia bestallt, und nach Florentz mitt grosem unkosten verschreiben lasen, was solchs fur eine Musica gewesnn, weill die italianische Musici doch sher beruemett, mag ein jeder verstendeiger und liebhaber der Musica bei sich selber abnhemen und nachdenckenn." Ibid.

63. "Wir hetten gern die gelegenheitt wie solchs möcht regirt werdenn, aber es whar ernstlich verboten, das man solches niemand soll sehen lasenn. Ist also dis die beschreibung der Comoedi oder vielmher der Intermediorum der Comoedi." Kümmel, "Ein Deutscher," 19, and Katritzky, "Aby Warburg," 244.

Appendix 3

1. The bulk of Cavallino's description here refers to *intermedio* three; however, by way of reference to the disappearance of the three mountains (from *intermedio* two) his description appears to blur the two interludes.

2. Cavallino treats the hell scene as a separate *intermedio,* thus referring to *intermedio* five here, instead of four. The acquatic *intermedio* thus becomes his sixth *intermedio,* and his description of "il settimo & ul[ti]mo intermedio" corresponds with the final, concluding *intermedio* of the set of six.

Appendix 6

1. The text of "Ò begli Anni del Oro" is drawn from Giambullari, *Apparato et feste,* 125.

Bibliography

Primary Sources: Manuscripts

B:Bc, ms. 704, pp. 15–16. Setting of Giulio Caccini's "Io che dal ciel cader."

D:W, Cod. Guelf. 67.6 Extrav., pp. 670–78. Account of the *Pellegrina* interludes by Barthold von Gadenstedt, transcribed in W. F. Kümmel, "Ein deutscher Bericht über die florentinischen Intermedien des Jahres 1589." *Analecta Musicologica* 9 (1970): 1–19.

F:Pn, ms. fr. 5550, ff.64v–68v. Account of the *Pellegrina* interludes by an anonymous Frenchman, transcribed in Luigi Monga, *Voyage de Provence et d'Italie.* Geneva: Slatkine, 1994.

I:Fas, Magistrato de' Nove Conservatori, filza 3679. Girolamo Seriacopi, *Memoriale e ricordi . . . 1588–1589.* Transcription included in Testaverde Matteini, *L'officina delle nuvole* (see "Secondary Sources" below).

I:Fas, Manoscritti, filza 130. Francesco Settimani, *Memorie fiorentine dell'anno MDXXXII . . . infino all'anno MDCCXXXVII.*

I:Fn, Conv. Soppr. C.7.2614, 353v.–358v. Description of the *Pellegrina* interludes in *Diario di tutti i casi seguiti in Firenze . . . dall' Anno 1500 All' Anno 1591.*

I:Fn, Magl. XIX.66. Includes setting of Giulio Caccini's "Io che dal ciel cader."

I:MOs, Archivio per materie, Spettacoli pubblici, b. 10. Appears to be a brief, untitled description of the *Pellegrina* interludes.

I:MOs, Cancelleria Ducale, Ambasciatori, Firenze, b. 31. Letters from the Ferrarese ambassador, Girolamo Gigliolo, at Florence. Transcriptions are included in Ledbetter, "Luca Marenzio" (see "Secondary Sources" below).

MüBHStA, Kurbayern Äußeres Archiv 4576, ff. 245r–252v. Account of the *Pellegrina* interludes by an anonymous Bavarian commentator, transcribed in M. A. Katritzky, "Aby Warburg and the Florentine Intermedi of 1589: Extending the Boundaries of Art History." In *Art History as Cultural History: Warburg's Projects,* edited by Richard Woodfield. Amsterdam: G+B Arts International, 2001.

Primary Sources: Published Material

Aristotle. *Metaphysics,* book 1. Translated and edited by W. D. Ross in *The Works of Aristotle,* vol. 8. Oxford: Clarendon Press, 1908–52.

———. *Politics. Books VII and VIII.* Translated with a commentary by Richard Kraut. Oxford: Oxford University Press, 1997.

Bellaviti, d'Andrea. *Panegirico . . . al Serenissimo Don Ferdinando Medici Gran Duca di Toscana.* Florence: Giunti, 1604.

Bermudo, Juan. *El libro llamado declaraciòn de instrumentos musicales.* Osuna, 1555.

Bocchi, Francesco. *Discorso . . . sopra la Musica, non secondo l'arte di quella, ma secondo la ragione alla politica pertinente.* Florence: Giorgio Marescotti, 1581.

———. *Le bellezze della citta di Fiorenza.* Florence, 1591.

Caccini, Giulio. *Le nuove musiche.* Florence: Marescotti, 1601.

Cartari, Vincenzo. *The Fountaine of Ancient Fiction*. London: Adam Isip, 1599. Reprint, Amsterdam: Da Capo Press, 1973.

———. *Le imagini . . . degli dei degli antichi*. Venice: Vincentio Valgrisi, 1571. Reprint, New York: Garland, 1976.

Cavalieri, Emilio de'. *Rappresentazione di anima e di corpo*. Rome: N. Mutii, 1600.

Cavallino, Simone. *Raccolta di tutte le solennissime feste nel sponsalitio della serenissima Gran Duchessa di Toscana fatte in Fiorenza il mese di maggio 1589*. Rome: Blado, 1589.

Cerreto, Scipione. *Della prattica musicale vocale, et strumentali. . . .* Naples: Iacomo Carlino, 1601.

Conforti, Giovanni Luca. *Breve et facile maniera d'essercitarsi a far passaggi*. Rome, 1593.

Dante Alighieri. *The Inferno*. Translated by Anthony Esolen. New York: Random House, 2002.

De' Sommi, Leone. *Quattro dialoghi in materia di rappresentazioni sceniche*. Edited by Ferruccio Marotti. Milan: Edizioni Il Polifilo, 1968.

Discours de la magnifique réception et triomphante entrée de la Grande Duchesse de Toscane en la ville de Florence, avec les cérémonies de son couronnement et esponsailles. Lyons: Benoist Rigaud, 1589.

Discours veritable du marriage de la fille du Duc de L'orainne, avec le Duc de Florence. Avec les Ceremonies de son Coronnement et espusailles, les Theatres, Arcs Triomphaux, Statuës, Inscription, Devises, Tournois, Musiques, et autres singularitez. Paris and Lyons: Denis Binet, n.d.

Ficino, Marsilio. *Meditations on the Soul: Selected Letters*. Rochester, Vt.: Inner Traditions, 1996.

Florio, John. *Queen Anna's New World of Words*. London: Bradwood, 1611. Reprint, Menston, Eng.: Scholar Press, 1968.

Galilei, Vincenzo. *Dialogue on Ancient and Modern Music*. Translated by Claude V. Palisca. New Haven, Conn.: Yale University Press, 2003.

Giambullari, Pier Francesco. *Apparato et feste nelle noz[z]e dello Illustrissimo Signor Duca di Firenze, et della Duchessa sua Consorte, con le sue Stanze, Madriali, Comedia, et Intermedii, in quelle recitati*. Florence: Benedetto Giunta, 1539.

Giraldi, Giuliano. *Delle lode di D. Ferdinando Medici Gran Duca di Toscana*. Florence: Giunti, 1609.

Gualterotti, Raffaello. *Descrizione del regale apparato per le nozze della Serenissima Madama Cristiana di Loreno moglie del Serenissimo Don Ferdinando Medici III Granduca di Toscana*. Florence: Padovani, 1589.

Hewitt, Barnard, ed. *The Renaissance Stage: Documents of Serlio, Sabbattini and Furttenbach*. Translated by Allardyce Nicoll, John H. McDowell, and George R. Kernodle. Coral Gables, Fla.: University of Miami Press, 1958.

Il corago, o vero, alcune osservazioni per metter bene in scena le composizioni drammatiche. Edited by Paolo Fabbri and Angelo Pompilio. Florence: Leo S. Olschki, 1983.

Ingegneri, Angelo. *Della poesia rappresentativa e del modo di rappresentare le favole sceniche*. Edited by Maria Luisa Doglio. Modena: Edizioni Panini, 1989.

Le ultime feste et apparati superbissimi fatti in Fiorenza nelle nozze del Serenissimo Gran Duca di Toscana. Bologna: Alessandro Benacci, 1589.

Li artificiosi e dilettevoli intermedii rappresentati nella comedia fatta per le nozze della Serenissima Gran Duchessa di Toscana. Rome: Tito and Paulo Diani, 1589.

Li sontuosissimi apparecchi, trionfi, e feste, fatti nelle nozze della Gran Duchessa di Fiorenza: con il nome, e numero de duchi, precipi, marchesi, baroni, et altri gran personaggi: postovi il modo di vestire, maniere, e livree. Et la descrittione de gl'intermedii rappresentati nella comedia nobilissima, recitata da gl'Intronati Senesi. Aggiontovi l'ordine, e modo che s'è tenuto nel coronare l'Altezza della Serenissima Gran Duchessa. Florence and Ferrara: Baldini; Venice: Larduccio, 1589.

Longinus, *On the Sublime.* Translated by James A. Arieti and John M. Crossett. New York and Toronto, 1985.

MacClintock, Carol, trans. *Ercole Bottrigari: Il desiderio; Vincenzo Giustiniani: Discorso sopra la musica.* Rome: American Institute of Musicology, 1962.

Malvezzi, Cristofano, [ed.]. *Intermedii et concerti, fatti per la Commedia rappresentata in Firenze nelle nozze del Serenissimo Don Ferdinando Medici, e Madama Christiana di Loreno, Gran Duchi di Toscana.* Venice: G. Vincenti, 1591.

Ovid. *Metamorphoses.* Translated by Charles Martin. New York: W. W. Norton & Co., 2004.

Passignani, Giovanni. *Descrittione dell'intermedii fatti nel felicissimo palazo del Gran Duca Cosimo, & del suo Illustriss. figliuolo Principe di Firenze, & di Siena. Per honorar la Illustris. presenza della Sereniss. Altezza dello Eccellentissimo Arciduca d'Austria.* Florence: B. Sermartelli, 1569.

Patrizi, Francesco. *Della poetica.* Edited by Danilo Aguzzi Barbagli. 3 vols. Florence: Istituto Nazionale di Studi sul Rinascimento, 1969–71.

———. *Lettere ed opuscoli inediti.* Edited by Danilo Aguzzi Barbagli. Florence: Istituto Nazionale di Studi sul Rinascimento, 1975.

Pavoni, Giuseppe. *Diario . . . Delle feste celebrate nelle solennissime Nozze delli Serenissimi Sposi . . . Nel quale con brevità si esplica il Torneo, la Battaglia navale, la Comedia con gli Intermedii, & altre feste occorse di giorno in giorno per tutto il dì 15. di Maggio.* Bologna: Giovanni Rossi, 1589.

Peri, Jacopo. *Le musiche . . . sopra L'Euridice.* Florence: Marescotti, 1601. Reprint, New York: Broude Brothers, 1973; and Bologna: Forni Editore, 1973.

Plato. *The Republic.* Translated by Alexander Dunlop Lindsay. New York and Toronto: Alfred A. Knopf, 1906.

Raccolta di tutta le solennissime feste nel sponsalitio della Serenissima Gran Duchessa di Toscana fatte in Fiorenza il mese di maggio 1589. Rome: Paulo Baldo, 1589.

Rossi, Bastiano de'. *Descrizione del magnificentis. apparato. E de' maravigliosi intermedi fatti per la commedia rappresentata in Firenze nelle felicissime Nozze degl' Illustrissimi, ed Eccellentiss[i]mi Signori[,] il Signor Don Cesare d'Este, e la Signora Donna Virginia Medici.* Florence: Marescotti, 1586.

———. *Descrizione dell['] apparato e degl'intermedi. Fatti per la commedia rappresentata in Firenze. Nelle nozze de' Serenissimi Don Ferdinando Medici, e Madama Cristina di Loreno, Gran Duchi di Toscana.* Florence: Anton Padovani, 1589.

Serlio, Sebastiano. *Tutte l'opere d'architettura, et prospetiva. . . . Diviso in sette Libri.* Venice: Heredi di Francesco de' Franceschi, 1600.

Strozzi, Giovan Batista. *Della famiglia de' Medici.* Florence: B. Sermartelli, 1610.

Treitler, Leo, and Oliver Strunk, eds. *Source Readings in Music History.* New York: Norton, 1998.

Vasari, Giorgio. *Le opere di Giorgio Vasari.* Edited by Gaetano Milanesi. 9 vols. Florence: Sansoni, 1906.

————. *The Lives of the Artists.* Translated by George Bull. London, 1965.

Vieri, Francesco de'. *Compendio della Civile et Regale Potestà.* Florence, 1587.

Secondary Sources

Aguzzi Barbagli, Danilo. "Humanism and Poetics." In *Renaissance Humanism: Foundations, Forms, and Legacy,* vol. 3, edited by Albert Rabil. Philadelphia: University of Pennsylvania Press, 1988.

Aiazzi, Giuseppe. *Narrazioni Istoriche delle più Considerevoli Inondazion dell'Arno.* Florence: Piatti, 1845.

Alazard, Florence. *Art vocal, Art de gouverner: la musique, le prince et la cité en Italie à la fin du XVIe siècle.* Paris: Minerve-Centre d'Études Supérieures de la Renaissance, 2002.

D'Ancona, Alessandro. *Origini del teatro italian.* 3 vols. Turin: Ermanno Loescher, 1891. Reprint, Rome: Bardi Editore, 1966.

Berner, Samuel. "Florentine Political Thought in the Late Cinquecento." *Il pensiero politico* 3/2 (1970): 177–99.

————. "Florentine Society in the Late Sixteenth and Early Seventeenth Centuries." *Studies in the Renaissance* 18 (1971): 203–46.

————. "The Florentine Patriciate in the Transition from Republic to *Principato,* 1530–1609." *Studies in Medieval and Renaissance History* 9 (1972): 3–15.

Berti, Franco. "Studi su alcuni aspetti del diario di Girolamo Seriacopi e sui disegni buontalentiani per i costumi del 1589." *Quaderni di teatro* 2 (1980): 157–68.

Biagioli, Mario. *Galileo, Courtier: The Practice of Science in the Culture of Absolutism.* Chicago: University of Chicago Press, 1993.

Bianconi, Lorenzo. *Music in the Seventeenth Century.* Translated by David Bryant. Cambridge: Cambridge University Press, 1987.

Bizzarini, Marco. *Luca Marenzio: The Career of a Musician between the Renaissance and the Counter-Reformation.* Translated by James Chater. Aldershot: Ashgate, 2003.

Bloch, Marc. *The Royal Touch: Sacred Monarchy and Scrofula in England and France.* Translated by J. E. Anderson. London: Routledge and K. Paul, 1973.

Brown, Howard Mayer. *Sixteenth-Century Instrumentation: The Music for the Florentine Intermedi.* Neuhausen-Stuttgart: Hanssler Verlag, 1973.

————. "The Geography of Florentine Monody: Caccini at Home and Abroad." *Early Music* 9/2 (1981): 147–68.

Brown, Judith C. "Concepts of Political Economy: Cosimo I de' Medici in a Comparative European Context." In *Firenze e la Toscana dei Medici nell'Europa del '500,* vol. 1. Florence: Leo S. Olschki, 1983.

Bryson, Norman. *Vision and Painting: The Logic of the Gaze.* New Haven, Conn.: Yale University Press, 1983.

Burke, Peter. *The Italian Renaissance: Culture and Society in Italy,* 2nd ed. Princeton, N.J.: Princeton University Press, 1986.

————. *The Historical Anthropology of Early Modern Italy: Essays on Perception and Communication.* Cambridge: Cambridge University Press, 1987.

————. *Eyewitnessing: The Uses of Images as Historical Evidence.* Ihaca, N.Y.: Cornell University Press, 2001.

Burrows, David. "On Hearing Things: Music, the World, and Ourselves." *Musical Quarterly* 66/2 (1980): 180–91.

Butchart, David S. "The Madrigal in Florence, 1560–1620." Ph.D. diss., University of Oxford, 1979.

———. "The Letters of Alessandro Striggio: An Edition with Translation and Commentary." *Royal Musical Society Research Chronicle* 23 (1990): 1–78.

Cantini, Lorenzo. *Legislazione Toscana*. 32 vols. Florence: Fantosini, 1800–1808.

Carter, Tim. "A Florentine Wedding of 1608." *Acta Musicologica* 55/1 (1983): 89–107.

———. "Giulio Caccini (1551–1618): New Facts, New Music." *Studi musicali* 16/1 (1987): 13–32.

———. *Jacopo Peri, 1561–1633: His Life and Works*. 2 vols. New York: Garland, 1989.

———. "Finding a Voice: Vittoria Archilei and the Florentine 'New Music.'" In *Feminism and Renaissance Studies,* edited by Lorna Hutson. Oxford: Oxford University Press, 1999.

Certeau, Michel de. *The Mystic Fable.* Translated by Michael B. Smith. Chicago: University of Chicago Press, 1992.

Clark, Stuart. *Thinking with Demons: The Idea of Witchcraft in Early Modern Europe.* Oxford: Oxford University Press, 1997.

Classen, Constance. *Worlds of Sense: Exploring the Senses in History and Across Cultures.* New York: Routledge, 1993.

Cochraine, Eric W. *Florence in the Forgotten Centuries, 1527–1800: A History of Florence and the Florentines in the Age of the Grand Dukes.* Chicago: University of Chicago Press, 1973.

Contini, Alessandra. "Aspects of Medicean Diplomacy in the Sixteenth Century." In *Politics and Diplomacy in Early Modern Italy: The Structure of Diplomatic Practice, 1450–1800,* edited by Daniela Frigo and translated by Adrian Belton. Cambridge: Cambridge University Press, 2000.

Couliano, Ioan P. *Eros and Magic in the Renaissance.* Translated by Margaret Cook. Chicago: University of Chicago Press, 1987.

Cox-Rearick, Janet. *Dynasty and Destiny in Medici Art: Pontormo, Leo X, and the Two Cosimos.* Princeton, N.J.: Princeton University Press, 1984.

Cummings, Anthony M. *The Politicized Muse: Music for Medici Festivals, 1512–1537.* Princeton, N.J.: Princeton University Press, 1992.

Cusick, Suzanne. "Dancing with the *Ingrate.*" In *Gender, Sexuality, and Early Music (Criticism and Analysis of Early Music),* edited by Todd Borgerding. New York: Routledge, 2002.

———. "Performance, Performativity, and Politics in Early 1600 Florence." Paper presented at the conference "Structures of Feeling in Seventeenth-Century Cultural Expression," part 4, "Performing Bodies." University of California, Los Angeles, June 3, 2005.

———. *Francesca Caccini at the Medici Court: Music and the Circulation of Power.* Chicago: Chicago University Press, 2008.

Damisch, Hubert. *A Theory of Cloud: Toward a History of Painting.* Translated by Janet Lloyd. Stanford: Stanford University Press, 2002.

Daston, Lorraine, and Katherine Park. *Wonders and the Order of Nature, 1150–1750.* New York: Zone Books, 2001.

Debord, Guy. *Society of the Spectacle.* Detroit: Black and Red, 1983.

DeFord, Ruth. "Marenzio and the *villanella alla romana.*" *Early Music* 27/4 (1999): 535–52.

Del Vita, Alessandro, ed. *Il libro delle ricordanze di Giorgio Vasari.* Rome: R. Istituto d'archeologia e storia dell'arte, 1938.

Diaz, Furio. *Il Granducato di Toscana: I Medici.* Storia d'Italia 13, no. 1. Turin: Unione Tipografico-Editrice Torinese, 1976.

Dizionario biografico degli italiani. 44 vols. Rome: Istituto della Enciclopedia Italiana, 1960–.

Donington, Robert. *The Rise of Opera.* London: Faber and Faber, 1981.

Durante, Elio, and Anna Martelloti. *Cronistoria del Concerto delle dame principalissime di Margherita Gonzaga d'Este.* Florence: Studio per Edizioni Scelte, 1979.

Enciclopedia dello Spettacolo. Edited by Francesco Savio et al. 9 vols. Rome: Casa Editrice le Maschere, 1960.

Fabbri, Mario, Elvira Garbero Zorzi, and Anna Maria Petrioli Tofani. *Il luogo teatrale a Firenze.* Milan: Electra Editrice, 1975.

Fenlon, Iain. *Music and Patronage in Sixteenth-Century Mantua.* 2 vols. Cambridge: Cambridge University Press, 1980.

———. "Preparations for a Princess: Florence 1588–89." In *In cantu et in sermone: For Nino Pirrotta on his 80th birthday,* edited by Fabrizio Della Seta and Franco Piperno. Florence and Perth: Leo S. Olschki and University of Western Australia Press, 1989.

———. "The Origins of the Seventeenth-Century Staged *Ballo.*" In *Con che soavità: Studies in Italian Opera, Song, and Dance, 1580–1740,* edited by Iain Fenlon and Tim Carter. Oxford: Clarendon Press, 1995.

Findlen, Paula. *Possessing Nature: Museums, Collecting, and Scientific Culture in Early Modern Italy.* Berkeley: University of California Press, 1994.

Fiorani, Francesca. *The Marvel of Maps: Art, Cartography and Politics in Renaissance Italy.* New Haven, Conn.: Yale University Press, 2005.

Foucault, Michel. "The Spectacle of the Scaffold." In *Discipline and Punish: The Birth of the Prison.* Translated by Alan Sheridan. New York: Vintage Books, 1995.

Fragnito, G. "Le corti cardinalizie nella Roma del Cinquecento." *Rivista Storica Italiana* 106 (1994): 5–41.

Franko, Mark. "Figural Inversions in Louis XIV's Dancing Body." In *Acting on the Past: Historical Performance Across the Disciplines,* edited by Mark Franko and Annette Richards. Hanover: Wesleyan University Press, 2000.

———. "Majestic Drag: Monarchical Performativity and King's Body Theatrical." *Drama Review* 47/2 (2003): 71–87.

Gargiulo, Piero. "Strumenti musicali alla Corte Medicea: nuovi documenti e sconosciuti inventari (1553–1609)." *Note d'Archivio per la Storia Musicale* 3 (1985): 55–72.

Geertz, Clifford. "Religion as a Cultural System." In *Anthropological Approaches to the Study of Religion,* edited by Michael Banton. London: Tavistock, 1966.

Ghisi, Federico. *Feste Musicali della Firenze Medicea (1480–1589).* Florence: Vallecchi Editore, 1939.

Goldthwaite, Richard A. *The Building of Renaissance Florence: An Economic and Social History.* Baltimore: John Hopkins University Press, 1980.

Gombrich, E. H. "Icones symbolicae: The Visual Image in Neo-Platonic Thought." *Journal of the Warburg and Courtauld Institutes* 11 (1948): 163–92.

Goodwin, Christopher, ed. "Some unusual lutes, a talk by Stephen Barber." *Lute News* 78 (2006): 16–19.

Grafton, Anthony, and Lisa Jardine. *From Humanism to the Humanities: Education and the Liberal Arts in Fifteenth- and Sixteenth-Century Europe.* London: Duckword, 1986.

Greenblatt, Stephen. *Shakespearean Negotiations: The Circulation of Social Energy in Renaissance England.* Berkeley: University of California Press, 1988.

———. *Marvelous Possessions: The Wonder of the New World.* Chicago: University of Chicago Press, 1991.

Greene, Thomas M. "Magic and Festivity at the Renaissance Court." *Renaissance Quarterly* 40/4 (1987): 636–59.

Greenlee, Robert. "'*Dispositione di voce*': Passage to Florid Singing." *Early Music* 15/1 (1987): 47–55.

Hackenbroch, Yvonne. "The Florentine Jewels: Buontalenti and the Dragon Theme." *Connoisseur* 169 (November 1968): 137–43.

Hale, J. R. *Florence and the Medici: The Pattern of Control.* New York: Thames and Hudson, 1977.

Halliwell, Stephen. *The Poetics of Aristotle: Translation and Commentary.* Chapel Hill: University of North Carolina Press, 1987.

Hanafi, Zakiya. *The Monster in the Machine: Magic, Medicine, and the Marvelous in the Time of the Scientific Revolution.* Durham, N.C.: Duke University Press, 2000.

Hanning, Barbara Russano. "Glorious Apollo: Poetic and Political Themes in the First Opera." *Renaissance Quarterly* 32/4 (1979): 485–513.

———. *Of Poetry and Music's Power: Humanism and the Creation of Opera.* Ann Arbor, Mich.: UMI Research Press, 1980.

Harness, Kelley Ann. "Nonaulic Intermedi in the Performance of Comedies in Florence (1550–1590)." M.A. thesis, University of Illinois at Urbana-Champaign, 1982.

———. *Echoes of Women's Voices: Music, Art, and Female Patronage in Early Modern Florence.* Chicago: University of Chicago Press, 2006.

Hathaway, Baxter. *Marvels and Commonplaces.* New York: Random House, 1968.

Hill, John Walter. "O che nuovo miracolo!: A New Hypothesis about the Aria di Fiorenza." In *In cantu et in sermone for Nino Pirrotta on his 80th birthday,* edited by Fabrizio Della Seta and Franco Piperno. Florence and Perth: Leo S. Olschki and University of Western Australia Press, 1989.

———. *Roman Monody, Cantata and Opera from the Circles Around Cardinal Montalto.* 2 vols. Oxford: Oxford University Press, 1997.

———. "The Solo Songs in the Florentine Intermedi for *La Pellegrina* of 1589: Some New Observations." In *"Et facciam dolçi canti": Studi in onore di Agostino Ziino in occasione del suo 65° compleanno,* edited by Bianca Maria Antolini, Teresa M. Gialdroni, and Annunziato Pugliese. Lucca: Libreria Musicale Italiana, 2003.

Hillman, David, and Carla Mazzio, eds. *The Body in Parts: Fantasies of Corporeality in Early Modern Europe.* New York: Routledge, 1997.

Hitchcock, H. Wiley. "Caccini's 'Other' Nuove musiche." *Journal of the American Musicological Society* 27/3 (1974): 438–60.

Hollander, John. *The Figure of Echo: A Mode of Allusion in Milton and After.* Berkeley: University of California Press, 1981.

Hotchkiss, Valerie R. *Clothes Make the Man: Female Cross Dressing in Medieval Europe.* New York: Garland, 1996.

Hudson, Richard. *Passacaglio and Ciaccona: From Guitar Music to Italian Keyboard Variations in the 17th Century.* Ann Arbor, Mich.: UMI, 1981.

Jones, Ann Rosalind. "New Songs for the Swallow: Ovid's Philomela in Tullia d'Aragona and Gaspara Stampa." In *Refiguring Woman: Perspectives on Gender and the Italian Renaissance.* Ithaca, N.Y.: Cornell University Press, 1991.

Kantorowicz, Ernst. "Mysteries of State: An Absolutist Concept and Its Late Medieval Origins." *Harvard Theological Review* 48 (1955): 65–91.

Katritzky, M. A. "Aby Warburg and the Florentine Intermedi of 1589: Extending the Boundaries of Art History." In *Art History as Cultural History: Warburg's Projects,* edited by Richard Woodfield. Amsterdam: G+B Arts International, 2001.

Kenseth, Joy, ed. *The Age of the Marvelous.* Hanover, N.H.: Hood Museum of Art, Dartmouth College, 1991.

Ketterer, Robert. "Classical sources and thematic structure in the Florentine intermedi of 1589." *Renaissance Studies* 13/2 (1999): 192–222.

Keyte, Hugh. "From De' Rossi to Malvezzi: Some Performance Problems." In *The Golden Age.* Program booklet for the 1979 performance of these *intermedi* in St. John's, Smith Square, London.

Kirkendale, Warren. *L'aria di Fiorenza.* Florence: Leo S. Olschki, 1972.

———. *The Court Musicians in Florence During the Principate of the Medici: With a Reconstruction of the Artistic Establishment.* Florence: Leo S. Olschki, 1993.

———. *Emilio de' Cavalieri "Gentiluomo romano": His Life and Letters, His Role as Superintendent of all the Arts at the Medici Court, and His Musical Compositions.* Florence: Leo S. Olschki, 2001.

Kümmel, W. F. "Ein deutscher Bericht über die florentinischen Intermedien des Jahres 1589." *Analecta Musicologica* 9 (1970): 1–19.

Ledbetter, Stephen J. "Luca Marenzio: New Biographical Findings." Ph.D. diss., New York University, 1971.

Le Goff, Jacques. *The Medieval Imagination.* Translated by Arthur Goldhammer. Chicago: University of Chicago Press, 1988.

Leppert, Richard. "Music as a Sight in the Production of Music's Meaning." In *Metaphor: A Musical Dimension,* edited by Jamie Croy Kassler. Third Symposium of the International Musicological Society, Melbourne, 1988. Sydney: Currency, 1991.

———. *The Sight of Sound: Music, Representation, and the History of the Body.* Berkeley: University of California Press, 1993.

MacNeil, Anne. *Music and the Women of the Commedia dell'Arte in the Late Sixteenth Century.* Oxford: Oxford University Press, 2003.

Mamone, Sara. *Il teatro nella Firenze medicea.* Milan: Mursia, 1981.

Maniates, Maria Rika. *Mannerism in Italian Music and Culture, 1530–1630.* Chapel Hill: University of North Carolina Press, 1979.

Marciak, Dorothée. *La place du prince: Perspective et pouvoir dans le théâtre de cour des Médicis, Florence (1539–1600).* Paris: Honoré Champion, 2005.

Marignetti, Barbara. "Gli intermedi della *Pellegrina*: Repertori emblematici e iconologici." *Rivista italiana di musicologia* 31/2 (1996): 281–301.

Marin, Louis. *Portrait of the King.* Translated by Martha Houle. Foreword by Tom Conley. Minneapolis: University of Minnesota Press, 1988.

Marongiu, Marcella. "Storia e cronaca nel Corridoio vasariano." In *Il Corridoio vasariano agli Uffizi,* edited by Caterina Caneva. Florence: Banca Toscana, 2002.

Marshall, Cynthia. "Bodies in the Audience." *Shakespeare Studies* 29 (2001): 51–56.

Martines, Lauro. *Power and Imagination: City-States in Renaissance Italy.* New York: Alfred A. Knopf, 1979.

Mason, Kevin Bruce. *The Chitarrone and its Repertoire in Seventeenth-Century Italy.* Aberystwyth: Boethius Press, 1989.

McClary, Susan. "Constructions of Gender in Monteverdi's Dramatic Music." In *Feminine Endings: Music, Gender, and Sexuality.* Minneapolis: University of Minnesota Press, 1991.

———. *Modal Subjectivities: Self-Fashioning in the Italian Madrigal.* Berkeley: University of California Press, 2004.

Mead, Andrew. "Bodily Hearing: Physiological Metaphors and Musical Understanding." *Journal of Music Theory* 43/1 (1999): 1–19.

Meyer-Baer, Kathi. *Music of the Spheres and the Dance of Death: Studies in Musical Iconology.* Princeton, N.J.: Princeton University Press, 1970.

Minor, Andrew C., and Bonner Mitchell. *A Renaissance Entertainment: Festivities for the Marriage of Cosimo I, Duke of Florence, in 1539.* Columbia: University of Missouri Press, 1968.

Mirollo, James V. *The Poet of the Marvelous: Giambattista Marino.* New York: Columbia University Press, 1963.

Molinari, Cesare. *Le nozze degli dei, un saggio sul grande spettacolo italiano nel seicento.* Rome: M. Bulzoni, 1968.

Monga, Luigi. *Voyage de Provence et d'Italie.* Geneva: Slatkine, 1994.

Mosco, Marilena. "The Medici's 'Meraviglie.'" In *Meraviglie: Precious, Rare and Curious Objects from the Medici Treasure,* edited by Marilena Mosco. Florence: Alpi Lito, 2003.

Mulryne, James R., and Elizabeth Goldring, eds. *Court Festivals of the European Renaissance: Art, Politics, and Performance.* Aldershot and Burlington: Ashgate, 2002.

Nagler, Alois Maria. *Theatre Festivals of the Medici, 1539–1637.* Translated by George Hickenlooper. New Haven, Conn.: Yale University Press, 1964.

Nevile, Jennifer. "Cavalieri's Theatrical *Ballo* 'O che nuovo miracolo': A Reconstruction." *Dance Chronicle* 21/3 (1998): 353–88.

———. "Cavalieri's Theatrical *Ballo* and the Social Dances of Caroso and Negri." *Dance Chronicle* 22/1 (1999): 119–33.

Newbigin, Nerida. "Epilogue: The Republican Heritage in Grand-Ducal Florence." In *Feste D'oltrano: Plays in Churches in Fifteenth-Century Florence.* Florence: Leo S. Olschki, 1996.

———. "The World Made Flesh: The Rappresentazioni of Mysteries and Miracles in Fifteenth-Century Florence." In *Christianity and the Renaissance: Image and Religious Imagination in the Quattrocento,* edited by Timothy Verdon and John Henderson. Syracuse: Syracuse University Press, 1999.

Newman, Karen. "The Politics of Spectacle: *La Pellegrina* and the Intermezzi of 1589." *Modern Language Notes* 101/1 (1986): 95–113.

Ossi, Massimo. "*Dalle macchine . . . la maraviglia:* Bernardo Buontalenti's *Il rapimento di Cefalo* at the Medici Theater in 1600." In *Opera in Context: Essays on Historical Staging from the Late Renaissance to the Time of Puccini,* edited by Mark A. Radice. Portland, Ore.: Amadeus Press, 1998.

Palisca, Claude, ed. *The Florentine Camerata: Documentary Studies and Translations.* New Haven, Conn.: Yale University Press, 1989.

———. *Studies in the History of Italian Music and Music Theory.* Oxford: Clarendon Press, 1994.

Paster, Gail Kern. *The Body Embarrassed: Drama and the Disciplines of Shame in Early Modern England.* Ihaca, N.Y.: Cornell University Press, 1993.

Paster, Gail Kern, Katherine Rowe, and Mary Floyd-Wilson, eds. *Reading the Early Modern Passions: Essays in the Cultural History of Emotion.* Philadelphia: University of Pennsylvania Press, 2004.

Perruccio, Francesca, ed. *Due scritti intorno alla musica nel principato mediceo di Cosimo I e Francesco I.* Naples: Centro Attività Musicali, 1989.

Pirrotta, Nino. *Li due Orfei: da Poliziano a Monteverdi.* Torino: Einaudi, 1975.

———. *Music and Theatre from Poliziano to Monteverdi.* Translated by Karen Eales. Cambridge: Cambridge University Press, 1982.

Platt, Peter G. " 'Not Before Either Known or Dreamt Of': Francesco Patrizi and the Power of Wonder in Renaissance Poetics." *Review of English Studies* 43/171 (1992): 387–94.

———. *Reason Diminished: Shakespeare and the Marvelous.* Lincoln: University of Nebraska Press, 1997.

Price, Leah. *The Anthology and the Rise of the Novel from Richardson to George Eliot.* Cambridge: Cambridge University Press, 2000.

Reinhard, Wolfgang. "Papal Power and Family Strategy." In *Princes, Patronage, and the Nobility: The Court at the Beginning of the Modern Age, c. 1450–1650,* edited by Ronald G. Asch and Adolf M. Birke. Oxford: Oxford University Press, 1991.

Rowe, Katherine. "Humoral Knowledge and Liberal Cognition in Davenant's Macbeth." In *Reading the Early Modern Passions: Essays in the Cultural History of Emotion,* edited by Gail Kern Paster, Katherine Rowe, and Mary Floyd-Wilson. Philadelphia: University of Pennsylvania Press, 2004.

Ruvoldt, Maria. *The Italian Renaissance Imagery of Inspiration: Metaphors of Sex, Sleep, and Dreams.* Cambridge: Cambridge University Press, 2004.

Saslow, James M. *The Medici Wedding of 1589: Florentine Festival as Theatrum Mundi.* New Haven, Conn.: Yale University Press, 1996.

———. Review of *La place du prince: Perspective et pourvoir dans le théâtre de cour des Médicis, Florence (1539–1600),* by Dorothée Mariak. *Renaissance Quarterly* 59/1 (2006): 147–49.

Satkowski, Leon. *Studies on Vasari's Architecture.* New York: Garland, 1979.

———. "The Palazzo Pitti: Planning and Use in the Grand-Ducal Era." *Journal of the Society of Architectural Historians* 42/4 (1983): 336–49.

———. *Giorgio Vasari: Architect and Courtier.* Princeton, N.J.: Princeton University Press, 1993.

Schiesari, Juliana. "The Gendering of Melancholia: Torquato Tasso and Isabella di Morra." In *Refiguring Woman.* Ithaca, N.Y.: Cornell University Press, 1991.

Schoenfeldt, Michael. *Bodies and Selves in Early Modern England: Physiology and Inwardness in Spenser, Shakespeare, Herbert, and Milton.* Cambridge: Cambridge University Press, 1999.

Seznec, Jean. *The Survival of the Pagan Gods: The Mythological Tradition and Its Place in Renaissance Humanism and Art.* Translated by Barbara F. Sessions. Princeton, N.J.: Princeton University Press, 1972.

Shearman, John. *Mannerism.* Harmondsworth, Middlesex: Penguin Books, 1967.

Shelemay, Kay Kaufman. "Toward an Ethnomusicology of the Early Music Movement: Thoughts on Bridging Disciplines and Musical Worlds." *Ethnomusicology* 45/1 (2001): 1–29.

Shemek, Deanna. *Ladies Errant: Wayward Women and Social Order in Early Modern Italy.* Durham: Duke University Press, 1998.

Sisman, Elaine. "President's message." *American Musicological Society Newsletter* 36/2 (2006): 2, 4.

Slim, H. Colin, ed. *A Gift of Madrigals and Motets.* 2 vols. Chicago: University of Chicago Press, 1972.

Small, Christopher. *Musicking: The Meanings of Performing and Listening.* Hanover, N.H.: University Press of New England, 1998.

Solerti, Angelo. *Le origini del melodramma.* Turin: Fratelli Bocca, 1903.

———. *Gli albori del melodramma.* 3 vols. Milan: Remo Sandron, 1904.

———. *Musica, ballo e drammatica alla corte medicea dal 1600 al 1637. Notizie tratte da un diario con appendice di testi inediti e rari.* Florence: Bemporad and Figlio, 1905. Reprint, New York: Benjamin Blom, 1968.

Strong, Roy C. *Splendor at Court: Renaissance Spectacle and the Theater of Power.* Boston: Houghton Mifflin, 1973.

———. *Art and Power: Renaissance Festivals, 1450–1650.* Woodbridge, Suffolk: Boydell Press, 1984.

Testaverde Matteini, Annamaria. *L'officina delle nuvole: Il Teatro Mediceo nel 1589 e gli Intermedi del Buontalenti nel Memoriale di Girolamo Seriacopi.* Musica e teatro: Quaderni degli amici della Scala, vols. 11/12. Milan: Amici della Scala, 1991.

Tomlinson, Gary. *Monteverdi and the End of the Renaissance.* Berkeley: University of California Press, 1987.

———. *Music in Renaissance Magic: Toward a Historiography of Others.* Chicago: University of Chicago Press, 1993.

Treadwell, Nina. "The Chitarra Spagnola and Italian Monody, 1589 to ca. 1650." M.A. thesis, University of Southern California, 1995.

———. "The Performance of Gender in Cavalieri/Guidiccioni's *Ballo* 'O che nuovo miracolo' (1589)." *Women and Music: A Journal of Gender and Culture* 1 (1997): 55–70.

———. "Restaging the Siren: Musical Women in the Performance of Sixteenth-Century Italian Theater." Ph.D. diss., University of Southern California, 2000.

———. "She Descended on a Cloud 'from the highest spheres': Florentine Monody 'alla Romanina.'" *Cambridge Opera Journal* 16/1 (2004): 1–22.

———. "Music of the Gods: Solo Song and *effetti meravigliosi* in the Interludes for *La Pellegrina.*" *Current Musicology* 83 (2007): 33–84.

Tyler, James. *The Early Guitar: A History and a Handbook.* Oxford: Oxford University Press, 1980.

Tyler, James, and Paul Sparks. *The Guitar and Its Music: From the Renaissance to the Classical Era.* Oxford: Oxford University Press, 2002.

Van Veen, Henk Th. "Art and Propaganda in Late Renaissance and Baroque Florence: The Defeat of Radagasius, King of the Goths." *Journal of the Warburg and Courtauld Institutes* 47 (1984): 106–18.

Walker, D. P., ed. *Musique des intermèdes de "La Pellegrina": Les fêtes de Florence, 1589.* Paris: C.N.R.S., 1963.

Warburg, Aby. "I costumi teatrali per gli Intermezzi del 1589: I disegni di Bernardo Buontalenti e il 'Libro di conti' di Emilio de Cavalieri." In *Gesammelte Schriften,* edited by Gertrud Bing. Leipzig: B. G. Teubner, 1932.

———. *The Renewal of Pagan Antiquity.* Translated by David Britt. Los Angeles: Getty Research Institute, 1999.

Weaver, Robert L. "Sixteenth-Century Instrumentation." *Musical Quarterly* 47/3 (1961): 363–78.

Weinberg, Bernard. *A History of Literary Criticism in the Italian Renaissance.* 2 vols. Chicago: University of Chicago Press, 1961.

Wind, Edgar. *Pagan Mysteries in the Renaissance.* London: Faber and Faber, 1958.

Winternitz, Emanuel. *Musical Instruments of the Western World.* New York: McGraw-Hill, 1966.

Wisch, Barbara, and Susan Scott Munshower, eds. *"All the World's a Stage . . .": Art and Pageantry in the Renaissance and Baroque.* 2 vols. University Park: Dept. of Art History, Pennsylvania State University, 1990.

Wistreich, Richard. "'Real Basses, Real Men': Virtù and Virtuosity in the Construction of Noble Male Identity in Late Sixteenth Century Italy." *Trossingen Jahrbuch für Renaissancemusik* 2 (2002): 59–80.

———. Review of *Art vocal, Art de gouverner: La musique, le prince et la cité en Italie à la fin du XVIe siècle,* by Florence Alazard. *Renaissance Quarterly* 57/3 (2004): 1093–94.

———. *Warrior, Courtier, Singer: Giulio Cesare Brancaccio and the Performance of Identity in the Late Renaissance.* Aldershot: Ashgate, 2007.

Wittkower, Rudolf. "Transformations of Minerva in Renaissance Imagery." *Journal of the Warburg Institute* 2/3 (1939): 194–205.

Yates, Frances A. *The Art of Memory.* Chicago: University of Chicago Press, 1966.

Young, G. F. *The Medici.* New York: Dutton and Co., 1926.

Zapperi, Roberto. "The Summons of the Carracci to Rome: Some New Documentary Evidence." *Burlington Magazine* 128/996 (Mar. 1986): 203–205.

Zika, Charles. "She-man: Visual Representations of Witchcraft and Sexuality in Sixteenth-Century Europe." In *Venus and Mars: Engendering Love and War in Medieval and Early Modern Europe,* edited by Andrew Lynch and Philippa Maddern. Nedlands: University of Western Australia Press, 1995.

Discography

Linde, Hans Martin. *La Pellegrina 1589: Intermedii et Concerti zur Hochzeit des Don Ferdinando Medici und der Madama Christiana di Loreno.* Stockholmer Kammerchor and Linde-Consort. EMI Reflexe 30 114/15, 2000 [1973].

Nevel, Paul van. *La Pellegrina: Music for the Wedding of Ferdinando de' Medici and Christine de Lorraine, Princess of France, Florence 1589.* Huelgas Ensemble. Vivarte S2K 63362, 1998.

Parrott, Andrew. *Una "Stravaganza" dei Medici: Intermedi (1589) per "La Pellegrina."* Taverner Consort. EMI 7 47998 2, 1988.

Index

Jove, *ii (cont.)*
208, 214; song text for, 214; sorceress's reference to, 114, 117, 212; spectators' identification of, 252n8
Judy, Susan, xv, xvi, 209, 213, 250nn36–37

Katritzky, M. A., 58, 239n9
keyboard instruments: lack of use in *Pellegrina intermedi*, 149, 235n24
Kirkendale, Warren, 53, 54, 176, 217n14, 222n85, 231n38, 252n3, 253n26
Kümmel, W. F.: on Gadenstedt, 61, 225n28

Landi, Antonio, 19–20, 48
lira da braccio: depiction of, xi, 148, pl. 24, *pl. 24;* mentioned in Rossi's 1589 *Descrizione*, 185, 190, 194–195, 196, 251n58; use on accompanying CD, 209, 210; in *intermedi*, 82, 95, 96, 112, 128, 240n33, 245n34, 253n16
lira viol, in *intermedio* four, 245n34; use on accompanying CD, 209
lirone, use on accompanying CD, 209, 210, 146–147; in *intermedi*, 140, 145, 253n16
Longinus: and Patrizi, 39
Longus: and Echo, 76
Lorraine, Christine de, 1, 11, 93, 133, 134, 145; as referenced in *descrizioni*, 60, 198, 200, 203; as referenced in the *Pellegrina* interludes texts, 74, 77, 121–122, 163, 166, 207–208, 236n35; association with Juno, 237n41; association with Minerva, 96, 181, 211, 236n35; at *Pellegrina* performances, 58, 227n77, 232nn54,57; her entrance into Florence, 61, 218nn30–32
Lucifer: in *intermedio* four, 104, 123–125, 133, 134, 193–194, 199, 246nn47–48, 247n59; in stage design for *intermedio* four, pl. 17, *pl. 17;* preparatory sketch for, xi, pl. 18, *pl. 18. See also* Pluto
lute, 148, 170, 254n36; in *intermedio* five, 140, 146, 250n30,34, 252n69; in *intermedio* four, 245n34; in *intermedio* one, 70, 71, 73, 82, 86, 148; in *intermedio* six, 253n16; in *intermedio* two, 96; in *Li artificiosi*, 204; in Pavoni's *Diario*, 236n34; in Rossi's 1589 *Descrizione*, 181, 184, 189, 190, 191, 195, 249; use on accompanying CD, 146–147, 209–210
Luzzaschi, Luzzasco, 107, 173

Machiavelli, Niccolò, 47
Macrobius: and Echo, 76–77; and Harmony of the Spheres, 76–77
magic, 32, 38, 40–43, 44, 71–72, 78, 81, 118–119, 122; 227n68, 161
magnificence, ix, 14–16, 21, 217nn19,23, 220n50, 223n1; in Cavallino's *Le solennissime feste*, 200; in De' Sommi's *Quattro dialoghi*, 15, 217n21; in Giraldi's *Delle lode di D. Ferdinando*, 26, 222n80; in Rossi's 1589 *Descrizione*, 14–16, 18,

30, 92, 177–179, 185–186, 194, 218n35; in Serlio's *Tutte l'opere d'architettura,*15, 217n19
magnificenza. See magnificence
Malvezzi, Cristofano, arranger and compiler of *Intermedii et concerti*, xvii, 3, 137–138, 215n10,14, 235n24; as composer, 81, 82–88, *84–86*, 137–138, 140–147, *141–143*, 157–158, 182; concerning *nono* partbook of *Intermedii et concerti*, 3, 86–87, 96, 100, 111, 112, 138, 140, 146, 147, 148, 157, 163, 164, 171, 172, 206–208, 210, 222n73, 235n24, 240n31,32,35, 241n41,46, 242n61, 245n32, 250n50, 252n69, 253n16, pl. 4, *pl. 4*, pl. 29, *pl. 29*
Marenzio, Luca, 174; as composer, x, 60–61, 94–95, 96–101, *99–100, 101*, 105, 107, *108–110*, 184, 186, 241n43,45
Medici, Cosimo I de', 11, 12–13, 14, 17, 20, 21, 22, 23, 33, 56, 178–179, 180, 216n8, 218n30, 221n58, 229n18, 252–253n12
Medici, Cosimo il Vecchio, 14–15, 20, 178, 220n48
Medici, Ferdinando I de': activities at the Port of Livorno, xi, 27, 162, pl. 2, *pl. 2;* aligned with a Christian god, 81, 133, 145; as Neoplatonic Magus, ix, 7, 29, 42–44, 122, 150, 161, 227n80; as referenced in the *Pellegrina* interludes' texts, 74, 121–122, 163, 166, 206–208; as theatrical arbiter 26–29; attendance at *Pellegrina* rehearsals, 28, 57; depictions of by Callot, pl. 1–2, *pl. 1–2;* his body, 44, 150, 228n87; military exploits of, 26–27, pl. 1, *pl. l;* naval exploits of, 145, pl. 21, *pl. 21;* prince-as-god, 20–25; interest in Ferrarese *concerto di donne,* 173–174
Medici, Francesco I de', 12, 13–14, 25, 43, 56, 78, 230n26, 243; and divine-right theory, 21; musicians of, 107, 173, 243n82; in Rossi's 1589 *Descrizione*, 179, 180; interest in Ferrarese *concerto di donne*, 107, 173; marriage to Bianca Cappello, 119, 221n68; marriage to Joanna of Austria, 23, 229n18, 236n28
Medici progeny: references to, 120, 146, 147, 162, 166, 207, 222n73
melancholy: and music, x, 126–128, 133, 247n62,64
Memoriale e ricordi, 7–8, 27; entries in, 27–28, 57, 58, 59, 69, 148, 219–220n45, 222n82,86, 223n87, 231n50, 232n57, 235n20, 236n27, 251n56. *See also* Seriacopi, Girolamo
meraviglia. See wonder (*meraviglia*)
meraviglie. See Uffizi Palace, *galleria* in
Muses: costume design for, xi, pl. 11, *11;* in *intermedio* six, 159, 252n3; in *intermedio* two, 89, 91–92, 94, 95, 97–98, 100, 184–185, 186, 239n15,16, 240n26,27, 245n20, pl. 8, *pl. 8;* song text for, 184–185, 212
musical instruments: decoration of, 148, 251n55; hybrid instruments, 148–149, pl. 24, *pl. 24, pl. 25–26. See individual instrument names*

NINA TREADWELL is Associate Professor of Music at the University of California, Santa Cruz. She is a musicologist whose research is informed by her experience as a performer on plucked-string instruments of the Renaissance and Baroque periods, and by her interest in gender studies.